Warfare State

Warfare State

World War II Americans and the Age of Big Government

JAMES T. SPARROW

OXFORD
UNIVERSITY PRESS

OXFORD

UNIVERSITY PRESS

Oxford University Press is a department of the University of Oxford.
It furthers the University's objective of excellence in research, scholarship,
and education by publishing worldwide.

Oxford   New York

Auckland   Cape Town   Dar es Salaam   Hong Kong   Karachi
Kuala Lumpur   Madrid   Melbourne   Mexico City   Nairobi
New Delhi   Shanghai   Taipei   Toronto

With offices in

Argentina   Austria   Brazil   Chile   Czech Republic   France   Greece
Guatemala   Hungary   Italy   Japan   Poland   Portugal   Singapore
South Korea   Switzerland   Thailand   Turkey   Ukraine   Vietnam

Oxford is a registered trade mark of Oxford University Press
in the UK and certain other countries.

Published in the United States of America by
Oxford University Press
198 Madison Avenue, New York, NY 10016

© Oxford University Press 2011

First issued as an Oxford University Press paperback, 2013.

Library of Congress Cataloging-in-Publication Data
Sparrow, James T.
Warfare state: World War II Americans and the age of big government /James T. Sparrow.
p.   cm.
Includes bibliographical references and index.
ISBN 978-0-19-979101-9 (hardcover); 978-0-19-993035-7 (paperback)
1. World War, 1939–1945—Political aspects—United States. 2. World War, 1939–1945—Social aspects—United States.
3. United States—Politics and government—1933–1945. 4. Politics and war—United States—History—20th century.
5. Political culture—United States—History—20th century. 6. Social change—United States—History—20th century.
7. Citizenship—United States—History—20th century. 8. Federal government—United States—History—20th century.
9. Legitimacy of governments—United States—History—20th century. 10. Military-industrial complex—
United States—History—20th century. I. Title.
D742.U5S7   2011
940.53'73—dc22   2010039420

For Simon Sparrow

CONTENTS

Warfare State

Introduction: War and the Mass Foundations of the Modern State

On January 11, 1944, Americans gathered around the radio hearth to hear their president, Franklin Delano Roosevelt, deliver a fireside chat. "There is only one front," he told his listeners. "There is one line of unity which extends from the hearts of the people at home to the men of our attacking forces in our farthest outposts."[1] It was a message Americans had heard often, repeated in one form or another by agencies concerned with their war-mindedness. After years of repetition it had begun to sink in. By conflating the actions of civilians "fighting" on the "home front" with the real battles fought by GIs overseas, wartime rhetoric reinforced rising expectations fostered by a buoyant war economy, and attached them firmly, if vaguely, to the government as a guarantor of basic fairness wherever it touched daily life—which was nearly everywhere during the war.

The fireside chat of January 1944 stuck in the minds of so many Americans because it was the one in which Roosevelt made his case for an "economic bill of rights" that would guarantee a genuine national citizenship to all Americans who had struggled together in war. Making the case for a definition of citizenship modernized to include a comprehensive range of social rights, without which the "true individual freedom" promised by political and civil rights "cannot exist," Roosevelt set the liberal agenda for the postwar period. His words resonated so widely because they articulated the fictive social contract on which so much of the war effort depended in order to justify the exertions of mass participation in the mobilization for total war. He further bolstered the universalistic implications of his promises by portraying the national project as an epochal moment in world history. "The nation," he said at the opening of his address, was "an active partner in the world's greatest war against slavery. We have joined with like-minded people in order to defend ourselves in a world that has been gravely threatened with gangster rule."

The rising expectations unleashed by the war did not amount simply to demands for entitlements. If citizens had "an individual stake in the preservation of democratic life in America," as Roosevelt put it, that stake could be claimed only through obligation and sacrifice. With each fireside chat, it seemed, the president made a point of reinforcing the direct moral obligation that bound ordinary citizens to the heroic soldiers who gave their lives for their country. It began as early as his "Four Freedoms" address before the war, in January 1941—a speech remembered less for its invocation of obligation than for its pledge to secure freedom of speech and expression, freedom of worship, freedom from want, and freedom from fear. In that landmark statement, which would shape wartime rights rhetoric, Roosevelt also asserted that the interests of individuals and groups "must give way to the national need," as must anything else that stood "in the way of speed and efficiency in defense preparations." It was the sovereign people who held the highest claim: "a free nation has the right to expect full cooperation from all groups." And that sovereignty was embodied by the federal government, empowered to place the collective good above all else.[2]

From the very beginning, then, the liberal ideals of freedom and rights championed by Roosevelt and his war administrators were predicated on the greater obligation to meet the requirements of national belonging. Contributing to the war effort might foster visions of national citizenship and even provide new guarantees of federal protection, but such claims were always to remain subordinated—practically, to the requirements of the war government, and symbolically, to the demands of the combat soldier. Americanism provided the language, imagery, and cultural logic by which clashing claims on the government could be made. In the end, Americanism went hand in hand with entitlement, policing as well as authorizing it.

The Americans who lived through the Second World War partook of a sweeping transformation in the foundations of national government. Internationally, American power leapt far beyond territorial bounds, inaugurating an era of globalism. Domestically, warfare replaced welfare as the central purpose of the national state. More than in any other period since the Civil War, changes in government politicized everyday life, touching nearly every American. For soldiers and civilians alike, the war instilled a sense of entitlement to full citizenship that the federal government increasingly would have to placate, if not always fulfill, in subsequent years. At the same time, and for related reasons, the integrity of the state and the loyalty of its employees and citizens became paramount concerns, subject to the increasingly stringent criteria of a normative and bureaucratized Americanism.

The obligations of national belonging that exponents of Americanism asserted, together with the rights of national citizenship to which ordinary Americans increasingly claimed entitlement, legitimized the federal leviathan erected during the war. Nationalism and social democratic egalitarianism had been contending impulses in American political life for decades, much as they had been for the other powers participating in the war. It took the ideological threat of a European continent ruled by German National Socialism, combined with the racial specter of an entire hemisphere of Asians united by imperial Japan, to fuse the two impulses into a new mode of American statism.

Total war changed the stakes of national government—even in the United States, where it brought full employment and economic mobilization rather than shelled-out cities and masses of refugees. Within the span of half a decade the United States departed from some of its longest and most dearly held political traditions. The first of these departures was the permanent peacetime draft, inaugurated in late 1940, which violated an aversion to conscription and large standing armies dating back to the Revolution. It shaped the most basic requirements of male citizenship for more than a generation, while providing a ready source of manpower for the vast military establishment erected in these years.

The United States' wartime alliance, the second major departure, represented a historic break with more than a century of international aloofness predating the Monroe Doctrine. Starting in the spring of 1941, Lend-Lease inaugurated a massive program of aid to Britain and, eventually, to other Allied nations fighting against the Axis powers. These provisional measures eventually pulled the United States into a constellation of long-term alliances whose entanglements persisted decades into the postwar period.

War finance, another dramatic policy departure, embedded the federal government more deeply within American society than had the regressive fiscal regime of the New Deal, whose attacks on the wealthy had never transcended purely symbolic gestures. Mass income taxation and vast structural deficits, both undertaken for the first time during the war, produced a revolution in public finance that fostered the affluent society at home and funded the American Century abroad. Eight generations after the Boston Tea Party, Americans not only taxed themselves—directly, substantially, and broadly—but also sent a large chunk of the resulting revenues back across the Atlantic to sustain the British Empire.

Even the mixed economy, on which the war effort's decisive "miracle of production" relied, represented a departure from New Deal regulation. The War Production Board's controls over vital materials, combined with the explosion of war contracts directed by procurement officials within the army and navy, directed the energies of entire industries toward public purposes with more vigor, success, and permanent impact than the short-lived National Recovery Administration (NRA) ever could have. Price and wage controls, rationing and manpower priorities, consumer protection and labor arbitration—these lasted longer and shaped the economy more profoundly than had the NRA's codes of fair competition. They involved the federal government more intensively in the affairs of management and labor than had been the case during the golden age of Wagner Act militancy in the last half of the 1930s.

The agencies that conducted the mobilization for the Second World War quickly dwarfed the New Deal programs that had seemed gargantuan only a few years earlier. They touched the lives of more than 85 million war bond holders (in a total population of 130 million); 42 million new income-tax payers; nearly all of the nation's 17 million industrial workers employed by war industry, and further millions who worked in supporting white-collar jobs; and more than 16 million servicemen and -women. Rationing was so widespread that registrations for ration books were used as a proxy for census information on population size and distribution in 1943.[3] By way of contrast, the Works Progress Administration employed just under 15 million people during its eight-year tenure; all of the New Deal emergency welfare projects combined reached a total of 28.6 million recipients between 1933 and 1943. Just one of the war programs, Lend-Lease, spent more in six years—$50 billion between 1941 and 1946—than all of the New Deal emergency programs had in a decade ($40 billion between 1933 and 1943).[4] As the larger trajectory of federal spending, revenue, debt, employment, and military deployment in the twentieth century makes clear, the Second World War, building on but also superseding the New Deal, was a critical turning point for the growth of the federal government within American society. (See Charts A.1–A.8.)

Not only did the federal government expand in sheer size during the war but, just as important, it dramatically extended the scope and nature of its authority. War agencies were far less beholden to state and local political interests than had been the case in the 1930s. This was due to the authority granted to the president by the Second War Powers Act of 1942—one of the biggest grants of executive discretion in U.S. history—which made for a state of emergency that did not officially end until 1952.[5]

The war also rehabilitated big business, returning corporate figures to the public service that had burnished the preeminence of market values in national life before the crash of 1929 shook their hold. Prior to the coming of war, the Roosevelt administration had sought to resuscitate and then discipline the marketplace through recovery measures, antitrust enforcement, and labor relations that many business leaders resented. With the coming of war the nature of the emergency shifted, redirecting energies from preserving national welfare to mobilizing for national defense.[6] Consequently, the nature of "mixed government" altered decisively.

The new compact with big business extended well beyond the offices of military purchasing agents and civilian mobilization officials, although that is where it began. "Dollar-a-year" men retained their corporate salaries and rushed into Washington to work for a nominal fee, setting the government into a new relationship with business. Within war plants, management regained the discretion and authority that had been challenged by years of sit-down strikes and shop floor militancy. In the culture industries admen and copywriters, radio and film producers, newsmen, and commercial illustrators all devoted their time and skill to public productions that sold the "Fifth Freedom" of private enterprise as much as they did the other four. Businessmen volunteered to run the war effort at all levels, from local car dealers selling war bonds all the way up to national figures such as Sears, Roebuck president Donald Nelson heading the War Production Board to guide the entire mobilization.

In this new iteration of the "associational state" that had been growing since the nineteenth century, the government was not simply "captured" by corporate liberals, as critics would claim at the time and for decades afterward. If federal power became critically dependent on business in the war the reverse was also true, making those business figures who entered public service at least as much creatures of the state as they were servants of capital. Neither was the government captured by conspiratorial warhawks bent on institutionalizing militarism.[7] Military contracts would come and go over the years according to congressional whim and cautious military priorities. The economy born in the war did produce a coherent network of defense-related businesses, but it did not lock in a triumvirate of businessmen, generals, and politicians bent on converting the United States into a "garrison state."[8] The leaders of the armed forces mobilization— men such as Allied Commander Dwight D. Eisenhower, Chief of Staff George C. Marshall, Secretary of War Henry Stimson, Assistant Secretary of War Robert Patterson, and Secretary of the Navy Frank Knox—were as skeptical of protracted military buildup as they were of civilian administrators' judgment.

Even if war was not simply the handmaiden of capitalist growth or the product of warhawks' dreams, these years did nonetheless establish a kind of "warfare state" rooted both in society and government. Over years of emergency that did not end in 1945 militarism took on its own life, providing "memories, models, and metaphors that shaped broad areas of national life" from the late 1930s onward.[9] The mixed economy proved exceptionally dynamic once militarized. Although business leaders then and now have bemoaned the ways in which state planning might foreclose market innovation, in fact war brought opportunities for "creative destruction" on a scale that has yet to be matched.[10] Furthermore, this furious innovation reordered social relationships and cultural meanings as much as it did market share or capital investment, requiring consumers and industrial workers, drafted soldiers and home-front families to reorient their productive energies toward reworking the nation. In the process they remade themselves through everyday exertions. It was this fluid environment, as much as the crusade against fascism, that permanently bent private lives and capital to public purposes and fostered a fusion of corporate and New

Deal liberalisms with exceptionalist nationalism. America entered into a warfare state that would last for decades, thanks to the continued emergency of the Cold War.

How was it that this massive new warfare state, with its global mission, attracted so little of the dissent that had marked the Great War and the debate over the League of Nations, even while it eluded the more recent quarrels that had hobbled the late New Deal and the debate over intervention? Given the traditions of individualism and decentralized governance that had long conspired to thwart a centralized national state in the United States, the triumphal and unimpeded ascent of "big government" in the 1940s requires explanation.

One part of the answer has to do with the ways in which the American mobilizers of the Second World War enlisted nationalism. Well into the twentieth century, Americans still had much to resolve on the question of national identification. In part the problem was structural. Due to the federalism and division of powers that have defined the American state since 1789, there historically have been multiple centers of community and power within which a citizen might realize his or her patriotic membership: militias, patriotic societies, veterans' organizations, civic and other voluntary associations, and similar institutions organized in local communities or within the several states. The federal government was only one among many competing centers of nationalistic affiliation.[11]

Traditions of regionalism, localism, and religious pluralism compounded the obstacles to a genuinely national polity. In the South and West, where memories of the Civil War lingered and populist resentments of metropolitan leverage over government and economy continued to fester, antistatism was such a vernacular indulgence that patriots easily looked askance at the national government, particularly when it challenged local or regional prerogatives regarding race relations, class conflict, or land use. Evangelical and dissenting religious denominations—often flourishing in the countryside and in regional hinterlands alongside sectional and local jealousies—continued to defend the First Amendment's check on government authority, managing to defy even the most basic oath of national fealty, the Pledge of Allegiance, in a time of war.[12]

Equally venerable traditions of individualism and private property further constrained the extension of federal authority. Until the twentieth century, few public institutions reached into everyday life and oriented ordinary Americans toward the nation in ways that could habituate them to the authority of the federal government. The most visible national institutions were private enterprises such as railroads, mass media, or vertically integrated industries, all of which fostered national connectedness in economic and cultural life, but also considered the prospect of a powerful federal government with indifference or open hostility. The War Industries Board and other corporatist improvisations of World War I had placed business "czars" in harness for eighteen months, although U.S. involvement had not lasted long enough, nor marshaled sufficient popular support, to buy the federal government the time and resources it needed to truly dominate and manage the national economy. Throughout the 1920s, it had remained unclear who wielded the whip hand of this associational state.[13]

The American political tradition thus militated against popular acceptance of the European-style statism that menaced large swaths of the globe at the dawn of the 1940s. Americans had adopted an approach to government that obscured or hid the greatest sources of its power, while abetting a liberal ideology predicated on the myth of a timeless "weak state."[14] Thinking themselves exceptional in the annals of world history—a habit only reinforced by the war, with its contrast between Allied freedom and Axis tyranny—Americans of nearly every political stripe chafed at the extension of government power when it did not seem somehow to extend their own freedom. This was true even of liberals devoted to the welfare state, which they viewed as a necessary means to secure a greater sphere of liberty within the modern economy.

Despite the precedent of federal growth in earlier decades, the project of building a state powerful enough to win a global war on two fronts was no foregone conclusion, as the protracted debate over intervention demonstrated. The leviathan that Americans rapidly erected to meet the challenges of this global cataclysm required *legitimacy*, accorded by citizens who were invested somehow—materially or ideologically—in the power of the national government.

How did citizens come to accept or reject the newfound authority the federal government exercised over their lives, and how did that cultural process of legitimation inform their sense of national citizenship? At heart this is a question of political culture—the set of customs, values, assumptions, attitudes, and images that together define what was politically meaningful and thus possible within the polity. For no democratic regime could have persisted (much less expanded) without widely shared perceptions of legitimacy to motivate continued political engagement among leaders and ensure popular compliance with the pragmatic requirements of ordinary governance. This question has largely been neglected by historians, who share with political scientists and most theorists a blind spot when it comes to the cultural foundations of the nonviolent coercions and collective political action that are so central to modern political life.[15]

By focusing on the interplay between state formation and political culture at the grassroots—rather than restricting analysis to ideology or to the presumptive interests of pressure groups—it is possible to uncover the shared assumptions that ordered both cooperation and conflict within the polity. Such an approach is attuned to the unique problems raised by the simultaneous dispersion and concentration of power within mass society. It unveils the ways in which ordinary Americans came to terms with massive structures of national power, adapting and appropriating language, imagery, symbols, and ideas in order to orient themselves and their ideological commitments toward politicized social arrangements.[16] As government expanded and demanded more of its citizens, they had to be habituated to new forms of authority and new social arrangements resulting from its growing power. This requirement held doubly true for the American involvement in World War II, when churning social changes and raw tensions constantly threatened military morale, industrial production, and the authority of new war agencies.

The broad patterns of political culture during World War II have received considerable scholarly attention. Scholars focused on liberalism as the central tradition in American political life have suggested that even during the "good war" the very nature of the liberal polity precluded any genuine sense of collective obligation. Propagandists invoked self-interest by casting war aims in images of domesticity and postwar affluence. Interest groups such as labor, business, and farmers wrapped their agendas within a "politics of sacrifice" that engendered flag-waving opportunism. The takings required to safeguard the public welfare were thus justified as simple extensions of private self-interest, down payments on liberties such as the "freedom from want" depicted in Norman Rockwell's bounteous Thanksgiving. When they were contested, wartime sacrifices were denounced as violations of the maxim that all interests be safeguarded by an "equality of sacrifice."[17]

Because scholars have focused so heavily on the limitations imposed by American political culture on reform and political obligation during the war and early postwar years, we have little sense of how the extraordinary state-building of the period was accomplished with so little opposition. No tax revolts, no draft riots, no postwar isolationism—the quiescence attending the dramatic policy departures of these years requires explanation. The answers that millions of Americans gave to the question of "why we fight" mattered deeply—for the personal and social meanings they attributed to the patriotism and national citizenship the war effort cultivated in them, and for the emerging structures of a national state that could not win the war without their compliance.

Of all the years of the twentieth century, federal legitimacy grew most dramatically during World War II, just when expanding state capacity most burdened the nation's citizenry. Even where war administrators were most constrained, as with matters of race, they held at least nominal authority over social arrangements that had been considered beyond the purview of the federal government since the collapse of Reconstruction more than three generations earlier. While this greatly expanded state presence did produce significant conflict, the resulting divisiveness did not so much threaten the federal government's authority as heighten the claims that citizens felt they could make upon it. The "good war" may not have been the uniformly noble crusade portrayed in the war movies of midcentury, but it was a period in which the basic goals of the government were widely accepted as valid and necessary.[18] Unlike earlier periods of dramatic government expansion, the basic legitimacy of the federal government's efforts in World War II were not successfully challenged within the political mainstream. Critics from the left and right generally chose to embrace federal power during World War II and afterward, seeking to bend it to their will (whether for reform or reaction) rather than protest or dismantle it.

In Max Weber's classic formulation, there are three kinds of legitimate authority on which states can draw to exercise power securely: charismatic, traditional, and rational.[19] During the Second World War, the federal government drew on all three as it consolidated unprecedented control over society. Franklin Delano Roosevelt concentrated all the force of his extraordinary charisma to become the only president in U.S. history to win four terms, earning the title of the "Great Communicator" with his rousing public oratory. At the same time, his patrician pedigree and constant invocation of liberal democratic tradition cloaked this charismatic authority in a traditional mantle. He presided over the creation of the New Deal state, which inserted the "rational" requirements of expertise and planning into national politics. Although Roosevelt's charismatic gifts, patrician aura, and bureaucratic empire could all become liabilities on the wrong occasion, when wielded together they were awesome to behold. As a war president, Roosevelt did not hesitate to use any of the tools available to him.

Many studies of the 1930s and 1940s have noted Roosevelt's exceptional qualities as a leader—indeed, the man still overshadows the age that bears his name—but few have explored the social, cultural, and institutional aspects of the authority that allowed his government to redirect the course of history.[20] In focusing on legitimacy, this study seeks to understand a dimension of politics and society that is often overlooked: the social politics of the state, where the great structures of the nation touch everyday life.[21] Formal politics is ordinarily the domain of organized elites: politicians, interest groups, policy makers, journalists, and their ilk. Occasionally the machinations of these political actors are constrained or overturned by large-scale developments in economy, society, or mass politics. Catastrophic events crystallize public opinion in ways that force new habits and commitments.[22]

This book is about just such an event—World War II—and its influence on the national political culture that set the boundaries of policy and normal politics. It reveals how the warfare state obtained its purchase on everyday lives of the American people, and what the consequences of that development were for the social power, political legitimacy, and institutional profile of the leviathan that ruled the postwar United States and led the "free world" for more than a

generation. Focusing on legitimacy as a cultural process of political accommo-
dation worked out within the social spaces and economic transactions of everyday life opens up the empirical middle ground within which the ideologies,
state structures, and political interests of national life were lived, negotiated,
and appropriated. The everyday, idealized messages that government authorities wished to impart—particularly liberal messages that they were fighting a
war for freedom, democracy, pluralism, and the American way—were shaped
at least as powerfully by the claims of nationalism as by the logic of liberal
"obligation."[23] At the grassroots, ordinary Americans produced a fusion of
nationalism and liberalism, Americanism and entitlement, that defined the
political culture of the war and shaped the contours of what could be imagined politically for more than a generation thereafter. Ideologically the fusion was paradoxical, verging on contradictory. But lived as a social politics
flowing from the governmentality required by the war, it was compelling
enough. By cloaking new obligations to the state in this fusion of liberalism
(with its valorization of freedom and equality) and nationalism (with its
demand for unity, order, and loyalty), the federal government could expand its
power radically without triggering opposition.[24]

Citizens expressed their acceptance of federal legitimacy in terms that
reflected the sensibilities of the time. They incorporated certain aspects of the
speeches and propaganda that the government and private industry sent into
their homes and workplaces to make them "war-minded." These messages encouraged all citizens to think of themselves as personally connected to the battlefront and to imagine the repercussions of their every action for the combat
soldier—a figure always idealized in the political culture of the war. In keeping
with the values of individualism, virtuous independence, and jealousy of centralized sources of power that had shaped American political culture since colonial
times, most Americans did not articulate their morally charged connections
to the government as obligations to the state or even to the nation (although
they did sing along heartily with Kate Smith when she belted out "God Bless
America"). Rather, they embraced an idealized figure of masculine virtue and
patriotic sacrifice—the combat soldier—as a proxy for both the nation and the
government protecting it.

Given the extreme diversity of the 130 million people who resided within the
continental United States when the war began, it is not surprising that citizens'
interpretations of what, precisely, they owed the GI and the government varied
significantly. The government found it necessary to "educate" its citizenry in the
specific details of their obligation. "The best way of dealing with the few slackers
or trouble makers in our midst," the president claimed in his "Four Freedoms"
speech, was "first, to shame them by patriotic example, and, if that fails, to use
the sovereignty of Government to save Government." During the war the federal
government would ultimately rely more on patriotism and shame than on its

sovereign power to coerce citizens into compliance with the war effort. Prosecutions for draft dodging, tax evasion, and black market activity were all strikingly low, given the scope and newness of government authority in these areas. In a country at war, the idealized figure of the combat soldier—and the millions of real servicemen for whom it stood—provided a unifying symbol through which

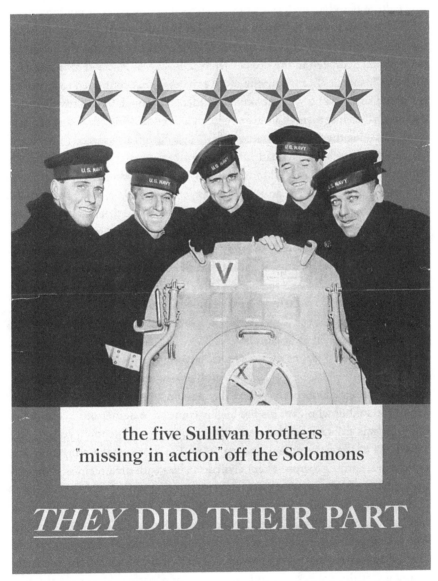

In November 1942, the light cruiser USS *Juneau* sank during the battle of Guadalcanal, taking the lives of all five sons of Tom and Alleta Sullivan: George, Frank, Joe, Matt, and Al. They were soon widely memorialized, putting a human face on the combat soldier who became a culture hero of the home front. (Courtesy of Northwestern University Library, http://digital.library.northwestern.edu/wwii-posters/img/ww1645-25.jpg)

diverse groups of civilians could be exhorted to meet their obligation to state and nation.[25]

The GI was a democratized update of the oldest model of citizenship, the warrior. Although more than 200,000 women served in the armed forces during the war, their contributions were eclipsed in public life by the masculine ideal of the "citizen-soldiers" who defended the nation. The masculine character of this new culture hero had enduring consequences. On one hand, it reinforced the claims black and other nonwhite soldiers could make on citizenship, allowing their manhood to be seen as a marker of patriotic virtue—not just the liability it traditionally had been in the eyes of whites. On the other hand, this claim by itself was insufficient to trump the racial privileges that continued to structure American society long after the war had ended—although it did provide openings for challenging them in a wave of civil rights action during the war and afterward. Elevating the GI to the status of first-class citizen also served to reinforce gendered hierarchies that had long shaped basic patterns of inequality in American society. Not only did white male World War II veterans enjoy guarantees of a fuller citizenship than everyone else, but the legal framing of those benefits reinforced the ideals and practices of the family wage that had kept women dependent and unequal for generations. The GIs' idealization in popular culture further reinforced traditional gender roles that would abet the resurgence of domesticity later in the decade. In light of the explosion of opportunities the war provided for women to enter public life and the workplace, this resuscitation of masculine citizenship came at a pivotal moment.[26]

The American soldier thus embodied national citizenship and legitimized government power in momentous ways. When citizens from various walks of life made increased claims on the federal government to guarantee what they saw as "fair" and "patriotic" solutions to problems raised by the war mobilization, they found their claims evaluated by way of comparison to the absolute sacrifice of the soldier who gave his life for his country. Whether the "sacrifice" in question was military service, war work, rationing, or income taxation, the legitimacy of the government's power to set the terms of the obligation was evaluated according to how it kept civilians in line with their reciprocal duty to the soldier.

This successful collective endeavor to build a national "imagined community" around the soldier had unintended consequences.[27] Government leaders who encouraged citizens to identify with the soldier did not anticipate that the cultural equation could work in reverse, as Americans visualized themselves as comrades of the soldier, patriotic members of a nation whose government owed them a diffuse but powerful right to full national citizenship. Despite this critical extension of public largesse, nationalism would set the terms of success for those who sought to claim its rights in the 1940s and beyond. As Americans rewarded the GIs with a Bill of Rights and applauded themselves for the triumph of freedom over fascist tyranny, they neglected to consider the foundations of government power on which their victory rested. In the end, the warfare state would prove less contentious and more durable than the liberties it ostensibly protected.

PART ONE

IDEOLOGY, POLITICAL CULTURE, AND STATE FORMATION

1

War Displaces Its Analog

In the late fall of 1939, with Europe descending into war after the Nazi invasion of Poland that September, the Magna Carta traveled to the United States for safe harbor and public display. In a carefully publicized ceremony, the poet laureate, dedicated antifascist, and recently appointed librarian of Congress, Archibald MacLeish, met with Lord Lothian, the British ambassador, to receive the Riverside copy of the Magna Carta. MacLeish pointed out the significance of "the turn of time which brings the Great Charter of the English to stand across this gallery from the two great charters of American freedom":

> The deposit of the Magna Charta in the library of the people's representatives in Congress is a plain and intelligible statement of a plain intelligible fact. . . . For generations we have taught our children in this Republic that our institutions of representative government were dependent on our constitutional charter for their existence. We have more recently learned, and now believe, that the opposite is also true: that without the institutions of representative government the charters of the people's rights cannot be saved.[1]

No matter that it had been a conspiracy of barons, not an uprising of the people, that had forced King John to protect their privileges at Runnymede in 1215; "the liberties of the people have often been established by those who had no interest in the people," MacLeish observed.

Franklin Delano Roosevelt was more mindful of the barons and their prerogatives. "Dear Archie," the president wrote earlier that November to approve this deft exercise in public relations:

> I think that in your remarks you can make the happy suggestion that there could properly be criticism if the Magna Carta had been turned over to the executive branch of government, i.e., the King John of modern days; but that as the library is the Library of Congress the

precious document has been retained in the safe hands of the barons and the commoners.[2]

With this strained metaphor, Roosevelt sought to portray the symbolic aid extended to Britain as an innocuous gesture steeped in the venerable Anglo-American tradition of liberty.[3] He was caught in the midst of a political firestorm over the question of aid to Britain and the other European nations fighting against Nazi Germany and fascist Italy. This battle over intervention was part of a larger struggle over the expansion of executive power that had begun in earnest after his reelection in 1936 and would continue to rage between New Dealers and conservatives through the war years and beyond.

The language of rights and freedom enjoyed a thoroughgoing revival during the Second World War, given flight by the brutalities inflicted by the Axis powers, sanctified by the sesquicentennial celebration of the Constitution, and

Librarian of Congress Archibald MacLeish, left, thanks British Ambassador Lord Lothian after accepting the Riverside copy of the Magna Carta for deposit on November 28, 1939. The Magna Carta was publicly displayed in a spot opposite the Declaration of Independence and the Constitution, a gesture intended to underscore the historical and ideological ties between the United States and Great Britain as Americans contemplated entry into the war. (Courtesy of the Library of Congress, LC-DIG-hec-27724)

hammered home to the majority of American households who regularly listened to Roosevelt's radio addresses.[4] The ruthlessness and speed displayed by the Axis lent a new urgency, and offered a qualitatively different conception of public welfare and national interest, to the meanings of statecraft in the late New Deal. As the Roosevelt administration shifted its political energies and institutional initiatives from welfare to warfare, it undertook a process of ideological transposition. It adapted the imagery and meanings of activist government to suit the requirements of a national interest defined by military security and international relations, rather than economic stability and social justice. As the purposes of government shifted from welfare to warfare, the foundations for its legitimacy shifted as well.

The New Deal on the Brink

By the autumn of 1938, it had begun to look as if "fear itself" might make a comeback. There were many signs, large and small, that the juggernaut of confidence, activism, and bluff that was the New Deal had run into dangerous territory. Ominous events threatened not only to undermine the reform program advanced by the Roosevelt administration over the course of the previous half-decade but also to strike at the very foundations of civilization itself.[5]

One such portent, oblique but telling, took place sometime after eight o'clock Eastern time on the night before Halloween. Frantic calls flooded the telephone lines in northern New Jersey and southern New York State as panicked radio listeners contacted family and friends about the Martians whose invasion they had heard "reported" with convincing if entirely fictional realism from the safety of their living rooms, courtesy of Orson Welles's Mercury Theater and the Columbia Broadcasting System.

The radio play to which they responded was a parable of social disintegration in which every authority figure misunderstood and quickly lost command of the situation, starting with the main character, an astronomer named Pierson who dismissed the mounting signs of alien invasion as innocent natural phenomena. Not long after Pierson finally began to confront the limits of his understanding, the head of the New Jersey militia announced martial law and an orderly evacuation, followed by a confident declaration by Captain Lansing of the Signal Corps that the situation was "now under complete control." Within moments, the seven thousand militia troops surrounding the Martian vehicle were incinerated. Soon thereafter, the secretary of the interior took to the air, urging listeners in unmistakably Rooseveltian tones to remain calm, place their "faith in the military forces" to deal with the invaders, and "confront this destructive adversary" as a "nation united." As more Martian cylinders were spotted landing throughout the United States, the air force dispatched waves of bombers only to see them incinerated by heat rays, while the invincible Martian war machines unleashed poisonous gas on urban centers and systematically destroyed power lines and other strategic infrastructure. "Their apparent objective," the announcer speculated, was "to crush resistance, paralyze communication, and disorganize human society." Two-thirds of the way into the hour-long broadcast, every last trace of government had been defeated summarily and the announcer had begun to send his last words from the roof of a building in New York City.

At least one million Americans reported being seriously frightened or "excited" by the broadcast, according to Hadley Cantril, the pioneering young Princeton psychologist whose study of the panic soon became a classic text. Many called their neighbors, local police, newspapers, or any other authority they could think of. That night, more than a third of the radio stations carrying the broadcast saw telephone call-ins jump by 500 percent over ordinary levels. In the area around Grover's Mill, New Jersey, where the first Martians "landed," some people became even more unhinged, speeding away in cars or seeking out neighbors in a frantic scramble.[6]

Experts in mass psychology such as Cantril worried that the *War of the Worlds* broadcast demonstrated Americans' vulnerability to manipulation by fear and uncertainty—precisely the sort of susceptibility that had already facilitated the seizure of power by the fascists in Italy, by the war government in Japan, and, above all, by the Nazis in Germany.[7] But not everyone who panicked resembled the man of the masses whose social insecurity, emotional lability, and authoritarian predilections social scientists in the late 1930s and 1940s would identify as the social dynamite waiting to explode within modern society.[8] A young white man privileged enough to attend college—a senior, no less—later admitted the broadcast had spurred him to a foolish sort of heroism. On hearing of the invasion, he tried to call his girlfriend in Poughkeepsie, New York, but was unable to reach her because of the jammed lines. He screeched off in his car and

> started driving back to Poughkeepsie. We had heard that Princeton was wiped out and gas was spreading over New Jersey and fire, so I figured there wasn't anything to do—we figured our friends and family were all dead. I made 45 miles in 35 minutes and didn't even realize it. . . . My roommate was crying and praying. . . . The speed was never under 70. . . . The gas was supposed to be spreading up north. I didn't have any idea exactly what I was fleeing from, and that made me all the more afraid. All I could think of was being burned alive or being gassed. . . . I remember thinking distinctly how easy it would be to get shot cleanly in a war.

In Newark, New Jersey, a black housewife heard her neighbors yelling "Get gas masks!" and drew a somewhat different conclusion. She dashed out of her house and ran up to passing cars, saying: "Don't you know New Jersey is destroyed by the Germans—it's on the radio." She assumed they had landed by zeppelin under cover of night, employing blitzkrieg tactics.[9]

The uncertainty and despair that revealed itself on that now infamous October night indicated just how brittle the structures of legitimate authority had become in the New Deal's darkest hour. The tumult of world politics cast a new pall over the economic catastrophe of the Great Depression, which stubbornly refused to end and indeed had deepened in recent months. By October 1938, Americans had been inundated by radio news bulletins and photographic images that made many of the scenes of *War of the Worlds* sound entirely plausible. In Manchuria, Abyssinia, and most recently the Chinese mainland, peaceful cities and villages had been invaded and mercilessly conquered in days, even hours, by columns of war machines employing the most advanced war technologies on land, at sea, and, most dramatically, from the air.

Even a country racked by the cruelties of civil war, as Spain was, discovered new horrors. In the spring of 1937, hundreds of civilians in the Basque town of Guernica, a Republican redoubt, had been incinerated in a few hours' time by the "thermite rain" hailed down by the German Condor Legion, which aimed its incendiary bombs at marketplaces and residential districts, and followed up with strafing runs on fleeing women, children, and clergy. The pilots demonstrated an "utter ferocity and scientific thoroughness" that had the calculated intent to sow terror and disorganize opposition in a fashion mimicked by Welles's fictional Martian war machines. By the time of the *War of the Worlds* broadcast almost a year and a half later, Guernica had become an international cause célèbre and Welles's listeners had encountered lurid depictions of the massacre in breaking stories, in editorials with headings such as "Death Rides the Wind," and in photos of the rubble-strewn city that reminded readers that "not one building escaped."[10]

Small wonder, then, that the college boy speeding to his girlfriend at Vassar College should have thought that gas and fire attacks might already have killed his college buddies, or that the Newark housewife believed Germany might be launching a blitzkrieg in the swamps of central New Jersey only six months after the *Hindenburg* had reached the blazing terminus to its transatlantic flight there. Even after the immediate excitement of the broadcast died down and embarrassed shock over the gullibility of certain radio listeners began to set in, some remained sufficiently unabashed to insist on preparations for invasions of a more terrestrial sort. On election day—which ushered in a cohort of conservative Democrats and Republicans whose studied opposition to Roosevelt would significantly limit the New Deal's last years—the *New York Times* reported that the War Department had recently been inundated with "countrywide requests for antiaircraft protection, renewed demands for coastal defenses, inquiries about the modernization of wartime cantonments," and other particulars of military preparedness. The "radio panic" prompted by Welles's broadcast was only the most dramatic manifestation of a mounting alarmism over the prospect of war.[11]

In the face of mounting recession and global catastrophe, Americans turned to a New Deal government that seemed inexplicably to be faltering at every turn, as if the magic decisiveness of its early successes had been inverted. Where government action previously had acted as a tonic on the body politic, restoring faith and inducing the first phase of an electoral realignment, now it sowed doubts and eroded confidence among the Democratic faithful while sparking opposition among conservatives determined to thwart Roosevelt at every step and roll back the New Deal.

When confronted with the geopolitical appetites of the fascist powers, the Roosevelt administration could respond only with a "policy of pinpricks and righteous protest," stymied as it was by domestic isolationist currents.[12] The political capital available to internationalist liberals by that time had been squandered in a disastrous sequence of missteps that followed on the heels of Roosevelt's landslide victory in 1936. Bitter fights over executive power battered the New Deal coalition in Congress—the proposal to "pack" the Supreme Court and plans to centralize power in the White House by "reorganizing" the executive were only the most galvanizing—shearing off conservative southerners, populists from the West and South, and sympathetic progressives within the Republican Party. The administration had relied on all of these camps to pass landmark legislation between 1933 and 1935.[13] But now it faced a global crisis that required even more political unity, and far vaster executive discretion, than the New Deal had ever asked of the coalition. To redress the situation, Roosevelt campaigned that very October against conservative Democrats whose "purge" from the party he hoped would transform it into a genuine party of reform. This move backfired, lending superficial credence to critics who accused FDR of dictatorial ambitions. Compounding the administration's woes was the self-inflicted wound of the "Roosevelt recession," widely understood to have been caused by FDR's decision to move toward balancing the budget in 1937. After dropping by half over the first four years of the New Deal, unemployment had spiked by a third in the year after FDR's budget cuts were announced, idling somewhere between 13 and 19 percent of those dogged Americans who were still looking for work.[14]

Those who tuned in to the *War of the Worlds* broadcast were sitting near the bottom of that second economic trough when they heard about the Martian invasion. They had reason to fear the worst, and to fret about the government's ability to save them from it. Global war was returning after a generation's respite. The nation remained impoverished, divided, and weakened, even after years of bold, nationalistic reform. Yet Roosevelt would emerge from this new, bellicose phase of world-historic crisis with his authority and popular support intact. One union loyalist wrote from San Francisco in April 1938, when the recession had been deepening for over a year, "You have not let us down. We know that. . . . But it's now become obvious that the fight wasn't over with our 27 million votes in 1936. . . . We have gained a better life—we mean to maintain this better life and extend it to others."[15]

The liberal crusade to bring the "American way of life" to more people, both within the United States and beyond its borders, would be propelled as much by the war that many on the left feared as by the Democratic votes they anticipated. Waging war shifted the foundations of government activism onto new social, economic, and institutional grounds, which in turn fundamentally altered the practices of national citizenship and the programs of national government on which the administration could draw. Geopolitics also split a New Deal coalition that had barely had time to form by 1938, when all three fascist powers began their expansive designs. As global war brought foreign affairs onto front pages and into living rooms, it placed further strain on the electoral pillars of the New Deal state—white and black working-class voters, nativist farmers in the South and German farmers in the Midwest, middle-class Democrats of varying ethnicities. The war pushed antifascists and interventionists in one direction—often for diverse reasons, as with Poles, Czechs, African Americans, and southern whites—pulled Axis sympathizers among Italians and Germans in another, and alienated dogged neutrals such as Irish Americans. The question of intervention was more than a wedge issue. It reframed the nature of government activism, redirecting interest and institutional innovation into an international realm that could just as easily obscure as energize domestic concerns. The internationalization of political energies and electoral orientation was most evident in the 1940 election, which Roosevelt won by reassuring voters that his record of government activism, though controversial, offered some kind of bulwark against the looming crisis in Europe. The voters chose Roosevelt largely because this argument was persuasive to them. Without the coming of war, he very well might have lost the election.[16]

It is ironic that the second coming of global war should have marked the end of reform, considering the extent to which the New Deal was beholden to the "analog" of World War I in establishing its bona fides and surrounding its reform program with a nationalistic aura in the 1930s. In its personnel, policy ideas, class politics, and foreign relations, the Roosevelt administration had been shaped by the legacy of the Great War. Nearly all the legislation passed in the initial burst of activity known as the "First Hundred Days," the first incarnation of the New Deal aimed mostly at economic recovery, enacted policies that either were lifted directly from the war or had been refined in the 1920s by policy makers building on the wartime government's foundations. Crop subsidies had their roots in Herbert Hoover's Food Administration; the industrial cooperation of the National Recovery Administration modeled itself on the War Industries Board and had as its director the World War I holdover General Hugh Johnson; the Civilian Conservation Corps echoed the values of the preparedness movement; even the Tennessee Valley Authority (TVA)—the poster child of the New Deal—had its origins in the nitrate plant established at Muddy Flats in the Great War.[17]

The approach of another global conflict brought the reminder that no moral equivalent could lay claim to national obligation more effectively than war itself. Men of Roosevelt's generation recalled vividly how the drums of war could drown out gentler hymns of reform. This lesson had been seared into FDR's memory during a critical episode in his political education. As the Democratic candidate for vice president in 1920, he had seen the harrowing defeat of the League of Nations guarantee his ticket's crushing loss. This time would have to be different, even though the makeshift alliances that had thwarted the League had grown into an organized coalition over the course of a generation, centered on "isolationist" opponents who found political capital and institutional momentum in the passage of neutrality legislation between 1935 and 1939.[18]

Treading carefully, Roosevelt built the case that chaos in international relations was analogous to the economic chaos the New Deal had partially vanquished. After Japan invaded the Chinese mainland in the summer of 1937, Roosevelt responded with his proposal to "quarantine the aggressors" in order to end "the present reign of terror and international lawlessness"—proposing "positive endeavors to preserve peace," although he did not specify precisely how the "contagion of war" would be stopped. Addressing an audience in Chicago, the capital of midwestern isolationism, Roosevelt did not refer to the aggressors by name. But his audience recognized that he referred not only to events in Shanghai but also to the Italian invasion of Abyssinia in 1935 and the involvement of Germany and the Soviet Union in the Spanish Civil War.[19]

Despite Roosevelt's caution the speech backfired, alarming the advocates of neutrality. Senator Hiram Johnson, who had campaigned for FDR against the orders of his own party in 1932 and gone on to support many of the early initiatives of the New Deal but had turned decisively against him in the court-packing episode, telegraphed presidential advisor Raymond Moley with a blunt assessment: "Levying sanctions means their enforcement . . . at once then you have war."[20] A firestorm of criticism fell upon Roosevelt. The implications of his speech made even some of his supporters quail. Brownie

Dressler of New York City, an admitted "admirer," opened her letter to the president with this: "Shades of Woodrow Wilson! The poor fellow must have stirred in his grave in efforts to warn you not to make the same mistake he did. *He* wanted to 'make the world safe for Democracy'—*you* want to make the world safe for 'civilization.' Heaven preserve us from our heroes!" Dressler felt the United States should first attend to its own problems ("numerous enough, you know"). "I'm sorry," she wrote, "for the first time since your election, that you are at the head of the government of this country." She hastened to add, "I'm not impugning your motives, which I still respect." But she had grown wary of his charisma—"of such personality stuff are dictators born, I suppose, even benevolent dictators such as you would be"—and wished he would change his mind before he brought on a cataclysm. "You have enough on your hands taking care of America," she closed. "Please don't try to 'save the world'!"[21]

Discouraged by the popular outcry at his quarantine speech, Roosevelt shied away from any overt gesture toward intervention for nearly three years, as German and Japanese aggression mounted. This sensitivity, which cost Britain, the United States, and the world dearly in the long run, reflected not only the seriousness with which Roosevelt regarded public opinion but also the underlying problem of implementing policies whose legitimacy was deeply contested.[22] But even if the quarantine speech proved politically counterproductive, it provided Roosevelt with an opportunity to adapt the oratory he had honed in domestic battles to fit the exigencies of foreign policy. Especially telling was his resort to the imagery of public health, one of the earliest and most indisputable examples of the expansion of police power to protect a broader public welfare. Considering that his most immediate, if unstated, point of reference was Japan, he may also have been invoking long-held racist associations of Chinatowns with filth, squalor, and contagion—associations that had also underwritten muscular governmental action since the early years of progressive reform in the nineteenth century.[23]

The United States was "fortunate," Roosevelt observed, for its distance from the aggressions in Europe and Asia allowed it to invest in "bridges and boulevards, dams and reforestation, the conservation of our soil and many other kinds of useful works rather than into huge standing armies and vast supplies of implements of war." But this peaceful, productive use of the nation's energies, he suggested, might not last beyond the "circumstances of the moment" if the unnamed aggressors were not checked. "There can be no stability or peace either within nations or between nations except under laws and moral standards adhered to by all." Isolation was impossible in the interdependent modern world. "International anarchy destroys every foundation for peace."[24]

References to lawlessness provided another link to the language of reform. In his September 1932 campaign speech to the Commonwealth Club in San Francisco, Roosevelt had traced the career of liberalism as a struggle to protect the individual against the "arbitrary power" wielded by the "man of ruthless force" throughout history—initially "ruling barons" in early modern Europe, then speculators, "financial titans," "princes of property," and other members of the "economic oligarchy" in industrial society. Not only was the Depression the work of such men, he argued, but so was its continuation, for in their opposition to efforts to restore the "public welfare," they threatened to "drag the industry back to a state of anarchy."[25] The modernized "economic constitutional order" he envisioned as a corrective was defined as much by its protection against the "Ismael or Insull whose hand is against every man" as it was by the positive regulatory measures that would prevent industrial society from destroying itself.

The bandit continued to play a useful role in legitimizing the liberal state throughout the 1930s. A crime wave presented J. Edgar Hoover of the Federal Bureau of Investigation with an opportunity to secure the place of federal policing within the growing New Deal state. Hoover's G-men bagged renegade bandits such as Pretty Boy Floyd even as they seized the public imagination in a series of films, pulp novels, comic books, and other effusions of popular culture, and captured the public purse under the rubric of a "New Deal" for fighting crime.[26] The tropes of gangsterism and criminality also remained useful for painting business opposition to the New Deal in hues of illicit activity. Roosevelt's loyal ally and secretary of the treasury, Henry Morgenthau Jr., found a delicious way to criminalize the "barons" by publicizing the bid by Alfred P. Sloan, chairman of General Motors, to evade taxes by incorporating his yacht.[27] With this negative publicity he hoped to evoke memories of Al Capone, another critic of the New Deal, who famously had been jailed on tax evasion. As late as the 1944 election, Morgenthau was still trying to find ways to bring up "my gangsters," as he put it, to retaliate against business opposition to Roosevelt.[28]

Roosevelt's opposition soon learned to criminalize domestic politics with more determination and thoroughness than he could ever muster. Not only southern Democrats and Republicans in Congress moved to block nearly all of the administration's legislative proposals since the disastrous court-packing and executive reorganization proposals of 1937, but determined foes on both sides of the aisle had begun to devise direct assaults on the New Deal. Leading Republican senator Robert Taft of Ohio worked effectively to deny FDR further successes, letting slip only two consequential initiatives—the creation of the United States Housing Authority in 1937 and the passage of the Fair Labor Standards Act in 1938. Texas Democrat Martin Dies chaired the House Select Committee on Un-American Activities, directing the lion's share of his inquiries into allegations directed at "internal subversion" by communists within New Deal agencies.[29]

The Dies Committee was not the only payback for FDR's attempted purge of southern conservatives from the Democratic Party. In 1939 and 1940, Senator Carl Hatch, Democrat from New Mexico, led the passage of the Act to Prevent Pernicious Political Activities, popularly known as the Hatch Act, which banned political activities by federal employees—including Works Progress Administration (WPA) workers implicated in efforts to get out the vote for liberal candidates in the attempted "purge" of 1938. Howard W. Smith, Democratic congressman from Virginia, added to the countersubversive tool kit by sponsoring the Alien Registration Act in 1940, which outlawed advocating the violent overthrow of the government, a net with which anticommunists hoped to catch the assortment of left-leaning intellectuals, economists, lawyers, and other public figures circulating within the Roosevelt administration who had flirted with the Communist Party during its Popular Front phase from 1935 to 1939.[30]

By the late 1930s, the basic legitimacy of the New Deal was under assault by political opposition at home and ominous developments abroad. As his overreaction to the criticism of the quarantine speech indicated, Roosevelt recognized the dangers of losing the public's confidence. To navigate the dangerously shifting currents of public sentiment, the administration took elaborate measures to monitor and shape public attitudes to avoid precisely that fate. These measures deserve attention in their own right, for they reveal both the means by which the administration sought to create a modern public sphere, and the liberal values its ideology was designed to instill.

Listening to the People

From the formative years of his political career onward, Franklin Delano Roosevelt demonstrated an exceptionally well-developed knack for taking the pulse of the people. He did this at first through political letter writing, which his handlers encouraged as a way of augmenting the "personal touch" so vital to retail politics. Louis Howe, the newspaperman who was Roosevelt's main political advisor from his Wilson days through the early years of the New Deal, helped lay the ground for his 1932 nomination by orchestrating an elaborate correspondence between FDR and the leading lights of the fatally divided Democratic Party over the course of the 1920s. Not only did this make for excellent public relations among both the party elite and the rank-and-file delegates, placing both classes of politicians in direct contact with Roosevelt over the heads of local and state machines, but it provided Roosevelt with a knowledge of political sentiments and policy commitments that was unrivaled in both national scope and local minutiae. During the 1932 campaign Howe helped set up a staff of six or so "dictators" and forty or fifty typists to expand the operation.[31]

Once in the White House, Roosevelt and Howe made the mail a vital part of the administration's political communications. A full-time staff of twenty-two handled the vast influx of correspondence, which crested at almost half a million in Roosevelt's first week in office but soon settled down to more than four thousand a week in ordinary times—higher in busier seasons, when as many as twenty thousand letters a week poured in, and the staff mushroomed to as many as seventy. In the twelve years of his presidency, Roosevelt received far in excess of the fifteen million letters that remain preserved in his presidential library.[32]

It was not just the spike in quantity that mattered but the way in which the mail was handled. Howe, Farley, and Roosevelt's other aides trained the staff to respond to every letter that was not completely negative, and to emulate the paternalistic, upbeat, engaged tone of the president in providing semicustomized responses. They also employed an extensive system of referrals to relevant agencies for actionable requests, such as those involving relief, loans, or information. The file cabinets of the New Deal agencies bulged with "Dear Mr. President" or "Dear Mrs. Roosevelt" letters forwarded from the White House for reply, staffers' blue pencil underlining certain passages that indicated why the letter was being forwarded to that particular agency.[33]

Something of the popular power of this chain of communication can be seen in the chaos that ensued in 1938 when the March of Dimes campaign to fund polio research began encouraging children to send dimes to the White House. The logistics of handling this mountain of change shut down the White House social calendar for two weeks during one especially large surge, as timely correspondence such as RSVPs could not be separated from the currency-laden envelopes. Nearly $27 million rolled into the coffers of the March of Dimes this way, ten cents at a time.[34] Since the creation of the U.S. Post Office and the franking privilege in the late eighteenth century, politicians had relied on the mail to test public opinion and shape it to their liking.[35] The Roosevelt administration's system of political communication surpassed all precedents. Here was a form of constituent service performed on a vast scale. It couldn't have made congressmen very happy to find out about this, as they invariably did.

Despite the availability of reliable polls, Roosevelt continued to lean heavily on the mail and his trips around the country to hone his unparalleled sensitivity to the shifting moods of the nation. Every evening a stack of fifty or so letters awaited perusal at his bedside. Often the president would dictate a reply in person. On a weekly basis, and after major speeches and events, he received regular "mail briefs" that broke down the contents of the mail by subject and separated out the obvious pressure campaign mail from the rest.[36]

President Roosevelt's March of Dimes campaign to fund a cure for polio demonstrated the scope of the communications conduit he had created between the White House and the American people. At times the flood of letters bearing dimes from ordinary Americans was so great it disrupted the Washington social calendar. (Courtesy of the Library of Congress, LC-DIG-hec-29294)

On the most basic level, Roosevelt used the mail as a feedback mechanism. When launching the National Recovery Administration (NRA) he sought to bolster the voluntaristic foundations of that program, urging his listeners to add their names to the "Roll of Honor" to be published in local post offices by sending letters or telegrams to the White House with a pledge to comply with the NRA codes. Tens of thousands of communications inundated Hugh Johnson from the mailroom.[37] The most dramatic case of a political feedback loop, though, was Roosevelt's policy retreat in the face of the outpouring of opposition to his October 1937 "quarantine the aggressor" speech.

Roosevelt could also use the mail as a weapon, encouraging his radio audiences to let their congressmen know how they felt about a particular issue. According to the *New York Times*, every surge of mail to the White House was accompanied by a surge of constituent mail to Congress, but "the name that appears in the letters more often than any other is that of President Roosevelt." Often such invocations were accompanied by threats of electoral defection if the president's program was threatened.[38] Roosevelt was most effective when harmonizing his own language and emphases with those of his obscure correspondents, as he did by regularly incorporating their letters to him in his fireside chats. This may help explain why so many of the letters written to FDR demonstrated an exceptionally intimate tone.[39]

This feeling Roosevelt had for the people has often been discounted as mere folksy affect, part of FDR's tool kit as the "Great Communicator." But beneath the extraordinary efforts devoted to cultivating this line of communication with ordinary people was a deeper philosophy of popular sovereignty and modern government that built on progressive efforts to craft a modern public sphere. Like his mentor and hero, Woodrow Wilson, Roosevelt sought nothing less than to transform the nature of popular sovereignty by creating a pipeline between himself and the people. His was a paternalistic vision that was closely related to what he saw as the government's obligation to respond directly to the economic needs of ordinary Americans.[40]

Beyond the White House's efforts, a second source of demand within government for systematically gathered political information came from administrators who increasingly needed to know what their clients were thinking in order to implement policy on a national scale. This evolved from the long-established practice of retaining knowledgeable informants, transforming over the 1930s and early 1940s into more systematic techniques.[41] The beginnings of the shift can be glimpsed in the vivid, information-packed reports that veteran journalist Lorena Hickok sent to Harry Hopkins, head of the Federal Emergency Relief Administration (FERA), over the course of a year and a half starting in the summer of 1933.

Hickok relied on her common sense and her reporter's ear, honed by years of following stories in courthouses and on city desks. Her reports were detailed letters, banged out on a typewriter after interviewing key local figures involved in the business of relief. She sought to make her accounts generalizable despite her many idiosyncrasies of temperament and belief. Also striking was how intertwined her political judgments were with her pragmatic insights on the challenges confronting relief. Not only did she warn Hopkins about external political threats from the likes of the Communist Party and pass along second-hand gossip—such as that Milo Reno, the gadfly organizer of the National Farmers' Holiday Association, was meddling with the treasury of the Farmers Union cooperative in Iowa—but she practically gave the name, rank, and serial numbers of local officials whose interpretations of the guidelines for relief varied from those in Washington.[42] These political nuggets arrived interspersed with sensitive evaluations of the mind of the farmer and why he might be vulnerable to the enticements of, say, the Farm Holiday movement. She must have felt she had earned her grasp of how local people, especially those in rural areas, felt about the New Deal, for she did not hesitate to give frank (and impolitic) advice, such as her insistence that

> somebody ought to explain a lot of things to these farmers. NOT General Johnson or Mr. Wallace or Mr. Peek making speeches—which they don't read—in Chicago, the Twin Cities, or Des Moines. But a missionary . . . Believe me, the Communists are doing it![43]

Hickok was also asked by Henry Morgenthau, the secretary of the treasury, to report back to him if she heard anything of use to his department, which had offices that tended to be located near FERA field offices. Irving Howe made a similar request regarding the NRA, Farm Credit Administration, and Home Loan Board.[44] Furthermore, Hickok was not the only scout sending reports back to Hopkins; there are sixty-seven boxes' worth of field reports produced by other informants.[45] Bureaucratic need pushed Hickok to her limits, but soon more systematic sources would have to be cultivated. Over time the instrumental value of her political observations must have outweighed that of her practical observations about the relief program. By early 1935 Hopkins had brought her into the reelection campaign, and her reports on relief ended.[46]

The Roosevelt administration cultivated every conceivable source of information with unprecedented diligence. Consider the routine requirement of field office reporting to Washington. Over the course of the 1930s, especially from 1935 onward, the task of coordinating these reports fell to the National Emergency Council (NEC). The state directors of the NEC, who were authorized to coordinate New Deal agencies in each state, sent regular reports back to Washington on the local performance of the New Deal. The sensitive nature of this information-collecting function is suggested by simply imagining how certain congressmen and senators opposed to intervention would have responded to the October 25, 1940, NEC memo reporting "complete approval of the Government's firm attitude toward Japan," with "almost unanimous sentiment in the 36 states reporting," all of which favored the fateful embargo on scrap iron.[47]

The NEC also aimed to attain a comprehensive review of public opinion through a clipping service that by 1940 had become vast in the scope and intensity of its coverage. It provided news clippings and brief commentary, broken down by agency and/or locality, to help guide New Deal administrators in their efforts to manage public relations. Notably, the clipping service was not available to congressmen or senators in any regular fashion, and so threatened their sway over constituent service, communication about government, and local awareness of broader currents of opinion. Despite attempts by conservative congressmen to kill it, it lived on within the wartime propaganda agency, the Office of War Information (OWI), under the auspices of the Bureau of Special Services, whose pioneering analyses would advance the method of content analysis.[48]

The WPA attempted to keep track of shifting public attitudes toward it by systematically analyzing the volume, geographic distribution, and content of its mail—gauging the precise proportions that were requests for employment, complaints about irregular pay, grievances about working conditions, and so on. This practice evolved from the more basic task of keeping lists of requests for employment begun by the WPA's predecessor, the FERA.[49] This constant and systematic routing of mail within the executive branch did not always endear the New Deal to its correspondents, but it did establish a direct line of communication—even when it alienated constituents and highlighted the challenge to established channels of constituent service. One such letter, which Marvin McIntyre forwarded from the White House to the WPA in early December 1938, proceeded for two single-spaced pages to outline a scheme by which idle WPA workers could be used to safeguard schoolchildren. Unsatisfied by the form letter the WPA sent in response, its author—a small businessman from Cleveland who specialized in the manufacture of souvenirs and other specialty items—upbraided the WPA and Harry Hopkins for the "aimless letter," whose boilerplate lacked any "sense or reason." "Do you realize," the author railed, "that my letter was regarding a matter that deals with tragedies swift and terrible? Unexpected and unnecessary?" He concluded that "the only way to handle such matters is to take them up direct with the elective representatives from my own state and district and let them bring the subject to you or maybe it would be considered important enough for them to pass some sort of resolution that will make it mandatory on your part."[50]

As the New Deal grew bigger and techniques of measuring public opinion grew more precise, administrators turned to emerging experts for assistance in gathering political information. The need for more precise and reliable measures of public opinion was pragmatic as well as political. Crop subsidies in the 1930s would not work if farmers did not understand the mechanics of domestic allotment. When gasoline rationing was introduced in 1942, it nearly foundered on the vast regional difference in acceptance of its necessity (oil was abundant in much of the West). Both policies were identified with a broader liberal program that administration figures viewed as essential to the New Deal, if not the survival of the nation itself. Popular misunderstanding or opposition could provide conservatives with just the ammunition they needed to torpedo liberal favorites. The surveying of clients and constituents reveals that this expensive and potentially controversial practice became increasingly indispensable, even if policy makers were not always able to make use of what they paid for.

Because government survey research was grounded in the need to make both material resources and citizens' subjectivities systematically legible, it came under the direction of men such as Rensis Likert.[51] As a psychologist at New York University, Likert had developed a five-point scale to measure intensity of attitudes and produced an influential study, *Morale and Agency Management*, which made him a leading expert on "scientific" attitude research and its application to government. His tenure at the Bureau of Agricultural Economics as director of the Program Surveys Division did much to shape the fledgling field of opinion research. When he was hired by the Department of Agriculture (USDA) in 1939, Likert took charge of an experimental unit that had conducted extensive scouting reports among farmers to determine a range of facts, from crop yields to farmers' opinions of New Deal programs. This work was initially quite similar to Lorena Hickok's: it entailed lots of travel to family farms and much front-porch conversation, which the scouts wrote down after driving away. Likert was able to convert these scouts into "scientific" survey researchers, training them to follow random sampling procedure and implement carefully structured instruments that left little or no room for the open-ended conversations that had been their bread and butter.[52] This kind of knowledge discipline was essential to bureaucratic efficacy, as the exploding demand for Likert's work outside the USDA demonstrated.

Roosevelt and his aides also had access to the most advanced polling, in addition to receiving information via back channels from influential figures working in the media. Often the key innovators here had been shaped by careers in political journalism, as were Howe and Hickok. Other journalists included Archibald MacLeish, who had written for Henry Luce's *Fortune*, and the CBS broadcaster Elmer Davis, who would succeed him as head of the OWI. The polling pioneers George Gallup and Elmo Roper were also creatures of the news business; both offered their services to the president on occasion. Most news veterans shared Gallup's optimism about managing the new public sphere, which he betrayed when he described public opinion as the very "pulse of democracy."[53]

At the same time that Roosevelt sought a direct line of communication with the people, while his administrators strove for client service and bureaucratic comprehensiveness, a third mode of popular knowledge evolved among the writers, photographers, muralists, and other artists who flocked to the New Deal's cultural programs—particularly the Farm Security Administration's rural photography, the Public Works Administration's mural projects, and above all, the WPA Federal Writers' and Federal Theater projects.[54] Individually, these artists found in the New Deal a wide variety of opportunities and ideals. But it is fair to say that collectively they were engaged in building a new kind of public sphere, one capable of countering the "totalitarian" threats to democracy that the Soviet show trials and the Nazis' Nuremberg rallies had monumentalized so vividly.[55]

MacLeish was a prominent leader in this project to fortify the "democratic mind." It was for this very reason that his name came to the attention of the White House when it sought to nominate a new librarian of Congress in the late spring of 1939. MacLeish's nomination had come with the decisive endorsement of Supreme Court justice Felix frankfurter, his old Harvard Law School mentor. Responding to a query from Roosevelt, Frankfurter had written in May 1939, "The librarians that have left the most enduring marks have not been technical librarians." A great librarian, he argued, should not only be a scholar and "a man who knows books, loves books and makes books," but also be equipped to face the cultural challenges of the day. "We are at the threshold of deeper problems" than ever before, he warned, due to the "educational influence" exerted by the "two new media, radio and the movie," which were already "competing for primacy with the printed page." MacLeish was the man for the job. In addition to being a trained lawyer and a poet laureate, MacLeish was the "father of the so-called radio play" and had done pioneering work on the film series Contemporary History. In closing, Frankfurter emphasized the distinctive "creative energy" MacLeish could summon in "making the Library of Congress the great center of the cultural resources of the nation in the technological setting of our time."[56]

Recognizing the enormous size of this challenge, MacLeish initially declined the librarianship. In a letter to Frankfurter he acknowledged the lure of advancing the "new and useful work of cultural dissemination," but worried his poetry would suffer. He accepted only after Roosevelt promised him time off to write.[57]

Upon MacLeish's nomination by Roosevelt in June, Republican representative J. Parnell Thomas of the Dies Committee immediately went on the attack, deriding him as a "fellow traveler" and observing that his candidacy was "a repetition of evidence that Communist influence had entered executive appointments lately."[58] Thomas and the other members of the committee had devoted hours to investigating and conducting hearings on "internal subversion" within the New Deal, which Thomas equated with fascism, Nazism, and Bolshevism—together, he claimed, they constituted "the four horsemen of autocracy."[59] Despite the vituperation, MacLeish's nomination passed Congress.

Once approved, MacLeish moved quickly to make the library an institution worthy of its mandate to rally all the cultural resources of the nation. One of his first initiatives was to invite his close friend the poet Carl Sandburg, author of the epic six-volume biography *Lincoln,* to be the library's first consultant in poetry. MacLeish had in mind the uplifting influence Sandburg could provide, particularly "your talk with members of the Library staff—particularly with Alan Lomax and the boys working with folksong and music—your educational influence upon the people's representatives in Congress, to say nothing of the Librarian of the people's representatives in Congress."[60] Sandburg declined, but the request reveals something about the nature of the working group MacLeish sought to assemble.

Within a matter of months, the library would provide safe harbor for a number of writers, folklorists, musicologists, and other scattered adherents of the Popular Front seeking shelter from domestic and international assaults on their intellectual commitments. Their rarefied world was in the process of being decimated by the dual hammer blows of Soviet deceit, which had become impossible to ignore after the show trials and the nonaggression pact with Germany, and the congressional attacks on "un-American subversives" in the WPA cultural programs and other New Deal agencies, which had been mounting since the beginning of the "little Red Scare" that was prompted by domestic responses to the Spanish Civil War.[61] Dies and his crew across the street in the Capitol could make life difficult for MacLeish's new staff, but until they could move their fellow representatives to cut their budget, MacLeish's intellectuals would remain to walk the marble hallways of the Library of Congress. When in the fall of 1941 Roosevelt also made MacLeish the head of his main propaganda agency, the Office of Facts and Figures (OFF, a precursor to the OWI), the line he and his culture workers would have to walk only became more fraught with peril and promise. The institution over which MacLeish presided may have been the "people's library," as he liked to think of it, but it scarcely deserved to be called the Library of Congress at that point.

The political and ideological stakes of the search for a Popular Front imaginary revealed themselves in the efforts of Alan Lomax, MacLeish's "assistant in charge" of the Library's Archive of American Folk Song. In the preceding decade Lomax had made a name for himself as a pioneering student of folk music, traveling throughout the South with his father, John, to conduct field recordings of "Negro folksong" by masters such as Huddie "Leadbelly" Ledbetter. Toward the end of the thirties, Lomax charged Americans with a democratic responsibility for the overlooked treasures of their culture, urging them to go out and capture the "music in your own back yard."[62] This romantic nationalism informed the approach that the folklorists working under Lomax took in their efforts to devise a democratic approach to war nationalism.

The people whom Lomax assembled around himself in the Archive of Folk Song—with MacLeish's full blessing—understood implicitly what his

ALAN LOMAX

**Authority on American Folk-Lore . . . Archivist to the
Library of Congress . . . Commentator and Artist on
"Columbia's School of the Air"**

The Library of Congress drew on the talent and expertise cultivated by years of New
Deal cultural programs to mold the messages intended to make American citizens
war-minded. Alan Lomax, a pioneer in the field of folklore, was one of the many Popular
Front figures who found employment in the Library. (Courtesy of the Library of
Congress, LC-USZ62-121915)

ambitions were and how they applied to the problem of a democratic morale.
His field worker in Virginia, Fletcher Collins Jr., wrote to him on December
11, 1941, to report he had been "mentally exploring the extraordinary possi-
bilities which this recording technique has in our wartime situation as well
as afterward":

It opens up a field which has not before been touched by the radio, and a field of enormous importance to Americans. It heightens their consciousness of themselves as Americans, and it contributes vitally to civilian morale in expressing what the common people of the nation are feeling and thinking, and expressions of others than governmental leaders, radio commentators, and newsmen.[63]

Collins had been recommended by Harold Spivacke, chief of the library's Music Division. In the eyes of Spivacke, Lomax, and the other staff of the Library of Congress, the interviews were to be part of a much broader "cultural strategy," in their words, that would democratize the nation's wartime morale.[64] As Lomax himself put it, the "total plan" was "to make it possible for the American people to explain for themselves what America means and has meant to them." By his reasoning, "the words and music have already been made by the people and presumably they like it." The library's role was simply to "put this material together and make it speak for the whole people rather than for any special region or group."[65] This vision of their task bore a curious if ultimately superficial resemblance to the role of the "organic intellectual" envisioned by the Italian radical Antonio Gramsci in his prison notebooks, on which he worked while held by the fascist government of Benito Mussolini. Whereas Gramsci's organic intellectual was supposed to emerge spontaneously from the life of the people through a process of authentic ideological selection, advancing class consciousness in the process, the library proposed to use the "science" of folklore as the basis for selecting representatives of the people in order to bend their voices into harmonies that could harness national consciousness. Only in the midst of the world-historic death struggle between communism and fascism could such a fusion of nationalism and proletarian realism suggest itself.[66]

A sense of the cultural strategy can be gleaned from a memorandum written around the time of Pearl Harbor by Pete Seeger's father, Charles, and Benjamin Botkin, his fellow folklorist and co-convener of the WPA folklore committee. In the memo the duo provided some organizational suggestions for how the library could assist the government in dealing with groups of various nationalities. Entitled "Tradition as a Factor in Cultural Strategy," it argued for an inclusive, pluralistic strategy allowing "the fuller realization of American cultural forces as they affect national unity and their fuller utilization in the present national emergency."[67] Botkin and Seeger sought funding to tailor education and information efforts to communities of different ethnicities, in hopes of avoiding the "severity of the aftermath"—presumably a reference to the outpouring of anti-immigrant, anti-German sentiment and the nativism of the Ku Klux Klan that followed World War I.

What was most striking about their memorandum was the ambitions it revealed for cultural work during the war emergency. Botkin and Seeger proposed to meet the emergency with a two-pronged strategy: first, the rapid production of "local and traditional material" capturing "the most characteristic reactions of the common man"; and second, a longer-term production "expressing and evoking the deepest-set, most universal potentialities of American cultures." The emphasis in the second prong was most decidedly on the plural. The proposed projects would subject "native" culture to the "same scrutiny" as "the minority groups and non-Anglo-American traditions." Further, "the American tradition" was to be presented "in its positive content and as an active force making for diversification as against the regimentation of collective social organization." The moment was propitious, they argued, because the rush of events was "shocking us into a new consciousness of our submerged cultural variations, as well as bringing into open conflict the strains and tensions, divisions and cleavages, latent in our composite ethnic, linguistic, regional, and economic heritage." It fell to the library to "direct" and "control" these "cultural trends" to preempt "their impending realignment and possible perversion."[68]

The library was specially equipped for the "analysis and control" of cultural "block resistances," the folklorists argued, because unlike "economic, political, sociological, statistical, psychological, and other techniques," theirs was a discipline devoted to the study of "unwritten and popular sources of American culture ('folk stuff')." Only this approach could allow the government to "penetrate through those layers"—"of 'print' and the abstractions of an all-leveling Americanism," as the memo's authors put it—to the core of our native-immigrant, indigenous-cosmopolitan "expression-spirit." Here was the "stuff" of the people itself: "at once collective and individual, stabilizing and plastic," these "unwritten materials" were the "nurture of a living and vital culture and the safeguard of democracy."[69]

The broader goals of this cultural strategy went unrealized, as congressional attacks and budget cuts eventually made its continuation untenable.[70] Some remnants of it can still be found in the archives of the Folklife Center: a proposal for a series of pocket-sized "American Songsters" with selected folk songs—"salty, swashbuckling, ironic, humorous and sentimental in the democratic vein of the American people"—appropriate to the cultural traditions of the major regions, for use in "conscription camps"; a plan for a pamphlet explaining the historical origins of "The Star-Spangled Banner"; lists of suggested "tunes good for marching or community singing"; a memorandum from Alan Lomax recommending that Spivacke hire an especially promising folklorist from Wayne University, who might prove useful in "morale building work in the Detroit area."[71]

The fate of one radio program of American folksong, aimed at GIs listening to military radio in the Pacific Northwest and Pacific Theater, suggested that military culture and folk culture—at least as conceived by the library—would not mix easily when war finally came. The idea was to overcome the commercialism of American popular culture through direct immersion in authentic roots music. Lomax, in a separate memorandum, had deemed both the beloved radio star Kate Smith and her signature rendition of "God Bless America" to be "extremely dull and mediocre" because "they have both been elevated to an artificially astronomical position by the power of mass advertising and the star system."[72]

Audience research in 1943 revealed that many, perhaps most, of the marines who eventually had the opportunity to hear broadcasts of American "folksong" from the South did not share Lomax or Spivacke's appreciation for the organic and lived expressions of the folk. Of seventy-two soldiers and sailors surveyed at one "spot check" at Dutch Harbor in Alaska, only eighteen admitted that they liked them, whereas twenty-three disliked them and thirty-one "were indifferent." While some "more or less informed men" liked hearing the songs for their authenticity, and others from rural areas "had a nostalgic liking for it," many were frustrated by the unfamiliar sound and style of group singing. In the words of one serviceman, "You can't understand what the hell they're saying." Spivacke was not surprised by this reaction, as it reflected the sad state "of our folk song situation" in an urbanized society.[73] Folk songs, poetry, and the native talent of the servicemen may have provided superior material for "the integration of the people and, specifically, of the conscripts," but too many of them wanted to understand immediately what it was they were hearing.

It was revealing that one of the folklorists' programs that did survive to gain a prominent place in the war effort was the Marine Corps Combat Recordings. The project was the brainchild of Spivacke, who worked with Brigadier General Robert Denig, wartime director of public relations for the Marine Corps. It entailed providing wire recorders to marines in the combat zones of the Pacific Theater in order to capture the immediate reflections of their comrades recently returned from battle. Though mainly comprised of "Joe Blow interviews" with ordinary marines, rather than more elaborate ethnographic fare, these recordings found their way onto radio and into Marine Corps publicity spots.[74] Unlike "the people," the combat soldier represented a figure whom wartime Americans would unhesitatingly embrace.

Transposing Ideology from Welfare to Warfare

Although the "cultural strategy" ultimately yielded mixed results at best for the Roosevelt administration, an alternative approach to building a democratic public sphere soon appeared with the rapid-fire succession of German annexations and invasions from 1938 onward, coupled with Japan's advances into China. Sensing an opening, the Roosevelt administration turned its energies toward "national defense" as an organizing principle of government action.

In making its case for the peacetime draft and the building of military camps, aid to Britain and other allies, and expanded military contracting for munitions and other war materiel, the administration found the criminalized caricature of external enemies useful. In this political climate, dominated by the skepticism of former progressives and the determined opposition of mobilized conservatives, and with isolationists still a force in Congress, it was essential to rely on the neutral language of national defense, and portray the conversion of government to purposes of war as if it were simply an expansion of the New Deal to larger and more pressing vistas, in order to safeguard "security" on a far grander scale. It was the analog of war inverted, with mobilization for military conflict cast as a New Deal for the world.

The fall of France in the spring of 1940 made this new framework stick. France, the proud builder of one of the wonders of modern military engineering, the Maginot Line, crumpled before the German blitzkrieg in a matter of weeks, sending waves of panic throughout Europe and beyond. In his May 26, 1940, fireside chat, Roosevelt reassured listeners of the soundness of his administration's preparations for national defense, and made the case for more ambitious measures. After trotting out the impressive numbers of ships and planes produced, and acknowledging the government's reliance on businessmen— "patriotic Americans of proven merit and of unquestioned ability in their special fields"—he moved on to make two interrelated points. The first was that "physical" defense relied on "the spirit and morale of a free people," which in turn depended on there being "no breakdown or cancellation of any of the great social gains which we have made in these past years." He warned against a "pincers movement" by those who would use the national emergency as an excuse to roll back the minimum wage, maximum hours, security against unemployment and old age, conservation of natural resources, agricultural assistance, and housing programs of the New Deal. His second point had to do with the threat of a "fifth column" that sought to sow "discord" by challenging defense and welfare policies so that "singleness of national purpose may be undermined." Echoing his now famous inaugural line about "fear itself," he warned that "faith and courage can yield to doubt and fear," making it easy for fifth columnists to induce a "state of panic." "The unity of the state," he concluded, "can be so sapped that its strength is destroyed."[75]

The same themes structured Roosevelt's fireside chat on December 29, 1940, which made the case for extending military aid to Britain, later known as Lend-Lease. He opened by comparing the world crisis to the banking crisis that had confronted his fledgling administration in 1933. With Germany ruling much of continental Europe, and recently joined together with Italy and Japan to form the Axis, the United States faced the prospect of "living at the point of a gun." All that stood between the United States and this banditry was Great Britain, fighting for its life against the Luftwaffe. Accordingly, it was a simple matter of "realistic, practical military policy, based on the advice of our military experts," that the United States should provision Britain and the other opponents of the Axis with "every ounce and every ton of munitions and supplies that we can possibly spare to help the defenders who are on the front lines." America should become the "arsenal of democracy." Roosevelt reassured his listeners that he would "ask no one to defend a democracy which in turn would not defend everyone in the nation against want and privation." Government would protect the "human dignity" of the worker—a canny counterposition of the "slavery" the Nazis imposed on their workers—but this was now a matter of national interest rather than social justice, since "the workers provide the human power that turns out the destroyers, and the planes and tanks."[76]

Redefining the national enterprise as building an arsenal of democracy, rather than attaining previous objectives such as economic "balance" or social justice, worked. A series of secret polls conducted for Roosevelt by Hadley Cantril showed a growing popular willingness from the summer of 1940 onward to aid Britain "even at the risk of getting into the war."[77] In pushing the public toward intervention FDR was assisted by a small but dedicated set of organizations and public figures, some of whose devotion to internationalism could be traced back to the 1920s, when the League of Nations Association, Woodrow Wilson Foundation, and allied interest groups had first sought to recover from the defeat of the League.[78] The effectiveness of these pressure groups impressed upon the president the need to keep a closer watch on public opinion. By 1942 Cantril was conducting biweekly polls with analysis aimed at the short-term policy ramifications of public opinion, while also tracking long-term trends in opinion on particular issues, such as attitudes toward the Allies and expectations of victory.[79] Roosevelt learned well from the battles over his legitimacy during the neutrality debate, and would attend carefully to his secret polls throughout the war.

By casting U.S. involvement in the war as a matter of national survival—indeed, part of a larger battle over the fate of civilization itself—Roosevelt drew on the language of rights and freedom that had long defined American civilizational discourse. This meant couching assistance to Britain as part of a defensive struggle to preserve liberty in a dangerous world. The domestic ramifications of this rhetorical move would become clear in the president's enunciation of the "Four Freedoms"—freedom of speech, freedom of worship, freedom from want, and freedom from fear—for which the war would be fought.

In his annual message to Congress on January 6, 1941, Roosevelt laid the rhetorical groundwork for America's gradual involvement in the war. The president warned that the "democratic way of life" so many Americans cherished was "at this moment directly assailed in every part of the world.... [T]he future and the safety of our country and of our democracy are overwhelmingly involved in events beyond our borders." The strength of his political adversaries, especially those advocating nonintervention, required that he cautiously build his case for greater material aid to the Allies without discussing specific repayment arrangements. Accordingly, Roosevelt skirted the many thorny questions surrounding Lend-Lease and stuck to the lofty idealism that had become the hallmark of his public oratory.[80]

Two of the Four Freedoms (from want and fear) would be incorporated into the Atlantic Charter—which formalized the alliance between the United States and Britain later that year—and the broad spirit of all four would inform the drafting of the United Nations' Universal Declaration of Human Rights after the war, in 1948.[81] On the home front, the Four Freedoms would come to represent "what we're fighting for," an idealistic vision of American war aims that had implications for freedoms at home as well as abroad, as revealed in their widely reproduced depiction by the painter Norman Rockwell.[82]

Having established a securely international frame for his reformist rhetoric, Roosevelt took pains to underscore the domestic ramifications of the Four Freedoms. Even as he rallied the nation to a "mighty action" that would defend America by aiding democracy around the world, the president acknowledged that such efforts could not "be based on a disregard of all things worth fighting for." "Those who man our defenses, and those behind them who build our defenses," Roosevelt reasoned, "must have the stamina and the courage which come from unshakable belief in the manner of life which they are defending." There was "nothing mysterious" about the sources of this belief in America, which formed the "foundations of a healthy and strong democracy." They were simply "the basic things expected by our people of their political and economic systems," of which he listed six:

Equality of opportunity for youth and for others

Jobs for those who can work

Security for those who need it

The ending of special privileges for the few

The preservation of civil liberties for all

The enjoyment of the fruits of scientific progress in a wider and constantly rising standard of living

"These are the simple, basic things that must never be lost sight of in the turmoil and unbelievable complexity of our modern world," Roosevelt noted, since America's power to protect democracy around the world depended on its capacity to "fulfill these expectations."[83]

While historians have emphasized the glaring gap between this high-flown rhetoric and the realities of the home front, the political culture of the period clearly betrayed the resonance of these ideals among a broad swath of the nation's citizenry. Americans raised their expectations of what the federal government should do to ensure fairness in their daily lives. However, they did not couch their expectations in lofty abstractions. Indeed, many Americans seemed unclear on what, precisely, the Four Freedoms were. When questioned by pollsters in early July 1942, most people expressed indifference rather than opposition—at least about the letter, if not the spirit, of the president's memorable rhetoric. Only 35 percent said yes to the question "Have you ever heard of the Four Freedoms?" Slightly more than 20 percent said they had heard of freedom of speech and religion, while just 5 percent had heard of freedom from fear or want. Awareness of the Atlantic Charter was comparably low, with a poll in late January 1942 showing that only 21 percent claimed to have heard or read about it.[84]

Despite this haziness, most Americans did respond positively when presented with the substantive ideas behind Roosevelt's memorable phrases. MacLeish informed the president in a May 1942 memo that an internal study of public opinion showed that "the Four Freedoms . . . have a powerful and genuine appeal to seven persons in ten":

> Thus the American people show themselves idealistically in favor of guaranteeing freedom of speech and religion all over the world, of maintaining a world police force to guarantee against future wars, of helping to secure better working and living conditions for people all over the world, and guaranteeing that all nations get a fair share of raw materials. Furthermore, four out of five people believe that this country should and will help to feed the hungry peoples of the world after the war is ended.

These affirmations coincided with an undercurrent of potentially corrosive expectations, MacLeish warned. "The same people who express these ideals," MacLeish cautioned, "have their private misgivings." Most of those surveyed expected lower wages and fewer jobs after the war. MacLeish put a positive spin on this apparent "storm warning" by concluding that the administration could bolster morale through appeals that both sharpened awareness of war goals and reassured the public that the goals were practical and would allay their personal concerns if accomplished. But the same findings could also be viewed as proof that most people paid only lip service to the ideals that Roosevelt, MacLeish, and other liberals within government promulgated during the war, and that the main concerns of ordinary people remained within the nonidealistic realms of self-interest and personal opportunity.[85]

Yet it was precisely self-interest that animated ordinary citizens' engagement with the political culture of the home front and elevated their expectations of government. Half a year after Roosevelt's 1941 inaugural address, the All Youth Club of Waterbury, Connecticut, sent an outraged telegram to General Lewis B. Hershey, head of the Selective Service System. "The ordered cancellation of striking defense workers' deferments is to be condemned as an arbitrary undemocratic attack upon a free trade union movement," it read, "and is inconsistent with President Roosevelt's self-declared Four Freedoms."[86] Somehow the right to strike in defense plants had been read into Roosevelt's declaration by this union-influenced youth group. Four years and an entire war later, on the day that the second atomic bomb was dropped over Nagasaki, a letter arrived in Washington, D.C., for Chester Bowles, head of the Office of Price Administration (OPA). It protested injustices perpetrated by a local rationing board in Willoughby, Ohio. "Just what do 'Four Freedoms' mean?" it began. "My . . . Board thinks that a man should crawl on his hands and knees in order to get what other people get—but we Jews are not liked in this KKK and German-American Bund County. What Say?"[87] Discrimination had likely burdened many aspects of this man's daily life in Ohio, yet the mundane matter of acquiring ration stamps had prompted him to write a complaint to the head of the OPA, invoking the Four Freedoms.

MacLeish's worries seem to have been misplaced. "Private misgivings" over government shortcomings and the many frustrations of wartime life would not so much discredit the broad ideals publicized by the administration as heighten citizens' insistence that they be met. Rarely did they reach, as the All Youth Club and the man from Ohio did, for lofty rhetoric or grand abstractions to articulate their expectations. But the war would bring changes that expanded the horizons of Americans' expectations. On that elusive line where the firm earth of daily experience met the blue sky of soaring hopes stood the federal government.

The Roosevelt administration's efforts to build a modern public sphere were constrained by its contradictory efforts to resolve an inherent tension between democracy and national security by defining the latter as if it were simply an extension of the former, as the phrase "arsenal of democracy" suggested.[88] In the end this tension was only a special case of the contradictions that had already emerged between the dream of a pluralistic, fully democratized polity and the romantic, nationalist construct of "the people."[89] Since 1933 New Dealers had faced the challenge of directly summoning the will of the people to confront an ongoing national emergency, even as administrators sought to steer the ship of state between the fractious attacks on public power waged by its ideological opponents on the left and right. The need to assemble and legitimize a political center around himself thus had become one of Roosevelt's foremost yet most elusive tasks, which he pursued not only through legislation aimed at key constituencies but also through a media strategy that claimed "the people" for the president.

Ordinary Americans may not have swallowed the New Deal line whole, but most of them did identify powerfully and intimately with Roosevelt, especially after Pearl Harbor. As part of that process of identification, they began to adapt the rhetoric of rights and freedom to their own lives. Most important, they did not challenge the war but accepted it as an uncontroversial matter of national interest. In this regard, the construct of a unitary national interest proved the administration's most enduring ideological accomplishment—far more significant than any of the putatively liberal ideological meanings the administration sought to encode into its war aims.[90]

Morale and the National Moment

"My God, I certainly want airplanes," remarked assistant secretary of state John J. McCloy in March 1941, "but we need this as badly as we need airplanes." By "this" he meant morale, the elusive fighting spirit whose cultivation among Germans, and destruction among their enemies, the Nazis had mastered. McCloy was no mystic, nor did he underestimate the significance of airpower, as his subsequent role in wartime strategy would reveal. His pragmatism and acerbity had vaulted him to the top ranks of corporate law in the interwar years. Within a few years his acumen would only increase his influence, marking him as one of the elect "wise men" who made Cold War foreign policy. When a man such as McCloy compared morale to airpower, he was saying something.[1]

McCloy made his remark in a meeting of midlevel defense bureaucrats assembled by Secretary of the Interior Harold Ickes to discuss the Committee for National Morale. His observation was a direct response to Roosevelt's media advisor Lowell Mellett, head of the Office of Government Reports (OGR), who dismissed the whole subject of morale as odiously German, and thus irrelevant. "No one could tell Americans what to do or how to think," Ickes recorded him as saying.[2] Mellett, a former journalist nicknamed "White Rabbit" for his timidity, found his opinion contradicted by subsequent developments. Not only would the government "tell Americans what to do" and how to think, but Mellett himself would work closely with Hollywood studios as the head of the Office of War Information's Bureau of Motion Pictures to incorporate those instructions into popular films. Mellett and the other propagandists would do so under the auspices of providing democratic "information"—hence the OWI's name.[3]

Retooling liberal ideology for total war required an operational framework and an institutional home. The enterprise of morale management provided both. It oriented war agencies toward a problem—inculcating "war-mindedness"—whose solution melded propaganda with surveillance. American efforts in this area appear feeble, even idealistic, when compared with the legendary "thought control" deployed by other combatants of World War II, particularly the apparatuses of propaganda and domestic spying that were so central to the Nazi and

Soviet governments. But American morale management marked a new stage of sophistication for the federal government. More importantly, it was well suited to the task it confronted, which differed dramatically from the exactions required of the Continental powers locked in their death struggle. To meet the central challenges of industrial production for the Allies and its own mobilization for wars in two separate theaters, the U.S. government had to secure mass compliance with a vast extension of state power, and it had to do so not long after political opposition to the Roosevelt administration's domestic and foreign policies in the late 1930s had brought it to a near standstill. The essential task, then, was to obscure the statist foundations of public power while insinuating them into the thoughts and lives of the citizenry.[4]

As it groped its way, the Roosevelt administration drew on progressive and Popular Front visions of a public sphere engineered for the modern age.[5] All the impressive resources of the New Deal's cultural, information, and education programs were available for the purposes of crafting democratic "war information." The persistence of the culture wars of the late 1930s, which had been central to conservative mobilization against the New Deal, profoundly limited the administration's efforts to adapt New Deal cultural strategy to the war—although not fatally. This impasse would open the door for other figures—military authorities, social scientists, experts drawn from the worlds of journalism, advertising, public relations, radio, and film—who had their own distinctive, if overlapping, ideas about how to monitor and manage mass compliance with the war effort. Consequently, a rough kind of ideological triangulation occurred, producing a liberal imaginary that drew on all but satisfied none of the contributors. Yet agreement or even coherence may have been less important than message repetition and organizational legacy. In the process of solving the problem of morale, the government produced an imaginary whose institutional and ideological contours would prove durable, setting the stage for the mixture of private sector organizations (such as the Advertising Council) and public sector agencies (such as the State Department's U.S. Information Agency) that would make "freedom" and the "American way of life" ideological calling cards for the United States in the Cold War.[6]

Pearl Harbor and the "Man on the Street"

When Admiral Isoroku Yamamoto launched his historic attack on Pearl Harbor on December 7, 1941, the moment had come to identify the greater purpose for which the American people could finally unify and rally behind muscular government. On December 9, as Roosevelt's speechwriters prepared the text of the fireside chat that would be broadcast to 80 percent of all Americans that evening, MacLeish wrote to FDR's speechwriter, Robert Sherwood, with his advice. "The American people at the moment are fighting mad," he observed, which brought the peril of defeatism because a sufficient military response would take months. At the same time, it presented an opportunity to forge national unity through identification with the recently embarrassed military. "If the American people fighting mad can lick the world," MacLeish reasoned, "then the American navy is part of the American people and the personification of the American people." Behind the navy and the "great fighting nation" was "the greatest and most rapidly available productive capacity in the world." In its audacity and risk, the raid on Pearl Harbor had revealed the unmistakable intention of the Axis to "knock us out of the war at one blow." Instead, it had "aroused and awakened us as a people," enabling "us to muster all our resources of heart and body for the greatest productive effort ever made by any nation."[7] Try as he might to cloak the old idols of militarism in the Popular Front imagery of the people, MacLeish was forgetting that war fever induced a jealous spirit that brooked no substitutes or moral equivalents once its engines were unleashed on the field of battle.[8]

Whether due to MacLeish's direct influence or to the broader sensibility Roosevelt shared with him, the president hit some of the same notes in his radio address.[9] He opened by invoking the image of an international crime wave:

My fellow Americans:

The sudden criminal attacks perpetrated by the Japanese in the Pacific provide the climax of a decade of international immorality. Powerful and resourceful gangsters have banded together to make war upon the whole human race. Their challenge has now been flung at the United States of America.

Drawing on effective tropes from the New Deal war on crime, he consistently referred to the actions of Japan, Germany, and Italy as "criminal," the work of "gangsters" and "bandits." In the absence of a formal declaration of war by Germany or Italy, which would come the next day, he also took pains to portray Pearl Harbor as part of "one pattern" of Axis aggression that played out on "one gigantic battlefield" spread across the globe. Some in his audience responded to this imagery. A gung-ho army private wrote to the president soon after the broadcast to inform him that "I prefer death th[a]n to live under a group of Bandits." Another supportive letter from Michigan urged him to use the only language the Axis knew, "FORCE," when dealing with "the treacherous yellow rats" and "mugs." "To hell with ideals," it urged, "until we have licked these international thugs."[10]

With industrial production at the center of the administration's strategy for winning the war, the earlier habit of demonizing big business and the "malefactors of great wealth" had become inadvisable. Although Roosevelt took care to invoke the Four Freedoms early on in the broadcast, intoning that "we are now fighting to maintain our right to live among our world neighbors in freedom, in common decency, without fear of assault," his emphasis on freedom from fear obscured the domestic antagonisms and economic justice that New Deal invocations of rights and freedoms had earlier emphasized.

The coming of war made obsolete earlier claims that full recovery was impossible without reform, even as it cast the captains of industry in a positive light—at least when they cooperated with the administration's program. Henceforth the business of business would be heroic production, rather than obstruction. This new reality came through implicitly in Roosevelt's rhetorical strategy to calm his audience. Despite the scope and coordination of Japan's "brilliant feat of deception," the president reassured his audience, all was not lost, thanks to the productive might of the nation's industrial sector. The defense policies enacted in the months since the fall of France allowed the United States to send "vast quantities of our war materials to the nations of the world still able to resist Axis aggression." "A steady stream of tanks and planes, of guns and ships and shells and equipment—that is what these eighteen months have given us." The years of bitter debate over neutrality were "now all past—and, I am sure, forgotten." Washington was now full of "recognized experts" working overtime to guarantee heroic levels of production. "We are going to win the war," he concluded, "and we are going to win the peace that follows."[11]

Roosevelt elaborated with his strongest emphasis on the point of national unity, leaning heavily on the venerable patriotic language of sacrifice.[12] This approach made sense two days after Pearl Harbor, when national resolve had to supplant dull shock. "Ahead," he intoned, "lies sacrifice for all of us." But it was "not correct to use that word," he immediately observed. When "the nation is fighting for its existence and its future life," he said, it is not a sacrifice "to give one's best to our nation . . . Rather it is a privilege." To help visualize what this sacrifice entailed, first he stated that it was "not a sacrifice for any man, young or old, to be in the Army or the Navy of the United States." Right behind them he itemized the list of civilians, all arrayed equally in their support of the men entering military service—"the industrialist or the wage earner, the farmer or the shopkeeper, the trainman or the doctor"—and none of whom would hesitate to "pay more taxes, to buy more bonds, to forgo extra profits, to work longer or harder at the task for which he is best fitted." Americans would do without in order to "retain all those great spiritual things without which we cannot win through."

The talk of national unity, with its spiritual overtones, resonated with Roosevelt's listeners. Lenore Parker wrote in from Pennsylvania to say, "God Bless you, sir . . . your frankness, honesty and sincerity makes us all want to fight to the bitter end for victory for this wonderful country of ours. . . . I believe the country is now united with one goal in mind and with you to lead us, we shall win, so help us God." Parker felt the nation looked to him as it had in the "terrible dark days" of 1933. He took encouragement in his "great faith in God and in this country." Another female writer, signing herself "Mamie O. Tew, Wife-Mother-and Secretary" from Gainesville, Florida, expressed a similar sentiment. As she listened to him on the radio she forgot that he was the president. Instead, she felt as she had "at times long ago, when things seemed all wrong and . . . fair-minded, lawyer-daddy would sit down with me and talk."[13] White women with Democratic sympathies were not the only ones who considered Roosevelt a father figure; indeed, the prevalence of this tendency was the reason his photograph graced so many mantles around the country. To many in those years and for decades thereafter, he was a kind of "Nordic father," a vivid, patriarchal embodiment of national authority.[14]

FDR addresses the nation over a national radio hookup, while Eleanor Roosevelt and the president's mother, Sarah, sit watching on the other side of the fireplace. This staged photograph captured the paternal authority Roosevelt conveyed in his fireside chats, while modeling the orderly synchronization between the private family and the public household that undergirded liberal conceptions of the nation. (Courtesy of Getty Images, #3252397)

The related theme of sacrifice also elicited a strong response from Roosevelt's audience. Private Juan N. Cavazos, the same man who wrote of his preference for death before life lived "under a group of Bandits," informed the president that even though he had to support an elderly father, a middle-aged mother, and two sisters, "I also have a country to defend and if I don't put all my streng[t]h to do so I will have a hungry family on my hands giving and working their last meal to a group of Bandits." Lenore Parker affirmed that "if my husband is called to protect his country, I know I shall be glad to make the best of the situation even though it means losing him, and he feels the same way about it as I do." P. H. Ryan of Kentucky wrote to say that the chat was *"just what we needed*. No task too great / No toil too hard / No cost too high / No blood too dear / Until the war is WON! All selfish aims / All petty ills / All politics / Put on the shelf / Until the war is WON!"[15]

In subsequent months, contending pressure groups would jockey for position using the language of sacrifice to castigate their enemies and wrap their interests in the flag.[16] Given the subdued nature of the "sacrifice" most Americans endured—as late as February 1945, nearly two-thirds of civilians interviewed by Gallup admitted they had not "had to make any real sacrifice for the war"—it was unsurprising that the language of sacrifice should lend itself so readily to political manipulation.[17] But in that raw moment after Pearl Harbor, the language and sensibilities of unity and unalloyed national obligation prevailed. What emerged was a conception of political obligation in which the self-interest ordinarily expected within the peacetime liberal polity had to be reconciled with a prior obligation to the nation. This was not to be confused with the effort, subsequently prominent in propaganda produced by admen, film producers, radio studios, and other corporate liberals, to equate obligation with self-interest—a theme that, government research suggested, did not resonate widely among civilians on the home front.[18] For most Americans, and within much wartime propaganda, liberal self-interest was not a substitute for national obligation, but rather had to be articulated within it, deferring to the thickening logic of patriotism.

Roosevelt saved his rhetorical powers for the theme of winning the peace in order to truly win the war, which received its fullest treatment at the culmination of the chat. Just as reform and rebalancing of the domestic political economy had been necessary to recover from the Depression, now it was the international community that needed reforming if the world was ever to see peace again. "Not only must the shame of Japanese treachery be wiped out," he asserted, "but the sources of international brutality, wherever they exist, must be absolutely and finally broken." From here on in, he asserted, "we can never again isolate ourselves from the rest of humanity," because "there is no such thing as security for any nation—or any individual—in a world ruled by the principles of gangsterism." Once the Axis was tarred with one of FDR's favorite rhetorical brushes, America's strongest allies, the British and the Soviets—the latter called "Russians," perhaps to mute the ideological dissonance—could be portrayed as comrades in arms, dispelling the aspersions cast on them by anti-imperialists and anticommunists over the course of decades. Together the allies were fighting "a war, not for conquest, not for vengeance"—as interwar isolationists had described the previous world war and the ensuing peace made at Versailles—"but for a world in which this nation, and all that this nation represents, will be safe for our children." Roosevelt obscured the questions of sovereignty that had torpedoed the League of Nations in 1919, instead portraying international cooperation as a simple matter of national and self-interest.

Whether Roosevelt's audience accepted his sophisticated argument for a latter-day Wilsonian internationalism is difficult to discern. Some letter writers gloated about his victory over the advocates of neutrality. William Gramfort of New Jersey sent a poem overflowing with praise: "And though some fools mock The New Deal / They'll praise it at a future date . . . / The world will know the worth of you / And call you the Real Prince of Peace!" Arthur Gahiner of Riverdale, New York, lauded the president's "courage, & your foresight." "Despite isolationists," he wrote, "despite 'copperheads' and despite a feeling of apathy . . . you insisted and persisted that safeguards be taken to protect our precious democratic inheritance." Though there would be a heavy burden in the years to come, "we are confident that you will guide us through these dark days with unerring wisdom so that the beacon of freedom and democracy will shine brighter than ever before when victory is won. . . . May God keep you . . . America and the world needs you!"[19] Neither of these letters explicitly embraced the Allies or internationalism, but their tone was consonant with Roosevelt's admonition that "it would serve us ill if we accomplished [victory over Japan] and found the rest of the world was dominated by Hitler and Mussolini." These affirmations reflected the biases of Roosevelt's listeners, who tended to be more interventionist and internationally minded than those who did not listen, and more inclined to think a victory would benefit them personally.[20] Some critics did tune in, though, such as the duo who telegraphed from the isolationist heartland to inform the president that they found his address "weak and cavillating." They, and "people of Iowa and Midwest," wanted to know the full extent of the losses, and demanded accountability: "Why not purge your navy and army of brass hats the same as you did the Supreme Court?"[21]

Contrary to common wisdom, Pearl Harbor did not produce a mass conversion to internationalism. It did, however, catalyze popular commitment to a total war effort.[22] By the fall of 1941, most respondents to Gallup's polls indicated a willingness to aid Britain, France, and other members of the Allies even if it led to war.[23] Secret polling for Roosevelt would confirm this during the war, although it would also confirm lingering distrust of the British and Soviets among large pockets of voters.[24] Couching intervention in terms of a unitary national interest, defined by the requirements of modern war, obscured its foreign policy consequences and thenceforth fused U.S. international relations with military policy.

Beyond the tidy columns of polling numbers, the responses of ordinary Americans to Pearl Harbor presented a less orderly but more immediate indication of what the national catastrophe meant for their sense of the purpose of the war and the government that waged it. On the same day that Roosevelt's Pearl Harbor fireside chat was broadcast, field workers for the Archive of American Folk Song in the Library of Congress received a telegraphic summons from Alan Lomax. With the bombing of Pearl Harbor, Lomax sensed a new opportunity to capture the inner workings of the mind of the folk. He redeployed field workers in ten locations, shifting them temporarily away from their interviews with Okie migrant laborers and carnival workers, to capture the elusive views of the "man on the street" in his own words. Perhaps by recording ordinary Americans' reactions to the event that finally had dragged the United States into war and great-power politics, the folklorists could provide some insight into morale. If Harry Hopkins could move from cutting checks for state WPA offices to authorizing Lend-Lease shipments to England and the Soviet Union, the Library of Congress could retool itself to study the people at war.

The "man-on-the-street" interviews captured some of the shock that still hung in the air. In Dallas, Texas, Dr. James Terrill reported first feeling "unbelieving surprise," followed by "the next realization that I personally was at war . . . [t]hat everything I had and all that I could do should go to war."[25] Frederick Hodge, a retired professor and chemical engineer living in Buffalo, New York, claimed he was "utterly astounded" when he happened to turn on his radio in his den that Sunday. His conclusion was that "we must revise entirely our whole national policy. We must see to it that the nations of the world have the necessities of life. But perhaps have the necessities for war restricted in some way."[26] These responses no doubt would have pleased Roosevelt.

A surprisingly large number of interviewees were not stunned or even surprised by the attack. As J. C. Brodie, a farmer in Austin, Texas put it, it was no surprise at all: "They just did what I thought they would do, attacked without any . . . warning whatsoever."[27] A Mrs. Whitaker told the same interviewer that "it's nothing more than what's to be expected. In other words, it's inevitable." For this woman, as for others who found the attack predictable if nonetheless shocking, the intentions of the Axis—not just Japan—had been clear for some time. As she put it, "I think they were influenced by Hitler in every way."[28] Here, too, were responses that echoed Roosevelt's argument that Pearl Harbor was simply one part of a larger Axis grand strategy.

Many of the man-on-the-street interviews captured a simple, overriding impulse to fight for national honor. Roosevelt had also been cultivating this defense mentality at least since the fall of France, in order to defend against isolationist attacks on his larger designs to aid Britain. As J. C. Brodie put it, "It's our duty as a nation to defend it and whip the aggressors."[29] For a group of men interviewed together in Burlington, North Carolina, the overriding need for security and honor blended together. They exchanged oaths, told jokes about hunting season ("no bag limit, kill as many as you want"), and indulged big talk about vengeance: "Two minutes would have been enough for me. I'd a killed that son of a gun [Japanese envoy Saburo Kurusu]."[30] One veteran interviewed along with a group of fresh draftees in Washington, D.C., provided a precise delineation of how his response to Pearl Harbor differed from his attitude toward U.S. entry into the previous world war:

> The last time I went to [fight] for democracy . . . They told me to fight for democracy. And I went over, and I volunteered. But next time I'm going to fight with the hate in my heart. What's in me, what's in my veins, I'm going to kill, slaughter . . . If I come across a wounded one, it wouldn't interest me. I'd kill my own father if he dare to fight against this country. I am American, not by birth, but by choice and I'm mighty damn proud of it. What we ought to do in this country to chase every damn skunk, German, Russian, the Japanese where they come from and never bring them back in this country. I wish I was the president for about one year, there'd be not a goddamned skunk left here in this country [laughter]. I tell you that right here and right now.[31]

Some interviewees were able to articulate ideological responses that went beyond unalloyed expressions of racial hatred. One Wisconsin mother, who was also the director of a state agency for community service, expressed her view that the war involved a clash between two different ways of life. Americans, and "all freedom loving peoples," believed in "tolerance, equality, and freedom for all"; "for over a hundred and fifty years" they had "acted closer to these ideals than any other" great power, and they believed that "these ideals should be followed in national and international relations." Japan and Germany, on the other hand, were "now exerting all their power to conquer other peoples so that they can suppress, exploit, and enslave the conquered peoples." The view of the war as an epochal clash of civilizations was a theme that Roosevelt had expounded at least since early 1940, particularly with the high language of the Atlantic Charter. The Wisconsin mother may have been susceptible to it due to her clear immersion in the tradition of maternalist patriotism (which had thrived since the preparedness movements in the teens); in her first words to the interviewer she confessed feeling that "American womanhood, as a whole, feels ashamed and humiliated" by the sole vote against the war resolution by Jeanette Rankin, "our one woman representative in Congress."[32] Edward Crane, a lawyer and veteran from Dallas, Texas, provided an extreme masculine counterpart to this attitudinal legacy of the Great War, stating bluntly:

> There are two civilizations involved. Both of which cannot exist. Frankly, my view is and I include the Hun or the Germans so-called in what I have to say about the Japanese. That is, we ought to extermi-nate both of them. There's no place for either of those races in the world today.[33]

In a similar vein, many interviewees strongly affirmed the need for sacrifice transcending self-interest—sometimes bringing it up themselves, without prompting. Mrs. Whitaker, the mother of two sons in Austin, Texas, explained, "If every mother, [from] the most selfish standpoint would say, 'No indeed, I'd rather let my [son] be sent to prison before I let him go into the marines or navy or army.' Why, how would our army stand . . . to defend our country. We'd be at a total loss. We have to act patriotic regardless of our love."[34] Joe Jirosik, a carpen-ter and union man in Austin, Texas, surprised his interviewer when he said he accepted the price of victory "even if it cost your son." Jirosik observed that his son had already served three years in the army and was being called back for more service. "I'm willing for him to go," he said, adding that "the country wouldn't be any good if we let them [the Japanese] have it." "Well," the inter-viewer answered, "that takes a whole lot of nerve to say that, especially when you ain't just hypothesizing."[35]

A few of the people interviewed by Lomax's field workers picked up on the liberal resonances beneath the surface of aroused nationalism in the immediate wake of Pearl Harbor. One interviewee was uniquely positioned to turn the theme of racial revenge, along with its ideological implications, on its head. In Nashville, Tennessee, a black minister and president of the local branch of the NAACP, the Reverend W. J. Faulkner, was quick to highlight the connection between the international and domestic dimensions of the war, which revealed "a tragic attitude of unpreparedness and selfish indifference" fostered by social divisions that had led the United States to dissipate "our vast strength" and strain "our national unity through labor conflicts and class bickerings" and "in prac-tices of stupid and costly racial recriminations," by which "our enemies have con-spired to destroy us."[36] Here was an early articulation of the "Double V," the call for victory over fascist racial supremacy at home as well as abroad, that would animate the rise of an early civil rights movement during the war. It was also an echo, almost certainly unintended by Roosevelt, of his pledge to wipe out "sources of international brutality, wherever they exist."[37]

Roosevelt's carefully cultivated theme of waging war to win a peace that would last beyond immediate victory caught the ears of a few interviewees. In the university town of Bloomington, Indiana, local merchant Merritt Calvert told his interviewer that the United States should declare war on all three Axis powers, not just Japan, in order to "start into this thing from scratch and really make them know that we are interested in doing away with their system." Calvert bemoaned "the way we did in the last war" (presumably the abandonment of the League of Nations) and argued that the United States should be the "leader" of a postwar order in which "policies, our democratic policies, our theories of life over here should be insisted upon in spots where it's possible at all to put it in force."[38] Frederick Hodge, former professor and chemical engineer, outdid Roosevelt himself in affirming New Deal principles for war. Rather than wreak "a vengeance upon Japan," as his interviewer put it, Hodge thought the United States should not bomb cities in Japan—"that's too much the Hitler way of executing hostages. That is the execution of the innocent for all of the evil that have been done by others." He did, however, support punishment for "the guilty." Hodge proved prescient, as both scenarios came to pass with the firebombing of Japan and Germany, as well as the war crimes trials at Nuremberg and Tokyo after the war.[39]

Many interviewees picked up on Roosevelt's depiction of the Axis powers as criminals or greedy villains, and agreed with his assessment that Japan's actions were part of a broader Axis design, but that did not necessarily lead them to follow his analogy to its fullest conclusion and embrace internationalist solutions. Most interviewees were far more inclined to agree with the Austin carpenter, Joe Jirosik, who was reluctant to talk about peace at all. In response to questions about the kind of peace that would prevail after the war, he simply declared that the United States would emerge victorious. After some prodding, he said that "they ought to set up a different form of government over there [in Japan]," and when asked if they should have "any power to govern themselves at all," he retorted, "Well barely."[40] J. C. Brodie expressed a similar view of what would be required for peace: "The only way to keep out of war with Germany is to do away with Germany entirely and put them under other governments and have no Germany at all. As long as there's a Germany there'll be wars."[41] Although Roosevelt's secretary of the treasury, Henry Morgenthau Jr., would propose a similar plan later on in the war, this view, like that of Jirosik, undermined the largest ambitions of the president's war aims.[42]

As might be expected, the man on the street reflected the biases of both the interviewer and the interviewee. At several points the recording captured an interviewer coaxing his subject toward expressions of war-mindedness, as when the black WPA employee and World War I veteran Willie Sorrels offered that he would "volunteer again, go out and fight for my country," and the interviewer, John Henry Faulk, replied "Good for you." To that Faulk followed up with the leading question, "You feel like America's worth defending?" only to hear, "Sure, because I was born and raised in the United States and I'm bound." It was unlikely that such a man required coaxing, but Faulk prodded him anyway for good measure.[43] Given labor's strong support of Roosevelt in 1940, it is likewise unsurprising that the carpenter, Joe Jirosik, agreed with Roosevelt that Hitler "had a direct contact" in the attack on Pearl Harbor, and that he reported that every last one of his fellow tradesmen in his local carpenters union was behind the president's declaration of war. He added that he thought the Japanese had been preparing for the offensive for years, and had done so with the help of greedy American businessmen who sold them scrap iron in a much-publicized transaction: "It was the capitalists that sold this stuff to them, they knew what they was using it for. But that wasn't a question at that time it was money, greed for money." The interviewer, Faulk, revealed his Popular Front sensibilities when he concluded the interview by saying, "I wouldn't be surprised if that's not a very sound opinion, Mr. Jirosik."[44]

Lomax continued to redeploy his field interviewers for purposes of monitoring morale into January and February 1942. He also began to identify interviewees who were suitable for a radio program inspired by the man-on-the-street interviews, entitled "Dear Mr. President." The administration had sought to dramatize the president's direct relationship to the people before, even producing a radio play of the same name in 1939 to generate popular support for the president's politically embattled budget message. This time ordinary Americans would play themselves. As they had for their field research, Lomax's roving folklorists drew their interviewees from all walks of life, choosing individuals for their representativeness of American "types." Asking interviewees to address th e president directly with the concerns and questions they had about Pearl Harbor, the interviewers were able to capture citizens' more considered efforts to make sense of the calamity. Interviewees completed the prompt that began "Dear Mr. President," speaking "privately [as] if they were given a short interview with him in his office."[45] Here was a simulacrum of the national family, redolent of the intimacy of the old town hall, but made for the radio age. Filled with high purpose, the participants in the "Dear Mr. President" interviews naturally built up the courage to cast their concerns in the loftiest of tones. Idealistic intensity replaced the rawness that Lomax's men had captured in those first few days. Anticipating the millions of other Americans who would listen to their testimony, the participants made their best effort to articulate the foundations of their patriotism to the nation's paterfamilias.

In early 1942, the Library of Congress conducted a series of interviews to be used for a documentary radio play titled "Dear Mr. President," in which ordinary citizens addressed the president about the war. This was not the first time the administration had used the new medium of radio to help mass audiences imagine their relationship to the president and the nation, as shown by this meeting of actors in the Interior Department's recording studio, where they enacted a play based on the president's January 1939 budget message that was broadcast by national hookup. (Courtesy of the Library of Congress, LC-DIG-hec-25890)

Some of the most poignant and eloquent testimonies came from black participants. Their voices emerged thanks to the sensibilities and contacts of the folklorists, whose work among African Americans had qualified them to conduct the interviews. According to one black veteran in Nashville, Tennessee, all he wanted was the right to do his duty as a citizen: "The only thing that we are asking is that we be given opportunity to fight, to live, and to die for the thing that we call democracy." In a blend of idealism and self-interest, nationalism and cosmopolitanism that marked many African Americans' expressions of patriotism during the war, he explained that democracy was "the thing that will cause this world to give the minority groups an opportunity to achieve all of the blessings of life, health, and happiness."[46] Carrie Timberlake, an elevator operator in Nashville, expressed a similar sensibility when she asserted that despite her humble station, "I am interested in the progress of our country." The administration's talk of Axis designs to "enslave" the free world resonated with her: "We are fighting for a democratic way of life for ourselves and for the people now enslaved by the demagogues of Europe."[47]

A man by the name of Smith, who proudly identified himself as "a Negro private in the United States Army," explained to the president why "the Negro soldier, as a whole, believes that he has something to fight for and believes in the outcome he will have more to fight for than he has now." He felt obligated to acknowledge to the president the bitterness caused by the lost promises contained in the "Declaration of Independence or in the declaration of the emancipation of slaves," both of which were belied by the ongoing insult of Jim Crow and by the abusive treatment he personally had experienced while stationed at Camp Hope, Louisiana. Despite all this, he felt that "no man can fight harder for victory than I can" because the adversity he had known only made him cling more tightly to the hope that "there is tomorrow":

> Because after all, the Negro when he is in the army is serving the same purpose that any other man is serving. He has the same duties to fill that any other man has to fill. And he feels that when he is in the service he should be given as much consideration as any other man . . .
>
> Because after all whatever any man do he can't do any more than give up his life. And that's what every colored soldier in the United States Army, that the flag's raised over, that wears the United States colors, he feel like he has only one life to live, and if it takes that life to make this country safe for democracy and the things that he hopes for and the things that has been promised to him, he is ready to give up his life. He know[s] that he may not enjoy these things, he may not be able to see these things happen, may not see a thing coming about, but he realizes in the future he have loved ones that is left behind at home. And he have friends that he would like to see enjoy these blessing[s] and he is ready to give up his life to make these things possible.

White interviewees also emphasized the need to defend freedom itself, although unlike their black neighbors they did so by emphasizing the personal liberties they already enjoyed. "My great-grandparents came to this country seeking religious freedom," said Reed Erikson of Minneapolis, "and they found it here." His family had flourished with the "chance to live in freedom, happiness, and contentment," which had allowed him to "live in a way of life that's proven to me to be greater than any other way of life than any other man could possibly ask for."[48] Robert Bruce Graham, a trim worker for the Ford Motor Company in Detroit, drew on the working-class Americanism that ran like a current through the industrial communities of the country, affirming the need to defend "the best possible way, the American way." He did not minimize the high price exacted by war, but "whatever the cost may be, our freedom is worth much more. Buy bonds and stamps and then buy more bonds."[49] Enos Francisco, who described himself as "a Papago Indian," related the current war to his tribe's past battles with the Apaches, linking their tradition of independence to the larger cause of freedom. The Papago had always followed their "old custom" and "never did want to go to war," Francisco claimed, but with the attack on Pearl Harbor, "we all feel different."[50]

Most of those who invoked the need to fight for freedom did so, like Graham, to emphasize the priority of sacrifice over taking "selfish" liberties. Mrs. John Henry Fault of Austin, Texas, spoke in the venerable cadences of populism when she worried about "war profiteering." "I have heard all my life about the millions of dollars that were made off of the last war," she reported. She reassured him that she was, "of course, wholeheartedly with the defense effort." But she closed by observing, "It seems to me that profiteering can only be a hindrance to it."[51] Frank W. McBee, also of Austin, thought that price gouging was "the biggest problems in this community," undermining the sacrifices of local folks who were "joining the military forces and buying stamps and bonds every day."[52] Some singled out particular groups for censure, already demonstrating the sensibilities that would drive the politics of sacrifice throughout the war. One student complained about strikers, claiming that United Mine Workers president John L. Lewis was "like Hitler only in the labor [movement]."[53]

Given the intimate nature of the exercise, it is unsurprising that participants emphasized the personal contributions they could make to the war effort. It was as if they were volunteering to Roosevelt in person. This had the effect of reinforcing the direct line of moral obligation Roosevelt and other government figures sought to draw between the home front and the battlefront. William Henderson, a barber in Bloomington, Indiana, used his barber's chair to "make every one of them [his customers] feel a little more his personal responsibility to his country in this war." He pressed them on whether they were doing their part, and demanded that, at the very least, they buy defense stamps and bonds. "I guess I've sold quite a few bonds right there in my chair that way."[54] George Sietsma, the operator of a gas station in Bloomington, acknowledged that "now in this time of emergency my obligation to the traveling public has tremendously increased," especially in light of the "comfortable living" he had been able to make despite the Depression. He emphasized the ways in which his work helped to limit "waste and inefficiency"—"two enemies we must vanquish before we can expect to defeat the others"—now that rubber was in such short supply.[55]

The theme of mass production as the signal contribution to the war effort, which Roosevelt had underscored since his "arsenal of democracy" speech, enjoyed considerable support. Bob Barker, a rancher, expressed his worries about the slowness of conversion to war industry. He blamed it on Donald Nelson, the head of the War Production Board (WPB), the civilian agency in charge of coordinating war production. "Now I think this man Nelson is a good man," he said, but he was "just anxious to see him and his men, his workers, get after this thing." His son, who lived near Randolph Field outside San Antonio, saw pilots being trained day and night. "You get after those men up there and tell them to get them [airplanes] right out."[56] Gerald H. Garrett, who owned a factory in Denver, spoke of his cooperation with the WPB to share a naval defense contract among his former competitors. Despite the cost-plus basis of the contracts, he claimed that the nature of the bidding process meant that "nobody is making any money out of it." That was all right, because "what's in the mind of all of us is getting more of these ships out." In a chipper expression of labor-management solidarity, he reported that "the boys in the shop have a very fine attitude." Like their employers, they just wanted to advance the production on which victory depended.[57]

Few of the participants in the "Dear Mr. President" interviews touched on the internationalist themes Roosevelt had used in his fireside chats. When they did, it was rarely done in a fashion that would have warmed FDR's heart. Jack Carlyle of Fairville, Arkansas, took Roosevelt's metaphor of Axis gangsters and ran with it:

> When guys like Dillinger and Pretty Boy Floyd and Clyde Barrow, they were some little two-bit outlaws we had down here, they got ready to quit, and we didn't let them quit. We went right on and got them. And I think that's the way we should do the dictator. Let's go in there and cut off a few heads, and blow up a few towns, and really show them what the losing end of a war looks like.

Carlyle added that after the war the United States should "take over the Western Hemisphere . . . we're going to have to police the world, why, we should at least have charge of half of it." To do the job right, the government should draft everything, "not only just people, let's take money and factories, and men, and women, and kids, everything." "After all," he concluded, completing the logic of national obligation, "this country's just a big family, and it's being threatened by a bunch of dictators."[58]

The man-on-the-street and "Dear Mr. President" projects both epitomized the way in which the cultural sensibilities and democratic aspirations of the Popular Front refugees in the Library of Congress adapted their work to the new needs of war. In keeping with this approach, Pete Seeger provided his own synopsis of the people's response to Pearl Harbor for the radio program with his

1942 song "Dear Mr. President," which he sang in the style of the "talking blues."[59] The song opened with a self-description that would have fit with any of the folk songs Seeger had sung in the 1930s. The narrator said he was "an ordinary guy, worked most of my life," and liked "being free to say what I think." True to his roots, Seeger took care to include the "Double V" in a bold stanza that explained "the reason that I want to fight": "a better America and better laws" to replace those that upheld Jim Crow, anti-Semitic discrimination, and union-busting. "There's a lot of things wrong," Seeger admitted, paraphrasing black boxing hero Joe Lewis, "but Hitler won't help 'em."

Despite these gestures, the central thrust of the song reached into martial registers that sounded unnatural to the idiom Seeger long had cultivated. Well before he got to the idealistic reasons why he wanted to fight, he opened the third stanza with "Now I hate Hitler and I can tell you why / He's caused lots of good folks to suffer and die." He figured "it's about time we slapped him down / Give him a dose of his own medicine . . . lead poisoning." Toward the end of the song he returned to this theme, reiterating the need to "lick Mr. Hitler" and "let no one else ever take his place / To trample down the human race." Then followed a direct request to the president: "You're commander of our forces / The ships and the planes and the tanks and the horses," so "give me a gun / So we can hurry up and get the job done." Before he closed the song out, Seeger sang a refrain that perhaps unwittingly captured the nature of the transposition he was attempting in writing that very song:

> I never was one to try and shirk
> And let the other fellas do all the work
> So when the time comes, I'll be on hand,
> And I guess I can make good use of my two hands.
> Quit playing this banjo around with the boys,
> And exchange it for something that makes more noise.[60]

In Lomax's estimation, Seeger's composition was a model "for a whole new approach to the basic morale problem in the United States."[61] He planned to use it as the centerpiece of a documentary radio program that would be composed of interview excerpts.[62] Just as liberals such as Roosevelt and MacLeish had to adapt their rhetorical idioms to suit the new war context, so too did the Popular Front stalwarts working in the Library of Congress find themselves singing a new tune.

To some ears, this transposition into the registers of war rang false. Seeger's "Dear Mr. President" was a far cry from the lines he had sung with the Almanac Singers on their spring 1941 album, *Seven Songs for John Doe*. In "C for Conscription," he had sung, "I'd rather be here at home / Even sleeping in a holler log /

Than go to the army / And be treated like a dirty dog!" The "Ballad of Billy Boy" included the quip "It wouldn't be much thrill / To die for Du Point in Brazil." Appearing just weeks before the Nazis abrogated the Molotov-Ribbentrop pact, the "Ballad of October 16" (the draft registration date) had gone even further: "Franklin Roosevelt told the people how he felt / We damn near believed what he said / He said, I hate war, and so does Eleanor, / But we won't be safe till everybody's dead . . . But now I'm wearing khaki jeans and eating Army beans / And I'm told that J. P. Morgan loves me so." *Time* magazine's review accused the Almanac Singers of toeing the Moscow line. By 1943 the FBI would agree, attempting to track down the original masters and opening a file labeled "Gramophone Records of a Seditious Nature."[63]

Managing Morale, Building the Imaginary of Freedom

Outside the halls of the Library of Congress, a less rarefied approach to mobilizing popular involvement in the war prevailed. It involved managing "morale," a bureaucratic construct with military and psychological roots whose cultivation by war agencies in the 1940s owed much to the efforts of the Committee for National Morale (CNM), an ad hoc group of social scientists and allied academics convened after the fall of France by a Yale scholar named Arthur Upham Pope.[64] Pope was an archeologist and historian of ancient Persia who had worked for the Personnel Division of the General Staff in the War Department in World War I. By early 1941, with his trips to Persia blocked by the outbreak of war in Europe, Pope again took up his concern with morale.[65] At the solicitation of Ickes and Knox, the committee produced a survey of German psychological warfare that concluded with recommendations aimed to bolster the United States' ability to respond in kind.[66] Setting a pattern that would inform much of the government's propaganda work during the war, the CNM used Nazi propaganda as a negative template, studying German techniques closely to identify the most devastating methods and their underlying ideas about human psychology, then either exposing them in documentary style or fashioning antidotes that pursued what Archibald MacLeish termed "the strategy of truth."[67]

Morale was an especially pressing concern in World War II because the vast majority of Americans never had more than an indirect involvement in the actual fighting of the war, and so had to participate vicariously. Most were fighting the war on imagination alone. Yet the government desperately needed civilians' compliance with its new efforts to manage the economy. Morale shaped the critical machinery of war mobilization just as tangibly as did shortages of rubber or aluminum, causing bottlenecks and production shortfalls when demoralized workers failed to show up for work, threatening runaway inflation when consumers grew tired of "sacrifice" and bought clothes instead of bonds, and generally weakening the civic glue on which so much of the war effort relied in the absence of sufficient enforcement capacity. If morale fell too low, that reliance would become a grave liability. This was what McCloy meant when he said the United States needed morale as badly as it needed airplanes.

Morale was more than a purely pragmatic consideration, although that was what propelled it to the forefront of government attention during the impending national emergency. As Pope explained in the opening to his aptly timed article "The Importance of Morale," published in December 1941, "morale wins wars, solves crises, is an indispensable condition of a vigorous national life and equally essential to the maximum achievement of the individual." Because "an army fights as the people think," he observed, civilian morale could not be divorced from that of the military. Merciless German application of the modern methods of psychological warfare to France demonstrated precisely how critical it was to foster "an intense and durable emotional and ideational unity that increases, sustains, and organizes all effort." The "sovereign role of morale in great crises" could not be left to the cautious cultivation of public opinion, even though he acknowledged that "our citizens are slowly making up their minds" to form "a genuine, even if tepid, unity." By the time his article made it into print, Pearl Harbor had mooted his point.[68]

Alexander Leighton provided a more articulated formulation of the conception of morale that predominated in the wartime administration in his 1949 study, *Human Relations in a Changing World*. This book drew on his wartime experience as the chief of the Foreign Morale Analysis Division of the OWI and on his postwar participation in the U.S. Strategic Bombing Survey of Japan, which studied Japanese civilians' responses to incendiary and atomic bombardment. Leighton's definition ran as follows:

> If morale is defined as *the capacity of a group of people to pull together consistently and persistently in pursuit of a common purpose*, then it is dependent upon preponderance of the following factors:
>
> 1. The faith of each member of the group in the common purpose;
> 2. The faith of each member of the group in leadership;
> 3. The faith of each member of the group in the other members;
> 4. The organizational efficiency of the group;
> 5. The health and balance of emotions in the individuals of the group.[69]

Where Lomax and Spivacke had emphasized cultural practices of pluralism and social gestures of organic solidarity, Leighton propounded a metaphor hinging on collective monism, atomistic psychological "health," and bureaucratic efficiency. MacLeish's democratic people and Roosevelt's nation gathered round the fireside chat could be squared with such a vision, but not without distortion.

Leighton was a trained psychiatrist and naval officer who, prior to his service in the OWI and the Bombing Survey, had served as a community analyst doing "applied anthropology" for the Bureau of Indian Affairs (BIA) and later the War Relocation Administration (WRA) at the troubled relocation camp in Poston, Arizona. His observations there, which helped guide the BIA's efforts to quell an uprising of imprisoned Issei and Nisei at Poston in November 1942, were summarized in his 1945 study, *The Governing of Men*. "Societies move on the feelings of individuals who compose them," Leighton wrote, "and so do countries and nations. Very few internal policies and almost no international policies are predominantly the product of reason. . . . The administrator's job is to accept these things as they are and to take them into consideration, turn them to advantage if possible, but never to ignore them."[70]

Under the direction of Roosevelt appointee John Collier, the BIA had been drawing on the insights of social scientists since the creation of its Applied Anthropology Unit in 1936, formed to conduct field research on tribal structure in order to facilitate assimilation under the Indian Reorganization Act of 1934. Since September 1941, Leighton and his wife, Dorothea Cross, had been working with the University of Chicago and the Interior Department on the Indian Personality, Education, and Research Project, studying culture and personality among the Navajo.[71] Their work connected them to a network of social scientists, primarily anthropologists and social psychologists, whose contributions to the war effort (mostly in the realm of propaganda) fused with their emerging innovation of "culture and personality" studies. These included the anthropologists Ruth Benedict and her student Margaret Mead, whose wartime work posited that the secrets of "national character" were hidden in plain sight, available to be deciphered and rearranged to preserve and fortify an essential ingredient of national power: morale.[72]

If military figures and social scientists led the way in conceptualizing civilian morale, journalists, admen, public relations executives, and other experts of commercial media were the ones who institutionalized it. Nearly every war agency, military or civilian, had at least some staff devoted to public relations. Many of these bright young men wound up working for or with the OWI, whose Domestic Branch sought to manage popular expectations of the war effort and monitor public opinion on behalf of the federal government as a whole, establishing bureaus for the major channels of communications.

The OWI was not to be a full-fledged ministry of information in the sense that term applied to the corresponding agencies of the major belligerents in the war, or even to its World War I predecessor, the Committee on Public Information.

Rather, it was to coordinate efforts throughout the war agencies, and by the end of the war it had come to rely heavily on the Hollywood studios, radio networks, and other privately owned media to produce the vast bulk of war propaganda. The News Bureau cleared, edited, and distributed between 250 and 300 releases a week to nearly 2,000 daily newspapers and just under 1,500 trade journals, using its *Magazine War Guide* to suggest topics for feature articles and other copy. The Radio Bureau reached as many as 100 million listeners when it placed roughly 350,000 "impressions," or war messages, each week, working with thirteen major networks through its Network Allocation Plan to coordinate and incorporate a vast outpouring of war-minded skits, jingles, daytime dramas, and plugs into shows that played on the radios of nearly all American families in the early 1940s. The Bureau of Motion Pictures advised Hollywood studios on ways to incorporate approved themes into films that were screened before 85 to 90 million viewers each week. The Bureau of Graphics and Printing produced posters and other images that were put up in subway cars, buses, factories, stores, and other public places nationwide.[73]

Attempting to gauge the effectiveness of these efforts and identify aspects of public opinion that needed remedying through new campaigns, the Bureau of Intelligence enlisted the efforts of leading social scientists to conduct ongoing national surveys of public opinion on a wide range of issues pertaining to the war effort. By using intelligence research in tandem with public relations efforts, war agencies sought to manage morale—or at least those aspects of public opinion that impinged on their specific role in the war effort. The federal government adopted these public relations techniques for the same reasons that private firms had—their need to plan and manage large-scale enterprises within national markets. Fortunately for the government, the techniques of publicity and attitude measurement had recently attained a professional level of sophistication accomplished by advertising agencies, corporate public relations departments, academic social science journals, newspapers, and, most recently, polling organizations. A small throng of social scientists, pollsters, admen, and journalists flocked to Washington in the early years of the war to provide their services to the war effort, many of them employed by the Program Surveys staff of the OWI's Domestic Intelligence Division.[74]

The apparatus for monitoring and shaping morale was both extensive and fragile. While it could draw on all the influence of the culture industries, its homes in the OWI and allied bureaus throughout the war agencies were vulnerable to political attack, and its leverage ultimately depended on the cooperation of a strong-willed private sector. Consequently, the substance of war propaganda often betrayed a consumerist or corporate liberal mentality. The core themes fostered by this institutional morass reinforced the ideological shift away from New Deal concerns with social justice and toward a more unitary and bellicose conception of national interest. Although corporate liberalism often overwhelmed New Deal liberalism in war propaganda, it just as often melded with it in the minds of millions of citizens who encountered both in the saturated media environment of the home front. Even in the minds of the message makers, the boundaries between the free market and the Four Freedoms could become blurred.

Wartime practices of voluntarism and the rhetorical emphasis on freedom and rights in official war aims obscured the coercive and statist components of the mobilization. On a very basic level, the reliance on voluntarism was a critical fact of state capacity. Without its five million volunteer salesmen, enlisted by thousands of civic groups around the nation, the tiny War Savings Staff of the Treasury could not have sold war bonds to more than 85 million Americans. Both rationing and price control likewise would have collapsed in the absence of the 300,000 unpaid volunteers who were organized into more than 5,000 local rationing and price control panels nationwide. While the War Labor Board handled formal processes of arbitration, thousands of local tripartite boards comprised of volunteers from management and labor worked together with government officials to resolve disputes and complaints before they rose to the level of legalized dispute. The armed forces would have been hard-pressed to register 45 million men and classify them for suitability to induction without 184,000 volunteers working on 6,000 local draft boards.

Compared with the tradition of vigilance still practiced locally by citizens as recently as World War I, the civilian volunteers of the Second World War were astonishingly passive and willing to leave the state to its monopoly on violence. As civic-minded civilians, they were by and large the willing servants of the agencies whose manpower needs they served. Pledge campaigns conducted by the Treasury to purchase a certain proportion of one's salary in bonds, or by the OPA to adhere to its guidelines for conservation, rationing, and price control, demonstrated that the forms of civic agency had become yet another channel of "mass persuasion." Local boards provided a nicely contained venue within which local elites could play a part in the administration of policies made in Washington. Most OPA chairmen presiding over their boards' handling of price violations or black market activity were overwhelmingly drawn from the ranks of local professionals and businessmen. Draft board chairmen exercising similar authority were often World War I veterans and nearly always prominent local civic figures. Tripartite boards in war factories contained individuals hand-picked by management and union leadership. Such figures could, for the most part, only adjust complaints to dampen discontent. In toeing the government line, case by case, the volunteers learned to identify with the government they represented. For ideological purposes the Roosevelt administration leaned heavily on both the practice and the ideal of voluntarism to run its war effort at the grassroots, but this made mass participation into more of a simulacrum of self-government than the real thing.

Infusing all this activity was an ideology of liberal nationalism that officials used to sell the war, completing the adaptation of Rooseveltian rhetoric to the purposes of war and melding it with a canny advertising and public relations sensibility that bolstered the public image of business and "free enterprise" as much as it did the Four Freedoms. Despite the capture of propaganda by corporate liberals in the middle years of the war, critical social democratic valences persisted due to the overriding ideological challenge posed by the fascist enemy. This survival was most evident in one of the dominant themes of war propaganda, the need to defend and articulate the virtues of a free, democratic society. Roosevelt worked this theme into many of his public addresses, notably the "Arsenal of Democracy" and "Four Freedoms" fireside chats defining U.S. war aims prior to Pearl Harbor; the Atlantic Charter, announcing the high principles that would animate the alliance against the Axis powers; and the 1944 "Economic Bill of Rights" promised by FDR as his agenda for comprehensive postwar social citizenship. Official propaganda and countless movies, radio plays, comics, and other effusions of popular culture promulgated the Four Freedoms and the virtues of "the American way of life." Along with this celebration of democratic freedoms came officially sanctioned Constitution worship, animated by the contrast between law-abiding nations and the Axis powers, which recognized no law beyond their own national will.[75] When they came from the government such messages indulged classical liberal metaphors, casting the war effort as the embodiment of the social contract that was necessary to avoid the descent into chaos and brutal domination sought by the fascist powers.

Related to this theme of a venerable American democracy imperiled by Axis tyranny was the constant tocsin that warned of the epochal stakes of the civilizational struggle driving the war. This struggle was often conveyed by depicting the irreligious abuses of the Axis powers or by counterposing generic religious imagery against scenes of Nazi brutality. MacLeish's decision to grant the Gutenberg Bible safe harbor in Fort Knox alongside the Magna Carta was a prime example of this. Norman Rockwell's illustration "Freedom of Worship" was another, depicting an assembly of congregants of varied confessions and skin hues, whose solemn devotion implicitly indicted the fanaticism, conformity, and racial exclusivity of the Nazis' Nuremberg rallies and the official emperor worship of Shintoism. One poster, "This World Cannot Exist Half Slave and Half Free," featured a clergyman alongside a threatened family crouching in the shadow of a Nazi officer advancing with a whip. The influential orientation film series Why We Fight conveyed a similar message. A preponderant amount of footage in its first installment, Prelude to

War (1942), evoked the horror of pseudo-religious fanaticism inculcated by fascism, visually underscoring the parallels between German schoolchildren taught to venerate Hitler as "our Savior, our hero . . . our Lord" and masses of Japanese assembled to worship the ostensible godhead of Shinto, the emperor. In another *Why We Fight* film, *The Battle of Britain* (1943), a quiet interlude surveyed the ravaged dignity of a bombed-out church, wordlessly signaling the full profundity of the Luftwaffe's depredations. Evoking a similar moral tone, the unforgettable climactic scene in the war's most popular melodrama, *Mrs. Miniver* (1942), assembled the townspeople of the blasted English countryside into a bombed-out shell of a church to hear their minister declaim:

> This is not only a war of soldiers in uniform. It is a war of the people, *all* the people, and it must be fought not only on the battlefield but in the cities and the villages, in the factories and on the farms, in the home and in the heart of every man, woman, and child who loves freedom. . . . Fight it then. Fight it with all that is in us. And may God defend that right.[76]

This vein of propaganda made clear that the fascist threat to democracy and its brutal disregard for the "Judeo-Christian" values of Western civilization were one and the same. It linked the spiritual and moral struggles of everyday life to the dramatic clashes of men and matériel on distant battlefields.[77] Civil rights organizations would draw on these associations throughout World War II and the postwar period, relying heavily on the moral authority of ministers who often made explicit appeals to the tolerance inherent in the new notion of a "Judeo-Christian ethic."[78] To those who saw the war through religious eyes, modern society's only hope for redemption lay in an updated version of an ancient and evocative imperative: sacrifice.

The emphasis on sacrifice that figured so prominently in wartime propaganda emerged from an early insight into the psychology of civilian morale. Government propagandists learned from confidential survey research that simply imploring civilians to "do their part" and "sacrifice" was not sufficient to motivate them to comply with the many requirements of the war mobilization.[79] The most effective appeals were those that personalized government messages while downplaying overtly ideological statements:

> Results indicated that for thoroughgoing support of the governmental program it would be necessary to create a different psychological atmosphere—an atmosphere based upon a conviction of the equality of sacrifice and upon personally relating the sacrifices on the fighting front to the everyday activities of the housewife in her shopping and household

management, or the wage earner in the disposition of his income. (Readers may recall the implementation of this notion in the car card of the soldier and the slogan: "Can they get by on my pay?")[80]

The thinking behind this observation captured the rationale for a dominant rhetorical strategy in wartime propaganda, the "home front analogy." This was the pointed evaluation of every conceivable aspect of civilian life according to its contribution to the war effort, most often by tracing the battlefront consequences of ordinary decisions at home with an appeal to the folk wisdom of the maxim "For the want of a nail, the war was lost." Within the home front analogy, mundane items such as kitchen fats were not simply the messy by-product of cooking meat; they were a source of glycerines whose salvage might mean another bomb that could bring Johnny home sooner. One WPB poster, "Save Your Cans, Help Pass the Ammunition," made the connection visually impossible to ignore, portraying a housewife's extended hand, shirtsleeve rolled up, adding a can directly to a magazine that fed into a machine gun manned by a soldier who blasted away at the enemy.[81]

In this rhetorical universe, defense workers were promoted to "soldiers of production," home gardens became "victory gardens," and young women willing to socialize with soldiers were called "victory girls." Even the most private or mundane aspects of life were made relevant to the war effort, usually by contrasting civilian concerns with the drastic sacrifices of idealized combat soldiers.[82] A poster from 1943 presented the ghastly image of a soldier facedown in the mud. Beneath his fallen body was the caption "What did *you* do today . . . for Freedom?" In another poster put out by the OWI in the same year, a band of grinning brothers looked out from the deck of a ship. They were the famous Sullivan brothers, all five of whom had perished in action in the Pacific. "*They* Did Their Part," it reminded the viewer (see p. 13). Such appeals worked their way into the conscience.[83]

It was this idealized symbol of nationalistic self-sacrifice, the combat soldier, that provided the master key to wartime political culture. The GI was a culture hero whose name came from the phrase "government issue," a joking reference to the standardized nature of the military in which he served.[84] He personified the new ideals of a changing social order. His ordinariness and common touch conveyed the democratic and humane nature of the American war effort, as opposed to the regimentation and hierarchy of the Wehrmacht or the fanaticism of Japanese dive-bombers.[85] At the same time, he represented martial virtues that supplanted the more social democratic conception of the Depression-era man on the street. The GI's appeal was also personal. He provided individuals with a model onto whom they could project a personal, intimate identification, as if he were a brother, father, son, or husband. He was a rugged individual. He

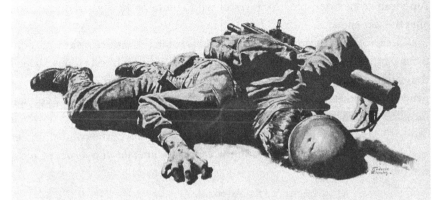

What did *you* do today
... for Freedom?

Today, at the front, he died ... Today, what did *you* do?

Next time you see a list of dead and wounded, ask yourself:

"What have *I* done today for freedom?

What can I do tomorrow that will *save* the lives of

men like this and help them win the war?"

To help you to do your share, the Government has organized the Citizens Service Corps as a part of local Defense Councils, with some war task or responsibility for every man, woman and child. Probably such a Corps is already at work in your community. If not, help to start one. A free booklet available through your local Defense Council will tell you what to do and how to do it. Go into action today, and get the satisfaction of doing a needed war job well!

EVERY CIVILIAN A FIGHTER

Civilians were constantly urged to think of their obligation to the soldiers fighting overseas by scrutinizing the consequences of their everyday actions, linking home front to battle front through analogies whose popular impact proved consequential. (Courtesy of Northwestern University Library, http://digital.library.northwestern.edu/ wwii-posters/img/ww1645-21.jpg) "did his part" but didn't get too sentimental about it. He was an "ordinary Joe." But most of all, the GI was a hero who dominated the society and culture of the American home front, and he was vested with a moral authority that did not fade after the war ended.

The rhetorical appropriation of the combat soldier's sacrifice by unions, politicians, and business advocates, among other contending interest groups, shaped the national political debate.[86] How far into the populace this elite discourse penetrated, and the degree to which it shaped the social experience and cultural meaning of the war mobilization, would depend as much on the ways in which ordinary Americans were able to appropriate the symbol of the combat soldier as it did on the marketing genius of the corporate liberals who designed most war propaganda.

In a Minor Key

Given the political tone deafness exhibited by Lomax and the other folklorists, it is unsurprising that the New Deal for war information gave way so quickly to morale management. The work of the Library of Congress and Office of Facts and Figures staff (particularly as the latter was absorbed by the OWI) fell before the budgetary axe and reorganizational requirements of Congress within a matter of months. By the time the veteran journalist and highly popular CBS radio commentator Elmer Davis agreed to take the helm of the OWI at its creation in June 1942, MacLeish's agency had already drawn the fire of newspapers, which jealously guarded their role in providing information about the war. The enthusiasm with which MacLeish and his like-minded colleagues had embraced the Four Freedoms and other articles of the liberal faith had undermined the objective, factual pretensions of the proclaimed mission to adopt the "strategy of truth."[87]

Aside from the political legacy inherited from MacLeish's battles, there were other restraints that further held the OWI in check, such as its small budget. It exercised no real authority over the actions of other agencies, especially those in the War and Navy departments, which jealously guarded their information and their public image. Worse than active resistance was the indifference of agencies such as the Treasury, which conducted major publicity campaigns and public opinion studies with as much or as little help from the OWI as they saw fit. Roosevelt's tendency to keep his own counsel on matters of publicity didn't help, as it undermined any official authority that OWI might have appeared to enjoy. Most threatening of all, however, was the vocal and bitter criticism by conservatives in Congress, who suspected the OWI of harboring radicals and New Deal holdouts seeking to build a propaganda machine for Roosevelt. In the summer of 1943, following the Republican victories of the previous fall's elections, Congress cut the budget of the Domestic Branch down to the bone at the same time that it eliminated or cut what remained of New Deal emergency agencies such as the WPA.[88]

It was no coincidence that the political assault on the New Deal included a devastating attack on the morale program that had been developed under MacLeish's OFF and Library of Congress. When Rufus C. Holman, the isolationist Republican senator from Oregon, began the final attack on the OWI in early 1943, complaining about an article in its publication, *Victory*, that bore the title "Roosevelt of America—President, Champion of Liberty, United States Leader in the War to Win Lasting Peace," he was simply firing one of the last shots in a cultural struggle that had been raging since the middle of the previous decade. Democratic senator Harry F. Byrd Sr. of Virginia happily fired off another, offering to extend the hunt for New Deal propaganda to other agencies through the investigations of his Joint Committee for the Reduction of Nonessential Federal Expenditures.[89]

The budget cuts spelled the end of the Domestic Branch's independence as a propaganda agency, but that did not prevent its skeletal remainder from continuing to work closely with the major media. OWI had always relied heavily on the media to produce the great bulk of war propaganda. Indeed, the movie studios, radio networks, and especially advertisers had exercised such independence and initiative from the start that they probably exerted more influence on the OWI than vice versa, even before the Domestic Branch's political comeuppance. Advertising executives and journalists assumed the helm of most important bureaus of the OWI by the early spring of 1943. The small staff remaining in the OWI's Domestic Bureau continued to work with private industry to help guide the making of movies, radio shows, and other efforts to bring the war home to Americans. One graphic artist who remembered the idealistic vision of the OFF under MacLeish provided a cutting indictment of the admen's approach in a sketch titled "The War That Refreshes: The Four Delicious Freedoms!" which featured the Statue of Liberty holding aloft four bottles of Coca-Cola. By the war's end, corporate America's public image had received an enormous boost from its role in war propaganda.[90]

As newsmen and public relations experts supplanted writers and artists in the OWI, the ensuing flight of Popular Front intellectuals traced the arc of a larger retreat of New Deal cultural mobilization, brought on by the logic of war nationalism. They had accepted MacLeish's summons to the Library of Congress and followed him into the OFF and OWI. Soon some of them would continue onward with him into the cultural bureaus of the State Department, where they would remain into the first years of the postwar period. Their battles made up only one front in a larger domestic struggle over the direction and meaning of government power as the United States turned away from domestic welfare and became preoccupied by war.

While advertisements placed through the War Advertising Council certainly emphasized commercial themes and even featured some thinly disguised consumer fantasies, they still connected the viewer with the ideals of the war. The home front analogy remained—indeed, it was often amplified, sometimes mercilessly, in the hands of copywriters who wholeheartedly embraced the idea of "selling" battle. The moralistic message of the home front analogy persisted even longer than the agencies that had first promoted it, working its way into the daily lives of ordinary Americans, where it could be reinterpreted to shape the needs of personal viewpoint and memory.

Even if the social contract on which the imaginary of freedom rested was entirely the product of the administration's conjuring, that did not deny its consequence. Grassroots participation in the war effort helped to inspire wartime rights consciousness, encouraging social movements pushing for labor rights, consumer rights, and civil rights. Without the imaginary of freedom, it would have been difficult if not impossible for the United Nations, the International Monetary Fund, and the World Bank to gain acceptance, given the legacy of the defeat of the League of Nations after World War I and the potent isolationism that had grown from that defeat during the two interwar decades.[91]

Yet this dynamic of identification and rising expectation necessarily operated within a cultural logic of nationalism that limited it, at least for the duration of the war. The liberal imaginary carefully constructed by the Roosevelt administration at war inspired visions of a greater New Deal in the world, but it was also, at base, a construct designed to obscure the coercions of a modern state capable of mobilizing for total war. Nationalism—spurred by a near-constant state of emergency generated by depression and world war—overrode the rights of the individual in countless ways. The most basic civil liberties were routinely denied to African Americans in the South, Mexican agricultural workers in the Southwest, Filipino guest workers on the West Coast, and—with the passage of the Smith Act in 1940—political radicals in all regions, whose activities increasingly fell under the scrutiny of the Federal Bureau of Investigation or military intelligence. The mass imprisonment of nearly the entire population of citizens and residents of Japanese descent served as unforgettable proof that the Constitution could be suspended summarily, regardless of individual merit, simply on the grounds of racial suspicion. Internment was a reminder as well that the defense of democratic ideals prompted by Nazi barbarities did not cancel out the greater priority most Americans accorded to the goal of prosecuting a race war in the Pacific.[92] The assurances offered by the Roosevelt administration's war propaganda fell quickly when they clashed with—or merely inconvenienced—raisons d'état.

Perhaps it was fitting, then, that in the days following Pearl Harbor, Archibald MacLeish moved to secure the Magna Carta, along with the Constitution, the Bill of Rights, and the Gutenberg Bible, within the vaults of Fort Knox. The dark symbolism of placing the charter of liberty under lock and key could not have eluded his poetic sensibilities.

In early October 1943, near the end of his celebrated tenure as Librarian of Congress, MacLeish wrote to James Allen, the assistant director of the OWI's embattled domestic branch, "You take it: I'm sick of it." His enemies—in the press, in Congress, and in the OWI itself—had won their fight against him. In so doing, MacLeish believed, they had ensured the ascendancy of dumb "news" over the "proposition that the people are entitled to know and to understand." The OWI's reliance on admen and journalists who stuck to "just the facts," in pointed neglect of the larger concept of national morale MacLeish had tried to cultivate as librarian, posed a danger that went beyond poor taste or low standards:

> Has it ever occurred to you that if you listen very carefully in the middle of any conversation or on the streets of any town in this country today, there is a huge and terrible silence within and beyond the words and sounds that fill your ears? Have you ever thought that that silence is as dangerous and inwardly explosive as a vacuum in the world of physical things?[93]

The OWI did, in fact, attend carefully—even systematically—to the portentous silences of which MacLeish spoke. But under Elmer Davis it listened with the ears of social scientists and bureaucrats, rather than those of poets and Popular Front intellectuals. A cultural strategy dedicated to the democratic cultivation of the voice of the people gave way to a more instrumental approach in which listening and understanding needed only to flow in one direction, through secure channels, while information and explanation streamed separately through others duly authorized.

3

Scapegoating the State

On the night of December 9, 1941, in his first radio address since the Japanese attack on Pearl Harbor two days earlier, President Franklin D. Roosevelt undertook to set the record straight. Early in his address he admitted unequivocally, "Many American soldiers and sailors have been killed by enemy action. American ships have been sunk; American airplanes have been destroyed." This statement of the obvious—in retrospect, a drastic understatement of the worst naval defeat in U.S. history—was necessary because rumor and speculation had spread nationwide in the hours since the surprise attack. Had the entire fleet been destroyed, granting Japan unchallenged supremacy in the Pacific? Had a Japanese destroyer been sunk near the Panama Canal, suggesting an impending invasion of the mainland? "These ugly little hints of complete disaster fly thick and fast in wartime," the president warned. "They have to be examined and appraised."[1]

Despite Roosevelt's admonition, the rumors continued to multiply as bad news poured in during the desperate early months of the Pacific War. By February 1942, speculations about the disaster had evolved into elaborate fantasies. One morbid story had become so widespread that Rear Admiral Adolphus Andrews, commander of the North Atlantic naval coastal frontier, was compelled to issue a formal debunking, although he had previously deemed it not "worthy of a denial." The "wild-eyed tale" claimed that a boat or boats bearing casualties from Pearl Harbor were stuck in harbor at New York because "no workman would take the job" of unloading the bodies. "No such ship" had entered New York harbor, Andrews reported, which led him to the conclusion that the rumor had been "deliberately planted by persons seeking to lower the morale of the American people," and that those "who give them credence or transmit them are playing into the hands of the enemy."[2]

Though animosity toward labor ran high in early 1942, the derelictions of duty attributed to unions paled in comparison with the incompetence or outright treachery that the Roosevelt administration's enemies attributed to it in the wake of Pearl Harbor. "Well, he got us in through the back door," spouted General Robert Wood, national chairman of the America First Committee, when fellow isolationist Charles Lindbergh picked up the phone on December 8. Such responses were simply common sense for the many Americans who had long feared Roosevelt was maneuvering the United States into war.[3]

In this climate of recrimination, the president returned to the airwaves on February 23, 1942, to deliver his "Map Room Speech." In it, Roosevelt sought not only to instruct his listeners on the geopolitics of the war but also to allay fears and uncertainties that had festered as bad news arrived from the Pacific Theater in the first months of the war. His grim task was to convey the global scope of the task facing the nation, while reassuring listeners that the job could be done. An audience of 61 million listened raptly, many with recently purchased maps in hand, tracing with their fingers a path that followed his words around the globe.[4]

After charting far-flung developments in broad strokes, Roosevelt turned his listeners' focus from the farthest reaches of the globe to the familiar terrain of their everyday lives, addressing once again the rumors about the losses at Pearl Harbor. "You and I have the utmost contempt for Americans who, since Pearl Harbor, have whispered or announced 'off the record' that there was no longer any Pacific Fleet" or made similarly exaggerated statements. These claims were worse than mistaken, the president remarked; they were practically treasonous, for they came "originally from Axis propagandists":

> The American people want to know, and will be told, the general trend
> of how the war is going. But they do not wish to help the enemy any
> more than our fighting forces do, and they will pay little attention to the
> rumor-mongers and the poison peddlers in our midst.[5]

Had he heeded his own counsel regarding poison-peddlers, Roosevelt would not have signed Executive Order 9066 five days earlier, authorizing the mass removal and confinement of more than 110,000 lawful residents and citizens of Japanese ancestry living along the West Coast. He had given in to mounting pressure for mass removal—despite intelligence from the Federal Bureau of Investigation (FBI) and the navy indicating it was unnecessary—only after a sustained campaign led by West Coast politicians and figures within the army's Western Defense Command suddenly gained political advantage in late January. Gordon Allport, pioneering Harvard social psychologist and preeminent wartime expert on rumors, later observed that the "desperate losses" at Pearl Harbor had attracted relatively "few rumors" until "the [news]papers themselves had published an official report on the disaster."[6]

That report, which assigned principal blame to Pacific commanders Admiral Husband Kimmel and Lieutenant General Walter Short, came from a commission led by Supreme Court justice Owen Roberts.[7] Resting as it did on the authority of a man whose reputation for independence and integrity was widely celebrated, the Roberts Commission report might have been expected to settle the matter. But its corollary finding, that Japanese espionage and other "fifth-column" activity in Hawai'i had abetted the attack, set off a wave of outrage and consternation when the report went public on January 24. By early February concern over a domestic fifth column and the possibility of a second strike, this time on the mainland, had reached a fever pitch. Suddenly it became impossible to dismiss the wild claims that West Coast nativists and their well-placed allies had repeated like a drumbeat since December—that "Jap subs" lurked just outside the Golden Gate; that formations of Japanese planes had been sighted over California cities; that Japanese farmers had planted their crops to point the way for an impending invasion. The rumors of an inscrutable and inherently treacherous Japanese community placed extraordinary political pressure on Roosevelt, to which he finally acceded in a telephone conversation with Secretary of War Henry Stimson on February 11. He authorized Executive Order 9906 a week later.[8]

Although it allayed the panic unleashed by Pearl Harbor, the mass removal and confinement of entire Japanese communities within bleak camps located in abandoned corners of the nation's interior did not squelch rumors of a Japanese fifth column. It only shifted the locus of the imagined treachery to the camps. Nor did it stanch the flood of paranoid speculation about how the world's mightiest nation could possibly have fallen prey to such "yellow treachery." In the coming months, skeptics would aver that the "same kind of mistakes that happened at Pearl Harbor" were still being made. How else could the steady string of defeats through the first six months of the war be explained? Suspicion was not reserved for the high and mighty. On the local scene, gossips speculated darkly about the behavior of questionable characters, such as the "shabbily" dressed "old woman who used to work for the Federal Writers' Project" in Salt Lake City and whose sudden disappearance soon after December 7 prompted allegations that she had lent her library card to "a man who is known to have borrowed about ten books on it, all pertaining to bombs and explosives." The two were alleged to have been seen together around town, although now she dressed "very well."[9]

Rumormongers nearly always inserted some telling detail, such as to the Federal Writers' Project, to signal implicit associations and resentments that couldn't be stated openly. Indeed, these details were what made rumors worthy of re-telling, propelling them beyond the confines of individual opinion and passing conversation. Far from dying down, the rumors about Pearl Harbor only grew stronger over time. During the war alone, cries of outrage and foul play forced the government to launch no fewer than five investigations of the attack. What was new about the Pearl Harbor conspiracy theories, and what made them so enduring, was not simply the use of conspiracy theory to discredit the powerful, although the government had increasingly become an object of such fantasies as it grew in capacity and authority. The "paranoid style" had long inflected discourse at both extremes of the political spectrum, dating back at least to the fears of royal intrigue and tales of conspiratorial Freemasonry that shaped the nation's early political culture in the eighteenth century.[10]

What made the Pearl Harbor conspiracy theories stick was their ability to draft race into the service of antistatism. With its attack, imperial Japan had accomplished much more than the demolition of the Hawai'ian base of U.S. naval power in the Pacific. The dawn raid was only a stratagem to buy time for a much larger maneuver deep into the heart of East Asia and the South Pacific. Within three months of the December offensive Japan had dislodged all the Western powers from their seats of colonial rule in East Asia—British Hong Kong, Malaya, Singapore, Borneo, and much of Burma; the Dutch East Indies; French Indochina; Australian Papua and New Guinea; Portuguese Timor; the American Philippines. The resulting pan-Asian order Japan established with its Co-Prosperity Sphere inverted the racial hierarchies on which Western power and notions of civilization had rested for centuries. While galvanizing to non-white peoples around the world, these developments appalled most whites, who readily demonized "the Japs" as a treacherous race in need of extermination. The geopolitical earthquake unleashed a racial Armageddon whose ferocity made the Pacific War one of the bloodiest in American history.[11]

Such a profound challenge to the most basic racial assumptions that structured everyday life in the United States required an explanation. By linking racial treachery to government incompetence and liberal subterfuge, critics of the Roosevelt administration hit upon a conspiracy theory that would last decades. They scapegoated the state, all the while deflecting accusations of sedition with a shield of nationalism fashioned from patriotism and racial outrage.

The significance of wartime rumors lay not so much in the truth-value of the stories they told as in the specific narrative features used to appeal to listeners, and the effectiveness of these features in boosting their retelling. Truly absurd tales were not worth remembering, much less passing on to friends and acquaintances. By inquiring into the reasons why Americans found obscure rumors, jokes, and tall tales compelling enough to pass along—and why government monitors considered them sufficiently threatening to track and analyze—it is possible to glimpse the coalescence of a national political culture around the mundane transactions between a society and its government girding for war. Politicized talk about the war effort formed a sort of folklore through which expectations and attitudes coalesced around the parts of the federal government that were suddenly brushing up against private spheres and preexisting power arrangements. Telling stories, whispering rumors, laughing at jokes, singing songs, and passing along gossip were small but meaningful ways in which Americans could talk indirectly about the myriad changes in their everyday lives brought about by war mobilization.[12]

Once they had adapted the ingrained racial folklore of their regions to cloak the aspersions they wished to cast on the government, those spreading rumors could draw on this coded language to undermine the legitimacy of government policies, even those that ultimately had little to do with race per se. By the end of the war, race continued to echo in the conspiracy theories cultivated by the right, but the state had been made a scapegoat in its own right, allowing anticommunists finally to gain the political purchase they had lacked during the "little Red Scare" prior to the war. In this way the cultural politics of rumor raised the stakes of the challenge that conservatives had been mounting against the New Deal state for more than half a decade, while opening up much more effective lines of attack. Despite this challenge to its legitimacy—indeed, because of it—the government only gained greater power over everyday life, as it trained citizens to monitor and report their own speech as well as that of their neighbors.

Bureaucratizing the Grapevine

Pearl Harbor was not the only topic suitable for scapegoating the state. The early years of the war, unsettled by the greatest military uncertainty and the most intense social upheaval, generated a profusion of rumors so striking that several government agencies felt obliged to respond to it. Federal officials were careful to avoid the vigilantism and mass arrests that had attended the politics of sedition in World War I. New Dealers such as Archibald MacLeish, first head of the OWI, or Francis Biddle, attorney general for much of the war, sought to contain or monitor speech rather than repress it. Bureaucratic infighters such as FBI director J. Edgar Hoover aimed to monopolize channels of communication about subversion in order to garner the political rewards of its exposure for themselves. The surveillance of everyday public discourse provided a new means by which the warfare state could make citizens' subjectivity legible, even as its propagandistic admonitions to self-regulate speech in the name of national security made citizens "war-minded," further disposing them to governmentality.[13]

Americans in 1942 and early 1943 were jittery. East Coast beachgoers in the summer of 1942 watched in dismay as German submarines sank Allied ships seemingly at will, bringing the Battle of the Atlantic within eyeshot of their children gamboling in the surf. In July and August, Americans read sensational headlines about the six German saboteurs who had landed by U-boat on Long Island and in Florida in June, equipped with weapons, explosives, maps, and plans to incapacitate industry and undermine the American war effort.

Their electrocution on August 8 could not allay concerns over the ease with which they had made their way into Chicago and New York, where they blended into German American communities.[14]

Sabotage now had a recognizable face, which set tongues wagging about suspicious local figures: Italians who flagged secret messages by referring to a relative named Roberto (an acronym derived from the Axis headquarters of Rome, Berlin, and Tokyo); local Japanese community leaders such as Kay Mukai, owner of a noodle shop in Ogden, Utah, whose yearly treatments for eczema were imagined to have been a cover for reconnaissance trips to photograph dams, canals, and copper mines elsewhere in the state; even recently arrived German neighbors of an elevator operator in Iowa who were "mean to the children in the neighborhood" and kept a large dog.[15]

The FBI investigated these sorts of allegations, despite their patent implausibility. Anticipating the need to protect defense plants from sabotage, it had by 1940 developed a "plant protection program" in which employees working in factories on the navy and War Department priority lists (which by 1942 included virtually every major industrial operation) were selected for their vigilance and encouraged to "be on the alert for any evidence of sabotage, espionage, or subversive activities." If they noticed anything suspicious, they were instructed to report directly to FBI special agents, who would follow up on their leads. Popular enthusiasm for spy hunting guaranteed that the FBI would not want for informants. Indeed, Hoover moved to deputize volunteers as semiofficial "contacts" in order to avoid the excesses of vigilantism and lawlessness that had nearly destroyed his early career in the aftermath of the previous war's Red Scare. Through an arrangement with the national leadership and local posts of the American Legion, the FBI had already secured more than forty thousand contacts just a month before Pearl Harbor. Within two years another seventeen thousand Legionnaires joined in, and by the war's end special agents recruited roughly seventy thousand Legionnaires from more than ten thousand posts around the county, providing at least one contact for each county.[16]

The scores of thousands of informants whom the FBI secretly deputized in communities around the nation in effect constituted a bureaucratized rumor mill. By the end of the war the FBI received 18,091 complaints of sabotage. Subsequent FBI investigations found "no successful foreign-directed act of sabotage" and only 568 domestic episodes producing enough evidence to secure a conviction. The FBI had to concede that the "vast majority" of even the 3,020 verified claims of sabotage "were due to spite, carelessness, and juvenile mischief." That the FBI received 15,071 false or mistaken reports of sabotage may be taken as an index of sorts to the politicized nature of talk, speculation, and everyday life during wartime.[17]

At the same time, the Office of War Information hoped to snuff out rumor through its security of information campaign, which made the phrase "loose lips sink ships" an official watchword of the home front.[18] Consistent with its home-front analogy, the OWI's campaign emphasized that information about the smallest detail of everyday life might prove vitally revealing to enemy spies, and so should be kept secret.

By constantly reminding Americans of the grave consequences of their un-regulated talk, the OWI hoped to regulate even the most elusive elements of citizens' lives. "Bits of careless talk" could be "pieced together by the enemy," one poster suggested, showing a swastika-ringed hand finishing a puzzle in which the final piece, labeled "England," completed the sentence "Convoy sails tonight for . . ."[19] Other posters in the series suggested the dire consequences resulting "because somebody talked"—an infantryman clutching his bloody face on the field of battle, a lifeless paratrooper descending amid a shower of flak, a sailor's hand grasping out as he sinks beneath the waves, a dog waiting vainly beneath a service star that indicates his master will never return home.[20] To ensure that such subtle messages did not pass over civilians' heads, one poster showed a photograph of a woman with the caption "Wanted! for mur-der: her careless talk costs lives," while another showed the hapless face of a sailor looking out from a porthole framed by the entreaty "If you talk too much, this man may die."[21] The provost marshal general went so far as to equate rumors with sabotage, reminding workers in a poster entitled "Warning, Sabotage" that violation of the Federal Sabotage Act could incur heavy fines and decades of imprisonment. In severe cases, it threatened, "treason is punishable by death!"[22]

Warnings against "loose talk" produced some crude responses, especially early in the war. The Veterans of Foreign Wars (VFW) publication *Foreign Ser-vice* encouraged its readers to "kill that rumor" and advised, "Rumor is the hand-maiden of propaganda and is never innocent in its inception. . . . Anyone repeating rumors aimed at disunity among us and to undermining our confi-dence in our fighting forces, the quality of our fighting equipment, or our gov-ernment, is serving the Axis enemies."[23] The illustration for the story, depicting an axe labeled "truth" swung by a burly pair of arms beneath the admonition "KILL," suggested the finesse with which veterans might handle such a job. Here was the reason J. Edgar Hoover had moved early to co-opt veteran assistance through the American Legion contact program. Small wonder, then, that OWI officials declined an offer extended by Victor Devereux, director of the VFW's Department of Americanism, to place six thousand VFW units at the service of the OWI, in continuance of its long tradition of "combating subversive activ-ities." Rather than revealing the sinister presence of enemy sympathizers, the OWI responded, "On the contrary, most rumors do begin quite innocently, and arise from the stress and tensions prevalent in the community or nation."[24]

WANTED!

FOR MURDER

Her <u>careless talk</u> costs lives

Popular stereotypes presumed that most gossips were women who could not control their "loose lips." Research on morale-threatening rumor showed otherwise. This poster was part of the federal government's security of information campaign to squelch leaks that might compromise production or troop movements. (Courtesy of Northwestern University Library, http://digital.library.northwestern.edu/wwii-posters/img/ww0207-80.jpg)

If the OWI rejected such crude efforts, it nonetheless acted on the assumption that rumors could be a deadly weapon when wielded by the enemy. The rumor control staff viewed rumors and other forms of speech as vectors for poisonous external threats to morale, originating in Axis shortwave broadcasts and the whispers of fifth-column subversives. The very language of rumor control, in which the OWI and others spoke of "inoculating" the public against Axis lies, treated rumors as if they were verbal viruses, plagues transmitted orally and capable of causing epidemics of panic, such as had happened in 1938 after Orson Welles's *War of the Worlds* broadcast.[25] Germany had demonstrated the devastating effectiveness of its psychological warfare techniques, sowing pestilential terror to "soften" Poland, France, and other prospective victims before the blitzkrieg. Though invasion of the North American mainland came to seem unlikely as the war progressed, the possibility of panic and demoralization posed a real threat to the war effort.

As the OWI probed further, it discovered just how subtle and complex the threat of propaganda and "defeatist thinking" might be. An internal report prepared by the Enemy Sources Section of the OWI's Intelligence Sources Division compared the content of Axis shortwave broadcasts to the rumors that were reported to the government in the first week of August 1942 and found a "striking parallelism" between the two. Enemy Sources claimed that "a majority of the most frequently occurring 'rumors' are also found in Axis propaganda content," which in turn indicated an active intent among Axis propagandists to "implant" the stories in the United States, with fifth-column assistance.[26]

A review of the rumors that the Enemy Sources group linked to Axis broadcasts reveals the inherent slipperiness involved in identifying smoking guns. Commonly voiced anti-Semitic allegations, such as "No Jews are volunteering for war service," shared much prejudice, but little precise verbal content, with far more vitriolic Nazi slanders against "the international Jew," "crooked-nosed Kikes," and their supposed connections with "international bankers" that allowed them to rule the world without having "sacrificed themselves." The Axis broadcasts singled out by Enemy Sources railed obsessively against Jews, New Dealers, and the British. More mundane rumors concerning wartime policies such as rationing, price control, scrap collection, the draft, government waste, and black market activity were at least as common on the home front as were slanders resembling the philippics featured in the broadcasts. Indeed, rumors of waste, privilege, and injustice produced by the war effort most likely outnumbered the "wedge-driving" slanders by a significant margin, yet these topics received little or no treatment in the broadcasts analyzed by Enemy Sources. In the case of one of the most divisive classes of American wedge-driving stories, Axis propagandists surprisingly made discrimination against African Americans a major theme, playing to their discontents, while largely neglecting the prejudiced anti-"Negro" rumors that dominated rumors of domestic origin.[27]

Another group of analysts within the OWI, dedicated to rumor control, took a more cautious approach, observing that "although these stories may not be actually planted by enemy agents, the important point is that they are the rumors which the Axis powers are desirous of having in circulation in this country."[28] Here was a fundamental challenge to wartime democracy: how could democratic morale be preserved against the sinister predations of fascism—with its ruthless employment of psychological warfare—without indulging in regimentation?[29] Rumors were an unavoidable possibility in an open society whose freedom of expression could allow mischief makers to sow widespread confusion, uncertainty, and lies. The liberal answer was to safeguard the American public through a campaign of "straight facts." Truth was the proper democratic antidote to Axis psychological warfare, according to the OWI's philosophy. The American mind needed only the facts to remain free.[30]

Accordingly, the OWI rumor control group, coordinated by Eugene Horowitz in the Bureau of Public Inquiries and Leo Rosten, the deputy director for military information, focused its energies on public information campaigns. These efforts often involved little more than working with other OWI staff on poster campaigns, newsreels, and the like, to highlight certain morale-building facts or slogans that rumors had cast into doubt. Horowitz, a social psychologist, came to this work from a scholarly grounding in black culture and interracial relations.[31] Rosten had established himself as an authority on Jewish American culture and language by writing, pseudonymously, *The Education of H*Y*M*A*N K*A*P*L*A*N*, whose protagonist's humorous efforts to learn English at night school appeared in serialized form in the *New Yorker* in the 1930s.[32]

Local communities of like-minded journalists, social scientists, and civic leaders followed the example of Harvard social psychologist Gordon Allport, forming "rumor clinics" in cities around the country to preempt rumors by defusing them with facts. Between the fall of 1942 and the following summer more than thirty rumor clinics were established in civilian defense offices and newsrooms around the country, soliciting responsible citizens to write or call in with suspicious stories. Especially troublesome stories were publicly dissected in newspaper features and radio shows, where authoritative statements could be used to debunk them by way of contrast. These efforts may not have been very effective. One study indicated that debunking a rumor actually tended to promote acceptance among readers who had no prior exposure to it, especially on radio, where listeners tended to turn the dial sporadically.[33]

The OWI also conducted some covert investigations of rumors, going so far as to launch a nationwide study in the first two weeks of August 1942 that asked civilian defense "morale wardens" and local federal officials to report any rumors they overheard.[34] The Washington office could call on its field staff, working out of eleven regional offices around the country, to provide a quick and effective canvass of local conditions. For more extensive investigations it could augment field reports with passive intelligence garnered by a broad range of federal agencies in the course of their daily operations. Social scientists drafted into the OWI for the duration complemented the formidable scope of the OWI's bureaucratic purview with an arsenal of maturing research techniques.[35]

Unsurprisingly, the meaning of rumors proved difficult to pin down. Unlike the views expressed to government interviewers and pollsters, rumors were shared and recorded surreptitiously to avoid public accountability. They were expressive, ambiguous, usually told for curiosity's sake rather than to establish clear beliefs or points of view. Furthermore, government officials and social scientists recorded only those utterances they considered to be morale-threatening. For these reasons, the rumors recorded by rumor clinics and the OWI staff were artifacts of opinion formation, rather than exact representations of underlying attitudes.[36] A willingness to pass along a story did not necessarily indicate absolute belief in its contents. Wartime estimates of the proportion of individuals who believed the rumors they heard varied as widely as a fifth of all hearers to two-thirds, verging on four-fifths in some cases.[37]

Rumor researchers found that the proportion of rumors believed generally increased with "exposure," although in some special cases where respondents had no prior exposure—mostly to rumors of special privilege—they indicated belief anyway.[38] One OWI study found that rumors circulated most among the socially active: 60 percent of respondents with "many social contacts" mentioned high numbers of rumors (between seven and twenty-six), while 72 percent of the "socially isolated" mentioned very few rumors (from zero to six). The stereotype of the uneducated peasant woman gossiping within the ethnic warrens of the great cities proved unfounded. Rather, it was the newspaper-reading male high school graduate who considered himself well informed who posed the greatest danger to public opinion.[39] Even if the numbers were imprecise, the general picture painted by this analysis suggested not only that rumor clinics ran a grave risk of feeding verbal kindling to those most in need of having their inflammatory tendencies dampened, but also that the social conditions of the war made rumor control a Herculean task.[40]

Despite the best efforts of government officials, rumor and other forms of talk remained elusive and difficult to measure much less control during the war. Top-down strategies came up against the long American tradition of free speech and the abiding suspicion of central government. Aside from the highly flawed trials of a small group of native fascists, prosecutions for sedition were limited and speech remained relatively free for the duration, forming a semiprivate sensibility beyond expert control.[41] It turned out that Americans had their own internalized censor: patriotism. This internal censor required that disgruntled citizens find ways to vent antigovernment sentiment indirectly. Time-worn stereotypes and scapegoats offered the path of least resistance. With a little imagination and a dose of suspicion, wartime rumor tellers could focus their frustrations on familiar figures they had already learned to hate. In scapegoating the state, the teller's patriotism thus remained unquestioned. It was this dynamic, rather than the "penetration" of Axis propaganda, that explained the proliferation of racially inflected rumors that Allport, the OWI, and others worried were planted as "wedge drivers" by agents provocateurs.

Three types of rumors were especially widespread and potent during World War II, deriving from distinctly regional sensibilities: anti-Semitic rumors, which occurred in all parts of the country but assumed their most vitriolic and concentrated forms in the industrial communities of the Northeast and Midwest; rumors of black conspiracy, confined almost entirely to the South; and stories of Japanese American privilege and government subversion, which circulated mostly in the western states.[42] Each type of rumor appealed to well-established regional stereotypes of race and ethnicity to garner the interest of its listeners. Yet all three contained allusions, punch lines, and outright condemnations that sought to link the federal government's newly intrusive activities to well-established caricatures and epithets.

Anti-Semitic Conspiracy Theories in the Industrial North

Concern about morale-threatening prejudice and its possible agitation by Axis propaganda led the liberals within the OWI to be especially attentive to popular expressions of anti-Semitism. This was sparked not only by the prominence of anti-Semitism in Nazi propaganda, but also by the wave of prejudice that washed over the United States during the war years. Polls showed that while most Americans were appalled by the Nazi persecution of Jews, ingrained suspicions led a plurality—which grew during the war to become a majority—to accept the proposition that American Jews had "too much influence" or power.[43] Generic suspicions of Jews evading the draft were among the most commonly repeated rumors on the American home front, and they persisted long after other rumors subsided.[44] Stories abounded of Jews using "pull" to evade the draft or obtain officers' commissions. In countless rumors they were accused of using their notorious wealth to bribe draft boards and induction officers. Other accounts depicted Jews maneuvering to avoid the draft so they could profit from the war boom. The basic point of all such stories was to impugn Jewish manhood and patriotism. Rumors of Jewish draft evasion were so widespread that General Lewis Hershey, head of the Selective Service, found it necessary to issue a statement denying that Jewish men served any less frequently than other men.[45]

The most extreme versions of anti-Semitic rumor and slander clearly emanated from within the ranks of the native fascist communities that still festered in the cities of the industrial North, most visibly in Boston, New York, Detroit, and Chicago. Gerald L. K. Smith, the wartime publisher of *The Cross and the Flag*, launched the America First Party in the middle of the war, years after the eponymous committee and its cause of neutrality had become defunct. From his base in Detroit Smith issued invectives against the secret dealings of Jewish bankers, British imperialists, and New Deal liberals, drawing large audiences who responded to the nativist and isolationist themes that had been so effective in rallying opposition against the Roosevelt administration in the years before Pearl Harbor. It was in Detroit that he befriended Henry Ford, whose earlier publication of *The Protocols of the Elders of Zion* he would eventually reissue, after renaming his party the Christian Nationalist Crusade in 1944 and running as its presidential candidate several times. His followers lapped up the constant diatribes he issued in his broadsides, passed out in the streetcars, subways and defense plants of northeastern and midwestern industrial cities.

In these ethnic enclaves some of the most vitriolic rumors circulated, bolstered by a popular preoccupation with Jews and their place in American society.[46] An illustration of their approach may be observed in an excerpt from a poem that caught the OWI's attention in November 1942. It was passed out on streetcars and subways, as well as in defense plants, and told the story of "America's fighting Jew."

> They are fighting at the race tracks / To place their show bets down
> They'll fight for ring side table / At the Swanky joints in town
> They fight like hell at Jordan's / And cousin Filene's too
> Wherever there's a bargain / You'll find the FIGHTING JEW
> Onward Christian soldiers! / That is their battle cry.[47]

Another poem, "Onward Christian Liberals," presented a similar juxtaposition of Jewish materialism and Christian sacrifice. It showed its colors before the reader could complete the first couplet, taunting tolerant liberals for their willingness to "give the Jew his Rights . . . while you fight his fights." Yet even this clumsy piece of agitprop had to make some attempt to catch the eye of an audience broader than the true believers. The Christian liberals in the poem were not simply guilty of letting "Jewish bankers rile you from abroad," or allowing "the Jew" to "hog our business." They sent their "sons to fight [Jews'] wars" while back home Jews profited by controlling everything from the manufacture of "ammunition, sausages and booze" to the movies of Hollywood and the shows on "radio, a plaything for the Jews."[48]

The caricatures in these pieces of doggerel had grown tired after a decade of Depression-inspired extremism, but their strained effort to contrast the figure of the Jew with that of the soldier revealed the pressures wartime patriotism had placed on native fascists. They had somehow to affirm the American soldier while tarring his government with a "Hebrew" association, a strategy that invested Jewish scapegoats with ridiculous amounts of power or absurdly picayune control over mundane aspects of the war effort, such as rationed tires or scrap metal.

Smith's star began to wane during the war, especially once the Justice Department began to pursue its sedition prosecution of prominent native fascists, including William Dudley Pelley, the self-proclaimed "American Hitler" who led the Silver Shirts, the most menacing fascist group. When in March 1942 Pelley published the claim that the U.S. had "aggressively solicited" the "Japanese bombers" who "made Pearl Harbor look like an abandoned W.P.A. project in Keokuk," Roosevelt immediately wrote Attorney General Francis Biddle, ordering him to "indict the seditionists." Like the Enemy Sources analysis of Axis shortwave propaganda's influence on domestic rumors, the attorney general's prosecution of Pelley and his comrades on the right hung on the charge that the defendants conspired to "follow the Nazi blueprint" in their publications, repeating Nazi phrases, themes, and propaganda, most distinctively those featuring anti-Semitism as an "indispensable revolutionary ingredient."[49]

The provocations of the native fascists explain the preoccupation with anti-Semitism that guided much of the rumor monitoring conducted by OWI and Gordon Allport's outfit in Boston. Because of the agitators' conspicuous efforts to use hatred of Jews to sow discontent with the Roosevelt administration, they drew the attention of rumor monitors to all such expressions of prejudice, regardless of their tellers' political leanings. Consequently, we have a surprisingly detailed picture of the less overtly ideological stories, gossip, jokes and rumors that expressed currents of anti-Semitism persisting into the middle years of the war.[50] These ordinary slanders and other expressions of prejudice assumed less dramatic formulations than the agitators' doggerel, but shared many of the same themes and associations, if in diluted form.

In the late winter of 1943, OWI rumor control began to track the alarming national circulation of a piece of doggerel variously entitled "The First American," "A Little Difference in Americans," and "It's Great to Be an American," whose formula had become notorious in northern cities by late 1942:

> The first American soldier to kill a Jap was MIKE MURPHY
> The first American bomber to sink a Jap battleship was COLIN KELLEY

The first American flyer to bag a Jap plane was EDWARD O'HARE...
The first American to get four new tires was NATHAN GOLDSTEIN

The litany of "The First American" had spread nationally, thereby attracting the attention of the OWI rumor staff, who thought it might be evidence of fifth-column activity. Subsequent investigation determined that no Axis-inspired conspiracy could be found. Nathan Goldstein was not the only butt of the joke; the federal government was, too, as it had allowed him to get the rationed tires while "real" Americans killed "Japs."[51] A nationally popular joke about draft dodging contained a similar punch line. When Mannie Harper was granted three wishes, his first two (for one hundred suits of clothes and $100,000 cash) satisfied him enough that he "decided to do something for humanity" by wishing "that Hitler be exterminated." At that very moment the phone rang with a call from the draft board, informing Mannie his deferment was cancelled: "You are now 1-A."[52]

While most Americans couched their anti-Semitism in jokes and other accepted forms of bigotry, some citizens had no qualms about addressing their prejudices directly to public figures, despite the heightened suspicion of Nazi ideology. "Investigate the case of Sidney Goldberg," wrote one woman to the *Philadelphia Inquirer*'s rumor clinic. She claimed that Goldberg's father, who owned a local "meat and grocery store," was "a rich jew" who used his "pull with the navy yard" to exempt his son from the draft by securing him an essential war job there testing acid. "I am a mother of a boy who enlisted in the navy and I don't think it is right for a rich man's son to be able to get a good job and be deferred." Her accusation was personal—she knew Sidney Goldberg from the neighborhood—but she articulated her resentments using language and imagery drawn from a broader set of wartime rumors.[53]

The less ideologically extreme the rumor, the more likely it was to finger the mundane hassles of wartime life as evidence of Jewish influence. A druggist in Wilkes-Barre, Pennsylvania, claimed that old toothpaste tubes collected for government scrap drives were in fact "sold to Jewish junk dealers," who then profited by selling them "at four times their cost." A New Yorker recently arrived in California claimed that "in Yonkers the Jews did not turn in their scrap rubber. They preferred to wait until a better price could be offered." In Athens, Pennsylvania, there was alleged to be "a man with nine carloads of tires," a commodity made scarce by government rationing; "He is a Jew. All the tires and gas bootleggers are Jews."[54] In the eyes of the rumor tellers, the Athens man was not alone. This specific allegation—that Jews were profiteering from government scrap drives—was reported from many locations around the country, accounting for 11 percent of all anti-Semitic rumors reported to the Boston rumor clinic by the early spring of 1943.[55]

When it appeared outside the Northeast, the accusation of profiteering adopted the familiar features of a conspiracy by "New York Jews." A policeman in Maricopa County, Arizona, reported that he had heard talk "that the Jews in New York are sorting the rubber turned in during the rubber drive and are getting $400 a ton for some of it."[56] A barbershop patron in St. Paul, Minnesota, argued that rationing was unnecessary: "If they ration gasoline here, it is on account of the Jews in New York City who want it."[57] These accusations, which drew on enduring regional tensions, allowed local citizens to vent their frustrations with rationing, scrap drives, and other controls over their daily economic transactions, without pointing the finger at anyone in particular.

By fingering Jewish corruption and invoking old images of a Jewish cabal to manipulate the economy, anti-Semitic rumors transformed frustration into suspicion, thereby suggesting that the war effort was being undermined. Such suspicions necessarily implicated the federal government, which apparently had been manipulated from without by schemes to profit from war conditions, and corrupted from within by sinister figures who had "taken over" the government. A Newell, Iowa, woman dismissed the rubber, scrap iron, and tire drives by saying "the rubber was all sold cheap to three prominent Jews who resold it to the government at an enormous profit."[58] If it was unclear why the government would allow itself to be manipulated in this way, the uncertainty could be cleared up by another rumor circulating in Maryland, Massachusetts, Michigan, Minnesota, and California: "Three Jews in Washington own all the scrap rubber collected in the big drive."[59]

Rather than grapple with the difficulties of shortages and inflation, it was easier to assume a plot. "The cost of shoes and clothes have gone up every week for months," observed a pinched consumer in Buffalo, New York. OPA director Leon "Henderson and his pals blame it on inflation. If you want to know the truth, I'll tell you. Those Jews are to blame." Likewise, rationing could be transformed from a necessary allocation of scarce goods to a plan for regimentation. An embittered citizen of Indianapolis, Indiana, echoed the Buffalo consumer when he confided, "Did you know that the G.D. Jews and Henderson are ruining this country. This whole war is a farce. There's plenty of sugar and plenty of rubber." Yet his bitterness did not prevent him from wondering aloud if "the Government" had "any good jobs in Mexico. I want to get out of this country and the sooner the better."[60] The mixture of antigovernment resentment and government-oriented entitlement could not have been more absurd, but it reflected how personally many citizens responded to the government's new role in their lives.

A penchant for global conspiracy transferred naturally from one target to another, especially among anti-Semites familiar with an extensive conspiracy lore. To some, it appeared that Jews were not simply capitalizing on the moment from their secret councils in New York City and the other financial centers of the world; they had begun to exert their corrosive influence from within the highest seats of power in the federal government. The Boston rumor clinic and the OWI rumor staff closely tracked the proliferation of countless claims that Jews—the president's "intimate advisors," who "ran" Washington—had "blackmailed Roosevelt" into the war. A simpler explanation for the "mess" in Washington was that "Roosevelt and his whole cabinet are Jews." In the most tortured twist of logic, one rumor alleged that Jews were providing covert aid to the Germans to prolong "their war," while another confided that "Jewish political bosses control President Roosevelt. . . . Hitler is really on the best of terms with the Jewish people who are backing him financially." Such rumors were similar in form to, and sometimes overlapped in both substance and audience with, other contemporary claims that "the British are running everything in Washington, having everyone fingerprinted, etc.," as an informant reported to the Boston rumor clinic in early spring of 1942. Here were echoes of interwar conspiracy theories about the international Jew, Jewish-backed "merchants of death," and the British connections of the House of Rothschild, all of which had stoked isolationism and helped stymie Roosevelt in the interwar period.[61]

When people told anti-Semitic jokes like the one about the Jewish man who made a living "smuggling Christians" into Washington, D.C., they were reinforcing a broad set of implicit associations.[62] On a few occasions these associations slipped out in flat statements of belief: "The streets of Washington are so filled with Jews and they are so aggressive that they fairly push you off the sidewalk. Jews hold nearly all the public offices. Roosevelt is putting Jews everywhere. Jewish doctors are on the Examining Boards and they exempt their own boys."[63] The state of affairs was downright un-American. "Imagine Lincoln and Washington being advised by men like Harry Hopkins," griped a Pittsburgh businessman within earshot of an OWI rumor warden. "They've got too many Jews down there. . . . Henderson's real name is Horowitz. . . . and Morgenthau . . . and a bunch of other ones."[64]

As extreme as these statements were, they merely expressed in crude stereotypes the widespread sentiment that Jews had "too much influence" and power. Anti-Semites were simply more willing to make explicit statements such as "There are too many Jews in the various federal agencies and bureaus in Washington and they have too much control over our national policies." Interviews conducted by Daniel J. Levinson for The Authoritarian Personality showed that affirmative responses to this specific statement were highly correlated with other expressions of anti-Semitism. Levinson's interviews occurred both during and immediately after the war, which suggests that the associations on which such rumors played remained resonant even after the period of early war mobilization.[65]

Ice Picks and Eleanor Clubs in the "Solid" South

We have a detailed picture of southern rumors thanks to Howard Odum, a sociologist and folklorist at the University of North Carolina. In the first months of the war Odum, a prominent southern liberal, became concerned by the proliferation of extreme rumors concerning African Americans. Like Rosten and Horowitz in the OWI, he hoped to preempt racial violence by defusing misunderstandings and dissipating venomous fictions.[66] To that end, Odum wrote to colleagues and students in colleges and universities, asking them to report such stories to him. Letters poured in recounting tales told over dinner tables and in corner stores throughout the South. Odum used the reports to produce his wartime study *Race and Rumors of Race.*[67]

The rumors reported to Odum expressed racial anxieties among southern whites about the intentions of African Americans whose expectations had been raised by war conditions. The Great Migration, military service, and industrial war work, as well as the emphasis on racial pluralism that dominated much official propaganda aimed at the Nazis, all had broadened the horizons of African Americans and were helping to unleash the early stirrings of the modern civil rights movement.[68] White southerners perceived this and, through the rumors they told, tried to divine the significance of the new assertiveness among their black employees and neighbors.

In Washington, D.C., rumors of race drew special notice. The FBI's wide-ranging investigation of "Axis influence" and "agitation" among black organizations, code-named RACON, was launched in mid-December 1941 as part of a larger effort to root out a domestic fifth column and deflect attention from the cataclysmic failure of intelligence prior to Pearl Harbor. J. Edgar Hoover, raised in the southern tradition in Washington, D.C., shared many of the suspicions of the rumor tellers and sought to develop dossiers that would transform those suspicions into documentation of seditious libel to discredit "radical" agitators for racial equality.[69]

Many of the rumors were simple observations that black help had become more difficult to keep and discipline due to tight labor market conditions. "They say that by June all but the old Negroes will no longer be servants," one report relayed. "This includes both men and women whose labor the gov't needs."[70] A landlady near Tulane stated that "Negro women quit work." Her maid "confessed" to her that "Negro defense workers with plenty of money are now supporting them."[71] An outraged housewife in Georgia claimed to have learned the same intelligence from a washerwoman she interviewed for a job. The interviewee informed her potential employer that "she does not have to work as her son is in the army and her husband on a defense job." She planned to cease working altogether after the war.[72] This sort of withdrawal from the labor market to increase the independence of the black family had provoked outrage among southern white employers since the days of Reconstruction. Consequently, economic independence seemed to them more like laziness or impudence: "b/c of the opp. in war industries, the Negroes . . . could afford to be independent. [Maids and cooks] were quitting work and *letting* their husbands support them."[73]

The OWI rumor staff tracked the same kinds of statements circulating in the South. But since their primary goal was to safeguard morale, the transcripts preserved by the OWI's network of rumor wardens revealed more sharply the antigovernment sentiment that tinged many such racially charged complaints. "You can't get a decent maid any more with all these defense factories," complained a Birmingham housewife. "If those Northern people don't quit coming down here and over-paying the Negroes and hiring them for work that White people could do—we're going to have a war that's worse than Hitler's war, right in our own back yards."[74] A bridge party in Valdosta, Georgia, departed momentarily from the usual light banter when one participant complained, "If the government doesn't stop giving relief and old age pensions we won't be able to get any help. I've trained five cooks in six weeks and I don't have one now. There are plenty of jobs for those able to work without government spending money feeding them." Federal employees sometimes agreed with criticisms of the government. One official in Birmingham commented on Fair Employment Practices Commission (FEPC) policies against discrimination by intoning, "this business of trying to get jobs for negroes and put them in charge of white people is going to start trouble. We are going to have violence yet."[75]

Vague comprehension of who actually ran the different parts of the government could produce unintentionally ironic rumors. One carpenter from Dade County, Florida, suspected an unlikely administrator. His carpooling companion, a fellow painter, said that the painters union had received a letter from J. Edgar Hoover ordering Jim Crow signs removed from public places "to give equal rights to the colored people in all public places, including those now used exclusively by the white people."[76] For the painter, the long shadow of the FBI and its association with the federal government obscured the actual racial politics of its director.

Some of the gossips and rumor mongers overheard by the OWI attempted to draw connections between southern racial tensions and larger wartime developments. A couple recently returned from Miami were overheard in the Chicago Public Library discussing the problems the South faced due to the improved standard of living for African Americans. Locals there thought it "terrible" that black workers constructing cantonments received "white man's wages, same scale as given in the north." This development raised "the now unbearable national debt unnecessarily," despite the "much lower standard of living in the South." Worst of all, it pushed up inflation "because the Negroes are not used to having so much money and are spending wildly."[77]

The FEPC was sometimes singled out for censure when southern conversationalists chose a target more specific than "the government."[78] "It's this committee on fair employment and other things Washington is doing," complained a train passenger overheard en route to Montgomery, Alabama, "that are putting so many ideas in the Negroes' heads and making them think they are as good as White people."[79] Most such claims were purposely vague about which part of the government was at fault, as it was assumed that the problem lay with racial liberals who had infiltrated nearly all civilian war agencies. A rumor warden in Jacksonville, Florida, reported a conversation in which the central complaint was that racial tensions were "inevitable," "caused by the pampering of negroes by various Government agencies. It is getting to the point where it is almost impossible to discuss the negro question without the name of Mrs. Roosevelt as their champion being brought into the matter."[80] Derisive accusations of "pampering" and "coddling" provided coded language for conservatives seeking to tar the government by claiming it gave succor to dangerously insubordinate groups, such as labor unions or civil rights organizations.[81]

Suspicions of Eleanor Roosevelt's influence went beyond the commonplace awareness of her prominent efforts to advance racial pluralism. Like their counterparts in the industrial states of the North and Midwest, southern rumor mongers worked their uneasy suspicions into a conspiratorial narrative. In states throughout the South, society women told tales of black women "organizing in secret," sometimes in "their churches," to form "Eleanor Clubs" that would "force white women" to work "in their own kitchens." This rumor was so persistent that the OWI rumor control team and the FBI RACON agents mounted separate investigations to check into the fictive cabals. The two agencies concluded independently that no Eleanor Clubs could be found.[82]

Instead of a conspiracy, what they found was a highly condensed parable about the reliance of white womanhood on a racial caste system that forced African Americans to the bottom of the southern labor market. Such stories expressed the anxieties of white southerners already leery of being "invaded" by the FEPC and northern unions.[83] The Eleanor Club rumors, as well as the less stylized rumors of "uppity" black public behavior, reflected resistance to Jim Crow on the part of African Americans. Many similar rumors told of "bump clubs" of black men jostling whites on buses or pushing white pedestrians off downtown curbs. Likewise, black domestic workers had become less interested in working for white women as the war economy opened new opportunities. To local whites, the sudden assertiveness of their black neighbors seemed suspicious, amounting to a conspiracy, and the threat to Jim Crow assumed the appearance of an insurrection by force: Eleanor Clubs would "*force* white ladies into their kitchens by Christmas of 1942."[84]

Fictive members of the Eleanor Clubs threatened to turn the southern caste system upside-down. They were not content simply to ask for higher pay or more lenient work conditions, although some stories had black women learning from their local Club to make such demands.[85] In numerous versions, white women offered work to black women, only to have the tables reversed. When asked by a white woman where a "laundry girl" could be found, a black woman was said to have retorted, "I couldn't say; I've been looking for some white trash to do my washing for the longest." Nothing could have been more insulting to a southern lady.[86]

The white homemakers' circulation of the Eleanor Club rumors demonstrated their own resistance to the unwanted power of the federal government. Even though the upper-middle-class white men and women telling these tales enjoyed significant power relative to the African Americans in their midst, this power derived from the social and economic arrangements of Jim Crow that subordinated black lives to theirs. The sudden presence of the federal government as an "outside" force drawing African Americans into higher-paying defense work, recognizing CIO unions bent on interracial organizing, and nominally defending their right to equal employment opportunity through the FEPC, all threatened that control. Even though the Eleanor Clubs were fictional, the implicit threat was not. In time, this federal presence would become a strategic factor in the ultimate success of the civil rights movement in dismantling the legal components of Jim Crow.

That these clubs were allegedly organized by Eleanor Roosevelt made sense, given her liberalism on race issues, but the choice of the crusading First Lady had an added meaning. Other racial progressives might have been named as the archconspirator behind the "uppity" behavior of black southerners. But Eleanor's progressive racial agenda was perfectly suited to tar her husband's activist, expanding federal administration.[87] Some rumors put the association in the words of defiant servants. In Georgia it was said that a Negro couple quit their positions after twenty years of service in protest over a guest's disparagement of the Roosevelts.[88] A related tale pinpointed black loyalty to the First Family more explicitly. A maid overheard her mistress's tea guests criticize "the government and various policies of the President during the war." Indignant, she confronted the ladies by blurting out, "President Roosevelt is a personal friend of mine and I won't have you talking about him." She added, "I won't work for you any more if you don't like my friends," and slammed the door on her way out.[89]

The clearest statement of the role played by Eleanor Roosevelt and her invading forces of organizers was revealed in the rumors spread by white employers. The same women who complained about losing help to government jobs and defense work summed up their frustrations in the machinations of the Eleanor Clubs. One well-to-do Georgia woman made the connection reflexively. She was angry at her butler, who had quit to earn war wages "twice as high as she could pay"; but she was also "indignant at . . . the government, the war, and Mrs. Roosevelt b/c he would not yield to her pleas to return to his place as her servant."[90] Seen within the context of the other racial rumors circulating in the South at the time, the Eleanor Club rumors presented an opportunity to deflect and concentrate growing resentments of federal influence in daily life onto a figure many considered grotesque and detestable. Eleanor Roosevelt had become a scapegoat for the activist liberal state.

As Odum observed, rumors blaming southern racial conditions on liberal agitators "reflected very well the South's reaction to the New Deal and to the general theme of outside interference."[91] James Woodall, the regional representative to the U.S. Employment Service in Richmond, Virginia, captured this mentality when he reported to the OWI in the summer of 1942 that a former state commissioner of public welfare had warned him of an impending race riot by Christmas 1942 (the same date by which the Eleanor Clubs were rumored to strike). The view among many of the Virginians Woodall interviewed was that it was all the fault of "the present administration," which "was attempting to place Negroes on a basis of equality with whites with respect to all forms of employment."[92]

The specter of the outside agitator had a long pedigree dating back to the rumors of slave insurrections that had swirled throughout the antebellum South.[93] In antebellum times the agitator had been a northern abolitionist, or sometimes a new slave who brought intelligence of slave revolts from Haiti and other distant places. In World War II, the Roosevelts and their liberal minions in Washington, D.C., were fitted for this role, and in the most extreme rumors they were tied as well to tales of fifth-column intrigue.

To many southern whites, the presumptive northern conspiracy to end the southern way of life was proof of a conspiracy to undermine white American morale. In the eyes of J. Edgar Hoover, another southerner concerned with the role of outside agitators, such views of racial equality as sabotage were not far from the mark. Although the FBI built its wartime cases of indictment for sedition around extreme groups such as the tiny Ethiopian Pacific Movement in Harlem—which included "Ras de Killer," later fictionalized as Ras the Destroyer by Ralph Ellison in *Invisible Man*—it also investigated racial liberals in government. During the war the FBI built thick files on Eleanor Roosevelt, Judge William Hastie, the black civilian aide to the secretary of war, and William Pickens, the racial advisor to the Treasury, among other advocates of racial equality. This investigative investment had long-term consequences, forming the groundwork for the FBI's COINTELPRO program against the civil rights movement in the postwar period, and feeding popular southern assumptions that race liberals were un-American dupes.[94]

The Specter of Racial Inversion in the West

A curious story ran in the June 1, 1943, edition of the *Los Angeles Times* under the headline "Inquiry Opened on Charges of Jap 'Pampering.'" According to Robert E. Stripling, investigator for the Dies Committee, the "Japanese in the camps are possibly the best-fed civilians in the United States." Stripling had been sent to investigate rumors that Japanese Americans interned in the camps of the WRA were "enjoying large quantities of foods seldom available to civilians." A stockpile of scarce and rationed goods allegedly sent by the army to stock the camps tantalized the imagination of *Los Angeles Times* readers. With the announcement of Stripling's "findings," the Dies Committee began hearings in Los Angeles to pursue the matter further.[95]

Why did the Dies Committee adopt the alleged misuse of canned vegetables and gasoline as its cause in the summer of 1943? One reason was the pursuit of publicity, the lifeblood of the committee, which it pursued wherever it could harm the political enemies of its members. New Deal social workers accused of "coddling" racial enemies provided political bait every bit as tempting as the Popular Front artists of the WPA and the Library of Congress.

Chairman Martin Dies was an old hand at the game of race-baiting, having been trained at the knee of his father, Martin senior—also a congressman from Texas, well versed in the countersubversive tradition that had gained a boost from nativism at the turn of the century.[96] In 1940, after less than two years investigating un-American behaviors for the committee, the younger Martin had published *The Trojan Horse in America*, warning of Communists and other subversives burrowing from within the federal government.[97] Immediately following Pearl Harbor, Dies had further burnished the family tradition by claiming that thousands of Japanese nationals on the West Coast and in the Pacific islands were spies of imperial Japan and that their treachery could have been thwarted—and a national tragedy prevented—if only the government had heeded his warnings. These charges helped whip up the public uproar leading to evacuation and internment.[98]

John Costello, another leading light on the committee, had also had a hand in the politics of internment, heading the California delegation that successfully pushed for exclusion legislation in Congress. He introduced the House version of the bill whose enactment into law on March 21, 1942, gave legal sanction to Executive Order 9066. With this new investigation of the WRA, Costello was resuming the committee's challenge to the legitimacy of liberal administrators

During a hearing on August 12, 1938, Martin Dies, chairman of the House
Special Committee on Un-American Activities, passes on to his son, Bobby, the
counter-subversive tradition he inherited from his father. The Dies Committee,
as it was called, perfected the politics of rumor and innuendo that would become a
mainstay of anti-communism in the 1940s. (Courtesy of the Library of Congress,
LC-DIG-hec-24949)

such as WRA head Dillon Myer, a veteran of the left-friendly New Deal agencies
within the Department of Agriculture.[99]

Recent developments created an environment that made the committee's
findings potentially explosive. Beginning in late 1942 the WRA had begun the
gradual process of releasing some Japanese Americans from the camps for
induction into military service, work, and resettlement in the nation's interior.
This outraged many local communities and regional politicians throughout the
West, lending ammunition to the foes of the Roosevelt administration. The
committee's inquiry seized on this moment of outrage, which had reached a
fevered pitch in the late spring of 1943 because of unrest and resistance among
some in the camps to an oath pledging unqualified loyalty to the U.S. government and willingness to register for military service.[100] ·

Political posturing can explain the timing of the hearings, but it cannot account for their substance. For all the sniping, the claims publicized by the Dies
Committee were oddly mundane. Unlike the secret "Black Dragon" societies or

fifth-column spies that populated the imaginary life of West Coast demagogues, canned peaches and muttonchops hardly posed an imminent threat to the American people. Most telling, though, was the sheer implausibility of the charges. Japanese evacuees were as far from pampered as any group of civilians could have been—they lived in Spartan conditions exactly the opposite of the portrait Stripling and the committee painted for the press.[101]

The committeemen running the hearings took pains to paint a vivid picture of what "pampering" and "coddling" entailed. Oddly enough, this portrait centered around fantasies of consumer indulgence. At critical points in the hearings, the conditions in the camps were compared invidiously to those endured by American soldiers. A disgruntled former employee, H. H. Townsend, claimed that the three WRA camps at Poston had "every modern convenience . . . very superior to many of our modern Army camps." Some of the barracks were air-conditioned, he claimed, and all of the camps had swimming pools. The mess halls served "58 tons of food daily, the finest quality that money can buy, all grade A, top brands," based on a menu established in the WRA's Washington headquarters. He made a special point to say that the evacuees' food was "superior in every way" to the food served to American soldiers, "about 25 percent better than that to the Army." They got the "finest cuts and grade A meats; quarters and full carcasses of lambs and pork, and the best cuts of beef were brought in; on an average of one refrigerator car a day." A committee member pressed the point, asking if the food "was better than that obtained by our own citizens in the markets and stores." "Very much better," Townsend replied. Furthermore, there "never was a shortage" of meat, as there had been in California during the previous winter, even though "the Japanese chefs did not serve left-overs."[102]

As an aside later in his testimony, Townsend added that the evacuees had used WRA tractors "as playthings," driving them in races and burning up gas. They were also given credit cards to pay for gasoline and authorized to take long "pleasure trips" driving "these big sedans . . . into these metropolitan centers out there," all the while "giving the boys [soldiers on post] a big horselaugh" as they drove by in "big Government cars." All in all, life was sweet for the evacuees in the camps he described; those who were allowed to leave "were very happy to get back into the camp."[103]

Townsend viewed life in the internment camps through the racial lens he had developed while working as a juvenile officer in Indian Territory in Oklahoma prior to statehood. He did not like what he saw as chief supply and transportation officer for the war relocation camp situated on a reservation near Poston, Arizona. The reason for this state of affairs, in Townsend's opinion, was a treasonous laxity on the part of the administrators who ran the camp. The social workers running the Social Services Department were in complete sympathy with their charges. One "very vicious Japanese supporter"—Miss Findley, the head of the Welfare Department at Poston—told the male director "what to do, and when to do it, and how to do it." Findley, he claimed, "has some very definite pull in Washington, and she wields a very heavy stick." He described a camp shot through with corruption, ranging from the smallest infractions of administrative procedure to the most serious matters of treason. At one point Townsend took care to mention the "Jewish firm" Finkelstein & Co., which sold old broken-down dump trucks to the WRA for $2,400 apiece when their real value was closer to $400.[104]

Because of the permissive stance adopted by the social workers in charge, Townsend explained, the "Japs" controlled "everything" in the camps, especially the warehouses over which he unsuccessfully tried to assert control. A "gestapo" consisting of Kibei—American-born citizens educated in Japan, whom Townsend oddly claimed were trained by German agents—controlled the others in the camp. They had set up a system by which vital goods were systematically diverted from the warehouses. Not only did Japanese warehouse employees pilfer gasoline and other supplies from the government, but they were "hoarding" dried bread "and other supplies, for parachute troops and for invasion forces." "They [the Japanese] are not great bread eaters," he noted, although the camp purchased 3,750 pounds of bread daily. This sinister invasion toast was stored away with the other supplies in desert caches and in cellars dug beneath the barracks.[105]

The liberal administrators' laxity, self-indulgence, and "softness" toward their Japanese charges was a recipe for disaster, Townsend explained, and had made inevitable the riots that occurred at Poston in November 1942. More than a third of Townsend's testimony described, in horrified detail, the national "shame" enacted by the rioting prisoners: the "enemy seizure," under "mob rule," of "Government property,"

> taking complete control away from Government appointees, belittling and lowering our flag, cursing our Government . . . holding under siege and riot, under threat of death, for more than a week one of the largest semimilitary posts; with the poor simpleton, cowering Caucasians employees standing around like whipped children, lucky to be spared.[106]

The upshot of the riots was that "on the Poston battle front the Japs have won all the battles." Asked to sum up the reasons why the evacuees had been able to take control of the camp, Townsend did not hesitate:

> Well, my interpretation was that at the beginning Mr. Head [the project director of the camp] was operating under W.R.A. orders, and the orders of Mr. Collier of the Indian Agency, that they had started an

experiment and that they were endeavoring through the Indian Agency to give the Japanese the same freedom and the kind of careful attention that they were giving the Indians, believing that they were a mild group of American citizens.

His solution for the state of affairs was to "put it entirely under military control, and when the Japanese are told to do something, see that they do it, instead of laughing at the instructor, the management, and the Government."[107]

Townshend's claims proved thoroughly false, a fact the committee might have gathered from his quick flight from the country following his deposition. By the end of the summer Townsend's allegations had been thoroughly refuted by WRA officials.[108] Nevertheless, the full text of Townshend's testimony was released, providing ammunition to critics despite the efforts of camp administrators, whose testimony established the far less sensational facts of the situation.[109] WRA head Dillon Myer used part of his appearance before the committee to upbraid it for so blatantly disregarding the truth. The committee's members could barely conceal their indifference to his anger. In response to the WRA's documentation that the hearings had publicized at least forty-two "lies or half-truths," Costello corrected him: "We find only thirty-nine."[110]

If the committee's investigation rested on a premise that was so patently false, even absurd, why did it enjoy so much public attention? An answer can be found in the curious ways in which the requirements of sacrifice could backfire. The thought of evacuees burning gas in tractor races or on pleasure trips would enrage a war worker who barely had enough points of rationed gasoline to commute to a job in an essential industry. Vaguer but no less galling frustrations about the standard of living made tales of air-cooling systems and refrigerators provocative rather than absurd. The war boom had put more money in the pockets of all civilians, but the resulting demand had raised the consumer price index by 25 percent between 1939 and 1943. Combined with the shortage of materials available for civilian industry, this trend decreased the availability of housing and consumer durables just when they seemed within reach for the first time in more than a decade.[111]

Meat held a special significance for Americans during the war, signifying a high standard of living and providing the nutrition required to ensure the vigor "red-blooded" Americans needed for war work or fighting.[112] Government propaganda often explicitly tied meat consumption to the success of soldiers facing battle, as in the text of one pamphlet, which explained:

American meat is fighting food. It's an important part of a military man's diet, giving him the energy to outfight the enemy. It helped the Americans drive the Japs from Guadalcanal. . . . Meat from our farms and packinghouses is playing a part almost on par with tanks, planes, and bullets.[113]

Touching on this association, time and again the committee inquired about the quality and quantity of the meat available in the WRA camps, falsely suggesting that evacuees got "first call" on the choicest cuts while soldiers were stuck with lesser grades and civilians endured shortages. Committee interrogators conducted endless, detailed exchanges concerning the lavish menus supposedly dictated by WRA heads in Washington. One such exchange led committee member Karl Mundt to conclude in disgust, "It seems to me the OWI should beam that news to Tokyo by short-wave radio, and maybe they will treat our prisoners a little better when they find out we are feeding their Japanese better than our white citizens."[114] Upon reading the testimony that the average evacuee dined on excellent food and wine, Dies Committee veteran J. Parnell Thomas arrived at the conclusion he and his colleagues had sought from the beginning: "Are we to release this fat-waisted Jap while our boys on Guadalcanal are barely receiving enough food with which to keep alive?"[115]

In some western communities where anti-Japanese feeling ran high, the mere sight of Japanese Americans in consumer environments was violently provocative. When the deputy sheriff of Yuma County, Arizona, testified before the Dies Committee that white citizens were fed up with evacuees from a local camp coming into town on "shopping sprees," he reported more than mere frustration over crowded shops and restaurants, although a violated notion of consumer entitlement was crucial to the story's meaning. Evacuees had been stirring up trouble in town, the deputy sheriff explained:

> You have got a number of people here that have got boys in the Army— got several of them that have boys in the Army that have been killed by the Japanese and they walk into a drugstore for a Coca-Cola or something and the Japanese have all the seats, and they walk into the grocery store and the Japanese are crowded in there and you have got to mill your way around them and they resent that.[116]

One soldier had become so upset when he saw a "Jap" in the local drugstore that he nearly managed to "clean him out." The deputy sheriff's testimony conveyed an outrage at the very presumption that Japanese people might take a place at the counter of American life, thereby displacing white Americans.

The allegations the Dies Committee aired may have been fictional, but they represented more than the fanciful embellishments of a political circus. During Myer's testimony, Congressman Karl Mundt countered Myer's accusation of holding an entirely frivolous investigation by saying: "Mr. Townsend did not start all these rumors about food in these relocation centers. There were a lot of them going up and down the coast before the Committee went into hearings." "I agree with that," Myer replied, adding with ironic sympathy, "I appreciate what the hearing was up against."[117]

Months before the committee began its investigation, rumor mongers traded many of the same wild stories it would later elect to investigate. By that time, Townsend found it easy to compress these rumors into a master plot that conveniently distorted the uncomfortable details of his own career at the camps while serving the political agenda of the Dies Committee.[118] He chose the details of his story carefully, so they would fit the broader climate of suspicion he knew so well.

Transcripts recorded in August 1942 by OWI rumor wardens captured stories that anticipated Townsend's testimony in nearly every detail. In the late summer of 1942, almost a year before the hearings and five months before Townsend's departure from Poston, a mining engineer living in Phoenix, Arizona, confided that "a number of stories" were circulating concerning conditions in the relocation centers, including "one that says there are air-cooling systems and aluminum refrigerators in every apartment." Although he felt compelled to add, "That is just a little too far-fetched to believe," he passed it on just the same. Thanks to the OWI's covert efforts to monitor national rumors in early August 1942, we know that such far-fetched stories were not restricted to Phoenix.[119] "You just can't get good meat anymore," went one complaint in Boise, Idaho. "It just makes me sick. That good beef, that the beet tops and stuff is fed to, is being given to those damned Japs at Eden."[120]

Local resentments and regional folkways of race provided much of the material that made its way into the rumors about Japanese internees. Legionnaires shooting the breeze at a convention in Phoenix, for example, complained that evacuees could fish without a permit. The freedom to fish, apparently on a par with the Four Freedoms, struck a chord because of the water and fishing rights that had long been entangled in political battles over both Indian and Japanese community settlements before the war.[121] A service station attendant on the other side of town drew on another venerable stereotype when he made the off-hand observation that, despite a local beer shortage, "the Japs have all they want for 5 cents a bottle because they do not have to pay any Federal tax, being located on Government ground."[122] The assumptions that linked federal land, taxation, and unrestricted alcohol consumption by a suspect minority population under government supervision reflected an old regional variant of antigovernment sentiment pervasive in the western states.

Work, a critical source of racial formation, prompted special attention from the critics of the WRA. An OWI rumor warden recorded the musings of a Phoenix businessman who wanted to know why "several thousand Japs are sitting around at Sacaton with nothing to do." He had heard a rumor that "a recent meeting of social workers" ruled out the idea of using them for labor "because living conditions were not suitable." "It's strange," he concluded, "that such accommodations are good enough for the white migratory cotton-pickers but not for the Japs."[123] This observation zinged westerners whose racial assumptions had been built on the axiom that nonwhite labor was inherently degraded and threatening to whites—an old fear at the source of much anti-Asian sentiment in the West going back to the Chinese Exclusion Act of 1882. The thought of reversing this "natural" inequality was alarming, particularly to those who agreed with the likes of J. W. Buzzell, secretary of the Los Angeles Central Labor Council, who testified before Congress that the early release of internees would threaten white standards of living. He proposed that the government should instead force the Japanese to do agricultural work—at which they had "proven themselves to be excellent"—and then appropriate "all they produce . . . to feed the military forces in this country."[124]

Rumors invoking the hardships endured by "our soldiers" cast the injustice of "Jap pampering" in the starkest terms. Some of these traced their provenance to the Hearst press, which alleged that evacuees were "paid much more than the American soldiers fighting the country's battles overseas."[125] The influence of this attempt to discredit the WRA can be seen in rumors that repeated its basic assertion, adding small details for emphasis. An echo of the Hearst accusation cropped up in Milwaukee, bemoaning "them Japs . . . why they earn more than our soldiers and they don't do nothin' but set."[126] The same rumor also surfaced in El Paso, Texas, only this time it was less coy in suggesting the real culprit: "The Government don't make 'em work and they feed 'em better than they do our Army." Such talk sometimes could assume the ominous tone adopted by a bus passenger en route from Alamogordo, New Mexico, to El Paso, Texas, who confided that "the Government ain't tellin' us nothing about it but this whole country is going to be filled with Japs—and the Government is feedin' them better than our own soldiers."[127]

Assumptions about consumer entitlement could be particularly powerful because they were implicitly tied to the visions of full citizenship promised by market society—what was reflexively termed "the American standard of living."[128] Americans took for granted that they were the freest people in the world, that they were fighting to defend this freedom, and that this state of grace was reflected in the abundant goods and services they were free to buy with their ample incomes. Rumors of Japanese privilege revealed the significance of market ideology through inversion, suggesting how the country would be transformed and life turned on its head if the American standard of living were to be undermined by government "experiments" altering the racial and economic status quo.

No component of this consumerist vision of the American way of life was more sacred than the home, that refuge from the public world that merged property and privacy so completely. The home has been central to ideologies justifying a wide range of social relationships throughout American history. For this reason, white women from middle- and upper-middle-income families were especially frustrated by the unavailability of new consumer durables, such as refrigerators and electrical appliances, that maintained the level of living to which they felt entitled. Rather than express their frustration over this state of affairs directly, some worried instead that the perquisites they had "sacrificed" in support of the war were secretly being lavished on the "pampered" Japanese. One lady prominent in Phoenix society expressed her outrage within earshot of an OWI informant, relating, "I have heard that at the relocation center in Sacaton, Arizona, the Japs have electric dishwashers and white cooks, and I would like to find out about that." Women of a slightly lower station imagined the threat to their domestic primacy in different tones. "Well," huffed one Minneapolis housewife to another, challenging her defeatist attitude, "are you getting prepared to be a Jap's housemaid or something?"[129] Much like the southern women who spread the Eleanor Clubs rumor, these women were exercised by the prospect of toiling under the direction of their racial inferiors. The reversals they imagined revealed a need to defend class privilege without questioning the assumptions of sacrifice, something only an easy jab at an impudent "pampered Jap" could accomplish without raising eyebrows in the egalitarian home-front culture.

The rumors of pampering were so poisonous because they menaced the much broader insistence on government guarantees of racial subordination that mass internment had already validated. By claiming the government had botched the job, these rumors did more than finger authorities for leniency. They purported to unmask a hidden world of government-sanctioned privilege in which "the enemy" was practically running the camps, manipulating the "soft," feminized WRA to their benefit, all of which amounted to a subversive plot that undermined the sacred sacrifice of the combat soldier. This vision of a world turned upside down by hidden forces fostered a cynicism that corroded the legitimacy the federal government had worked so hard to establish. In this sense, pampering became the mirror image of sacrifice, and in the process cast aspersions on the discipline exerted by the wartime government over American society.

Rumor as Politics

In the hothouse atmosphere of the home front the politics of rumor gained a coherence over the course of the war, as Americans learned to monitor their own speech and police that of their neighbors by following the instructions provided by the OWI's security-of-information campaigns and the FBI's contact program.

At the same time, the highly encoded meanings within individual rumors gradually coalesced into a sort of meta-rumor about the state and its subversion by internal enemies.

The old racially inflected slanders lived on, of course. This was made clear by an artless joke that circulated among FDR's opponents during the 1944 campaign, condensing the regional scapegoating rumors into an electoral plot. In it, the First Couple were envisioned indulging a sort of campaign duet, with the president chiming in: "You kiss the niggers / and I'll kiss the Jews / and we'll stay in the White House / as long as we choose." Offering this "slanderous rumor in rhyme" as a classic "hostility rumor" with a direct kinship to the Eleanor Clubs, Gordon Allport observed that in it "three antipathies have fused. The hatred is tripronged."[130] Prejudice also flowed through official channels of communication. At the direction of Henry Luce, whose disaffection with Roosevelt had been festering for a decade, *Time* ran a long profile of Sidney Hillman that highlighted his origins in Jewish socialist labor circles.[131]

As the campaigning grew more contentious through the fall, appeals to prejudice gave way to a more ideological take on subversion. Increasingly the Republican presidential candidate, New York governor Thomas Dewey, began to hammer away at the theme of communists in government, putting his reputation as a prosecutor of racketeering to full use. In October he warned audiences from the stump that war agencies were "little by little" converting America into "our own corporate state," much to the approval of men such as Hillman— whom he unhesitatingly depicted as a lib-lab Shylock bent on constitutional ruin, "stalking the country squeezing dollars for the Fourth Term Campaign."[132] Only days before the election, Dewey warned a crowd at the Boston Garden that a "Red Menace" would rise if Roosevelt were reelected. "Now, by the self-same tried and familiar tactics and with the aid of Sidney Hillman," Dewey asserted, "the Communists are seizing control of the New Deal, through which they aim to control the Government of the United States." He concluded by fusing the abiding wartime concerns of Roosevelt's bitterest critics into one sinister pattern: "In Russia a Communist is a man who supports his Government. In America a Communist is a man who supports the fourth term so our form of government may more easily be changed."[133]

Dewey's gambit was desperate, but it lent a new respectability to the whispers and allegations that previously had been couched only as slander or rumor, emboldening other critics of the administration to revive old rallying cries— particularly the suspicion that Pearl Harbor was a stab in the back by men in high places, perhaps by the president himself. Representative Forest Harness of Indiana shared with his colleagues in the House a rumor that the Australian government had repeatedly relayed messages to the U.S. government—at precise intervals of seventy-two, forty-eight, and twenty-four hours in advance of the attacks—warning of a Japanese force headed toward Pearl Harbor. Before making their choice in the upcoming election, Harness argued, voters should know whether Roosevelt had been "culpable in directing our military activities in Hawaii."[134]

Conservatives followed up on this lead, pushing for investigations whose reports finally gave the Pearl Harbor conspiracy theory an official imprimatur. Throughout 1946 a congressional committee held hearings on culpability for Pearl Harbor, allowing its two dissenters, Owen Brewster of Maine and Homer Ferguson of Michigan—both Republicans—an opportunity to publish, in their minority report, the long-simmering allegation that Roosevelt had baited the Japanese into striking the first blow at Pearl Harbor in order to provide a "back door" by which the United States could be dragged into the war.[135]

In this climate of mounting revanchism, counter-subversion would have its day back in the sun, institutionalizing the politics of rumor during the postwar resurgence of the permanent committee popularly known as HUAC. In the postwar hearings on communists in government, the most compelling scapegoats would no longer be scheming Japs, surly Negroes, or conspiring Jews. Echoes of those figures would certainly be invoked: by Westerners leading the Asia First lobby in its protests over the "loss" of China; by Dixiecrats denouncing the communist influences of racial progressives within the federal government; and by McCarthyites deriding the "effete" intellectuals and striped-pants boys who had gone "soft" on communism in the State Department. But more salient than the prejudiced caricatures of the war years would be the sinister figure that haunted Americans in the tense years that followed: the corrupted and corrupting communist sympathizer or "dupe" who had allowed the government to be hollowed out from within by a vast "communist subversion." These "fellow travelers"—many viewed as "soft-headed" liberals who had snuck into the federal government under the New Deal—would also be attacked by slander, innuendo, rumor, conspiracy theory, and a generalized suspicion. And like the WRA social workers, Eleanor Club organizers, and conspiring Jews, their softness would seem to threaten the American way by handing the reins over to a sinister alien power.

The popular machinery of surveillance set up to track down wartime rumors of subversion was another legacy that would survive into the postwar period, transformed and energized. Ironically, the cultural politics of scapegoating the state had only given the government a firmer toehold in American life. In enlisting citizens to monitor their own speech as well as that of their neighbors, the government instilled not only acceptance but also faith in its surveillance. During the war, a cigar store manager in New York City had expressed this confidence when he declaimed within earshot of an OWI rumor warden, "J. Edgar

IF YOU TALK
TOO MUCH

THIS MAN
MAY DIE!

Americans internalized wartime prohibitions on "loose talk," disciplining their own speech and monitoring that of their neighbors. Private Ivan A. Smith, editor of the *Camp Hood Panther*, Camp Hood, Texas, devised this mirror after reflecting on the message in the Office of War Information poster, "If you talk too much, this man may die." (Courtesy of the Library of Congress, LC-DIG-fsa-8b09830)

Hoover knows where every spy is. He can take them all in any old time he wants to. There's no reason why we should be afraid to talk in public places. We don't have anything to worry about." At a Wings for Norway rally in Minneapolis in the summer of 1942, one audience member echoed this sentiment. When her friend remarked, "I suppose there is espionage going on right at this meeting," she replied, "Yah, they know it is, but they make allowances for that," an exchange that her local librarian wrote down and mailed to the OWI.[136] This trust in the competence of the FBI would only grow stronger in the following years.

By bureaucratizing the grapevine, the FBI, the OWI, and the rumor clinics had bolstered the legitimacy of one part of the federal government—the agencies associated with national security—at the expense of the others. The business community also took opportunities to rehabilitate and consolidate its public authority, sometimes by affirming government authority with security-of-information messages and civic-minded gestures such as the rumor clinic columns, at other times undermining it with Hearst-style sensationalism. Regardless of their political valence, rumors served to bolster government authority over public discourse without setting off alarm bells regarding the First Amendment. The government accomplished this feat even as it instructed Americans in the art of spying on their neighbors, a skill whose dissemination would amplify the social power of the anticommunist purges in the postwar period.

PART TWO

ENCOUNTERING THE STATE
IN EVERYDAY LIFE

To understand the influence of the Second World War on ideology and political culture within the United States, it is essential to place political beliefs and expectations within the war's dynamic social context. One reason that full citizenship seemed so imminent and rights so natural in these years was the substantial loosening of the social structure at all levels. Mass conscription and economic mobilization for total war fostered dramatic personal mobility with great suddenness. Each of the "four mobilities" that tend to corrode local solidarities—geographic, social, marital, and political—accelerated during World War II.[1] As the war propelled millions to escape the confines of their local circumstances and pursue broader horizons, it also placed them in new contact with the federal government, whose ideological guarantees suddenly had concrete ramifications in their everyday lives.

Geographic mobility was the most immediate and vividly experienced form of personal freedom fostered by the war. More than twenty-five million Americans, or roughly a fifth of the nation, moved across county lines between 1940 and 1947, with half of them doing so in order to relocate to other states. Just under sixteen million men and a quarter of a million women traveled to the far corners of the nation and the globe for military service. Millions more civilians followed jobs and drafted spouses into war centers, where they encountered all the frustration and unsupervised freedom of U.S. history's greatest boom.[2]

Freedom of movement had often been taken for granted, especially by white male migrants, but thanks to the recent appointment of New

Dealers to the Supreme Court, freedom of movement across state lines, regardless of economic status, was reaffirmed as a constitutional right with the ruling in *Edwards v. California* (1941). By the time the case was heard by the Court, what had begun as a matter of local versus national welfare jurisdiction had evolved into one with new valences for the defense mobilization. As Justice Robert H. Jackson wrote in his concurring opinion, "Rich or penniless, [a person's] citizenship under the Constitution pledges his strength to the defense of California as a part of the United States, and his right to migrate to any part of the land he must defend is something she must respect under the same instrument."[3]

African Americans, who suffered the petty tyranny of local authority more acutely than most other citizens due to their concentration in the Jim Crow South, often had to claim "freedom of movement" before chasing the Four Freedoms promised by FDR. Despite the concerted efforts of southern planters and other large employers to keep black workers on the farm with debt peonage laws and Selective Service classifications, among other measures, millions of African Americans were able to claim their freedom of movement because of the unprecedented demand for labor in the war mobilization.[4] More than one million of the roughly ten million African Americans living in the South in 1940 moved north or west during the war, the latest and one of the greatest chapters of migration in a long history of mass movement for freedom dating back to emancipation. Additionally, more than 1.1 million black men from around the country entered military service, leaving their hometowns for boot camp, followed by assignment to troop units that often were stationed overseas. Awaiting these black migrants were underemployment, job discrimination, and relegation to segregated military units. Even so, departure from the South represented relative advancement for the vast majority of migrants.

Social mobility, like its geographic counterpart, flowed directly from the unprecedented demand for labor created by the war mobilization. After a decade of depression in which the incomes of full-time employees had remained largely stagnant while as much as a quarter of the labor force was unemployed, the opportunities of ordinary Americans suddenly improved dramatically starting in mid-1940. The GDP rose from $101 billion that year to $223 billion in 1945, an increase of almost 73 percent after inflation. With this rise in the general prosperity of the country came a staggering 30 percent increase in real disposable personal income, an improvement that buoyed the entire labor force. Underwriting the vast improvement of economic fortunes was the federal government, whose annual expenditures for national defense reached nearly $83 billion by 1945, accounting for 37 percent of the GDP and two-thirds of all industrial production.[5]

Booming economic growth and rising personal earnings obviously made life easier for most workers. Two other developments—full employment and declining inequality—transformed this prosperity into something more. With industry at full capacity by 1943–44, unemployment rates fell to 1.2 percent, or 670,000 in a labor force that had grown by 17.8 percent since 1940, to 66 million.[6] An explosion of largely unionized industrial employment represented a considerable expansion of better-paying jobs providing new opportunities for personal advancement, which workers often pursued by leaving jobs, quitting at the astronomical rate of over 5 percent a month by the war's end. As many as fifteen million workers shifted jobs for higher pay or better working conditions during the war, reflecting a confident optimism.[7]

Not only were more jobs available to those who sought them, but income disparities were shrinking along some of the most salient lines of social inequality: class, occupation, and race. Families in the bottom quintile of the national income distribution saw their average annual incomes rise from $450 in 1941 to $982 by 1946, twice the proportional improvement of those in the top quintile.[8] Wartime income redistribution did not amount to a social revolution, but a 3 percent shift in the income structure of a nation as vast and prosperous as the United States was in the 1940s still represented a palpable opening of opportunity among citizens whose economic horizons had been severely constricted in the previous decade. Furthermore, the shift in incomes was accompanied by a permanent and significant flattening in the distribution of wealth—a far more intractable source of economic inequality. Between 1939 and 1945, the richest 1 percent of Americans saw their share of wealth drop by 8.9 percentage points, from 35.9 to 27 percent of all assets. (Their share continued to drop after the war, falling as low as 17.3 percent by 1976.) As the national structures of income and wealth shifted, ordinary workers could sense that their lot was improving. The hard numbers that ruled the family budget told them so with each growing paycheck.[9]

The impact of two other kinds of mobility—marital and political— also broadened personal horizons during this period. A marriage boom mounted throughout the war years, peaking in 1946 at a rate that was 62 percent higher than in 1939, and producing the first wave of the baby boom that would so define the postwar period. Along with the wartime marriage boom came a divorce boomlet, which peaked one year earlier, in 1945, with the rate spiking to double the prevailing rate in the 1930s.[10] So much flux in the basic realities of personal allegiance must have had some effect on local attachments, particularly for women whose wartime migrations and newfound employment had already dislodged them from their families and hometowns.

Political attachments were also in flux. While the 1930s are generally seen as a period of monolithic realignment resulting in the New Deal coalition, in fact the reconstitution of both parties continued well into the 1940s, as Harry Truman's near defeat in the close-run elections of 1948 demonstrated. Here again, the African American experience placed broader developments in sharp relief. While established black voters had swung over to the Democrats for Roosevelt during the 1930s, hundreds of thousands of new voters gained the ballot after the Supreme Court struck down the white primary in *Smith v. Allwright* in 1944. For the newly enfranchised, the choice of partisan alignment was a wartime opportunity. Southern black voter registration, mostly urban, jumped more than fivefold (from 3 percent to 16.8 percent) during the 1940s. Meanwhile, hundreds of thousands of new black voters in the North joined the rolls as a result of the Great Migration, making their exercise of the franchise a new experience associated with the war as well.[11]

Not until the 1940s did African Americans constitute a national swing vote, eventually allowing Truman to retain the presidency in 1948 without the Dixiecrats, whose seniority and gerrymandered staying power had defined the party (and killed black civil rights) since the end of Reconstruction. The black political journalist Henry Lee Moon captured the political self-consciousness this partisan reorientation produced when he wrote that the "Negro citizen [in 1948 is] possessed of the greatest ballot potential in his history."[12] Political realignment, like geographic and social mobility, reoriented African Americans toward a federal government whose tentative responsiveness to their interests—demonstrated by Truman's creation of the Civil Rights Commission and his executive order to desegregate the military—held out the hope of fuller citizenship.

The fluidity and opportunity unleashed by the war could be daunting or exhilarating, disorienting or liberating, depending on one's outlook and position. Much of what fueled revanchist efforts to stem the tide of social expansion and entitlement drew on these same social energies, but from a stance of outrage and determined opposition rather than enthusiasm or acceptance. The sensibilities of Americanism provided a language and a political tradition on which to draw in efforts both to unleash and contain social democratic energies fed by the war economy.

The war mobilization unleashed violently clashing tendencies that directed politicized consciousness toward the government, whose encroaching presence had done so much to bring about these rapid changes. Consequently, the meanings that fiscal citizenship, war work, or military service held were formed by the ways in which these new obligations situated Americans within a shifting political economy and a dynamic society.

4

Buying Our Boys Back

Just after eight o'clock in the morning on Tuesday, September 21, 1943, singer and radio star Kate Smith addressed her national audience with a personal story that set the tone for the marathon bond drive she would conduct over the next eighteen hours. In her usual self-effacing manner, she began by recounting the words of a man whose speech at a recent bond rally in Utica, New York, held special meaning for her audience:

> You know, friends, when we buy War Bonds, we're not buying tanks and guns and shells and planes. What we're really doing is buying our boys back . . . bringing them home to us, safe and sound once again. Now I know there isn't a person listening to me who wouldn't give everything he has to buy his boy back. . . . I'd give anything . . . all my money, or my health, or my own life . . . to buy my boy back from the War. But I'm afraid I can't do that now. You see, I got a telegram from Washington this morning. My boy isn't coming back.

"That is what War Bonds are to every one of us," she concluded, "a chance to buy our boys back. We've all of us got boys we want back . . . and here today, is our chance to do something about it. Just pick up the phone, and call the local War Bond Number." With personalized anecdotes and appeals such as these sprinkled liberally in short spots throughout that entire day and long into the night, Smith raised a record-breaking $39 million.[1]

Later in the broadcast Smith announced an important call that came into the CBS studio from a veteran who had been saving his money to purchase artificial replacements for the two legs he had lost in the Great War. The man "made himself a hero all over again," in Smith's eyes, because he pledged the money to the Third War Loan Drive instead of spending it to "escape being shut in twenty-four hours a day." When he heard Smith on the radio he made up his mind: "My artificial limbs can wait . . . but this war can't."[2] Immediately after this spot aired came the largest surge of the entire marathon. As the pledges

The popular singer Kate Smith had a virtual monopoly on maternal patriotism thanks to her famous rendition of Irving Berlin's "God Bless America." In this photo unidentified Marines pose with her during her appearance with the Navy Band on a CBS radio show, *Spirit of '42*. (Courtesy of AP Photo, #420425025)

poured in, she implored, "When you think of these wounded and suffering boys who are paying so great a price, can you honestly think that any sacrifice *you* have made is enough?"[3]

Weighing their own sacrifices against those of the idealized combat soldier, Americans would consent to buy their boys back in record numbers during

World War II. Unlike in any previous war, nearly all Americans were drawn into the very sinews of the state: its financing. For the first time in history, most families paid income taxes and owned their own portion of the national debt in the form of savings bonds. While banks, corporations, and the wealthy would continue to provide most of the government's funding through taxes and other mechanisms of public finance, the great majority of ordinary Americans joined them in financing a significant portion of war expenditures, setting a pattern that would bolster the postwar fiscal regime and democratize the meaning of fiscal citizenship.

Facing a time of unprecedented crisis, when the cost of global war vastly exceeded the demands of any prior emergency, policy makers authorized measures that would raise federal expenditures to unrivaled heights—$98.3 billion by 1945, nearly half the war-swollen gross national product.[4] (See Chart A.2.) The resulting fiscal revolution would have profound implications for the growth of the economy and the federal government's power to manage it. By far the greatest part of the recovery from the Great Depression was due to the fiscal policies adopted in 1941 and 1942 to meet war costs.[5] The fiscal state these policies erected was durable, forming a solid basis on which the federal government could embrace deficit spending and other measures to manage the macro performance of the economy.[6]

Without the tax payments and bond purchases of millions of Americans, and their subsequent votes to elect Congresses that would sustain the new fiscal system rather than dismantle or undermine it, the postwar state would have stood on feet of clay, ready to crumble at the slightest challenge. Growth politics, and the global ambitions it bankrolled, depended on the economic and political compliance of ordinary Americans.[7]

Mass participation in the new fiscal regime was, contrary to common wisdom, far from automatic. Enforcement and patriotic peer pressure were insufficient to goad a populace not yet habituated to the instruments of public finance—although they were of course necessary. Bondholders and taxpayers had to be persuaded to do their duty. Like the callers who responded so viscerally to Kate Smith's radio marathon, they were most strongly persuaded when they could envision themselves as directly assisting the combat soldier. When the complexities of policy eluded citizens' sense of direct obligation to the soldier or threatened their standard of living, as was the case with inflation in the first half of the war and again in the late 1940s, bond purchases declined and taxpayers grew resentful. But when patriotism was fused with a sense of entitlement to an American standard of living—underwritten by government-managed economic growth—the obligations of fiscal citizenship proved quite durable, lasting decades beyond the war emergency and funding the explosive growth of the postwar state.[8]

The Public Household at War

Popular participation in the fiscal policies of the federal government was crucial in a "total war" whose magnitude threw a long shadow over even the world's most prosperous economy. The Second World War was ten times more expensive than its predecessor. In five years the U.S. government spent $304 billion on defense alone, almost twice as much as it had devoted to all expenditures, military or otherwise, in all of the preceding budgets since the nation's founding. Annual federal outlays jumped more than tenfold, from $8.8 billion in 1939 to $98.3 billion in 1945, by which time they consumed almost half of GNP.[9] (See Charts A.2 and A.4.) Such a burden overwhelmed the prewar fiscal system, which was based on government securities, excises, tariffs, corporate taxes, and individual income taxes on the wealthy. Consequently, the mainstays of public finance shifted permanently from class to mass taxation, while public debt also became a popular concern. In a matter of four years, taxpaying became a nearly universal obligation, making it a prominent feature of national citizenship. A series of tax laws permanently expanded the federal tax base by lowering exemptions to poverty levels, raising marginal rates for all income brackets, and instituting a pay-as-you-go system of withholding. War bond drives and other mass-marketing devices made an even larger portion of the citizenry owners of the national debt.

For the first time, a factory worker, clerk, or stevedore was likely to stake some financial claim, however modest, on the federal government. The resulting sensibility—"that's my tax dollar"—has resonated throughout the national political culture ever since. By 1943 nearly all working American families paid income taxes, which were deducted directly from their regular pay.[10] Partly as a result of the expanding tax base, federal revenues grew to $133 billion during the war and paid for 45 percent of all war-related expenditures, compared to 30 percent of war expenses paid by revenues during World War I. The rate of revenue growth increased by a factor of 8.8 between 1939 and 1945. Although it exacted an overall tax burden that was still considerably lower than that shouldered by the citizens of most other warring nations, the new system's rate of growth outstripped the increases accomplished by allies such as Canada and Britain.[11]

Both Roosevelt and his longtime secretary of the treasury, Henry Morgenthau Jr., protested what they considered to be the regressive features of the new tax regime. In 1935 the Treasury, under Morgenthau's leadership, had drafted the "soak the rich" tax bill that had done much to give the New Deal its reputation among conservatives for being a radical experiment gone awry. Morgenthau hoped to redistribute the burden of taxation even further onto the shoulders of the wealthy during the war. Yet he was far from radical, as his left-leaning opponents within the administration would note, nor was he a liberal in the sense that other close advisors in Roosevelt's brain trust were.

Morgenthau was at heart a fairly conservative man with strong moral commitments to what he considered matters of justice and fair play. His father, a domineering man, had made his own fortune in real estate after an early legal apprenticeship in which he specialized in foreclosures and title searches. The son would build his own career in public life, at one point—when he was head of the Farm Credit Administration—saving farmers from foreclosure in the darkest years of the Depression. Throughout his public career ran a thread of economic moralism that drove his commitment to use financial and other economic tools to protect those within the market, rather than unleash the market in all its brutal efficiency, as his father had.

The same economic moralism that led Morgenthau to advocate a sharply graduated tax structure also convinced him that government should be lean and efficient and that budgets should be balanced. The first of these convictions allowed him to create a highly efficient and decentralized war finance program. However, his belief in balanced budgets had led him to encourage Roosevelt to cut spending in 1937, an action that exacerbated the sharp "Roosevelt recession" of that year and earned him the undying contempt of New Deal deficit spenders. Until the end of his time as secretary of the treasury in 1945, Morgenthau would assume a unique place in the Roosevelt administration. Neither conservative nor liberal, he would play a central role in the formation of enduring liberal policies, both monetary and fiscal, despite his lack of expertise in economics, law, or finance. Relying on his close personal connection with Roosevelt (they had a regular lunch every Monday) and his own independent sense of the right thing to do (what he called his "educated elbow"), Morgenthau left a deep mark on the "New Deal order" that could not be reduced to ideology or interest. Consequently, two dominant strains of contemporary liberalism—New Deal and corporate—coexisted within Morgenthau's Treasury, along with older producerist and civic sensibilities touting the virtues of thrift, independence, and voluntary association. Rather than clashing, the divergent perspectives worked in combination, reconciled by the sheer force of Morgenthau's personality.[12]

Consequently, Morgenthau was aghast when Congress proposed a bill in late 1943 that would lower the normal exemption even further, to $1,000, and raise effective rates on annual incomes under $2,000 to well over 10 percent, while taxing incomes of $5,000 or higher at the same or lower rates as the previous year and opening glaring loopholes for special interests. His old friend Roosevelt was of the same mind, famously denouncing it as tax relief "not for the needy but for the greedy." But Republicans and conservative Democrats in Congress proved stronger than the Roosevelt administration on the question of the tax code and its progressivity. Roosevelt vetoed the Revenue Act of 1943, only to see Congress override it in a political firestorm that briefly shook up the Democratic leadership in Congress. For the first time in U.S. history Congress overturned a veto of a revenue act, dealing Roosevelt a decisive defeat that sealed political debate over taxation. No further revenue acts were passed for the remainder of the war. This state of affairs left federal revenues higher than ever before, but still too low to cover the remaining $185.7 billion in war expenditures, a shortfall that pushed the national debt to record levels.[13]

Though the new mass tax regime erected in World War II fell far short of the reform agenda of progressive taxation that Roosevelt and Morgenthau had pursued on and off since 1935, it nevertheless represented a profound break with the past. In the previous 150 years of the federal government's existence, very few Americans had felt the tug of the Treasury's purse strings directly. Excises and tariffs dominated revenues until the first part of the twentieth century. While such imposts taxed the incomes of consumers and limited the earnings of export-dependent farmers in significant ways, they lacked the personal impact produced by income taxes, partly because of the indirect manner in which they were inserted into market transactions. Taxes on corporations and wealthy individuals had provided new sources of federal revenues during World War I, but they had bypassed the vast majority of Americans.[14] For most of the interwar period, the proportion of the labor force paying federal income tax wavered between 3 and 5 percent, or 1.25 to 2.5 percent of the residential population. As late as 1939, 93 percent of the labor force paid no federal income tax. In that year there were 3.9 million taxpayers, half as many as the number of residents in New York City—this in a nation whose workforce numbered 55.6 million and whose total resident population was 131 million. More than half of the Depression labor force, some 24 million workers, did have a brief experience with mass taxation in the form of their contribution to Old Age and Survivors' Insurance, which most states had not begun withholding from paychecks until the constitutionality of the Social Security Act was established in 1937. But this tax was so recent, modest in size, and unobtrusively collected that workers were not likely to have registered its deduction from their paychecks. Not until their retirement decades later would they deal directly with the government.[15]

Then, in five years of war mobilization, the tax base exploded by 1,000 percent. By 1944 roughly two-thirds of the American labor force paid income tax—42.7 million in a peak wartime workforce of 65.3 million—while another fifth of the labor force filed tax forms without owing anything.[16] (See Chart A.5.) Effective rates of taxation rose quickly across nearly all income brackets, consuming 11.13 percent of personal income and 8.98 percent of GNP by 1945.[17] (See Chart A.6.)

Not only did the wartime revenue system reach far and wide into the homes of ordinary Americans, but it also raised the average tax burden each year even as it expanded to include families of modest means. Average income tax payments (in both current and constant, inflation-adjusted dollars) were higher in 1944 and 1945 than had been the case for most of the fifteen-year period before the war, when a much smaller number of far more affluent citizens paid taxes.[18]

By the last year of the war the personal income tax had surpassed the corporate income tax as the largest source of federal revenue, providing almost 44 percent of all receipts. Unlike the tax system created in World War I, this new tax regime would continue to claim significant portions of American incomes for years to come. Over the next two decades, a steady two-thirds of the labor force would continue to pay personal income taxes that would consume 8 to 9 percent of personal income and 10 to 11 percent of GNP. (See Charts A.5 and A.6.) As GNP grew, this stream of money would increasingly overshadow other sources of federal receipts, providing growth-oriented policy makers with an unparalleled fiscal tool.[19]

Despite the broadening of the tax base to include even the poorer ranks of the working class, these were also the most progressive years for federal income taxation.[20] Consider the examples of a decently paid factory worker and a well-compensated professional. For the sake of comparison, imagine that their incomes did not rise during the war. If the worker was married with no dependents and earned $2,000 a year, he owed the U.S. government nothing in 1940, as had been the case for his entire life. He made his first federal income tax payment of $42 in 1941, his tax bill rose to $140 in 1942, and his payment peaked at a high of $245 in 1945—the latter an effective rate of 12.3 percent. A married professional without dependents making $5,000 a year would have had a long experience of paying income tax. But like the factory worker, nothing in his experience, not even the previous war, would have prepared him for the steep rates introduced in 1941 ($375), followed by even steeper ones in 1942 ($746) and 1943 ($894), peaking in 1945 ($975) at an effective rate of 19.5 percent, almost ten times higher than his largest prewar income tax.

The burden of sacrifice extended out to weigh heavily on the extremes of the income spectrum. Even rather poor workers, such as those married with two dependents and making between $600 and $1,000 a year, paid a small income tax in the last three years of the war. The wealthiest also paid a considerable share of the burden, with effective rates as high as nearly 70 percent for those earning $100,000 and 90 percent for those earning $1 million or more.[21]

The speedy extension of the federal tax base relied on voluntary compliance to an astonishing extent. Much as the war agencies regulating work were forced to hope for the compliance of employers and unions to carry out the great bulk of their rulings, so too did the Treasury lack the state capacity to coerce or even audit most of the millions of citizens who owed income tax for the first time in their lives. At its wartime peak in 1945, the Bureau of Internal Revenue (BIR) employed 49,814 people. This staff was twice as large as in 1940, but the number of taxpayers had grown so dramatically that the average number of taxpayers for every BIR employee had tripled, rising from 305 to 1,107 in 1943, then dropping to 856 in 1945.[22]

Even with the best of intentions, taxpayers posed a serious challenge to enforcement due to their inexperience. Realizing that the unfamiliarity of filing might pose an obstacle to the millions of new taxpayers, the Treasury conducted a study to evaluate a simplified version of the 1040 form. The results were discouraging. Most respondents were unsure of how to complete the form, in part because of the way it defined terms such as *dependent* or *head of household*. Some thought it "nonsense" that a wife was not classified as a dependent in the special reckoning of the tax form. One puzzled taxpayer asked in consternation, "How can you be the head of a family if you don't have any dependents?" As a Treasury researcher put it, the government's attempt to distinguish the economic components of the household through individual filing contradicted "the customary meaning deeply ingrained in their habits of thinking."[23] These habits reflected adherence to a gendered "family wage" that had developed over generations of budgeting and expenditure barely touched by the federal government's fiscal policies.[24] Combined with the abiding resentment of taxation that had marked American political culture since the colonial Stamp Act riots, the confusion about tax filing posed a significant threat. The Treasury faced the monumental task of educating Americans about taxpaying duties that, for many, clashed with basic notions of economic citizenship.[25]

In early March 1943, Morgenthau learned that millions of new taxpayers did not know whether they had to pay income tax in a matter of days. Convening his staff, he asked a bleak rhetorical question: "Suppose we have to go out and try to arrest five million people?" A staffer reassured him, "That is what we do, about four million" enforcement actions in a tax year. But everyone in the meeting knew that the dilemma was potentially much greater: there were to be more than 12.5 million new and apparently confused federal taxpayers in 1943. To educate its new citizen stakeholders, the Treasury would be forced to rely on a national network of volunteers, ranging from local participants in the war savings program to advertising executives donating their firms' expertise through the War Advertising Council.[26] The newness of popular participation in public finance would blur the boundaries ordinarily separating bondholding and taxpaying, merging both obligations into a transaction between citizens and the national state.

In sharp contrast with the scrutiny it exercised over tax policy, Congress largely ignored the specific measures taken by the Treasury to borrow money, leaving it free to manage the public debt as it saw fit.[27] Every year following Pearl

Harbor, Congress passed with little debate laws lifting the ceiling on the debt, permitting the limit to rise from $49 billion in 1940 to $125 billion in 1942 and $300 billion in 1945, while deficits pushed against the boundaries of past experience, reaching $270 billion by June 1946. The wartime budgets provided a dramatic and quite unintentional demonstration of deficit spending's effectiveness in prompting economic growth.[28]

In the long term, wartime spending would make the federal debt a permanent and major feature of the economic landscape. At its peak in 1946 the federal debt amounted to 129 percent of GNP for that year—the highest level ever attained in the history of the United States. It took more than a generation to pay the debt back down to 40 percent of GNP, a level equal to that accomplished by the "emergency spending" of the New Deal years, and still considerably higher than the 34.45 percent resulting from World War I deficits. (See Chart A.8.)

In the short term, the federal government's wartime deficit spending set loose inflationary forces that undercut the purchasing power of civilians. Fiscal policies were unable to damp down all of the demand caused by the $290 billion in disposable income that grew in excess of civilian goods and services over the course of the war. Taxes absorbed $67 billion of this inflationary gap and ownership of government securities removed another $49 billion from consumers' wallets, but inflation surpassed each of these, reducing discretionary income by $84 billion. It remained for the Office of Price Administration to fight a rearguard action against inflation with price controls and rationing, a task that lacked most of the advantages in psychology and morale exploited by the bond and tax programs.[29]

To encourage popular involvement in the war and help absorb inflationary purchasing power, the Treasury in the spring of 1941 broadened the "baby bond" savings program that had been operating since 1935 with the dubious aspiration of promoting thrift in the midst of depression. Beginning in May, the series D baby bond was replaced by the new series E "defense savings bond," later renamed "war savings bond," whose non-negotiable terms, low denominations, and premium annual interest rate of 2.9 percent were aimed squarely at Americans of ordinary means. This change would form the popular basis of the savings bond program for the duration of the war and into the immediate postwar period. Between May 1941 and the end of 1945 small investors purchased 997 million E bonds. These amounted to roughly $40 billion, a sum that financed 8 percent of federal expenditures and accounted for 15 percent of the deficit.[30]

War savings bonds may not have dominated the Treasury's borrowing program, but they did dominate the way in which it was experienced by the public. E bonds were what most Americans had in mind of when they thought of war bonds. Since nearly every family owned at least one bond, this nearly universal participation in war finance helped justify a radical experiment in deficit spending. In combination with the income tax payments made by most American families, bond ownership represented an unprecedented personal stake in the war—and, by extension, the government.

Americans devoted to war bonds a portion of their personal income that was comparable to what they spent on income taxes, especially during years of peak mobilization. In 1944, Americans spent just under 10 percent of their personal income on war bonds and just over 11 percent on income taxes. Over the entire period of defense, war, and reconversion spanning the years 1941–46, bonds absorbed 6.7 percent of personal income, an impressive feat considering that the initial war loan drive did not take place until the end of 1942.[31]

War savings bonds thus reinforced the democratic overtones of the war finance program, distributing the national debt so widely (if not evenly) that hardly any family emerged from the war without at least a handful of stamps. For the first time, most American wage earners began to save a portion of their incomes, often in small but regular increments. Small-denomination issues of $10 and $25 consistently accounted for over a fourth of all E bond sales during each of the eight promotional war loan drives. If $50 and $100 denominations are counted, Americans of ordinary means absorbed between three-fourths and four-fifths of total E bond sales during the eight drives.[32]

Although Treasury records preserved a fairly clear picture of aggregate bond sales during the war, the number of individuals who bought and held on to bonds was a far murkier question. The Treasury and its sales organization repeatedly touted the same number of bond owners—eighty-five million—despite bond sales that increased right up until the end of the war and thus presumably included at least some individuals who had not previously bought a bond. Henry C. Murphy, director of research and statistics for the Treasury, later explained that this number was based on an estimate that stuck in the public's mind sometime in the middle of the war, and was not revised later because of the cost involved in deriving the estimate. "In the latter part of the war," he explained, the increase of both new bond sales and old bond redemptions made this number misleading: "the 85 million figure was probably much too low as an estimate of the number of purchasers and much too high as an estimate of the number of holders" for the entire war finance effort.[33] This was a rate of bond ownership at least double the rate of income-tax paying.

The nearly universal ownership of war savings bonds was a phenomenal accomplishment considering the relatively weak form of state capacity established to run the program. If the Treasury did not have the power to police the exploding numbers of taxpayers, it also lacked the political will to coerce investment in war bonds through mandatory savings. Morgenthau consistently emphasized the voluntary nature of the program in promoting national morale. "We must persuade people to buy . . . willingly and enthusiastically," Morgenthau exhorted his sales staff, "by bringing them to realize that in doing so they serve their country today and themselves tomorrow." No pressure or intimidation could be accepted. Voluntary bond sales he viewed as a civic glue that would bring Americans together in a patriotic affirmation of the war and the democratic traditions for which it was being fought. In contrast with the coercive atmosphere that had surrounded Liberty bond drives in World War I, Morgenthau cannily chose "to use *bonds* to sell the *war*, rather than vice versa." Thus it was crucial that bond purchases remain voluntary, in keeping with the rhetoric of liberty that suffused bond sales efforts.[34]

A group led by Marriner Eccles, head of the Federal Reserve, Harold Smith, director of the Bureau of the Budget, and later James Byrnes, head of the Office of Economic Stabilization, pushed for mandatory savings at every step in the confrontation with Congress over taxes. As conservatives in Congress, led by the House Ways and Means Committee and the Senate Finance Committee, increasingly asserted their prerogative to write tax law as they saw fit—by 1943, tax levels were several billion dollars below what the administration considered necessary to combat inflation—the embattled Treasury clique insisted that mandatory savings was the only route left to bridge the "inflationary gap" between escalating earnings and the modest output of civilian goods, which had been preempted by war production. After much internecine struggle between Smith and Byrnes, Morgenthau finally prevailed in convincing Roosevelt that the war bond program should remain voluntary.[35]

To realize Morgenthau's agenda, the Treasury organized a massive network of volunteers who served as a national sales force during the eight monthlong campaigns, or war loan drives, between 1942 and 1945. In each of the drives local War Savings Committees called on the services of nearly six million volunteer "Minute Men" and women who canvassed their local communities to drum up sales during bond drives. These foot soldiers in the Treasury's civic army outnumbered the entire civilian payroll of the federal government by more than two million. Their efforts may have been the most effective of all the publicity devices in the government's arsenal. Internal studies of each drive repeatedly showed that personal solicitation was the single most decisive factor in motivating citizens to buy bonds. Half of all E bond sales occurred during the eight bond drives. More than simple salesmanship was at work here, however, since 61 percent of all E bond sales occurred within twelve states whose economies had surged due to major military contracts.[36] The opportunities opened by the war boom economy provided the economic leavening necessary to drive mass participation in the fiscal state.

The atmosphere of patriotic persuasion in which bonds were sold made individual decisions to purchase them something less than voluntary. Nearly universal rates of bond buying reflected the tremendous pressure that public expectations of war-mindedness could place on ordinary citizens. In light of this pressure, it would be more precise to characterize wartime bond buying as "semivoluntary" or "associational." Considering the Treasury's lack of enforcement capacity and reliance on public relations to persuade taxpayers to meet their obligations, the same characterization fits the paying of income tax. The Treasury asked citizens to buy bonds and prepare income tax returns on their own initiative, but it worked hard to organize a wide range of intermediary organizations that would provide the structure most citizens needed to understand their new obligations and transform them into patriotic habits.[37]

The most significant example of the semivoluntary basis of wartime finance was the role adopted by employers and unions, who enrolled workers in payroll plans for bonds as well as taxes. By 1944, these plans automatically diverted a portion of the regular paychecks of more than twenty-five million workers and soldiers into funds that employers turned over on a regular basis to the regional Federal Reserve Bank. Payroll reductions provided for the purchase of nearly half of all war savings bonds, and allowed the collection of income tax from roughly 70 percent of all taxpayers. Some employers became issuing agents for bonds. Others simply pooled employees' money to purchase bonds en masse. Most devoted some effort to promote workplace bond drives in tandem with national loan efforts. Unions cooperated in plantwide bond drives and canvassed their local shops intensively, helping to raise enrollment in payroll plans. When management and labor worked in tandem, participation in payroll plans soared, making it possible for 80 percent of all industrial workers to purchase bonds on a regular basis by April 1943. One government study done in mid-1943 found that nearly half of the companies that produced the highest volume of payroll bond sales had labor-management committees.[38]

The many voluntary societies that organized American civic life also devised innumerable ways to sell bonds to the war-minded and remind citizens to pay their taxes. Participating associations included women's organizations ranging from the Daughters of the American Revolution to the Women's Supreme Council of B'nai B'rith; fraternal and civic groups such as Kiwanis Clubs and the Knights of Columbus; national labor organizations such as the American Federation of Labor, the Congress of Industrial Organizations, and the thousands of union locals organized in war plants around the country; local branches of national farm organizations; business and trade associations, including local chambers of commerce and national professional societies such as the American Medical Association; organizations for racial advancement, including the National Association for the Advancement of Colored People and the National Urban League; and religious organizations of nearly all denominations.[39] A small staff of a few dozen staffers ran the national sales effort from the Treasury's

War Savings Division in Washington, providing state and local sales organizations and allied voluntary associations with guidance, promotional materials, public relations support, and any other logistical assistance the small central staff could muster. The Treasury relied on the voluntary organizations as a way to perform (rather than just trumpet) "democracy in action," allowing the direct personal experiences of millions of volunteers to instill liberal lessons about self-government in a free society.

The efforts the Treasury made to mobilize the voluntary energies of the black community revealed the problems inherent in couching fiscal citizenship as a simple matter of civic virtue that demonstrated the freedom of association for which Americans were fighting. This was because of the basic contradiction involved in asking African Americans to take on the obligations of citizenship when they could not enjoy many of its rights. Because black families were disproportionately poor, and because such a large proportion lived on farms where eligibility for income taxes and disposable income for war bonds was low, they were unlikely candidates for special attention. It was their ideological significance, not their fiscal clout, that drew the attention of the Treasury.

In 1941 the Treasury asked William Pickens to leave his post as field director for the NAACP to join the Defense Savings Staff, where he became the head of the Interracial Section in early 1942—the first black official appointed to the department since the Wilson administration.[40] Before the war, Pickens had not hesitated to highlight the unfair treatment of black citizens by emphasizing how little they got for their tax dollars. In one among many public criticisms featuring taxes as markers of citizenship, he had highlighted the injustice of requiring blacks to "pay taxes without getting receipts" necessary to establish voting eligibility, even as the same taxes funded segregated schools, buses, and other amenities that subsidized white privilege.[41]

Pickens changed his tune once he became head of the Interracial Section, ignoring or downplaying the ways in which black taxpayers and bondholders might use their leverage to get more for their money, while continuing to emphasize the rights that ought to accrue to fiscal citizenship. Where before he had underscored the categorical injustice of paying taxes for a Jim Crow government, now he presided over press relations and public events that celebrated the civic spirit and good financial common sense of black participation in the war bond program. The 1944 annual report of the Interracial Section was a virtual catalogue of boosterism. It celebrated the outstanding initiative taken by individual black citizens to promote the sale of bonds, such as the "elderly colored widow, with no sons or daughters to fight or join the armed services," who sold her home for $15,000 and converted the proceeds into war bonds. Pickens understood well how to channel aspirations for national recognition of black contributions to the war effort. Rather than dwell on segregation, he flipped the meaning of citizens' obligations and observed, "In our democracy any citizen of any race or color has the privilege of buying his bonds through all the issuing agencies."[42] If rights were not yet equal, obligations were becoming so.

By their nature, then, bond promotions could do little more to address the racial dimensions of citizenship than continually emphasize equality of sacrifice as a marker of patriotic merit. This was because the Treasury liked to think of itself as operating on a civic plane that transcended race. Tellingly, it refused to keep any systematic or official records of bond holders' racial background. Pickens captured the spirit of this refusal when he corrected the *Survey Graphic* in 1941 for mistakenly identifying him as the head of a "Negro Division" in the Treasury. He chided that the department had never had such a division—and, he concluded, "I sincerely hope that it never will."[43] This refusal to acknowledge race reflected a broader tendency to affirm the status quo, a tendency that paid great political dividends.

The Treasury earned political points because its organization did not intrude on existing power structures. Unlike the war agencies that drew the ire of congressional conservatives—most notably the Office of Price Administration—the Treasury did not expand dramatically during the war. Its reliance on local civic leaders to direct bond sales, combined with an effective use of patriotic appeals to promote bonds, may explain why Congress devoted so little scrutiny to the vast propaganda efforts mounted to sell bonds and encourage citizens to file their new taxes. It didn't hurt that the Treasury took special pains to clear appointments to field positions in state sales organization with appropriate members of Congress. Finally, bonds did not threaten well-organized political interests the way taxes did; they were voluntary and did not redistribute income downward.[44]

Despite enormous strides made to bring the better part of the national citizenry into the fiscal state, taxing and borrowing policies would move much of the financial burden of the war onto future generations. The Treasury's reliance on voluntarism ruled out stringent solutions such as the compulsory savings scheme put forth by Byrnes, Smith, and their allies, while the New Deal's declining political fortunes made steeper or more progressive taxation impossible. Yet bondholding and taxpaying accomplished an important goal. These fiscal obligations inculcated a sense of national citizenship. Just as important as the part of the national debt financed by war savings bonds or the rising portion of federal revenues contributed by income taxes was the role bonds and taxes played in promoting and sustaining widespread identification with the war effort. "There are millions of people," Morgenthau explained to the press in a candid moment off the record, "who say, 'What can we do to help?' . . . Right now, other than going in the Army and Navy or working in a munitions plant, there isn't anything to do. . . . Sixty per cent of the reason that I want to do this thing is . . . to give the people an opportunity to do something."[45]

Selling the War

To accomplish mass participation in war finance, the Treasury had to overcome a formidable cultural challenge. It had to persuade the majority of working Americans that paying federal income tax and buying war bonds were the legitimate duties of citizens. It had to do more than simply administer the various laws identifying new sources of revenue and authorizing higher levels of debt. It had to create a new "taxpaying culture" among Americans unaccustomed to federal income taxation. The same may be said of popular bondholding: ordinary citizens were not accustomed to thinking of the national debt as their personal property. Americans had to be persuaded to alter habits of spending and personal finance that—after a decade of frustration during the Depression, followed by the sudden recovery of the war boom—threatened to mushroom the inflationary gap beyond all control.[46]

To accomplish its monumental task of bringing the better part of the nation into the fiscal state, the Treasury adopted an encyclopedic public relations strategy. Morgenthau infused this strategy with a combination of liberal rhetoric, civic boosterism, and public relations commercialism that resembled the OWI's approach.[47] Much like the group of writers and artists who had rallied to MacLeish's New Deal vision of government information, Morgenthau and his staff pushed to portray bond buying and taxpaying as democratic duties that would ensure Americans a stake in a secure future guaranteed by the Four Freedoms. But like the admen and corporate executives who came to dominate war propaganda after the New Dealers' departure from the OWI, Morgenthau also placed great trust in the effectiveness of modern marketing techniques, working closely with advisors such as the advertising executive Fred Smith and his colleagues on the War Advertising Council. As a result of this astute move, the Treasury was able to rely for its public relations almost entirely on advertisements and other propaganda whose development, management, and placement in print, radio, and motion pictures was paid for by private industry.[48]

The corporate liberals who gladly took over direction of government propaganda by the middle of the war tended to pursue what one account executive bluntly called "selling America to America." They favored ads that treated consumerism, free enterprise, and affluence—"the American way"—as an essential "Fifth Freedom" on par with the Four Freedoms and the broader ideological goals of the war.[49] Certainly this optic applied to much of the free advertising and publicity that placed the Treasury's bond drive slogans, such as "Back the Attack," at the bottom of full-page advertisements informing the reader of "what this war is all about": "hastening the day when you . . . can once more walk into any store in the land and buy anything you want!" Many advertisements featured dubious equations of consumer behavior with fighting, exhorting consumers to adopt war-minded habits such as using "Gillette blades which last longer and thereby conserve steel for national defense." In these pitches and their subtler cousins, there was no conflict between consumer self-interest and going all out for the war.[50]

The Treasury's partnership with the Ad Council, Hollywood, and the radio networks produced an outpouring of such messages, saturating public life with appeals that painted taxes and bonds in familiar hues of consumerism. During the first three years of the bond program alone, the Ad Council arranged for approximately a quarter of a billion dollars' worth of free advertising, which translated into roughly 218,000 bond ads run in daily papers and 157,000 in weekly papers during the second, third, and fourth loan drives. Beyond this direct contribution, private industry worked with the War Savings Staff to produce countless pamphlets, posters, radio spots, outdoor advertising, and comic strips, whose placement was coordinated by the OWI. At the more glamorous end of the promotional spectrum, the staff of the Treasury's Special Events division arranged for celebrity appearances, such as the Stars Over America tour, which brought Humphrey Bogart, Judy Garland, Cary Grant, Rita Hayworth, and scores of other well-known actors to more than 360 communities around the country. To guarantee national distribution of its film shorts, the Treasury worked with the motion picture industry's War Activities Committee to show them before feature films in some sixteen thousand theaters nationwide. On the local level, individual theaters often agreed to screen movies for patrons who purchased bonds as the "price of admission." No portion of the sales chain was too insignificant to be enlisted by the Treasury: newspaper boys and automobile salesmen joined the volunteer sales force (the latter at Morgenthau's personal prodding), while department store windows featured displays that asked shoppers to add a bond to their day's purchases.[51]

As a result of its reliance on the machinery of consumerism, the Treasury produced or condoned propaganda that often represented the war, and especially the military equipment used to fight it, as if it were a consumer item only bonds and taxes could buy. An example of this commodification of the war could be found in a portfolio prepared by the Amos Parrish Company to guide retailers for the Fourth War Loan Drive in January 1944. After a quick reminder that stores had only "25 selling days to pile up the great volume of *sales* and *good will* that War Bonds are capable of producing for your store," the portfolio got straight to its pitch:

If War bonds *were fashion items* in one of your departments, you'd *adver-tise* them as you would any outstanding, fast-selling item, wouldn't you? You'd feature their *selling points* . . . their *value* . . . your *assortments* of them . . . the *dependability of their label* . . . what they do for the *customer*.

The pages that followed contained ideas for posters, store displays, and advertisements that capitalized on this insight. One reassured customers that the store in question stocked only reliable, well-known brands. "But of all the *famous name* merchandise we carry," it continued, one name—"the United States of America"—"stands behind the greatest *value* ever offered." What other brand "*ever sold* you anything with an unconditional guarantee that you could return it in ten years for 25% *more* than it cost you?" Another began with the tag line "We always have YOUR size in stock!" and proceeded to reassure shoppers that while the store might have trouble keeping "important fashions" in stock due to war shortages, they always had "plenty of junior size bonds here at $18.75" as well as a "splendid collection of larger sizes . . . every one selling at 25% below its true value." "Come on in tomorrow," it closed, "and let us fit you for a happy, secure and victorious future." A third ad concept took the bargain sale idea one step further, announcing a "five star special" available "at 25% reduction." This "mer-chandise" was "crisp, new, never handled," and it came with a free "combination offer": "Freedom from Want . . . Freedom from Fear . . . Freedom of Speech . . . Freedom of Religion."[52]

Jingoism often augmented the sales pitch for self-interest. Hatred's market value seemed unlimited, particularly when branded with a Japanese visage. That is to say, some commercial promotions took a predictable tack, portraying bonds as the purchase price for dead enemies, usually Japanese. One bond poster pre-sented viewers with a cartoonish depiction of Tojo, encouraging them to "buy this man a Hari-Kiri Kit on December 7, 1944," the anniversary of Pearl Harbor. The list of items in the kit included a "pearl handle dagger," "velvet kneeling pillow," and "handy enamel basin," which together cost a total of $75, the price of a $100 bond.[53]

During the winter of 1942, the Special Events Division worked with local war savings committees to present bondholders with a more tangible trophy of the defeated enemy. It organized a national tour of a captured Japanese subma-rine, which curious citizens could inspect after paying for a bond. In just one month, people in seventy-five municipalities throughout California bought over $1.6 million in bonds for the privilege of clambering around the hull on a cat-walk and peering inside to witness its "suicidal design." With no diving tanks and a cruising range of 150 miles, the sub and its apparently fanatical operators com-pleted a mission by transforming themselves into a "giant depth bomb" that they would ram into the side of the nearest American ship.[54]

Like the "Hari-Kiri Kit," the submarine display was intended to highlight the racially barbaric nature of the enemy—a ubiquitous theme in much anti-Japanese propaganda—and make symbolic evidence of his obliteration available for easy consumption by civilians.[55] As the narrator of *What Makes a Battle*, a Treasury film short produced for the Fifth War Loan Drive, explained while footage of blasted Pacific islands played before civilian moviegoers, "The Germans would have quit right away, but Japs are . . . Japs. . . . They crept behind wreckage. . . . They dug into the ground like rats." Victory against such a demonic foe was costly, requiring the purchase of more war bonds. "Each success leads to another and larger battle which cannot be won, cannot even be launched, until the mountains of equipment earmarked for it are actually dockside."[56]

The deeper point in selling images of the demonized Japanese foe was sometimes made explicit, as in *My Japan*, a Treasury short whose appearance in theaters in 1945 betrayed increasing government concern that civilians would become dangerously complacent after the decisive victory at Iwo Jima and the bombing of the Japanese home islands.[57] It featured a glowering Japanese officer who taunted American viewers, scorning their "soft bellies crying for beefsteaks and butter and candy." "You say you can destroy us by making sacrifices. How we suffer when you do not have a full tank of gasoline. . . . How we tremble when you have to wait to get into movies, restaurants, nightclubs." Japanese victory was inevitable, he boasted, since unlike sentimental Americans, they realized that "it is a fact that human lives are cheap. Unlike you, we have no cowardly illusions . . . so we spend lives freely. Yours, and ours."[58] Chastened moviegoers, motivated by their hatred of the narrator, were thus prompted to spend their remaining consumer dollars on bonds rather than popcorn. At the same time, viewers could relish the superior civilization their bonds "bought," perhaps reflecting that the value a society placed on human life was related to a high standard of living, and both were worth at least a little personal sacrifice.

Even though they were mandated by law, income taxes also posed a public relations challenge, one that was surprisingly similar to that confronted by the bond sales effort. In some instances it was possible to promote taxes and bonds at the same time, as on the *Treasury Star Parade*, a radio variety show that interspersed guest appearances by musicians and other celebrities with messages coordinated to meet the exigencies of bond drives and tax filing deadlines. Lighter fare included Irving Berlin's "I Paid My Income Tax Today," whose lyrics echoed much of the Treasury's egalitarian advertising copy: "You see those bombers in the sky / Rockefeller helped to build them—so did I." As with bonds, the Treasury promoted taxes in all media where industry cooperation could be enlisted. Thus, moviegoers were treated to movie shorts such as *The New Spirit*, which featured a beleaguered Donald Duck attempting to file the taxes due on his actor's salary. By the end of the reel Donald had completed his form and been transported to Washington, where he witnessed the guns, planes, and other war matériel funded by his taxes.[59]

Propaganda directed at children drew on civic themes and patriotic associations to impress upon students their stake in democracy. A concise expression of this civic traditionalism may be seen in the statement of principle that introduced the handbook *School Savings in Action*:

> A United States Savings Bond is more than an investment; it is a share in America. Like casting a ballot, the purchase of a Bond is the exercise of a right, the enjoyment of a privilege, and the performance of a duty. It gives the individual a true citizen's share in maintaining a strong national economy, and in preserving the American way of life.[60]

The Education Section of the War Savings Staff distributed this handbook and other such publications through state and local committees as part of its Schools at War program, which advised school administrators and teachers on curricular changes and special activities that would promote bondholding and teach students about the economic dimensions of citizenship. The main goal of the program was to involve students in war finance directly, through a regular program of stamp purchases in a school savings club. The Education Section promoted the Schools at War program with a flood of materials that surpassed the promotional output of all other offices of the war finance program, save the Division of Press, Radio, and Advertising. With the help of the U.S. Office of Education, which provided advice and mailing lists, the Schools at War program established an impressive national distribution network. Its official organ, *Schools at War*, was issued in batches of more than one million each quarter and distributed through bulk shipments to local schools whose cooperative superintendents placed them in the hands of "nearly every teacher in the land." By the end of the war, the Education Section had garnered more than $2 billion in sales of war bonds and stamps. Considering that the vast majority of participating students worked their way toward this goal one dime at a time, this figure suggests significant participation in the program.[61]

An equally important goal was encouraging students to reflect on the significance of their war savings in discussions that explored "what we are fighting for." In this emphasis on civic patriotism the Education Section reinforced a tendency among wartime educators and child experts to promote patriotic civic-mindedness as an essential part of a child's development. "It isn't enough" for "youngsters to do their part in the war effort," explained *Parents' Magazine* in November 1944. Children "must learn to understand and live by the principles for which this country fights." This view echoed the resolves of the National

Education Association (NEA), whose Wartime Policies Commission encouraged curricular reinforcement of "the ideals of freedom and equality for which we are fighting." By working closely with influential educators in associations such as the NEA, the American Council on Education, and the National Catholic Welfare Conference, the Education Section ensured that its educational message would spread far beyond the confines of the Schools at War program.[62]

That message centered on a liberal nationalist ideology that suffused the materials distributed by the Schools at War program. Teachers directing savings clubs were invited to integrate bond sales into their curricula, using them as object lessons to raise such questions as:

1) What are we fighting for? At home? Abroad?

2) What are we fighting against? At home? Abroad?

3) What are the reasons for rationing, price control, war bond purchases?

4) What is inflation and how can we fight it?

5) What can individuals do to help win the war quickly?

6) What are our responsibilities as consumers? As voters? As members of families?

7) How can enemy inspired rumors be recognized and refuted?

8) What sort of peace is necessary to guarantee us the things we are fighting for? Will the present program in citizenship, War Savings, etc., help us in any way to make a permanent peace?

9) What are the characteristics of Fascism and Naziism? Are there any who advocate similar measures for the U.S.A.?[63]

A wide range of assignments in mathematics, home economics, social studies, and civics could be adapted to instruct students on the many facets of war finance. Some of these were obvious and mundane, such as "budgeting and consumer problems," to be taught in home economics, or "making change, handling money," in mathematics; others strained to make a connection to the syllabus, such as "voluntary savings as democratic practice," which ostensibly related to social studies.[64]

Extracurricular activities allowed more leeway to dramatize the significance of economic citizenship in a time of war. The Educational Section provided, on demand, reprints of "tested" plays that students could act out for their schoolmates. In *Good Intentions*, one of the skits recommended by the

Educational Section, children were tempted by a windfall of 40 cents to spend it all on candy, soda, and nail polish. Luckily, they had been listening to the radio and playing war-minded spelling games with their mother that day, so they "suddenly all realize[d] that all day they ha[d] been wishing they had some money for just one purpose—War Stamps."[65] Contrasting selfish consumerism with the virtuous purchases of bond buyers was a common device used in Treasury propaganda to underscore the significance of personal spending habits during war.

A more powerful if heavy-handed technique asked students to follow the ramifications of their selfish decisions to the battlefront, where even the smallest margin of laxity could mean life or death. This was the moral of *Message from Bataan*, a melodrama that linked private and public households, mundane activities and the most heroic fighting of the war. It told the story of young Johnny Rand and his older brother, Bill, whose assignment to the unglamorous Quartermaster Corps disappointed the entire family. Bill soon warmed to his new job, explaining in letters home that without the supplies his outfit provided, and "the money to pay for them," "our Army would starve to death and freeze to death, or rather, down south here, bake to death in the open sun." Despite their good intentions, the Rand family remained disappointed until Bill found himself in Bataan. Trapped on Corregidor, Bill had to run dangerous missions across enemy lines in a desperate bid to supply the troops, even while "Japanese bombs dropped death." Not until the end of the play, when Bill was ominously reported as missing in action, did Johnny, still at home, finally accept the importance of his brother's role in the war and the corollary significance of home-front sacrifices, both of which he had scorned. In the final scene, Bill's last letter to Johnny arrived along with the army's telegram reporting that he was missing in action. In it he asked his younger brother the question that concluded the play:

> And . . . your stamp collection, Johnny . . . how is it? You young fellows and girls can't fight or work in war industries yet . . . but whatever else you do, you can buy War Savings Stamps and Bonds, and keep on buying, and buying, and buying . . . and so lend your country the money it needs to pay for so many planes and ships and tanks and guns that we soldiers and sailors and flyers will never again be caught short by our enemies.[66]

By constantly drawing connections between the ordinary decisions of child protagonists and soldiers facing battle overseas, the plays recommended by the Educational Section employed a rhetorical strategy far more effective than abstract idealism or crass commercialism. Indeed, the Treasury's efforts to reach schoolchildren may have been too effective. For boys and girls, the obligation to buy bonds presented a very personal responsibility that figured prominently in their socialization to wartime community expectations and patriotic norms. Every week students brought dimes to school to purchase stamps to fill their savings books. Like their contributions to scrap drives and other patriotic activities that occupied much of their time both in school and out, the regular purchase of stamps tied students' daily lives to the war. These experiences had a profound impact on the outlook of the cohort of Americans born between 1932 and 1941, instilling a deep patriotism and identification with the "good war" that would stay with them for life. Materials from the Schools at War program, such as *Message from Bataan*, forged that identification in an abiding guilt. While such guilt was clearly the effect intended by the Educational Section, and indeed by the entire War Savings Staff, it posed a dilemma in the case of poor children whose families could not afford sizable bond purchases.[67]

Messages aimed at adults often attempted to tug at the same heartstrings, reminding civilians of the battlefront repercussions of their smallest actions. Many of the most affecting messages flashed out at Americans from the silver screen. During the war some eighty-five to ninety million Americans went to the movies on a weekly basis, making the Treasury's film shorts a potentially influential channel of information and persuasion. Like other "Victory films" produced for various government agencies, the Treasury shorts enjoyed quick and nearly universal distribution to theaters nationwide. Most of these shorts took a direct approach to propaganda, using battle footage and voice-overs to illustrate the vast quantities of war matériel destroyed in combat.[68]

Battle footage had a visual effect akin to the scenes described by Roosevelt in his fireside chats: it placed the viewer in the midst of the fighting, thereby tying the equipment soldiers used for fighting to the money civilians were expected to spend on bonds.[69] One early film, *Bonds at War*, simply replayed footage of battle scenes featuring the ships, guns, planes, and other matériel paid for by war bonds.[70] Another, *Mission Completed*, tallied up the cost of a plane crash on an aircraft carrier out at sea:

> Mission completed. The plane, $80,000. The pilot's training, $50,000. Pete Eriksen's life . . . we can't put a value on a man's life, but we can make sure that all the Pete Eriksens have the best tools to fight with. We can make sure by buying war bonds and more war bonds. Only then is our mission completed.[71]

Most films displayed more ingenuity than this, especially as the war drew on and audiences became more skeptical. *This Could Be America*, produced in 1945, opened with footage of American planes strafing Japanese cities, while the narrator observed, "These could be Jap planes diving on Main Street. . . . This could be a small town in Iowa. . . . This could be the Fourth of July anywhere in America. . . . But it's not. Instead, it's twelve thousand miles away." The film closed with the narrator asking, "How much does it cost to fight a war twelve thousand miles away? Well, before you begin counting the billions of dollars, remember, it cost this man his life. We can cut down on the cost of life by buying war bonds." Another film appearing in the last year of the war, *Midnight*, presented its audience with a similar visual equation between their bond purchases and the combat soldier's idealized sacrifice. At midnight "navy time," it was 10:00 p.m. in Greenland, and American forces were blasting Nazi weather stations. On the other side of the globe an admiral ordered "one advance base, size ten, and a city [was] shipped overseas" to an island in the Pacific. On the high seas all over the world navy men would "strike the enemy" wherever they roamed, with "carriers your war bonds built." The film closed with the instantly recognizable image of the men on Iwo Jima, over which an animated *7th* pivoted upward as if it were the flag being raised, while the narrator made his final pitch for the Seventh War Loan. "We pay for this and the cost is monstrous, in blood and sweat and war bonds. Our enemies thought that we ... would not, dared not, face this cost. We answered, and your war bond must keep on answering so that they will not make the same mistake again."[72]

The Treasury's visual strategies all came together in the fictional plot of *It Can't Last*, a film short written by MacLeish and shown during the Sixth War Loan, at the end of 1944. In it, a complacent Mr. Squires reassured the local paperboy, Freddy, that he should not worry about his brother Quince, who was serving as a gunner on a navy bomber. "War's almost done," he explained as his thoughts turned toward a new car. At that very moment out over the vast Pacific flew Quince, whose thoughts turned back longingly to his sleepy Connecticut hometown. His reverie was interrupted when the bomber reached its target. His crew helped sink two Japanese destroyers in an intense firefight whose scenes were taken from actual battle footage. Their bomber was downed in the fighting, leaving Quince adrift in a life raft with the plane's radioman. As they floated out at sea with no land or ship in sight, Quince was overcome with despair as he thought of what he had seen and what he might never see again—particularly "the WAVE with curling black hair on her neck." The radioman reprimanded Quince, urging him to keep up his spirits:

> Haven't we got the squadron? And haven't we the flattop back of the squadron? And back of the flattop, the fleet? You think they'll ever forget us? And back of the fleet, the whole country, everyone one in it ... they're all part of this, too. There isn't one of them who wouldn't be with us.

The film ended on an ambivalent note with Quince and the radioman still at sea, while back home Mr. Squire picked up the paper Quince's kid brother had thrown onto his stoop in Old Lyme. The headline gave the film's ending an ominous tone: "Yanks Bag Nip Cruiser, Two Destroyers. Only One American Plane Failed to Return."[73]

Even more persuasive than propagandistic depictions of combat, however, was the opportunity to see and touch the real thing. Morgenthau went to great lengths to arrange for special events in which military personnel would present the public with equipment that had been used in battle. In a letter to Secretary of the Navy Frank Knox that sought to make such promotions a permanent feature of the bond sales effort, Morgenthau related that among the more than five million volunteer bond sales personnel, "there is highest praise for the effectiveness of Navy personnel and equipment in presenting to the people an understanding of the costs of war." By the spring of 1944 both the army and the navy would act as regular partners in promotional campaigns and special events, assigning liaison officers to work directly with the Treasury's staff.[74]

Army and navy promotions were especially effective because they combined personal solicitation with direct, tangible evidence of how bonds made their buyers a part of the war. The navy took this approach to an extreme on Navy Day, January 27, 1944, when six hundred sailors and officers "took over strategic points, bridges, [and] traffic intersections" in Chicago to stop civilians individually and remind them to buy an extra bond.[75]

Most army and navy participation in bond sales events was not so intrusive, but all such displays of military personnel and equipment were intended to "bring the war home" so that civilians could more concretely visualize the war, and thus participate vicariously. Parade-like displays in squares and other public spaces allowed children and adults alike to approach the real thing—stalwart men in uniform guarding and demonstrating guns, tanks, and other equipment that had seen battle—while feeling that they were a small part of the action. Often, outstanding bond buyers could win the chance to participate even more directly. A war show taking place in Wilmington, Delaware, during the Third War Loan Drive sold rides on a Sherman tank for the price of a $1,000 bond. In Reno, Nevada, the honor of riding on an M3 tank was awarded to four-year-old Michael Crawford, who with the help of his parents had saved up to buy a $50 bond during the Fourth War Loan Drive in the spring of 1944.[76]

Few events approached the military war show more comprehensively than "Here's Your Infantry," an outdoor exhibition produced by the Army Ground Forces that toured a hundred cities around the country as part of the Sixth War Loan Drive in December 1944. As its title suggested, the show was intended to present bond buyers with "a vivid picture of how their War Bond money is being used." Depicting "war at its grimmest," eight separate infantry units, manned with decorated soldiers freshly returned from overseas combat, conducted maneuvers for local townspeople in a "realistic display of actual battle conditions." Each unit demonstrated a separate phase of battle—assembling a mortar, advancing through enemy fire, mounting an assault on a fortified position—which led to the climax, the destruction of a Japanese pillbox by an "infantry

The most effective method of selling war bonds relied on direct, personal solicitation. "Here's Your Infantry," one of the Treasury's most successful sales promotions, provided a compelling personal sales pitch by having actual soldiers conduct maneuvers and re-enact battle scenes. (Courtesy of the National Archives Still Picture Records Section, ARC #515366)

jungle assault team armed with flamethrowers, dynamite and other deadly weapons." This miniature war, a hometown spectacle of genuine heroes and their authentic "killing weapons"—used "in actual combat against the Germans and the Japanese"—delivered to bond buyers the product for which they were happy to spend their windfall wages.[77]

Why They Bought

For all the fanfare, the Treasury's monumental public relations machinery may have missed its mark, at least in part. Early in the war, research sponsored by the Treasury revealed a mismatch between the Treasury's promotional messages and the motives of bond buyers. A survey conducted by the Psychological Corporation, a New York–based research firm, in early January 1942 found a "striking difference between the reasons which have been given to people through promotion and the reasons they give themselves" for buying bonds. Although all respondents had heard or seen at least one ad for war bonds, 81 percent of respondents gave reasons for buying bonds that were featured in only

6 percent of advertisements. Subsequent research would confirm that most people bought bonds for reasons that were independent of, or even opposed to, the pitches most often featured in war ads.[78]

Overexposure posed another problem. Not only did bombastic propaganda show bad taste, but by trumpeting "successes" in mounting public relations campaigns, it was possible to obscure ongoing problems. One study showed the bias inherent in gauging propaganda's effectiveness by the scale of its public exposure: although 5 percent of all adults in one northeastern industrial city attended a movie promoting bonds in the spring of 1944, interviews showed that those who attended were already highly motivated to buy bonds (while the 95 percent of adults who stayed away were considerably less so).[79]

Marketing techniques alienated enough people to present a problem in motivation, especially as the war dragged on. A significant minority of respondents resented high-profile events in which celebrities and prominent figures sold bonds or presented "rewards" to lucky bond buyers. These people felt that bond buying was a duty that should be expected, not applauded, and that promotional gimmickry cheapened a serious duty of citizenship. Repulsed by the mounting chorus of self-congratulation and commercialism, one conscientious advertising executive warned his colleagues as early as the summer of 1942 against the dangers of swinging "on the trapeze of war emotion."[80]

Perhaps sensing the peril of profaning the sacrifice of American soldiers with the techniques of marketing, sales, and merchandising, Morgenthau and his associates attempted to draw a line of integrity around bond sales. In the first month of the war, New Deal veteran Marriner Eccles established the principle that it was preferable to use "the word 'investment' rather than 'sale' wherever possible in discussing War Savings Bonds." Ted Gamble, national director of bond sales, acted on this principle when he advised Morgenthau against a promotion conducted in early 1945 by a local utility that offered to buy back used electrical appliances from its customers by exchanging them for bonds. Gamble insisted that "we should not, from Washington, encourage the sale of either stamps or bonds in connection with a merchandise transaction of any character."[81] These careful distinctions revealed a defensiveness on the part of government officials made uneasy by the bond program's wholehearted embrace of consumer culture. Because E bonds were non-negotiable and non-transferable, the War Savings Staff could use its discretion to restrict transactions involving bonds. Broader considerations of legitimacy, not simple calculations of revenue streams, shaped the ways in which the Treasury could effectively "sell" war finance.

Although bond and tax propaganda abounded with references to freedom and democracy, it is not clear that strictly ideological appeals worked any better than did commercialism. Take the example of *Our America*, a pamphlet of motivational images, articles, and stories widely distributed in January 1942, before the full tide of war propaganda had suffused public life with idealistic rhetoric. On its cover a class of schoolchildren saluted an American flag. The caption read, "One nation indivisible with liberty and justice for all." The first story, "Do We Deserve Them?" ran beneath a half-page photo of General Douglas MacArthur in full salute, followed by shorter pieces by Senators Carter Glass (D-Va.) and Warren R. Austin (R-Vt.). Glass advised the reader that bonds helped "to crush the enemy and save the lives of our fighting men." Austin began by posing the question, "Freedom or slavery? It's up to us." Throughout the pamphlet, photos of local volunteers and bond buyers alternated with photos of American leaders and heroes. For good measure, a Ripley cartoon depicted a ruthless German soldier tearing a blanket from the hands of a Norwegian girl whom he had jolted awake.[82]

A few months later, the Treasury conducted a study to gauge the effectiveness of *Our America*. It found that only 17 percent of people interviewed even remembered having received the vivid bond pamphlet, while a mere 11 percent had taken the time to read any part of it. This poor showing was not for lack of effort. The Treasury had enlisted the nation's post offices in an extensive campaign in which forty-five million copies were distributed to families around the country.[83] Despite this comprehensive effort, the recipients of *Our America* largely ignored its carefully crafted message.

The indifference that greeted *Our America* demonstrated the difficulty of conveying ideological messages to a mass audience. As a postwar summary of the Treasury's research findings concluded, much of the propaganda produced by and for the bond program produced "little actual change in people's beliefs," because most people had stable prior beliefs. Ironically, the rising glut of propaganda actually reinforced preexisting beliefs, rather than overcoming them, because it overloaded citizens, forcing them to selectively devote limited attention to a small proportion of the messages they encountered.[84] This was not to say that the Treasury's public relations campaigns were in vain; rather, they promoted a broad if vague awareness that needed to be transformed into a more pressing sense of obligation if they were to motivate citizens to buy bonds and pay taxes.

In order to tap more effectively the wellsprings of civic duty, the Treasury funded an extensive body of research on bonds and taxes, most of it conducted by Rensis Likert at the Bureau of Agricultural Economics. Thanks to this work, it is possible to determine with unusual precision the meanings fiscal citizenship held for most Americans.[85] One of the most striking findings of Likert's research was the discrepancy that lay between the actual motivations of ordinary citizens and the substance of Treasury propaganda. Rather than asking citizens to sacrifice for abstract ideals or for a future where they could once again pursue their self-interest, the most effective propaganda simply confronted audiences with someone with whom they could identify or sympathize, the GI. Those remaining behind on the home front could join him in battle, indirectly, by doing their part—buying bonds and paying taxes. Here was a way to sell the war by playing on the tension between obligation, as represented by the soldier's sacrifice, and the entitlement civilians felt in pursuing their personal self-interest.

Starting with the Second War Loan Drive in April 1943, Likert's staff conducted extensive batteries of surveys that asked bond holders about various aspects of their purchases, including their reasons for buying bonds. In these surveys, a few basic considerations emerged in respondents' rationales for bond purchases. First among the reasons for buying an extra bond was to provide the soldiers with the money they needed to win the war. Stated in various ways, this reason accounted for somewhere between a half and two-thirds of all answers given when respondents were asked why the government wanted people to buy bonds.[86] Roughly 95 percent of bond buyers consistently specified throughout the war that they bought bonds for "patriotic" reasons—no great surprise. But what qualified as patriotic was revealing. Interviewers recorded that the most common of the patriotic reasons was "to pay for the war, to furnish the Government with money," a response accounting for a steady 50 percent of all patriotic reasons given during each drive study. Considering that respondents were allowed to give more than one reason for buying bonds, this was a remarkably high proportion.

The second most common patriotic reason for bond purchases, the generic "to win the war," grew in popularity toward the end of the war, when it was mentioned by almost half of all respondents; however, this reason understandably disappeared during the loan drive after the war. Fewer respondents said only "to help the government," which was mentioned in roughly 20 percent of all patriotic responses. A surprisingly low proportion said only "to help the boys," which accounted for approximately 30 percent of patriotic responses in the Fourth, Fifth and Sixth War Loan Drives. This pattern of response, which remained essentially constant throughout the war, suggested that citizens felt they were doing more than simply meeting their obligation to the government or even to the soldier; they felt they were personally helping to win the war. The infrequent mention of "patriotic duty" or idealistic phrases such as "to preserve the American way of life" most likely reflected a resistance to the banalities of wartime propaganda. Yet neither did bondholders buy their bonds simply "to get the war over sooner," the nonideological motivation many historians ascribe to civilian participation in the war effort: no more than 10 to 14 percent ever gave this reason.[87]

A related patriotic sensibility also guided taxpayers. Income taxes were not paid only because they were required by law, although that certainly set them apart from war bonds. They were accepted as legitimate by the vast majority of the population, even after most wage earners had begun feeling their bite. Starting in February 1943, the Gallup organization asked its respondents whether the amount of their income tax was fair, to which 86 percent of new and 84 percent of seasoned taxpayers said yes. The proportion who felt their income tax was fair actually increased as the war went on and taxes grew larger, reaching 90 percent by February 1944 and dipping only slightly to 85 percent in March 1945.[88] Much like enthusiasm for bonds, willingness to pay income taxes was a key "index of war-consciousness" that was high among citizens with strong morale, the OWI concluded, citing the common sentiment among such stalwarts that "folks at home should pay the taxes if the others do the fighting." Tellingly, the most common reason given by respondents for cashing in their bonds prematurely (a widely held taboo broken by a small proportion) was to pay income taxes. Cashing in bonds for other purchases was shunned, suggesting the moral valence the two fiscal obligations shared.[89]

Aggregate patterns of patriotic endorsement for bonds and income taxes indicated their importance, but such patterns could do no more than suggest *why* they were important. A key to their moral significance lay in the imaginative emphasis that Americans placed on the equipment their bonds and taxes would provide for soldiers in battle. Much like workers who identified with soldiers through the products of their work, bondholders and taxpayers imagined themselves as part of the national community fighting the war through a special form of consumption that "bought" equipment that was placed in the hands of the soldier.[90]

Equipment for the GI provided a satisfying representation of citizens' obligations. Consumers could easily adjust their patterns of shopping and spending to accommodate, by analogy, the purchase of a well-defined and tangible "product" such as a howitzer or even a tank. Most had never made a tax payment or bought a government security before Pearl Harbor, but the majority had purchased consumer durables ranging from electrical appliances to automobiles, often on credit or an installment plan whose arrangements resembled payroll withholding plans. With consumer credit restricted and durables in short supply due to the war economy, Americans flush with war wages turned their eyes to a more symbolic type of durable good, one that satisfied consumers' desires to buy into soaring dreams beyond their means.[91]

The Treasury accordingly worked the theme of equipment into as many promotions as possible. Bond drives and special promotions featured an ingenious array of equipment "sales" in which bond buyers could attach their purchases to a specific piece of matériel. Indeed, promotions featuring equipment were such a regular feature of the War Savings Staff's activities that it maintained an accurate price list of munitions, vehicles, vessels, and other matériel as a reference for the Special Events Division and the state committees. Large items, such as a bomber, could serve as a tangible quota that a war plant or community could try

The Treasury's strategy of tying bond sales to particular items needed for combat allowed bondholders to "buy" military equipment in place of the consumer durables on which they spent their disposable income in peacetime. (Courtesy of the National Archives Still Picture Records Section, ARC #513992)

to "buy" over the course of a drive. The small town of Windsor Locks, Connecticut, population 4,300, "bought" its own bomber during a forty-seven-day drive in early 1943 that netted more than $175,000. It was unusual for such a small town to make such a large "purchase," which was a more plausible goal for cities the size of El Paso, Texas, or Napa, California.[92] Students at Union

Endicott High School were electrified in December 1943 when school officials received an official press service wire describing how the "Endicott Special," an Airacobra fighter they had sponsored through bond purchases in the Schools at War program, had "bagged three bombers and a fighter on its maiden combat flight in the South Pacific." After praising the "grand little ship" the students had paid for, the captain proceeded to describe in satisfying detail the fighting that had downed the four "Jap planes." The news inspired the students to buy yet another fighter—their fourth—during a special holiday bond drive.[93]

This approach to setting drive quotas became quite popular, stoking competition between rival towns, local organizations, and even different shifts working in war plants. In May 1942, the Treasury found itself in the difficult position of having to explain an unfortunate navy policy to state sales organizations wanting to have their names affixed to large ships they had "bought" with bonds. Even if they could raise the bond sales commensurate with a $6.5 million submarine or a $65 million aircraft carrier, the navy would not release the name of a vessel until twenty-four hours prior to its launch. The Treasury devised a solution that allowed organizations to hang a plaque on the bow. Army policy likewise allowed "decalcomanias" to be affixed to mobile equipment such as tanks and jeeps that schools, towns, and organizations had "bought" with bonds.[94] Treasury research found that stoking competition through such concrete goals was an extremely effective sales technique employed in the war plants attaining the highest quotas.[95]

Individual bond buyers enjoyed an abundance of opportunities to "buy" equipment in a more personal fashion. Students could "adopt" a soldier by saving stamps toward bonds in amounts that would pay for his food, clothing, ammunition, or rifle, each of which could be displayed along with its price on a wall chart that fit nicely on a bulletin board.[96] For those adults who wanted their bonds literally to outfit a friend or relative in the service, the V-mail Christmas bond letter was a perfect opportunity. It proved so popular during the 1944 holiday season that Morgenthau ordered it to be made available year-round as a "V-mail gift certificate."[97] President Roosevelt, once again showing his finely tuned understanding of popular sensibilities, forwarded to Morgenthau a promotional idea to help civilians identify more directly with the machinery of war in April 1943. Why not follow the example of the British, the letter asked, and allow citizens to paste their war savings stamps directly onto bombs that would be dropped over Germany?[98]

The figurative provisioning of the combat soldier was more than just an extension of consumerism. It was also an atonement that partially redeemed, or at least distracted attention from, the drastically improved living standards most civilians enjoyed.[99] Even the payroll savings plan, a seemingly impersonal mechanism, could be used as a sales channel that released the mounting guilt and peer pressure. One Cleveland union member described for a Treasury-sponsored labor-management conference the approach he and his fellow unionists adopted to encourage the high levels of extra bond sales that distinguished their plant:

> The fellow would say he is a little bit hard up, he can't do it, and we would explain to him, not pressure, telling the fellow after all, you may have a son, you may have a nephew, may have a cousin or some of you a brother or even a sister that is going in as a nurse ... Supposing you were in there and you were on the other side of the continent and you had no material there, you had your heart and soul in the fighting and you actually didn't have anything there to help you fight along? Wouldn't you think to help your brothers and so forth that it would [not] be a bad idea if you did sign up and start sending out ammunition over there to those boys to see if they come back as soon as possible and then, in the long run, to be on the safe side, you could always have a nice little bank account when the war was over; not so much the bank account, but to get these boys over there a real help.[100]

Confronted with the mental image of a friend, neighbor, or family member facing the enemy without ammunition, fellow workers often found it impossible to refuse to sign the proffered card authorizing deductions for yet another bond. When the bond arrived at the plant, the volunteer sales person would present it to the buyer in person, reaffirming its moral and personal significance. For buyers who had spent 10 percent of their income in bond purchases, a "10%" button would further reinforce their identification with the war effort while instilling guilt in those who spent less. This "person-to-person, bench-to-bench canvass of every worker" was the most effective way to sell bonds to factory workers, but it could also be used to encourage taxpaying.[101] It was one of the first solutions that came to Morgenthau's mind when he learned that millions of taxpayers might default on their taxes out of confusion. Not only would having union people "going around asking others, 'Have you paid your taxes'" allow their locals to report to the Treasury the proportion of their membership planning to pay taxes, but, as a staffer suggested, it would be "the best kind of propaganda."[102]

Personal solicitation was an extraordinarily effective sales technique. It consistently produced purchase rates 200 to 400 percent higher than other approaches, such as advertising, and its persuasiveness persisted even after repeated appeals.[103] It was a specialized version of this personal approach that made the Kate Smith marathon broadcast in September 1943 so effective. The sociologist Robert Merton dissected Smith's guilt-inducing personal sales pitch in his landmark study of this marathon, *Mass Persuasion*. The central challenge for the war bond program, Merton's team of survey researchers found, was that to commit a new pledge, listeners needed a specific reason to act on the day of the broadcast. This reason had to resonate with their deepest feelings about the war and allow them to feel they personally were "buying our boys back," as Smith put it in the dramatic opening to her radio drive.[104]

Kate Smith provided that reason with her voice, the things she said and the way that she said them, the many overlapping reasons she gave for buying a bond, and her persona. She projected a matronly, patriotic image due to the popularity of her rendition of Irving Berlin's "God Bless America," which she belted out at great volume, aided by the heft of her decidedly unglamorous figure. In this respect she outdid even Betty Grable, the actress with the girl-next-door look whose wartime popularity helped motivate American men to serve their country.[105] Roughly 60 percent of the men and women interviewed for the Merton study identified Smith as their first choice of a celebrity to sell war bonds on the radio; Grable and Frank Sinatra tied for last place with 7 percent each.[106] "It's that plain ordinary way," explained one of the bond purchasers interviewed by Columbia University's Bureau of Applied Social Research. "She's just an ordinary person." Another interviewee implicitly damned much of the Treasury's publicity effort, observing: "There is really no one like her, there is no competition, none of these slim women or commentators."[107] Smith understood how to use her maternal image to induce a sense of guilt and obligation that would transmute simple self-interest into nationalistic identification. For the listeners gathered around the radio hearth, she provided a maternal counterpart to FDR's paternal presence.

Smith was able to assert her moral authority repeatedly to invoke the soldiers' "sacrifice"—and demand it of her listeners in the form of bond purchases—because she had "earned the right to utter" that sacred word, according to Merton. In contrast to the cheap blustering about sacrifice so often bandied about in the wartime consumer culture, her authentic patriotic style struck listeners as genuine, and thus legitimate.[108] Smith constantly drew listeners' attention to the men in combat who made "the supreme sacrifice." She pointedly relegated her own devoted exertions, and the "sacrifice" of the civilians who called in new pledges, to a lesser (if crucial) supporting role.

Merton termed this rhetorical strategy the "triangulation of sacrifice." It elicited a powerful guilt in uncommitted listeners because "only by matching the sacrifices of the other three"—the soldiers, Smith, and bond buyers who had already made a pledge—"could tension be relieved." One listener explained to Merton's team how she would have felt if she hadn't bought a bond from Smith:

> I would have felt just terrible. To tell you the truth, I would have
> borrowed the money if I hadn't had it. They (meaning the soldiers) do

really so much every little bit counts. And I really would have thought "Here she stands all day"—and the boys—they go through so much. (My daughter's intended husband, he was in the desert maneuvers and they didn't eat for three days—only drank cold water. He lost 30 pounds....) It wouldn't do them no good if we just feel sorry.[109]

No less than the listener's sense of honor was at stake. Accordingly, Smith mentioned nothing about the material rewards provided by investing in government bonds, a significant departure from the approach of most bond appeals. To do so would be to confuse the "profane" interests of ordinary life with the "sacred" matter of identifying with "the boys" fighting the war.[110] This decision turns out to have been astute. Only a small proportion of bond buyers (between 10 and 15 percent) surveyed in all of the Treasury's extensive research ever mentioned economic considerations as the most important reason for buying.[111]

Tax messages sought to invoke a similar dynamic of guilt, identification, and obligation. Celebrity gossip columnist Walter Winchell took to the airwaves just before the filing deadline in March 1943 to remind Americans of their duty:

> Attention Mr. and Mrs. United States . . . Your income tax blank is not a bill from your government. It is your share in America. Our nation is composed of one hundred and thirty million shareholders—shareholders in civilization. . . . Civilization, like money, must be earned. It is earned by men, not by dollars. Our civilization was earned at Bunker Hill, New Orleans, Gettysburg and the Argonne. It is being kept at Guadalcanal, New Guinea and Tunisia. Your tax dollars go to support what other Americans died to create. To those who complain that the tax is a heavy burden, remind them that a soldier's pack on his back weighs sixty pounds.[112]

President Franklin D. Roosevelt reminded his listeners later that year that "the money you lend and the money you give in taxes buys that death-dealing, and at the same time life-saving, power that we need for victory."[113] Supportive listeners appeared to embrace the message of the fireside chat for reasons similar to those motivating Smith's phone-in pledgers. A woman from Chicago responded to FDR's fireside chat in a letter: "Go ahead—tax us, take our cars for as long as they are needed, tax our payrolls, take bonds out of them, take the married men, or the eighteen-year-olds, or both! We are willing, nay—*eager* to sacrifice for good things. . . . Don't let us *down* by not *cracking down*."[114] Although few Americans were as gung-ho as this letter writer was, the letter does capture the importance of fairness and equality of sacrifice ("cracking down") to securing the legitimacy of mass income taxation.

Roosevelt astutely drove home the equality-of-sacrifice theme as early as 1942, when he pushed a popular labor proposal to cap annual wartime salaries at $25,000, with a 100 percent marginal tax rate above that level. The cap was ostensibly to curb inflation, but it mainly served to answer labor's demand that profits and salaries be limited along with industrial wages. Polls showed that the majority of Americans (64 percent in early 1942) endorsed this proposal—a likely reflection of old working-class suspicions of war profiteers, which predicated labor support for the war government on a symbolic, if not actual, equality of sacrifice.[115] Support for the tax drew on a mounting politics of class resentment dating back to the Wobblies and the populists. But the cap also reflected the seriousness with which many working-class Americans, recent participants in the mass income tax, viewed their obligations. A couple wrote to FDR after his fireside chat demanding he not allow the war to create "a flock of millionaires, as the last one did." "The people of this nation are *not* afraid of sacrifice," they asserted, "but that sacrifice *must be borne by all*."[116]

Labor editors, advising the OWI on working-class opinion, were even more vehement about the need for equality of sacrifice. "The cost of government should be born by those best able to afford it," wrote one typical labor editor in Detroit, advising the OWI on workers' feelings about a proposed national sales tax. "To tax the backs and stomachs of the common people while we are making a new group of millionaires hardly seems fair." Instead, he concluded, the government should tax industry's "excess profits" that in any event would only be used to fund a postwar "grab."[117] Another editor in St. Louis agreed, writing, "I believe that neither large incomes nor corporate profits have been taxed as much as they should be," an opinion he believed to be held by "literally everyone I have spoken to," whether unionist, businessman, or housewife.[118] This demand for class equity had mixed results. The salary cap never made it through Congress, but neither did a proposed excise tax that prompted outcry against its regressivity.

The Treasury's efforts to inculcate the obligations of fiscal citizenship through moral earmarking of income unintentionally fostered a sense of entitlement that placed firm limits on what could be accomplished through either bondholding or income taxation.[119] By touting bond purchases and tax payments as necessary to preserve the high standard of living so central to the "American way of life," the Treasury inadvertently fostered expectations of economic security, even prosperity, that formed a boundary to the sorts of sacrifices ordinary Americans were willing to make.[120] This boundary could be seen in the ways most bond buyers and taxpayers misunderstood the anti-inflationary purposes of their transactions with the fiscal state. Early in the war OWI and Treasury research had discovered that most citizens, even the very educated, were thoroughly confused about inflation and their personal contribution to it.[121] After more than three years of propaganda touting the benefits of socking away money in bonds where it couldn't push up prices, preventing inflation still only accounted for just under 20 percent of all reasons respondents gave for buying bonds during the Sixth War Loan Drive in 1944. The proportion would remain the same until the war's end.[122] A similar confusion beset taxpayers. Among even the most educated, only a minority understood how their personal taxes helped dampen inflation.[123]

The failure to appreciate the value of bond purchases in fighting inflation might not have mattered if bond buyers had simply accepted the Treasury's line that they should be "buying bonds and more bonds" until they had committed all discretionary income to the war effort. But consumers did not obey this dictum. The burgeoning inflationary gap they produced represented purchases that would not have occurred if consumers had accepted the Treasury's zero-sum logic of sacrifice.[124]

Civilians bought bonds when they felt they could afford them, which depended on their perceptions of basic economic factors such as wages, the cost of living, and government controls. These perceptions had mostly to do with the way people felt about the "fairness" of their economic fates, which in turn reflected how much they had prospered because of the war economy. The mobilization had lifted the horizons of most labor-force participants, fostering a mounting sense of entitlement to a government-sanctioned American standard of living. These expectations were encouraged by the very language and imagery of war propaganda—most notably by FDR's 1944 proposal for an Economic Bill of Rights, which promised a "fair and stable economy" designed for "winning a lasting peace" and establishing "an American standard of living higher than ever known before."[125]

The willingness to buy extra bonds thus depended heavily on an individual's success in the war economy. One Treasury study in the late spring of 1943 showed that more than 55 percent of household heads earning $46 per week or more—the approximate boundary between good factory jobs in war industries and less desirable work—reported devoting at least 6 percent of their income to bond purchases. Those earning less bought bonds at lower rates and with less regularity. The differences in commitment became even starker when respondents were grouped according to whether their incomes had increased in the previous year, regardless of absolute pay: 51 percent of those who said their finances had improved devoted a steady 6 percent of their income or more to war bonds, while 38 percent whose finances were the "same" and 26 percent of those whose finances were "worse" reported making the same commitment. An even sharper division separated war workers—62 percent of whom devoted 6 percent or more of their regular pay to bonds—from other civilian workers, of whom 31 percent made the same regular purchases.[126] In the differentials of these patterns may be discerned both the uneven paychecks and the uneasy consciences of civilians swept forward by the war economy.

For those whose standard of living was less secure, fiscal citizenship could also foster uncertainty, suspicion, and resentment, which further limited acceptance of anti-inflationary measures. Those predisposed to skepticism suspected that all the talk about combating inflation was just another way to put the burden of the war on their shoulders. As a worker in Seattle explained to a Treasury interviewer regarding his reasons for not buying more bonds:

> One of the reasons they try to get people to buy bonds is so we won't have inflation; well, that's the same reason they give for not raising our wages. If you want to really know how I look at it, I just figure that the raise they didn't give us is the bonds I'm buying.[127]

Such complaints did not, in the main, represent a rejection of the fundamental legitimacy of war bonds, as citizens' actual behavior and more general attitudes testified. Indeed, factory workers as a group purchased bonds at the highest rate, spending an average 11 percent of their wages on them by December 1944.[128] People of even more modest means, earning as little as $25 a week, made extraordinary efforts to buy bonds with what little money they had, and looked on their bonds "almost as sacred items."[129]

Standard of living also provided a boundary to obligation at the other end of the income spectrum, as one of Merton's respondents who didn't buy a bond from Kate Smith explained:

> Since I had already purchased as many bonds as our family could afford, I felt no OBLIGATION to make a response to her appeal. . . . I had heard other appeals for pledges—doing without that extra fur coat or not taking that extra trip, but putting your money into bonds. And since I wasn't going to buy any luxuries which were not essential in any case and since I had bought and was buying all the bonds which I could afford which represented for our family a taking up of the slack between what we had to have and what we wanted, I didn't feel like telephoning her.[130]

Despite her decision not to buy, and her indifference to Smith as a radio personality, this woman displayed a defensiveness that revealed how even the unpersuaded recognized the moral claim of patriotic obligation. "I've always felt a bit ashamed because we weren't buying more bonds," she admitted later in the interview. "You hear of workers buying a bond every week, yet we buy only a bond a month." Her guilt notwithstanding, she held off because "I felt I had done all I could do."[131] In this regard she was like most bond buyers, who felt their obligation to buy bonds should not threaten their standard of living.

The heart of the inflation control problem lay in what one 1942 report termed the "spending as usual mentality." When probed, nearly all respondents indicated they would curb their consumption only "after a certain level of living has been satisfied," well above basic necessity. Only 14 percent of all respondents said they would cut their spending habits during the war. It was a question of maintaining "adequate" living standards: 65 percent expected that their standard of living would not drop significantly, if at all. Those in the top income brackets intended to preserve their high standard of living, and accordingly limited their bond purchases to 10 percent of their incomes, the proportion often specified in Treasury messages. Middle-income families felt that their quality of life demanded that they pay off debt and purchase long-deferred items, and so such families often found themselves torn between spending and saving because, as one OWI interviewee put it, "there is more to lose—things like electric refrigerators and automobiles, and T-bone steaks have become necessities, and the threat of losing them is a serious one."[132]

Locking in Mass Participation for Military Keynesianism

By the time of Kate Smith's marathon broadcast in September 1943, bond buying and taxpaying were stabilizing into patterns that would last the duration of the war. The Third Loan Drive held that fall sold more than fifty million E bonds, worth nearly $2.5 billion. Subsequent drives in 1944 and 1945 would sell somewhere in the range of fifty million to seventy million bonds and raise between $3 and $4 billion each. By that time nearly all industrial workers had a regular portion of their pay withheld automatically to purchase war bonds and pay a regular increment of their income taxes.[133] More than forty million citizens had paid income taxes the previous spring, and roughly that many would continue to do so until end of the war. Attitudes toward bond buying and taxpaying were likewise stabilizing into coherent patterns that would prevail from late 1943 until the summer of 1945, patterns that reflected the underlying meanings citizens attributed to these transactions. Right until the end of the war, bond buyers and taxpayers visualized themselves lending aid directly to soldiers through their contributions to the moral economy of the war.

With the war's end in August 1945, ordinary citizens almost immediately altered their patterns of bondholding and purchasing, buying far fewer new bonds and for the first time cashing in old bonds at significantly higher rates. Loan drives, always the most sensitive register of fluctuating citizen morale and identification with the war effort, revealed the shift most clearly. The Seventh War Loan Drive had tallied the highest E-series sales of all the wartime drives, bringing in just under $4 billion in the late spring and summer of 1945, despite the fact that American prospects for victory were better than they had ever been, with Germany defeated and Japanese forces on the run. Just four months later, however, the Victory loan drive yielded only half the amount of its predecessor; at $2.2 billion, it was the least successful drive since the early days of the war loan program.[134] With Japan defeated, fears of unemployment returning, and most wartime controls lifted or about to be lifted—including rationing and price controls, which most recognized as essential to containing the cost of living—it is not surprising that Americans in November 1945 should have cut back on their bond purchases in order to keep liquid a maximum amount of disposable income.

Total E bond sales would continue to decline dramatically through the end of the decade, regardless of the fluctuating state of the economy. After a wartime peak of $11.8 billion in 1944, followed by a slightly lower total of $11.6 billion in 1945, E bond sales dropped sharply to $6.7 billion in 1946, finally bottoming out in 1947 at around $4.3 billion. Adjusted for inflation, annual sales had by 1948 declined to roughly a fourth of what had been accomplished during the peak wartime years of 1944 and 1945. Where E sales had amounted to 5.6 percent of the roaring GNP in 1944, they consumed little more than 1.6 percent of the more attenuated peacetime GNP in 1948. Not only did the total amount of money invested in Treasury savings bonds decline, but the unit volume of sales dropped even more dramatically to roughly a fifth of its wartime peak, from 305,986 E bond issues in 1944 to 64,304 in 1950, so the size of the average E bond purchase rose sharply in a few years, from $38.63 in 1944 to $68.27 in 1948. This was a 30 percent increase after inflation.[135]

The reasons bondholders gave for buying bonds also shifted, starting with the highly successful Seventh War Loan Drive in the summer of 1945. The proportion who said they bought bonds for patriotic reasons remained roughly the same as it had been for drives in the previous two years, at 93 percent. But the types of patriotic motivations had changed. The proportion saying they bought bonds to "help the boys" or "buy equipment" dropped from 27 and 26 percent to 17 and 19 percent, while other reasons rose a few percentage points. The big break in bond buyer motivation came with the Victory Drive, in November and December 1945, which attracted just half of the sales of its predecessor in the previous summer. Over 30 percent of bondholders from the Victory Drive said they bought bonds to bring the boys back, 17 percent said "to help the boys," and 8 percent said "to provide for veterans, widows' pensions, [or the] G.I. Bill." A large proportion, 17 percent, said they bought bonds "to provide medical care [or] hospitalization," while for the first time more than 10 percent gave no patriotic reason at all.[136] The concrete connection between bonds and battle was ebbing, while economic conditions deteriorated at home.

Within a year of V-J Day, bond redemption rates shot up to 82 percent of current bond sales, while the Bureau of Internal Revenue announced that tax evasion had peaked at $3 billion a year. In 1947, with bondholders cashing in $4.4 billion worth of previously purchased bonds, the redemption rate for war savings bonds ranged from 65 percent for the popular $25 issues to 54 percent for $50 issues. The small-denomination savings bond was quickly and rather unceremoniously dropping out of popular currency, for not only were redemptions concentrated among small-denomination E bonds, but also new sales tended toward high-denomination E bonds, as well as the larger issues of the F and G series. By the eve of the Korean War, far fewer Americans were buying bonds, and they were making much larger consumer purchases than had been the case when bonds were considered a universal obligation.[137] The great majority (well over 80 percent) of respondents surveyed at the behest of the Treasury in 1948 and 1949 said they did not purchase bonds, whether they had been exposed to bond advertisements or not.[138]

As moral suasion and patriotic appeals rapidly lost their effectiveness, the Treasury shifted back to its earlier reliance on a small number of relatively wealthy investors and institutions to finance the federal debt. Immediately following the Victory Drive, the War Finance Division was reorganized and drastically cut back, while sales promotion efforts ceased. Treasury appeals, to the extent that they still reached the public at all, stressed themes that must have seemed a dim echo of the war campaigns: self-betterment through financial gain; patriotism by fighting inflation and curbing spending; planning for impending recession; and a democratic distribution of the public debt.[139] Meanwhile, the Bureau of Internal Revenue adopted a desperate publicity campaign that dramatized the travails of ordinary "tax cheats," who invariably ended up in jail, as a way to bluff the taxpaying public into overlooking its inadequate enforcement staff.[140]

Yet even after the savings bond program shifted away from the astronomical levels of popular participation in World War II, the war continued to leave its mark. Savings bond sales were still high at $5 billion in 1949, a twenty-five-fold increase over the $200 million invested in savings bonds during 1941, largely due to the Treasury's continued reliance on the payroll plan.[141] Mass taxation also remained in place, despite its more tenuous status in demobilization. Federal income tax payers never fell far below 60 percent of the labor force, nor did income tax receipts fall much below 8 percent of personal income after the war—levels that were at least four or five times higher than interwar levels. (See Charts A.5 and A.6.) Voters accepted that major postwar commitments, such as the military occupation and reconstruction of Japan and Germany, European food relief, and Marshall Plan aid, all precluded fiscal retrenchment, Republican platforms notwithstanding. The egalitarian ethos instilled by war finance may also help explain the new tax regime's durability. The distinctive progressivity of the tax structure may have retarded welfare expenditure by alienating policy-influencing elites, as some scholars have suggested, but it also helped ensure the popular legitimacy of the mass fiscal citizenship on which postwar government rested.[142]

The revival of national security concerns in the late 1940s reawakened fiscal citizenship. At the height of the Korean War, in June 1951, half of all respondents to a study by the Survey Research Center at the University of Michigan reported owning at least some bonds—not quite as dramatic as the track record established in World War II, but impressive nonetheless.[143] Within a few years, the wartime tax structure was placed on a permanent footing with the tax code enacted in 1954.

Between World War II and the Korean War, mass taxation came under political strain, while popular ownership of the national debt waned but did not disappear. But the central supports for a fiscal regime capable of sustaining the unlimited mobilization for which National Security Council Directive 68 called in 1950 remained in place long enough for the Cold War to revive the cultural logic on which mass fiscal citizenship rested.

5

Work or Fight

Toward winter's end in early 1944, a newsreel appeared in theaters around the nation bearing good tidings: "New ships bring U.S. Navy to twice pre-war strength." The clip opened with a sweeping shot of the launching of the aircraft carrier *Ticonderoga*, the sixty-fifth carrier added to the fleet since the beginning of the war. Slowly the camera followed the line of the massive prow up from the water, letting the viewer take in the sweeping, monolithic balance of the ship's hull. Finally the decks flanged out far overhead, and with the full immensity of the vessel arrayed before the viewer, the carrier slipped backward into the water of the launch. It was an awesome sight, suggesting in one visual moment the limitless industrial might of the nation.

Suddenly the scene cut away to newly released footage of the U.S. invasion of the Marshall Islands by "the most powerful navy task force ever assembled." As battles near Kwajalein raged onscreen in a shuddering, sea-swept collage of shell-rocked destroyers and tracer bullets streaking through steaming chaos, the narrator informed the viewer that American forces had blasted the islands with fifteen thousand tons of bombs and shells over the previous two months. In three minutes the viewer had been transported from the cathedral-like austerity of the shipyards, teeming with the power to make massive vessels of war on record-breaking schedules, into the maw of a Pacific hell that swallowed men and machines almost as quickly as they could be produced.[1]

In the eyes of industrial workers, images such as these, released by the federal government to buoy their morale, powerfully affirmed the significance of their daily contributions to the war effort. They had "enlisted" to win the "battle for production," a heroic undertaking that transformed hard, tedious work into patriotic productivity vital to winning the war. Workers conceptualized their involvement in the war by tracing connections between their personal efforts and the fighting overseas. Many worked in shops that produced munitions, military vehicles, and other equipment used on the battlefield, while most others could draw some connection between their jobs and the making of war matériel. Despite this easy source of identification, the ultimate usefulness of a particular factory job was often obscure, and always too many steps removed from the actual fighting to satisfy fully the urgent wartime need for patriotic display.

A real-life scene from the Kaiser shipyards in Richmond, California, recorded earlier in the war by an OWI field worker, laid bare the complex feelings produced by workers' identification with the war effort. In its externals the event was almost identical to the ship launches and other scenes of heroic producerism depicted in the many newsreels that bombarded movie-going audiences during the war:

> The crowd on the launching platform was made up of workers off duty, their wives, children and friends. It was a group of homely people, quiet, though excited and deeply thrilled in anticipation. About five minutes to six, the launching time, workers on ships in the ways on each side of the completed hull, crowded to the sides of their ship to see her slide away. Feeling was intense, yet there was no shouting or clapping, only a deep silence, as she hit the water, flags flying. Not one person in my hearing spoke of the ship's ultimate mission. The feeling was for the ship herself. However, this aspect of shipbuilding is not overlooked by the workers. One . . . said: "I wish we could know how many times our ships, the ones *we* build, make it across and where they go."[2]

This yearning for a connection between ordinary industrial work and the historic battles raging on distant seas lent a bittersweet edge to workers' identification with the war effort. It seemed that war workers were perpetually being scrutinized for every conceivable aspect of their lives—the high wages they earned, the hours of overtime they logged, the regularity of their work habits, their lifestyle and consumer choices. Everything they did was measured against the idealized sacrifice of the combat soldier. Yet they could look back at the end of the day and form a concrete picture of exactly what they had produced for victory.

Caught between guilt and pride, obligation and entitlement, workers looked to the federal government to protect the vague but resonant rights they felt they had earned as partners in the battle for production. For most workers during and immediately after the war, these expectations were indistinct, concerned mostly with improving the personal opportunity that had opened so drastically with the booming war economy. Increasingly, they came to see the federal government as a source of leverage in taking hold of this opportunity and protecting its corollary, a secure standard of living.

The pervasive rhetoric employed by federal officials encouraged ordinary workers to think of themselves as "soldiers of production," entitled to a higher standard of treatment due to the moral bonds tying them to the war effort, the soldier, and the nation through virtuous work. Yet the same enframing of war work restricted workers' assertiveness, casting it as near-treasonous subversion of the soldier's sacrifice. The conflict between the worker's pursuit of private gain within the labor market (what he or she ought to receive as compensation) and his or her public obligations as a citizen (how he or she ought to carry out the basic duty to work) required a balance of rights and obligations. The cultural work of this contest over the claims of war workers would shape their prospects for social citizenship during the war and in the decades afterward.[3]

Whether they viewed the product of their labor in movie theaters or in their neighborhood war plant, workers saw arrayed before them concrete proof that they were indeed soldiers of production whose efforts were second only to those of the combat soldier. The pride swelling within their hearts derived from a feeling of moral authority and worth as Americans and as citizens. Yet even as their participation in war production established the centrality of their labor to the moral economy of the war, and thus emboldened them to expect a greater degree of security and opportunity than had been the case before the war, war workers met with rising hostility as the war progressed. It was precisely this rising sense of entitlement, and the aggressiveness with which workers made their claims in the workplace, that alienated public sympathy for labor by the end of the war, inflaming class resentments and ultimately threatening workers' ability to assert their claims on the federal government.

The Wartime Labor Regime

War workers held jobs whose wages, work conditions, and job classifications were subject to the authority of an overlapping set of agencies. The National War Labor Board (NWLB) was charged with resolving labor disputes and stabilizing wages. The War Manpower Commission (WMC), together with the United States Employment Service (USES), sought to match available workers to the war jobs for which they were best suited. The Fair Employment Practices Commission (FEPC) investigated discriminatory hiring and employment practices among firms with war contracts.[4] The degree to which these agencies penetrated the workplace was unprecedented, even when compared with the presence of the National Labor Relations Board (NLRB), authorized by the Wagner Act in 1935. Before 1941, the NLRB had simply certified elections for bargaining agents, leaving the work of enforcing federal standards to those unions whose militancy was sufficient to hold employers' feet to the fire. Similarly, wage and hour standards guaranteed by the Fair Labor Standards Act (FLSA) of 1938 were not vigorously enforced in the first few years, but the need to guarantee full production and the third shift made overtime work and overtime pay a problem to be managed carefully by tripartite factory boards.

Government regulation of the workplace affected workers' personal lives directly. The increasingly egalitarian wage structure was partly influenced by the NWLB, whose rulings on wage stabilization tended to restrain increases for high-wage jobs, while allowing wage rate adjustments for groups of workers deemed to have substandard wages. Roughly 15 million of the 17 million industrial workers and 17 million of the 28 million nonindustrial employees in the civilian labor force worked at jobs whose wages were subject to NWLB wage stabilization. Over the course of the war the NWLB ruled on nearly half a million voluntary wage adjustment requests affecting 26.1 million employees. In roughly the same period it issued directive orders or otherwise closed 17,650 labor disputes, 83 percent of which concerned wages and affected the livelihoods of more than 10 million workers. It was nearly impossible to work at a war job in which wages were not somehow controlled by the federal government.

The increasingly global application of NWLB rules became a sore point for industrial workers after July 1942, when the board adopted the "Little Steel formula," named after a wage settlement for employees of the independent Bethlehem, Republic, Youngstown, and Inland steel companies. This formula limited wage increases to 15 percent above levels that had prevailed in January 1941. As prices continued to rise sharply until effective price controls took effect nearly a year later, workers grew increasingly restive and began to protest in wildcat strikes.[5]

Just as critical to workers' opportunity was their ability to leave their jobs for new positions with better conditions and higher pay. War workers quit their jobs in West Coast airplane factories at such a rate that by 1943 some plants were able to retain only 60 percent of their workers over a one-year period. Factory workers outside the war industries were even less likely to stay put, quitting at rates 29 percent higher than those for war workers by 1944. In war centers such as Los Angeles, Detroit, and the San Francisco Bay area, the situation quickly became desperate for employers, who sent recruiting agents to distant states in search of new workers.[6]

While such churning mobility was a boon to workers, it posed severe problems for military production schedules. The WMC sought to limit this turnover and adjust labor supply to the needs of war industries by arranging more than thirty-five million job placements through the USES over the course of the war. Starting in the fall of 1942, the WMC worked with employers to create "employee stabilization plans" for major industrial centers, which controlled referrals for workers seeking to enter or leave essential industrial jobs. By September 1944 the WMC plans determined the hiring and firing practices for 4.6 million essential war workers living in seventy-eight centers of war industry around the country, and by August of that year the plans' coverage extended nationwide. In addition to setting the basic terms for movement between industrial jobs, the WMC coordinated more than two million interstate job transfers and located positions for two million veterans.[7]

In an effort to stabilize the workforce for maximum production, both the NWLB and WMC rulings touched on long-standing inequities within the workplace. On November 24, 1942, the NWLB adopted Order No. 16, which ruled that there should be no difference in pay for men and women performing the same work. For the remainder of the war this principle of equal pay for equal work guided its decisions. Around the same time, the WMC also issued guidelines instructing employers to train and hire women without discrimination. Government officials endorsed the policy on equal treatment, as secretary of war Henry Stimson did by issuing a pamphlet titled *You're Going to Employ Women*. At the same time the OWI worked with government agencies and private advertisers to promote its "womanpower" campaign, which stressed the ability of women to do men's work—for the duration.[8]

In June 1943 the NWLB ruled against race-based wage differentials. Thereafter it would apply (with limited success) the principle of equal pay for equal work to cases involving racial discrimination in hiring and employment. WMC head Paul McNutt made public pronouncements against "our greatest waste," prejudice in the workplace. He frequently issued supportive statements to the black press and denounced discrimination as "a threat to the lives of American soldiers" in newsreels that were distributed across the country. As with gender-based discrimination, the WMC exhorted employers to abandon racially exclusive employment practices. For nearly a year, between the summer of 1942 and the spring of 1943, the WMC absorbed the FEPC, which was charged with investigating racial discrimination among employers receiving war contracts. This move ostensibly was made to increase the effectiveness of Executive Order 8802, which had prohibited racial discrimination in government employment and authorized the creation of the FEPC a year earlier. By September 1943 the WMC had issued a policy directive prohibiting local USES offices from making racially biased job referrals.[9]

These high profile federal policies did little to improve the lot of women and minorities, however. Because the NWLB's rulings only *authorized* the equalization of wages, rather than enforcing it, they resulted in a mere handful of voluntary wage adjustments by employers. As late as January 1944, no more than sixty thousand women enjoyed wage increases as a direct result of NWLB rulings. The federal government could not even rely on its own field representatives to carry out its policies. Local USES offices, especially those in the South, continued to fill race-based job positions submitted by employers even after being explicitly prohibited from doing so by the national WMC office. Even the national office fell short of its own high standards, as demonstrated by the complete cessation of FEPC hearings during its months under WMC control. Even without these hesitations and evasions by the government, unions and employers could easily circumvent federal policies by creating new job classifications and separate union locals for female and black employees, or by hiring outside the factory gates rather than in USES offices.

A lack of state capacity and a failure of political will lay at the heart of the federal government's inability to directly alter racial and gender inequities in the workplace. It is true that the civilian agencies charged with managing the labor force extended well beyond the reach of their World War I and New Deal predecessors: at its peak the NWLB employed 2,613 full-time staff in Washington and the field, and the WMC relied on 1,500 local USES offices. But these civilian agencies lacked the enforcement power needed to compel significant change in long-standing employment practices. If an employer or union chose to ignore such rulings, there was not much the WLB or WMC could do about it, since military procurement officers were unlikely to cancel or even suspend contracts to discipline recalcitrant firms. When the FEPC singled out twenty companies and seven unions as especially egregious and ordered them to cease discrimination in September 1943, sixteen of the companies and three of the unions refused outright, claiming that to do so would undermine worker morale and upset production. None of the companies or unions was ever punished for its transgressions.[10]

The FEPC and other federal agencies pursued racial policies largely according to strategic considerations intended to protect vital war production, concentrating efforts to redress racial discrimination in the industrial centers of the North and West, where industry most desperately needed to attract and retain employees. In the South, home to relatively little war industry but as much as two-thirds of the black labor force, fair employment policies took a backseat to other priorities, such as the army's concern that its many southern camps and bases not be disrupted by racial conflict. Where concentrations of southern industry did pose a vital concern, regional mores and political considerations trumped the limited influence the FEPC and WMC were able to exert elsewhere. This reality was clearly exposed when the yards of the Alabama Dry Dock and Shipbuilding Company in Mobile exploded into a race riot on the morning of May 25, 1943, in reaction to the management's sudden decision to integrate a welding crew with twelve black workers. To quell the unrest, four segregated work areas were created for the welders, a solution that revealed the severe limitations of fair employment policy when put to the test.[11]

Despite the limitations of the government's efforts, its broader intervention in the economy brought booming growth and demand for labor that accomplished the equalization it could not engineer in the workplace. Workers took full part in the rising prosperity of the war mobilization, enjoying an unprecedented share of the material benefits that the boom made possible. Basic wage rates for all workers in manufacturing industries rose by 24 percent between January 1941, when American industry had just begun its recovery, and July 1945, when war production entered its final phases. For urban workers the increase was even greater, 32.4 percent. But ceilings set by the federal government in its efforts to contain inflation restrained wages. Consequently, wage rate increases actually fell somewhat behind the rising cost of living, which jumped by 33.3 percent during the same period. Fortunately for workers, full production allowed them to work overtime, raising total earnings, if not wages. As a result, gross weekly earnings for workers in manufacturing increased by 70.5 percent, an improvement of 35 percent after inflation.[12] While this average obscures important differences in pay across industries, even workers with relatively low prewar pay scales enjoyed advances.[13]

By the time the war economy had reached its feverish extremes in 1943 and 1944, nearly all groups of American workers had reason to raise their expectations of what they could expect from their jobs. Black workers improved their economic standing relative to whites, entering higher paying manual work as well as some semiskilled and skilled positions that had never before been open to them. Women also assumed new roles and a new status in the factory by demonstrating that they could do much of what had been assumed to be men's work, even if their pay increased less rapidly than that of their male coworkers and their occupational mobility within industry was limited. Differences among white men also decreased, shrinking long-standing distances between skill levels, pay scales, and the ethnic boundaries that often reinforced occupational stratification. The combined influences of patriotism and rising egalitarianism among white ethnic workers, most of whom were male, produced during the war a distinctive feeling of common Americanness and working-class identity. If this new bond came at the cost of excluding women and racial minorities from its virtuous circle of masculine producerism and whiteness, it also prompted those who were excluded to use their own wartime advances as grounds to hope for an Americanism that would include them. The federal government, which stood at the center of all this change, provided a target of national identification on which these expectations could converge—and clash.[14]

The Arsenal of Democracy and the Ideology of Production

Above the din of the vast reshuffling of the labor force caused by the war mobilization, public leaders raised their voices to proclaim the meaning of war production. Military and civilian agencies, private industry, unions, and independent organizations all created propaganda that saturated the work-place with messages exalting the patriotic virtues of production, often imbuing the minutest aspects of workers' daily toil with deep significance. A variant of the rhetoric used to justify other obligations of wartime citizenship, such as buying bonds or obeying rationing restrictions, producerist propaganda encouraged patriotic citizens to embrace war work as their personal obligation to the combat soldier.

These appeals promoted a civic vision of work as democratic practice, emphasizing teamwork and cooperation to "get the job done," but the reality on the shop floor fell far short of this idealized vision. Workers mounted wild-cat strikes to protest poor working conditions and inadequate wages, and union leaders struggled with company officials and their own members to control hiring and other aspects of war work, while managers preserved their prerogative to control the production line during the war, backed by military procurement officials and civilian administrators nervous about disrupting production.[15] Even so, government-sanctioned representations of industrial work helped raise expectations about rights in the workplace by portraying it as a cooperative enterprise in which workers' contributions were tantamount to military service.

The production-oriented sensibility of workplace propaganda harked back to nineteenth-century ideals that identified producerism as a citizenly virtue fundamental to American independence.[16] Heroic depictions of production touched a deep chord, lending patriotic meaning and purpose to industrial work and tying workers' self-image to the government. The muscular worker straining bare-chested at the forge, Rosie the Riveter cocking her arm in determined confidence, the tireless production line workers turning out more and more—these and other images played on the "working-class Americanism" that emerged in these years.[17] If the combat soldier was the ultimate culture hero of the war years, then the soldier of production was his working-class helpmeet, a lesser but still central character in the national dramaturgy of sacrifice.

Roosevelt set the tone for these appeals, much as he set the tone and provided the imagery for wartime propaganda in general. From his very first efforts to articulate a vision of American involvement in the war, he highlighted the centrality of production, and the special status it conferred upon workers, in his widely remembered "arsenal of democracy" speech. After Pearl Harbor he declared to his radio audience that "ever-increasing," "quadrupled" production would be "the yardstick by which we measure what we shall need and demand." The "grueling work" ahead was not a sacrifice, he explained, but a privilege to be embraced by soldier and civilian in "working longer or harder at the task for which he is best fitted." With American entry into the war, the worker's charge had shifted to less abstractly ideological grounds, from provisioning the imperiled democracies of the world to backing American troops with vital production. "The lives of our soldiers and sailors—the whole future of this nation—depend upon the manner in which each and every one of us fulfills his obligation to our country."[18]

In fireside chats, Roosevelt returned repeatedly to the theme of sacrifice as a privilege whose value began with the soldier's service to his country and spread out in egalitarian fashion to encompass concentric rings of citizens doing their part for victory. In FDR's widely heard fireside chat of April 28, 1942, which reached 70 percent of urban households, he traced out the chain of national merit explicitly:

> Not all of us can have the privilege of fighting our enemies in distant parts of the world.
>
> Not all of us can have the privilege of working in a munitions factory or a shipyard, or on the farms or in the oil fields or mines, producing the weapons or the raw materials that are needed by our armed forces.
>
> But there is one front and one battle where everyone in the United States—every man, woman, and child—is in action, and will be privileged to remain in action throughout this war. That front is right here at home, in our daily lives, in our daily tasks.[19]

Roosevelt prodded his listeners' consciences with concrete examples that they could not help taking personally. The rhetorical device he employed was the visualization of a moral exchange: a wartime social compact between the soldier, offering the nation a sacred sacrifice, and the civilian, who reciprocated with a commitment to personal sacrifice in support of the soldier. The most effective way to cement this identification for workers was to trace the repercussions of workplace activities to the battlefield, where missed production quotas translated into casualty lists.

In late February 1942, the president took to the air to combat a pervasive sense of defeatism that had settled in due to the early, grim defeats in the Philippines. With a rallying cry for "production—uninterrupted production" (a phrase he repeated spontaneously for emphasis), the president made his charge to war workers:

> We are coming to realize that one extra plane or extra tank or extra gun or extra ship completed tomorrow may, in a few months, turn the tide on some distant battlefield; it may make the difference between life and death for some of our own fighting men.

Accordingly, he proceeded to enumerate "three high purposes for every American," the first of which he aimed directly at workers: "We shall not stop work for a single day. If any dispute arises we shall keep on working while the dispute is solved by mediation or conciliation, or arbitration—until the war is won."[20]

Propagandists picked up on Roosevelt's lead and made heroic production a central theme of their messages. The War Production Board as well as the army and navy worked out an arrangement with the small Art Pool within the OWI, which in turn arranged for graphic artists and other talent working in private industry to produce posters for specific government campaigns. Many of the same graphic artists, and their colleagues in corporate industrial relations departments, also produced posters directly for private industry. Despite this assistance, the production agencies in charge of managing the war economy lacked the marketing savvy and volunteer professional assistance lavished on the Treasury, and consequently tended to produce messages that translated the worker's obligation to the soldier in rather crude terms.

Production agencies were mostly interested in placing "production incentive" messages in factories where they were likely to affect workers' productivity directly. Private firms, whether they created posters for their own factories or collaborated with trade organizations to produce posters for public consumption, used such messages to discipline, or at least intimidate, a workforce grown unruly in boom times. Despite their diverse origins and purposes, most government and private posters designed for workers shared the underlying theme of a direct, personal connection between the worker, often portrayed as or labeled a "soldier of production," and the combat soldier. They also revealed the influence of OWI guidelines, which listed production and the need to work harder as one of the six main themes to emphasize in posters.[21]

Production posters had an extremely wide audience, one of the broadest enjoyed by any single channel of propaganda. As early as August 1942, more than 90 percent of war workers in one OWI study mentioned posters when asked about which production incentives they had experienced. None of the other production incentives—pep talks, bonuses, competitions, piece rates, or even the Navy E Award for excellence in production—was mentioned by more than roughly a third of respondents. A large majority of workers said they thought posters were an effective incentive to increased production.[22]

Just a few years earlier, workers' most vivid images of military men would have been of the national guardsmen and infantrymen who were sometimes sent to dispatch strikers. As recently as June 1941, 2,500 national guardsmen had been called by the president to break a strike against the aircraft manufacturer North American Aviation.[23] Industrial relations departments, labor-management committees, and government agencies symbolically redirected working-class aggression away from class conflict and toward nationalistic cooperation to fell the Axis powers. The War Department's 1943 poster "Your Ore Packs a Punch!"—printed in the year when the United Mine Workers' leader, John L. Lewis, would defy the no-strike pledge and lead his unionists in months of strikes—exemplified this transfer of aggression. In it, a white-haired unionist crouched by his radio in an animated boxer's stance, exclaiming "Atta boy! That's the ore we mined and smelted—*smackin' 'em!*" while news that "American tanks hit the Nazis a terrific blow today" blared from the set.[24] An Army Ordnance Corps poster from 1942, "Do It Right: Make It Bite," encouraged workers to channel stereotyped aggressions into war work. In it, a war worker flexed his muscle and released his spite as he tightened the head of an anti-aircraft shell. Superimposed over his image, a Nazi airplane crashed to the earth in a trajectory that followed his arm's violent downward movement.[25] Such images recast the shopworn iconography of the worker's clenched fist, bulging muscles and bellicose glare to represent national unity.[26]

In cementing the identification of workers with soldiers, it helped that production, like fighting, had long been understood to be a masculine activity. The continuing relevance of the image of the manly worker could be seen in the poster "Get Hot—Keep Moving," which featured a muscular, bare-chested man stoking a furnace beside the caption "Don't waste a precious minute."[27] The workers portrayed in the 1942 Army Ordnance Corps poster "Keep 'Em Coming" carried artillery shells as if they were rifles and marched forward in a straight line with an unmistakably martial bearing.[28] They man-handled the munitions with the same confidence and virility as the shirtless sailor in the 1942 navy recruitment poster "Man the Guns" or the bare-chested sailor in "Keep 'Em Fighting," whose subtitle reminded workers to stop accidents, which might impede the production that "wins wars."[29] The hypermasculine pose depicted in all three posters reflected the gender bias of producerism. Even Rosie the Riveter had to show some muscle to be a convincing soldier of production—at least in the eyes of middle-class women—although signs of her strength were usually softened by reassuring indications of an underlying femininity.[30]

Posters in this vein often suggested that workers and soldiers were simply men in different uniforms fighting the same battle on two fronts. One way to suggest that workers and soldiers faced the enemy together was seen in a General Motors poster from 1942, "It's a Two Fisted Fight," which portrayed two disembodied fists, one clasping a rifle and the other a wrench. A similar OWI poster from the same year portrayed three such disembodied fists: a distinctly feminine fist, raised above a rolled cuff and clenching a small monkey wrench; a gloved male fist clasping a much larger adjustable wrench that reached higher than hers; and in the center a soldier's fist clasping a rifle, which rose above the other two. The three arms thrust upward to form an arch of unified resolve, braced together against the enemy yet arrayed hierarchically so as to remind the viewer of the chain of virtue implicit in the shared sacrifice.[31]

Since it was the production of war matériel that linked the worker to the soldier and transformed labor into patriotic sacrifice, much wartime propaganda devoted itself to compressed depictions of the production process, linked or likened to military organization. The best production posters associated some of the glory and heroism of combat with industrial work, juxtaposing images of workers and servicemen and sometimes depicting an exchange of masculine potency, usually symbolized by artillery shells or ammunition. A typical example of this approach could be seen in a Navy Ordnance poster from 1942 promoting the E Award for excellence in plant production. In its foreground, a crew loaded an antiaircraft shell into one of the big guns on the deck of a ship, while enemy planes menaced from the clouds above. On closer inspection, the viewer found that one of the crew members was actually a worker dressed in overalls, handing the shell over to a sailor across the transition in a montage that merged a factory floor with the ship's deck. The nation, represented by a giant cumulus cloud formed in the image of Uncle Sam, nodded in approval. Below this scene was a pitch to work crews to "win the right" to fly the Navy E pennant and wear its badge. Such a reward combined the air of military decoration with a vague suggestion that workers earned rights to special status through heroic production.[32]

For all the camaraderie and symbolic cooperation that production posters displayed, most of them preserved a certain distance between the worker and the soldier. Some posters, however, deliberately erased the distance between the soldier and the worker in order to amplify the urgency of production messages. The most gripping way to accomplish this effect was to bring the viewer—presumed to be a worker, since most production posters were placed on factory walls—face-to-face with the soldier.[33] The 1943 War Department poster "Pass the Ammunition—The Army Needs Lumber" painted a scene that dropped the viewer just behind the front lines of battle, where artillery boomed in the near distance. In the immediate foreground a helmeted soldier lugged away a wooden crate marked "fuzes" that, his posture suggested, had just been handed to him by the viewer.[34] A similar intimacy underscored by urgency animated a 1942 entry in the WPB's More Production series. In it a soldier crawling on his belly through the brush turned momentarily from his rifle to wipe his brow and address his buddy, the viewer, with a sardonic request: "Kinda give it your personal attention, will you?"[35]

Such workplace propaganda placed a heavy burden on the worker's public image. If heroic production was tantamount to fighting, then anything short of full production was a dereliction of duty—or worse. The WPB tried to bring out this message in a constructive manner with its 1942 poster "What You're

War workers, regularly referred to as "soldiers of production" in official propaganda, relished their connection to the soldiers whom their work provisioned. The equation of working and fighting underscored the importance of the United States' reliance on its industrial might to win the war of machines. (Courtesy of Northwestern University Library, http://digital.library.northwestern.edu/wwii-posters/img/ww1645-80.jpg)

Making May Save My Daddy's Life," which featured a little boy who clutched a framed photograph of a man in uniform.[36] The same message—that soldiers' lives depended upon workers' productivity—could also be used to motivate workers in a more negative fashion. In this vein, some employers produced posters that placed the burden of delayed or threatened production on workers' shoulders. A 1943 poster by North American Aviation titled "Killing Time Is Killing Men" exemplified this approach. With wildcat strikes rising drastically throughout the war industries in 1943, the aircraft manufacturer confronted its workers with a soldier who stood on the moral high ground of the war economy. This high ground was the shallow grave of the battlefield, where a soldier lay facedown in the mud. Superimposed above the fallen soldier a craven slacker crouched, sitting down on the job for a smoke.[37] In the same spirit, a local plant placed a piece of twisted metal below a makeshift sign informing passersby that the metal came from a ship sunk "on the day you were absent from work."[38]

Such ghastly imagery offered war workers no constructive role, only the obligation to get back to work and produce without pause. The AFL and the CIO both sought, unsuccessfully, to counter such messages, but they lacked the necessary funds or the marketing expertise to conduct an effective publicity campaign.[39] In place of the positive identification allowed by government and union posters encouraging workers to think of themselves as soldiers of production, North American had substituted the figure of the traitorous slacker stabbing the soldier in the back. The contrast between positive and negative uses of the rhetoric of production hit at the very heart of workers' morale.

Soldiers of Production

How did workers respond to the propaganda aimed at them by businesses, government agencies, and unions? OWI researchers attempted to answer that question by investigating morale among defense workers. Convinced that a psychological predisposition to war-mindedness would be a major determinant of individual productivity, the OWI commissioned a number of studies probing the attitudes and perceptions that marked the war worker's outlook. This was an attempt at civilian morale management in its most instrumental form.

The most important determinant of morale, OWI researchers found, flowed from the deep commitment war workers had to raising the production record of the factories in which they toiled, which reflected the pride they took in their personal contribution to the output of war matériel.[40] Some workers expressed their feelings about the matériel they produced in terms that echoed the "soldier of production" theme featured so prominently in posters. As an OWI intelligence analyst summarized in the spring of 1942, their connection to the war "expressed itself in the recognition of a worker's job as equivalent to a soldier's." "Most of all," an OWI report from later that summer stated, "they desire to know more about the use made of the products on which they are working."[41]

Knowing about the ultimate use of their labor helped workers visualize themselves as genuine participants in the national effort. In assessing the relative effectiveness of various production incentives, one OWI report concluded, "Direct reports of the performance of their products in actual combat are the most favorably regarded of all appeals with which the workers have had experience." Posters—though far more commonly encountered and "consistently approved by workers as dramatizing their participation in the war effort"—did "not evoke the genuine feelings aroused by first-hand reports from the battle front."[42] One worker in an East Coast tank factory with high morale observed to his OWI interlocutor, "It seems to me the workers—all of us—worked a little harder after we were told our tanks were the best in Libyan fighting. That's what we wanted to know."[43]

The most effective way to provide the recognition that workers craved, the OWI found, was to present it in the person of a genuine soldier who had seen battle. Speeches and pep talks made by soldiers who had seen fighting were among the most rousing of all production incentives. A machinist in Milwaukee described to an OWI interviewer the impact an army captain made simply by walking among the workers and acknowledging their work. "He was very informal about it," the machinist noted. "There was nothing stuffy or military. After that, a guy can go around and really tell people what part he's playing in this war program."[44] When soldiers' speeches could be combined with a report on the performance of the equipment made in a worker's factory, the response was enormous. One worker remarked to his interviewer, "We should get reports to make the men realize the responsibility they have. Like Brigadier General Doolittle said, 'Your instrument guided us there.' That was thrilling."[45]

Workers took the production propaganda seriously—or at least selected aspects of it—and so increasingly expected the federal government to treat them as genuine soldiers of production. Wages, hours, work rules, opportunities for advancement, treatment by management—all of these aspects of industrial work were more than simple compensation, they indicated a worker's standing within the moral economy of the war. These were the perquisites of social citizenship to which workers increasingly felt entitled as soldiers of production. Their dramatically improved social and economic position further reinforced rising expectations, borne aloft on the rising currents of egalitarian wartime culture.

Thus, for more than obvious reasons, wages and earnings were among the most vital determinants of workers' morale. In a review of survey research on worker morale, an OWI analyst concluded that "wages appear to be a dominant factor in determining the satisfaction of men with their jobs." However, the relationship between morale and earnings was not linear. OWI interviewers found that 37 percent of workers in the lowest income group, earning between $16 and $45 a week, showed signs of high morale, not far behind the 43 percent with high morale in the next, considerably more comfortable bracket, those earning between $46 and $65 a week. The war worker's "attitude toward the war," explained the OWI report, "is closely tied up with the way in which his personal needs are satisfied and his modest goals achieved."[46] These needs and goals amounted to a stable, secure, and rising standard of living, which together with opportunities for employment and fair treatment at work seemed to be the essence of the "American way" for which the war was being fought.

With wage increases restricted under the Little Steel agreement, and with inflation rising throughout the first half of the war, workers came to depend almost exclusively on overtime work as a way to increase their earnings. Because overtime was a major source of both increased aggregate production and rising standards of living, it received widespread support. However, the exact terms of overtime work were the subject of considerable public debate. Disagreements centered on whether workers should be paid time and a half once they had worked forty hours in a week, as the FLSA mandated. For a small but influential minority of war workers—perhaps 10 percent, according to one OWI study—"the 40-hour week ha[d] become a right, much in the same sense as the right to speak freely and other 'inalienable rights.'" A somewhat larger proportion, roughly 20 percent, thought the forty-hour week was a natural and just state of affairs—no doubt reflecting a mentality forged in the long and only recently concluded struggle for the eight-hour work day. More than 70 percent supported overtime pay of time and a half for work beyond forty hours a week.[47]

While the sense of entitlement may have cemented war workers' patriotic image of themselves, it was not fully shared by other occupational groups. An OWI study in mid-July 1942 showed that only 61 percent of nonagricultural workers not contributing to the war effort, and between 55 and 57 percent of other occupational groups, felt that overtime pay was fair. The proportions for farmers, managers, and professionals fell below 50 percent.[48] Polls taken in November 1942 and again in January 1943 showed that most Americans felt overtime should not begin until forty-eight hours of work in a week, if at all.[49] In February, Roosevelt agreed to sign an executive order affirming a minimum work week of forty-eight hours. Although its wording was vague and the question of overtime pay was avoided, the order revealed shifting public sentiment.[50]

If civilians not working in war-related industries resented war workers' higher pay and rising standard of living, war workers often felt an equally strong frustration at the management running their factories. They felt that they were being asked to shoulder the greater part of the burden of production, working mandatory overtime shifts, devoting large portions of their earnings to war bonds and income taxes, accepting government-imposed wage caps while prices continued to inflate the cost of living, and putting up with the many frustrations of the crowded war centers in which they lived. Meanwhile, large corporations enjoyed cost-plus contracts that ensured unprecedented revenues and record profits, as business leaders enjoyed a renewed prominence running the war production effort.

These frustrations led the CIO to embark on a publicity campaign promoting an "equality of sacrifice" in which management would bear a greater proportion of the war's burden.[51] The single proposal from the campaign that stuck in workers' minds as most representative was the demand, adopted by Roosevelt, for a personal income limitation of $25,000 a year. This limit, which Roosevelt unsuccessfully sought to make law as part of his larger campaign for a national commitment to sacrifice, highlighted the imbalance many workers felt characterized the war effort; workers were forced to accept wage caps, while the "bosses" could earn as much as their "cronies" saw fit to pay them. An OWI analysis of public opinion in July 1942 showed that 64 percent of the public supported Roosevelt's proposed salary cap and only 24 percent opposed it, with approval increasing as one moved down the economic ladder. "To many workers," the OWI report concluded, "the $25,000 income limitation has evidently become a symbol of the idea of equality of sacrifice." Only three years earlier, at the tail end of the Depression, a *Fortune* poll had found that 72 percent of respondents of lower-middle economic status and 59.3 percent of poor respondents had opposed a law limiting annual incomes. The politics of sacrifice had encouraged workers to think of the national income distribution as a question of fairness that the federal government should guarantee—at least in wartime.[52]

The question of relative sacrifice may have faded as the war got longer—the proportion of respondents in OWI and commercial polls saying that "government has not asked people to make enough sacrifices for the war" declined steadily from 70 percent in August 1942 to well below 40 percent by early 1945.[53] But the underlying class resentments that animated the rhetoric of sacrifice only sharpened with time. The research that OWI conducted on war workers between the summer of 1942 and early 1943 revealed that relations with management were a major determinant of war workers' morale. Specifically, workers unhappy with the level of production in their local plants were nearly four times more likely to be unhappy with management than those who were satisfied with the output. Many other factors bearing on morale, such as workers' perceptions of the fairness of their wages or the conditions of their work, were by-products of this fundamental stance toward management and its production record. Asked by OWI interviewers in June 1942 about the causes of inefficiency in his plant, a Seattle employee of an aircraft manufacturer drew on the ideology of production to express a tangle of resentments:

> I think it is the higher officials. I think the company's out for money. Otherwise why don't they use the men they've got—let us all work full time. We could have turned out a thousand, or two thousand, even, more planes than we have.

Nearly half of all workers contacted for this study mentioned company profits in the course of their interviews.[54] This barely submerged hostility may explain why workers tended to blame management when they felt production was lagging, but gave government the credit when production seemed to be moving ahead at an acceptable rate.[55]

Such attitudes could have a powerful effect on war production. An OWI investigation in late October and early November 1942 noted that the gap between high and low morale could make a difference of 131 days of production. That was the difference between the average time required to lay a keel in Todd-Bath, a shipyard in southern Maine that took 76 days, and in the nearby South Portland Yard, which required 207 days. The main reason for the vast gulf in productivity that separated the two shipyards came down to how the workers were treated. Workers at Todd-Bath felt they were a vital part of the war production at their plant and that "a satisfactory earning situation and a sense of participation" compensated for the difficult conditions in which they worked and lived. South Portland workers, on the other hand, expressed an "intense feeling" of dissatisfaction with their work and a bitter envy of the high output of ships issuing from the Todd-Bath plant down the road, leading them to engage in unauthorized strikes, slowdowns, and walkouts.[56]

The findings of this study confirmed an earlier OWI study of war plants in the summer of 1942, which had concluded that workers' motivation to engage in maximum production hinged on five interlocking attitudes or perceptions: a sense that wages were satisfactory relative to previous earnings, or relative to the earnings of other workers; a feeling that working conditions were acceptable; an atmosphere that recognized an individual's contribution to production; a relationship with management that made workers feel they had a share in responsibility for production; and a feeling of security on the job and after the war.[57] The first and last of these would continue to shape workers' rising expectations, both economic and political, through the end of the war and beyond.

Fair Employment

The most dramatic example of federal authority in the workplace fostering rising expectations of a fuller citizenship was also the most toothless: the FEPC, created by President Roosevelt to head off the March on Washington organized by black labor leader A. Philip Randolph in 1941, but never provided with enforcement powers or a sufficient budget. Despite these liabilities, the FEPC proved to be a powerful catalyst of change that would destabilize local race relations in key war production centers. Roughly a million African Americans held defense jobs during World War II. As they found themselves systematically shunted to the lowest rungs of the war economy, many turned to the FEPC.

The process of filing discrimination charges with the FEPC helped forge a shared consciousness, activism, and tenacity among the working class that had been lacking in earlier civil rights activism. Like other complaints sent to the government during the war—most notably claims of peonage in the rural South

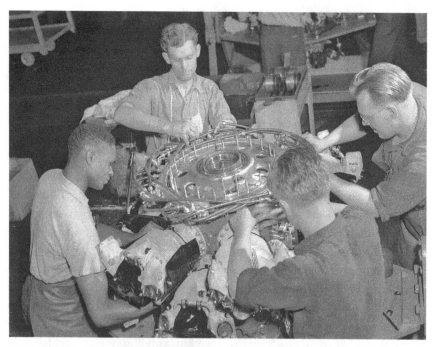

"Typifying American democracy at work, four soldiers of the production front assemble an airplane engine for Uncle Sam's soldiers of the battlefront. In this, as in other war factories throughout the U.S., prejudice pertaining to differences of race, creed, or color have been scrapped by those who recognize that victory must have priority over intolerance." The dismal reality of racial conflict in war plants belied the optimistic caption of this OWI photo. (Courtesy of the Library of Congress, LC-DIG-fsa-8e11119)

and violations of due process rights in employment in the North, both of which the NAACP helped claimants bring before the Department of Justice—the cases developed by the FEPC cultivated a precise sense of legal harm to the claimants. Failure to enforce fair employment only made those claims more insistent, highlighting the government's responsibility rather than negating it. If the timing of the FEPC's hearings or their uneven application to different industries revealed a set of priorities driven by the White House's need for "racial management" that would not upset the war effort, the simple existence of an avenue for grievance nonetheless legitimized the expectations of its claimants.[58]

Despite the FEPC's ineffectiveness, then, its case files spoke volumes about the rights consciousness and determination to achieve racial equality that it instilled. In 1942, for example, Timothy Hill provided an example of this new resolve when he wrote directly to Paul McNutt, the head of the War Manpower Commission, to complain about a supervisor who had thwarted his inquiries about promotion and advancement in the Paint Department of the Newport News Shipbuilding and Drydock Company. The supervisor had told Hill that he sought "too much money for a colored man." Hill pressed his case despite the hostility and threats he encountered, and the FEPC launched a full investigation that ultimately required the company's vice president to answer to the federal government.[59] Scores of similar complaints about stymied training and promotion flowed into the FEPC's Washington office when black workers' grievances were ignored by an internal commission at the naval air station.[60]

Such complaints could not be ignored, even if they were evaded by industry. The "battle for production" had become too central to both the ideology and the economics of the national war mobilization. A black worker in the Houston shipyards who been denied training and promotion to the position of mechanic echoed the sentiments of his Norfolk brethren when he wrote to the FEPC in March 1943: "We who have qualified to fill some important jobs in war plants would like to send fighting material . . . to our men in Service as fast as we can [but] they will not allow us because we are colored."[61]

FEPC claimants commonly drew on the official ideology of the war to make their case against discrimination. In June 1944 Herbert Cameron, field secretary of the Anderson, Indiana, branch of the NAACP, filed a report on the UAW-CIO's Delco Remy Local 662 accusing the local's officers of "collaboration with management" against its own members who were "men and women of color." Cameron, an employee at the Delco Remy plant, opened the report by quoting from Local 662's constitution, which repeated the words of the Declaration of Independence and guaranteed the equal status of all members "regardless of religion, race, creed, color, political affiliation or nationality." These ideals, he reported, were violated by the "lilly-white" local's failure across the board to guarantee equal treatment for black employees regarding pay, hours, seniority, working conditions, promotion, and the like. "You talk about appeasement!" Cameron exclaimed. "We Negroes here at Delco Remy are really being shoved around."[62]

The systemic discrimination at Local 662 was a matter of "un-Americanism" in Cameron's eyes, tantamount to treason. Anyone who discriminated against African Americans, he wrote, was "a fifth columnist" because he prolonged the "present world upheaval." What prompted him to complain to the FEPC was the indignity of black employees being banned from a banquet celebrating the success of the local's bond drive to purchase an army ambulance. The chairman of the entertainment committee had refused to sell tickets to black members because the banquet included a dance: "Brother Jack Daffron said that it would be social equality to let us in." The message sent was that their "money is good enough to buy bonds, to aid in the prosecution of this arsenals of war which these bonds buy," but that was as far as the local's commitment to its black members went. Furious, Cameron wrote:

> The boys on the 74 fighting fronts of the United Nations do not care whose hands, white or black, make the arsenals of war so long as they can receive them and fight on and on until victory is won.[63]

The FEPC informed Cameron that his case would not be pursued because it did not strictly relate to employment, despite the numerous incidents of discrimination in work he had catalogued in building up to the outrage over the ball. Instead of losing hope in the nation, the union or the FEPC, he issued a press release from his local NAACP office, throwing down the gauntlet to the local's officials:

> The recommendation of our executive committee (they must be in the employ of the Axis) which took place on the evening of the initial onslaught against the evils of fortress Europe, was, that in all social entertainments of the local, Negro and White workers be segregated![64]

It was not necessary to be NAACP field staff to recognize the ideological stakes of discrimination in employment and hold the FEPC—and the larger government—accountable for them. The testimony of Thomas Madison Doram before the FEPC in late 1943 provides a window onto the surging aspirations of many ordinary African Americans during the war, and what they were willing to risk in order to pursue them.[65] Doram worked at the California Shipbuilding Corporation, which industrial magnate Henry Kaiser had built in a massive facility on Terminal Island, right next to the major military installations for Los Angeles.

Doram had begun work for CalShip as a janitor three weeks after Pearl Harbor. Just over a month later he applied to the union, a local of the Boilermakers, Iron Ship Builders and Helpers of America, for authorization to become a welder's helper, a skilled position that had been almost entirely closed to African Americans before the war. The Boilermakers official, Hank Moses, granted the application without realizing that Doram was black, but reversed himself when Doram came to get his signature. Doram persisted anyway, convincing one of Moses's subordinates to sign the paperwork, which allowed him to begin training as a welder and automatically enrolled him in the Boilermakers local. After ten days of training, Doram requested to become a full welder's trainee, "hoping thereby to become ever more efficient in the production of Implements of War for my Country." Moses repeated his initial refusal, stating flatly "that Negroes would never be permitted to do that kind of work," and "that they were only wanted as janitors and custodial workers until the war was over."[66]

Refusing to accept Moses's rejection, Doram applied directly to the head of the training school for "burners," as welders were called. This individual also refused Doram outright, saying that the school was open only to white workers. Undaunted, Doram "studied madly" during his time off and practiced his new trade in secret, beneath the skids where the welding crews worked on the hull of the ship. Driven by what he said was an "unrelenting desire to serve my country better . . . whatever the sacrifice," he drew the approving notice of "many liberal and patriotic White Workers on the Job who were deeply moved" by his efforts. Moses eventually let Doram work on the graveyard shift "where other Negroes won't see you and therefore won't get the idea that they all can do the same thing," but "would NOT ever consent" to upgrade him to the status of instructor, where he would receive the same pay as whites doing the same work.[67]

By this time the Boilermakers had learned that Doram was black, and through bureaucratic maneuvering they attempted to force him to pay his dues to the "subordinate" black lodge of the local, rather than to the established white local in which he was enrolled. His race came to their attention because of his attempt to pay, in person, a mechanic's fee to the union that would reflect his de facto status as a welding instructor—a move that Doram acknowledged would have upgraded him "to the status where I would have gotten as a matter of course the salary of an Instructor." He "UNCONDITIONALLY REFUSED" to pay dues to the black auxiliary, whose members received half the benefits that white members of the main union enjoyed. In turn, the Boilermakers refused to accept his payments to the all-white local. Doram repeatedly pointed out to the union—and to other black workers—that "no word of Race or Color [was] mentioned" in the qualifications for membership listed in the union's constitution. Subsequently, fifty-three black workers applied to the executive board of the union to be installed as full members in the local, but they were turned down despite the fact that, as Doram pointed out:

> The Executive Order of the President of the United States, No. 9346, declared it Mandatory that "It is the duty of All Labor Organizations to eliminate Discrimination in regard, among other things, to Union Membership because of Race, Creed, Color or National Origin."[68]

With Doram spouting constitutional pronouncements and invoking the dreaded FEPC, the Boilermakers acted to stop him before he could cause any further trouble. Soon after the petition by the fifty-three black workers, he found himself menaced by coworkers, two of whom attacked him with a knife on the afternoon of June 29, 1943. Doram emerged from the fight unharmed, but it became the pretext for his arrest and eventual imprisonment in the local jail. His thirty-day sentence was to commence more than four months later, on the very day that FEPC hearings began in Los Angeles on discrimination in the West Coast shipyards.[69]

In spite of all that he had been through, and the evidence it provided him that "fair employment" was not so much a practice as a cruel promise usually broken, Doram continued to press his case from jail, submitting his testimony to the FEPC by mail. His belief that "the ultimate objective of the war was the unification of all peoples to a common ground of workmanship," fortified by an abiding religiosity, remained undiminished. Even though he was unjustly imprisoned and his wife lay "Quick with Child," he insisted:

> I, notwithstanding, still proclaim myself to be a brain-child of America and an ardent follower of Democracy, and like unto the ever-loyal Job devoted to the Christ, I say to you ... "Though he slay me, yet will I trust him."
>
> Thus shall I believe in America the beautiful. Thus shall I forever sing "My Country Tis of Thee, SWEET LAND OF LIBERTY of Thee I sing."

He closed with an appeal to the FEPC to "search for and find only the truth, the whole truth and nothing but the truth," and abolish "this ungodly and un-American circumstance."[70]

Doram obviously presented his case to the FEPC in the strongest possible light and deliberately used legalistic phrases and idealistic rhetoric to highlight the injustices in his workplace. Indeed, his reference to Executive Order 9346 (the second authorization for the FEPC), rather than to the more widely remembered Executive Order 8806, suggests that he probably had some experience in organizing that went well beyond what his uncomplicated narrative of personal determination acknowledged. Even so, his deliberate choice of language emphasizing the rights of citizens was telling, as were the connections he drew between the democratic ideals of the war and the particular details of his personal advancement and material opportunity. These were the terms in which he felt he could make the strongest claim on the federal government as well as on the broader public, which learned of discrimination through the hearings.

The FEPC hearings generated much publicity and outrage but no change in practice or policy by the Boilermakers: a court ruling in favor of the black auxiliaries arrived too late in the war to make a difference. Black workers in shipyards up and down the West Coast had been through experiences disturbingly similar to what Doram went through, in some cases joining together in organizations such as the East Bay Shipyard Workers' Committee, which called on rank-and-file workers to push for reform of the Boilermakers' auxiliaries in Kaiser's shipyards near San Francisco. Union leaders dismissed organizers and activists such as Doram as "professional agitators and negro uplifters who find it more profitable to dress well and live off the contributions extracted from the negroes . . . than it is for them to build ships and thus make a real contribution to the war effort." Sometimes the "agitators" made progress for individual auxiliaries, especially when they could rely on existing networks of activists drawn from organizations such as the Communist Party and the NAACP. But more often the complaints filed with the FEPC went uncorrected.[71] When the formal complaint mechanisms of local unions and FEPC boards failed, black workers also took direct action and staged their own wildcat strikes—though with less frequency than did whites. Such overt actions on the part of both blacks and whites were only the most visible tip of a submerged daily world of constant resistance and recrimination in the superheated wartime workplace.[72]

The largely symbolic nature of the FEPC's authority may seem severely circumscribed by today's standards. Yet that authority was taken very seriously by those most affected by its limitations, such as Charles Doram. When the FEPC appeared in danger of expiring in 1943, African American civil rights organizations raised money to campaign for a permanent agency.[73] After the war, the campaign for a permanent FEPC would remain a central concern of civil rights organizations, especially outside the South, where many fair employment councils were in fact created.[74] The inclusion of African Americans on local war boards provided a public voice, a vote, and a legitimacy whose memory could not be erased when the war ended. This role appears to have inspired an upsurge in civic activity in black communities around the country, including gutsy voter registration drives in southern war-boom communities such as Norfolk.[75]

Heightened expectations and politicized racial consciousness were not the only results of the politics of fair employment. A black fireman on the Norfolk

Southern Railway helped permanently alter national labor law in 1944, when the Supreme Court ruled favorably on his case in *Tunstall v. Brotherhood of Locomotive Firemen and Enginemen.*[76] Like many railway unions whose racial policies had been highlighted by well-publicized FEPC hearings, the brotherhood had signed an exclusive contract with the Norfolk Southern Railway. This resulted in Tunstall's replacement by a white employee, despite his three decades of seniority. With assistance from the Norfolk chapter of the NAACP, Tunstall appealed to the Supreme Court, which consolidated his case with a nearly identical claim brought by a black Alabama fireman. The court ruled for the plaintiffs, striking down racial exclusion in union membership. In his concurring opinion, Justice Frank Murphy pointed out that although the brotherhood was a private organization, the U.S. Congress had conferred on it powers of representation in the Railway Labor Act of 1934. In what must have been news to the white brotherhoods, whose restrictive practices had not troubled labor law for a decade, Murphy observed: "A sound democracy cannot allow such discrimination to go unchallenged. Racism is far too virulent today to permit the slightest refusal, in the light of a Constitution that abhors it, to expose and condemn it wherever it appears in the course of a statutory interpretation."[77]

Over time, the rulings in *Tunstall* and *Steele* would dilute the power of white brotherhoods to exclude black workers, linking a union's right to represent workers to the fairness of its practices. In a postwar political economy that channeled many of the most valuable public goods (such as health care) through private channels, this right to membership, though limited, was crucial.[78]

Wildcats, Hate Strikes, and Rising Expectations

The buoyant war economy unleashed conflict as well as hope. As sizable numbers of African Americans and other minorities began to find employment in war industries starting in late 1942 and early 1943, a rash of hate strikes broke out in war centers around the country. When twelve black workers at the Alabama Drydock and Shipbuilding Company, in Mobile, Alabama, complained to the FEPC about their exclusion from high-paying skilled work, and subsequently received upgrades in May 1943, they were attacked by more than five hundred white workers, some bearing pipes and metal tools, while company security guards looked on. Perhaps as many as fifty black men and women at the shipyard were badly injured. At the Packard Motor Company in Detroit, twenty-five thousand workers walked out in June 1943 on a weeklong strike when two black employees were promoted to nonmenial positions in the grinding department. Philadelphia in the late summer of 1944 saw its entire public transit system paralyzed by a citywide strike of white workers who refused to accept the upgrading of eight black workers into formerly white jobs. In both Mobile and Philadelphia, the strikers did not return to work until army troops were called in. The number of hate strikes cannot be determined precisely because of their spontaneous and unofficial nature, but their frequency appears to have peaked in the late spring and summer of 1943, providing an important context for the major race riots that broke out in Los Angeles, Detroit, and Harlem at that time.[79]

Fueling the antagonism caused by whites and blacks working side by side were the underlying issues of personal opportunity that the war economy had brought into sharp focus, intertwined with the racial inequities that had always shaped the labor force. Thousands of white workers were willing to leap to action at the advancement of a handful of black workers because such promotions threatened the existing structure of opportunities that had just begun to lift white workers out of the insecurity of the Depression. They feared black workers in "white jobs" would push whites out of work and erode wages after the war ended full employment conditions.[80]

OWI research on morale captured the clashing expectations that fed hate strikes and race riots. In a March 1943 study of attitudes in Birmingham, Raleigh, Oklahoma City, Chicago, and Detroit, "The Negroes' Role in the War," government researchers discovered that black and white views were sharply at odds. More than 50 percent of African Americans in northern cities and 78 percent in southern cities felt they were being "held back" and not "getting as much chance as they should to help win the war," while roughly seven in ten overall thought the government "should do more" to help them overcome discrimination. At the same time, two-thirds of whites thought African Americans were "well satisfied with things in this country," and only 9 percent felt the government should do more to assist them.[81]

Whites did not, in the abstract, oppose black workers taking war jobs: 63 percent said more African Americans should be hired to help the war effort, perhaps reflecting the belief that they had a "democratic right to work," which 50 percent of interviewees had affirmed in an earlier OWI study. In the North, white attitudes were even more accepting, at least on the surface: 61 percent in Detroit and 72 percent in Chicago said that more African Americans should receive training, and 69 percent said "it would not make a difference if a Negro were hired" to work alongside them. But such affirmations were contingent on black workers remaining subordinate to whites. More than two-thirds of white respondents in southern cities said it would make a difference if they were forced to work alongside African Americans, and 38 percent claimed they would quit under such circumstances. Northern whites came closer to the views of their southern brethren when it came to bread-and-butter issues of opportunity. No more than 31 percent of white respondents in northern cities and 12 percent in the South were willing to accept equal pay for black workers, while the proportions willing to allow "Negroes as good a chance at jobs" were even lower among northern city dwellers (7 percent) than among southern urbanites (15 percent).[82]

In the opinion of the OWI researchers, even the more general white affirmation of black employment in war industries depended on white perceptions that "Negroes are doing all they can to help win the war." If true, such a consideration would reveal the contradictory quality of the wartime moral economy, in which contributing to the war effort gave a worker a claim to special treatment, but by the same reasoning, that claim could be cancelled by any appearance of being unpatriotic. In the eyes of many whites, assertiveness by African Americans and other minorities qualified as unpatriotic behavior that might undermine the war effort. What could not be accepted under any circumstances were opportunities that allowed African Americans to gain greater social proximity to whites. Fewer than 0.5 percent of white respondents in cities both north and south said African Americans should be allowed a "chance to go to the same places" as whites. A poll taken a year later, in May 1944, asked, "If Negroes could get more kinds of jobs than they can now, do you think they would want to go more places white people go?" Only 65 percent of white respondents would concede that African Americans might indeed have such intentions, and 39 percent admitted that they "wouldn't like it" if they did. These attitudes were bound to come into conflict with the determination by African Americans and other minorities to improve their standard of living through conspicuous consumption and other lifestyle choices that put them into closer contact with whites.[83]

This clash of expectations has long been understood to have been the source of the wartime racial conflicts that assumed their most dramatic form in the race riots of 1943.[84] What has been less frequently observed is the underlying similarity of motive across the color line. Hate strikes and other racial conflicts occurred because both white and black expectations had been elevated by the war effort, and preexisting racial mores convinced most whites that economic opportunity was a zero-sum game in which whites could only lose if African Americans advanced. Seen this way, hate strikes represented a subset of a much broader and longer-lasting wave of unauthorized wildcat strikes.[85]

Ordinarily, wildcats were brief walkouts conducted to protest a range of local frustrations and complaints. Many were spontaneous, some were organized by shop stewards, but nearly all took place against the will of union officials who had pledged against wartime strikes in the emotional days after Pearl Harbor. Because of the threat that breaking the pledge would pose to unions' maintenance of membership privileges—which were subject to revocation by the NWLB—unions were in the awkward position of having to suppress rank-and-file militancy just at the moment when their membership was growing most dramatically. Unable to use their most potent weapon, the strike, unions often found themselves at a loss to address the mounting grievances of their members, millions of whom in the war's later years were drawn from communities without much sympathy for the labor movement. As a result, the number of work stoppages rose sharply throughout the war, jumping from 2,968 in 1942 to 3,752 in 1943, peaking in 1944 at 4,956, and then dropping slightly to 4,750 in 1945. Although these actions involved a large number of workers—roughly 7 percent of industrial employees in 1943 and 1944, and over 12 percent in 1945—most lasted less than a week. In 1944, the year of heaviest wildcat activity, 56 percent of strikes ended within three days, and the total production time lost per worker was the lowest for any year on record at the Bureau of Labor Statistics (less than .09 percent of available working time).[86]

This unusual development of strikes increasing in frequency but decreasing in intensity reflected the motivations of most workers, who wanted to protect their rights in the workplace but were not willing seriously to threaten production. Pay was the largest single cause of wildcat strikes, accounting for 51 percent of strikes in 1943 and 43.3 percent in 1944, and dwarfing the roughly 15 percent of strikes prompted by issues surrounding unionization in those years. "Money, money, and more money" was the reasons a Detroit plant inspector gave for the grievances where he worked. The wage controls established by the Little Steel agreement in July 1942 drew some of the most heated complaints from workers. Working conditions, including job security, shop conditions, policies, and workload, also figured prominently: they were the cause of roughly a third of all wildcat strikes in 1943 and 1944.[87] According to one analysis, workers engaged in wartime strikes mainly to protect "traditional practices or newly-won rights" rather than to assert control "at the point of production," as other historians have argued.[88] When workers' expectations were not met, the resulting disappointment produced assertiveness rather than defeatism. "Since when has it been necessary to destroy our promotional set-up to whip the Axis?" asked a local union man at Dodge Main in Detroit during a period of mounting tensions in March of 1943. "Our rights are something the boys coming home from the battlefronts of the world expect to find intact." By 1944 as many as two-thirds of the membership of the Michigan United Auto Workers and half of the national UAW membership took part in a wildcat strike, reflecting the rising impatience and frustration that permeated the factories of the late war years.[89]

Absenteeism was another sensitive barometer of workers' morale that became a serious problem. During the years of peak production, from 1943 to 1945, rates reached a fifth of the labor force in some industries, while industrywide rates ranged between 2.5 and 8.8 percent in early 1943. A number of situational factors, such as transportation or illness, influenced workers' tendency to miss work, but when these contributing factors could be held constant, one especially rigorous study discovered, it emerged that one of the most important determinants of absenteeism was job dissatisfaction.[90]

Both government and industry launched major publicity campaigns to discourage absenteeism.[91] Posters and advertisements regarding absenteeism almost inevitably cast "slacking off" in a harsh, semitreasonous light. Early in the war, one OWI poster showed two assembly line workers turning in shock to view an alarming scene outside the window. There stood a giant, angry soldier, knee-deep in mud and struggling forward with his bayonet lowered momentarily so that he could call back to the home front, "Who's holdin' up my supplies?!" A sign on an idle machine in the foreground explained the shortfall: "No operator today."[92] As the war progressed and professionals in advertising and journalism replaced the New Dealers who had shaped OWI propaganda before the domestic branch's pruning in 1943, the messages became even harsher. An advertisement placed by Jones and Lamson Machine Company in 1945 captured the hardening of sensibilities. It confronted readers with an illustration of a dead American soldier washed up on the shore of a nameless Pacific island. "*He's* not celebrating!" it stated, making an implicit reference to the lightened mood many felt in the summer of 1945, with the surrender of Germany accomplished and the defeat of Japan predicted to occur by year's end. "So you're celebrating . . . taking a few days off. having fun! Wait a minute, brother! Know what it's like to lie in a foxhole and hear the unearthly scream of 'Banzai' in the night? . . . For God's sake, get back to work. . . . Remember, *the shorter the war, the fewer American boys killed.*"[93]

Work or Fight

When viewed from outside the war plants, workers' attitudes could seem decidedly indulgent, if not unpatriotic. The thick wads of cash filling the pockets of defense workers stirred class resentments. As one Missouri farmer said within earshot of an OWI rumor warden, "It gripes us to hear about these defense workers demanding time and one-half and double time for overtime work. They ought to be glad they are not having to shoulder a gun on the front lines."[94]

A national study by the OWI in the late spring of 1942 reported that such expressions of "considerable envy" toward war workers were widespread. Workers were the only group whom respondents singled out as "the ones who are prospering conspicuously" in their communities.[95] Especially bitter were groups that had lost relative clout or prestige within the war economy: middle-class professionals paid on fixed salaries, farmers who worked long hours without overtime pay, and small businessmen swamped by the war economy's allocation of labor and raw materials to larger companies.[96]

Local resentments of the shifts in income distribution and social status resulting from war workers' improved economic position cropped up in the reports of OWI rumor wardens in the summer of 1942. Throughout the country, especially in the Midwest, unsympathetic observers decried the wasteful habits of "overpaid" war workers. In a beauty shop in Norman, Oklahoma, one warden overheard the scandalous tale of a war worker's wife who "just did not see how she was going to be able to buy that fur coat" now that her husband had cut back his overtime and was no longer earning $120 a week. "Now ain't it just too damn bad that she can't get by on 80 dollars a week." A farmer's wife in Osseo, Minnesota, claimed to "know a man and wife who both have defense jobs and who have a child and they spend their money in beer parlors." As further evidence of their violation of the conventions of the family wage, she added that "they don't pay their bills nor take care of their child."

One measure of the threat war wages posed to those not working in war industries was the degree of exaggeration in complaints recorded by OWI rumor wardens. Where specific figures were given to substantiate complaints of gross overpayment, the amounts tended to be at least twice as high as the actual pay for war workers, which OWI estimated at $53 a week after overtime in July 1942, the time when most rumors were reported.[97] The related theme of squandered money often cropped up to justify criticisms of workers' high wages: "They won't save their money . . . they are spending their money on booze," remarked a St. Paul watchman.[98] The vast majority of derogatory comments directed against war workers were made by members of the middle class who felt most threatened by the changing labor market. For small proprietors, it was simply a question of how much "cheap labor" was worth. Concerns about maintaining labor discipline and class prerogative worried others. A banker in Salt Lake City, Utah, warned: "When this money stops rolling in for these defense workers, we're going to have a bunch of Bolsheviks on our hands."[99]

The strongest indictments of war workers relied on a comparison, implicit or otherwise, between supposedly selfish workers and sacrificing soldiers. One version of the comparison simply asserted that war workers had an unwholesome interest in the war's continuation. One grumbler in New York City complained, "Most war workers are taking it easy. They don't want to see the war get over too soon because it would end their fancy jobs." A Minneapolis housewife sniped, "It certainly looks funny for soldiers to sacrifice their lives while defense workers are making big salaries at home." A Dr. Barnes, who manned a "listening post" in Cleveland, Ohio, sent the rumor control staff at OWI headquarters a report in the summer of 1942 on the "'special privilege' of the defense worker," which analyzed the spreading resentment of war workers:

The attitude of the average citizen whether rich or poor is very bitter. One of the best evidence of public hostility is the number of stories in circulation about soldiers, relatives, and men in ordinary walks of life beating up insolent defense workers . . . it is evident many of them are stock episodes. My studies in public opinion, however, have convinced me that the stories of this kind, because they are so often apocryphal, are the more convincing.[100]

The rising fortunes of war workers and of the other social groups benefited by the war economy seemed to some a threat to the American way of life. Such resentments showed that other civilians also located war workers within the national moral economy, but that location was often imagined to be opposite, rather than next to, the idealized combat soldier. An auto parts dealer put this view in the plainest terms: "You can't get people to fight when a soldier makes about $30 a month and has to make all the sacrifices and a defense worker makes around $100 a week and makes no sacrifices. There is a gross inequality of sacrifice."[101]

Little wonder, then, that war workers felt embattled. One measure of their beleaguered state appeared in April 1942, as American losses in the Pacific were at their worst. OWI survey staff stood outside the gates of Sperry Gyroscope in the Brooklyn Navy Yard and Hyatt Roller Bearing in Harrison, New Jersey, and asked workers for their responses to a poster that had been designed by the Office of Emergency Management for its "Don't Talk" campaign to discourage information leaks regarding war production. The poster featured a stylized portrait of a helmeted head, intended by poster designers to represent the enemy, peering out from above the admonition, "He's watching you."[102]

This cryptic phrase, combined with the ambiguous image of the helmet, elicited some telling responses. Most understood that it was meant to encourage them to "keep quiet, don't talk too much," while a large minority went further and thought they were being told to "be on guard against spies." A worker in the navy yard mixed paranoia with philosophy, speculating, "It's a Jap hiding under the liberty bell. It means that enemies can be hidden right behind the skirts of democracy."

Many made the mistake of thinking that the helmet, rather than suggesting the presence of spies, represented instead an American soldier. One Brooklyn worker gave this interpretation a positive spin that reflected the influence of government production propaganda, saying, "It means we are responsible for the war as much as the soldier is." This upbeat view was counterbalanced by a demoralized, even paranoid interpretation of the poster. "Sinister," said a navy yard employee. "Looks like an American soldier watching to see if we're backing him up or not. To remind us he's watching to see we are doing the best we can for

This government poster was designed to warn war workers against revealing vital production secrets within earshot of enemy spies. Many workers took the wrong message from it, thinking it represented their boss, or the glowering scrutiny of soldiers checking to make sure they weren't "slacking off." The confusion revealed the difficulty of conveying precise messages, ideological or otherwise, to mass audiences. (Courtesy of Northwestern University Library, http://digital.library.northwestern.edu/wwii-posters/img/ww0207-02.jpg)

him." To an employee of the roller bearing factory in New Jersey the poster seemed to mean that "the man at the front is watching the man in the defense plant to see that he keeps sending supplies."[103]

Of course, the workers who evaluated the OWI poster were right to assume that somebody was watching them. But rather than Axis enemies, it was the FBI that enlisted tens of thousands of volunteer "contacts" to watch their every move and listen for the murmurings of "loose lips" that might "sink ships," as the famous poster put it.[104]

The notion that workers were slacking off and in need of discipline was a common theme among labor's critics. Absenteeism attributed to job dis-satisfaction (or any other complaint, for that matter) seemed to many civilians not working in industry to reflect an unacceptable indulgence in a time of war—the result of "coddling" or "pampering" labor.

"There is no absenteeism in the fox-holes of the jungles of the Pacific or the burning sands of Africa," observed war hero Eddie Rickenbacker to a Los Ange-les audience in late 1942, demonstrating how easily the soldier of production metaphor could be reversed.[105] This much-publicized address was broadcast by radio and reprinted in papers. It polarized public opinion, according to an OWI analysis of correspondence with panels of individuals drawn from different walks of life. Those who opposed what they perceived to be the Roosevelt administration's lenient labor policy and agreed with Rickenbacker were ener-gized. "I do not think OWI could perform a greater service," wrote one enthusi-astic correspondent, "than to persuade him [Rickenbacker] to speak over the radio on future oc[c]asions on how we people at home can match the efforts of our boys in the Solomons." On the other side of the issue, one editor of a union newspaper fumed that "the normal, patriotic working man burns up at unfair criticism of all of us because of the actions of a tiny minority."[106]

Robert Patterson, the War Department undersecretary in charge of military procurement, called for the drafting of absentees, a position consistent with his advocacy of national service legislation. In a letter to Philip Murray, the head of the CIO, he admonished that "no consideration of personal convenience, no personal whim, can ever justify the production soldier in taking time off. . . . He must realize that he has as great an obligation to stay with his machine as the man at the front to remain at his post, come what may." Testifying before a hearing in Congress on a bill to have local draft boards receive quarterly lists of absentees at local shipyards, Patterson acknowledged the factors that contributed to absen-teeism, such as transportation, but he countered, "The men at the fighting fronts *have* to get there. If there is no transportation, they march, and if the weather is bad, they go just the same. If there is no housing, that is no excuse, they just stay out and take the weather as it is and risk life and limb doing it." Congressman Lyndon B. Johnson of Texas, the sponsor of the bill for which Patterson was testifying, claimed that "absenteeism sank forty-two liberty ships in December alone." The bill did not pass, but a large portion of the American public agreed with Patterson. When asked by the Gallup Organization in early March of 1943 what should be done with regular absentees, 48 percent of respondents said to "draft them."[107]

Since the first months of the war, large segments of the public had favored compulsory policies to manage labor market shortages and other manpower problems. At the end of April 1942, 79 percent of participants in a *Fortune* poll said that all men not in military service should be registered immediately for war work.[108] A "large majority" of civilians surveyed by the OWI in late 1942 felt that compulsory measures were "welcomed as a means of insuring equality of sacrifice."[109] When asked about their own willingness to be drafted into war work, however, civilians consistently showed less enthusiasm for compulsory measures. Only three out of ten respondents in an August 1942 OWI study said they would be willing to quit their current jobs for war work.[110] Thus there may have been less support for public calls to "draft" workers than sometimes appeared to be the case.

In such a climate, national service legislation of the sort that Patterson and others sought had little chance of passing. But this did not prevent large segments of public opinion from resenting workers' increasing assertiveness as it mounted toward the end of the war. A Gallup poll in early January 1944 asked whether respondents agreed with "an official in Washington" that "strikes and the threat of strikes have delayed the victory and will cost the lives of United States soldiers." Just under 80 percent agreed. A poll in June of that year asked whether there ought to be "a law to prevent strikes in war industries," to which 70 percent of the national sample said yes. As many as 64 percent of union members also agreed, reflecting the considerable ambivalence even among workers contemplating wildcats.[111] When poll respondents were asked in July 1945 what the government should do to prevent strikes, the three most common responses reflected a divided public opinion on the causes of wildcats: 11 percent said "put strikers in the army," 8 percent said "give better wages."[112]

Roosevelt expressed a mounting outrage at the rising assertiveness of the workers who walked out in wildcats. The vision of national citizenship he had presented for workers in his fireside chats and other public addresses throughout the war had always balanced duty and entitlement, with one producing the moral foundation for the other. In the dark days of early 1942, when many workers grumbled about the sacrifices they faced under wage controls while Detroit automakers and other corporations enjoyed guaranteed profits, Roosevelt had shot back in a fireside address, "Ask the workers of France and Norway and the Netherlands, whipped to labor by the lash, whether the stabilization of wages is too great a 'sacrifice.'"[113]

His retort reflected a basic conviction about the moral economy of the war, rather than a criticism of workers. Roosevelt consistently expressed sympathy for workers' concerns about inflation and its effects on their purchasing power under wage controls. When, in the fall of 1942, he addressed the need to institute stronger economic controls (including wage limits) to stabilize prices, he granted that if the cost of living continued to rise, workers would have the "right" to wage increases, as a matter of "essential justice and practical necessity." This was a strong statement, considering the summer's Little Steel agreement. But it was bolstered further still by the president's preceding remarks.

Roosevelt had begun the speech by describing a bomber pilot, Lt. John Powers, who was missing in action in the Coral Sea. Before he went down, the man said to the other pilots in his squadron, "Remember, the folks back home are counting on us. I am going to get a hit if I have to lay it on their flight deck." Roosevelt concluded the vignette by saying, "You and I are the 'folks back home' . . . have not those men a right to be counting on us?" That workers should have a right to such consideration when men like Lt. Powers gave their lives so selflessly was not a contradiction, nor a sign of Roosevelt "caving" to interest groups. He acknowledged that he might seem to be "overstressing these economic problems" when the proper focus of concern should be "news from far distant fields of battle," but he assured his listeners that a "vicious spiral of inflation" would mean more than just a rise in the cost of living or the cost of the war; it would threaten the "continued production of planes and tanks and ships and guns." He closed by reminding his radio audience, "Battles are not won by soldiers or sailors who think first of their own personal safety. And wars are not won by peoples who are concerned primarily with their own comfort, their own convenience, their own pocketbooks." In keeping with the moral economy of the war, he justified wage stabilization and other measures of economic control as a matter of equipment produced and lives saved.[114]

When the coal miners' strike began in the late spring of 1943, led by John L. Lewis, head of the United Mine Workers (UMW), the tone of Roosevelt's public discussion of workers began to change. After a strike by the UMW earlier in the year, which Roosevelt had ended by ordering the miners back to work, Lewis again called out his men on a general industrywide strike. That outraged the entire nation. While most people polled toward the end of the strike in June 1943 thought the miners should be given a wage increase—their wages had been frozen at rates considerably below those of other war workers—the defiance encouraged by Lewis was deemed unacceptable. By the time of the strike, Lewis was the most hated man in the country, according to polls.[115]

On May 2, 1943, Roosevelt took to the airwaves and addressed the striking miners directly in words that made their obligation to the soldier unmistakable, stating flatly that "every idle miner directly and individually is obstructing our war effort." Interrupting the movement of coal, even for a short time, amounted to a "gamble with the lives of American soldiers and sailors." He then shifted to a more intimate tone:

> You miners have sons in the Army and Navy and Marine Corps. You have sons who at this very minute—this split second—may be fighting in New Guinea or in the Aleutian Islands or Guadalcanal. . . . We have already received telegrams from some of our fighting men overseas, and I only wish I could tell you what they think of the stoppage of work in the coal mines.

The families and friends of millions of fighting men—"that includes all of us," he reminded listeners—were "also in the line of duty, the production line." Any failure there could mean a "costly defeat on the field of battle."[116]

Roosevelt let the moral implication of what he said sink in. He then switched rhetorical gears once again, speaking a language that would resonate among the miners and connect the moral obligations he had outlined to the concerns that had caused the strike.

> You miners have ample reason to know that there are certain basic rights for which this country stands, and that those rights are worth fighting and dying for. That is why you have sent you sons and brothers from every mining town in the nation. . . . That is why you have contributed so generously, so willingly, to the purchase of war bonds. . . . That is why, since the war was started in 1939, you have increased the annual production of coal by almost 200 million tons a year.

Because they had sacrificed for their country, miners and "all who do the nation's work" deserved a "better standard of living," a goal that had been "the objective of this government" for some time. The president acknowledged that the cost of living was "troubling" the miners, as well as workers all over the country, and he went through a list of steps the government had taken to avert the crippling inflation of the previous war. Roosevelt promised that the government would take immediate action to redress the problems that remained, rolling back meat prices to earlier levels and punishing price violators whenever they were discovered.[117] Yet in the end these concerns were trifles that could not justify blocking the all-important production needed to end the war quickly. He closed with the confidence that characterized his oratory at its most persuasive, predicting that the coal miners would end their strike.

Americans will not fail to heed the clear call of duty. Like all other good Americans, [the miners] will march shoulder to shoulder with our armed forces to victory.

Tomorrow the Stars and Stripes will fly over the coal mines, and I hope that every miner will be at work under that flag.[118]

In the end, even Roosevelt's powers of persuasion were not enough to convince the workers that they should return to work. More than other workers, miners felt that their low pay, harsh working conditions, and general standard of living in the company towns surrounding the mines were all violations of basic rights for which the war was being fought.

Soon after Roosevelt's fireside chat, as the UMW weighed its options, a striking miner learned that his son had been killed in action in the Pacific. "I ain't a traitor," he cried in response, "damn 'em, I ain't a traitor. I'll stay out until hell freezes over. Dickie was fighting for one thing, I'm fighting for another and they ain't so far apart."

If Roosevelt failed to persuade the miners, he had public opinion on his side. Most Americans probably would have agreed with the marine who asked the president in a letter, "What sort of traitors are those miners?" He had just returned on a plane full of men injured in battle, one of whom had lost his leg. "Imagine it must be rather bewildering to return from battle . . . to find the defenders of the homefront bargaining for another dollar or two to add to already mountainous wages."[119]

The president eventually prevailed after sending troops to seize the mine and threatening strikers with the loss of their draft deferments. Soon afterward Congress passed the Smith-Connally Act, which strengthened the president's authority to seize war plants, outlawed strikes in government-run facilities, required a thirty-day cooling-off period and secret ballot before a strike could occur, and prohibited political contributions by labor unions. Polls showed overwhelming public approval for at least some of these measures—nearly 70 percent of union members and almost 80 percent of all citizens polled in mid-May had agreed that it ought to be a "crime to urge workers to strike in companies taken over by the government." Opinion was even more extreme within Congress, where Roosevelt's veto of the bill was overridden in less than two hours. Neither the seizure of the coal mines nor the Smith-Connally Act could end the administration's labor troubles. Lewis led the miners out on strike again in October, part of a broader wave of illegal strikes that continued to spread through the major industries.[120]

A bridge was crossed that spring and summer of 1943 that left organized labor politically isolated and partially discredited as a full partner in the war effort—at least in the eyes of many Americans, especially conservatives. Reflecting this shift, Roosevelt came to embrace national service legislation after having opposed it earlier in the war. The change could be seen even in his most expansive and buoyantly reformist speech of the war.

In his annual message to Congress on January 11, 1944, the president pronounced the need for a new "economic bill of rights" to complement the existing constitutional guarantees enumerated in the Bill of Rights. "It is our duty," he stated, to plan for a "winning and lasting peace and the establishment of an American standard of living higher than ever known before." This was a vision that all citizens could accept. Of the eight rights he listed, the first was the right to a job, and the second was the right to a decent standard of living—mirroring the two biggest improvements in most citizens' lives during the war, and the two places where the government's presence had made the biggest difference. Two other rights promised a "decent living" to farmers and a "decent home" to every family.[121] This emphasis on standard of living was no accident. Hadley Cantril had prepared a memo in late 1943, just prior to the drafting of the speech, that showed Americans were overwhelmingly concerned with their standard of living, to the near exclusion of other issues. These data reinforced the earlier recommendations of the National Resources Planning Board, which FDR revised into language that trained the diffuse popular expectations of government onto a coherent and universalistic liberal agenda.[122]

To tie his new vision of national citizenship firmly to the moral economy of the war, Roosevelt closed his address by urging Congress to implement the economic bill of rights in legislation:

> Our fighting men abroad—and their families at home—expect such a program and have a right to insist upon it. It is to their demands that this government should pay heed rather than to the whining demands of selfish pressure groups who seek to feather their nests while young Americans are dying. . . . I have often said there are no two fronts for America in this war. There is only one front. There is one line of unity which extends from the hearts of the people at home to the men of our attacking forces in our farthest outposts. When we speak of our total effort, we speak of the factory and field, and the mine as well as of the battleground—we speak of the soldier and the civilian, the citizen and his government.[123]

This last note, of obligation, has often been overlooked in historical discussions of the economic bill of rights. Yet it was the major theme of the speech, dominating nearly all of what had preceded the eight rights Roosevelt enumerated. "The overwhelming majority of our people have met the demands of this war. . . . They have accepted inconveniences; they have accepted hardships;

they have accepted tragic sacrifices." But in their midst, a "noisy minority" of interest groups pressed for their selfish advantage to the detriment of the "nation as a whole." This led to "disunity at home—bickerings, self-seeking partisanship, stoppages of work, inflation, business as usual, politics as usual, luxury as usual . . . these are the influences which can undermine the morale of the brave men ready to die at the front for us here." Those who clamored for their own interests were "not deliberately striving to sabotage the war effort," Roosevelt explained; they were simply "laboring under the delusion that the time is past when we must make prodigious sacrifices."[124] To illustrate his point, in the draft version of his address he gave an example of such deadly overconfidence that pointed a damning finger at war workers:

> Last spring—after notable victories [overseas]—overconfidence became so pronounced that war production fell off. In two months, June and July, 1943, more than a thousand airplanes that could have been made and should have been made were not made. Those who failed to make them were not on strike. They were merely saying, "The war's in the bag—so let's relax." That attitude on the part of anyone— Government or management or labor—can lengthen this war. It can kill American boys.[125]

The passage was so damning, Roosevelt omitted it from his fireside chat that night.

To prevent such perilous complacency, and "to maintain a fair and stable economy at home," the president recommended that Congress adopt five major pieces of legislation. Two of these proposed to eliminate profiteering through taxation and contract renegotiation. The next two provided for measures to control food prices and maintain broader price stabilization measures.

After a perfunctory mention of the first four proposed measures to ensure the fair distribution of sacrifice among all citizens, Roosevelt turned to national service. Although he had "for three years hesitated" to support such legislation, long recommended by officers high in the armed services, he was now convinced of its necessity to ensure "an equal and comprehensive legal obligation of all people in a nation at war." Quoting from the text of one officer's recommendation, he read, "When the very life of the Nation is in peril . . . there can be no discrimination between the men and women who are assigned by the Government to its defense at the battlefront and the men and women assigned to producing the vital materials essential to successful military operations." Expanding on the point, Roosevelt claimed national service was "the most democratic way to wage a war." Like the draft, "it rests on the obligation of each citizen to serve his nation to the utmost where he is best qualified." Then, presenting the issue in a more personal light, he encouraged his audience to visualize themselves as part of a great nation united across generations:

> I know that all civilian war workers will be glad to be able to say many years hence to their grandchildren: "Yes, I, too, was in service in the great war. I was on duty in an airplane factory, and I helped make hundreds of fighting planes. The Government told me that in doing that I was performing my most useful work in the service of my country."[126]

While his embrace of national service was sudden and a surprise to even his closest advisors, Roosevelt stuck to it. He made it the topic of his last message to Congress and his last fireside chat in January 1945. The conscription of civilian labor was the only way to ensure the production needed to press on to victory, he asserted. And, as he had a year before, he pointed to workers who were making less than a total effort. "There's an old and true saying that the Lord hates a quitter," Roosevelt noted after observing that some workers were beginning to quit their jobs in the war industries, in anticipation of impending victory. These workers, and others who "lay down on their essential jobs," were exacting a price whose payment would have to be "made in the life's blood of our own sons." He urged Congress to adopt national service legislation to provide "our fighting men" with "supreme proof" that civilians were "giving them what they are entitled to, which is nothing less than our total effort back home." Almost as an afterthought, he reiterated his earlier commitment to an economic bill of rights, emphasizing "the most fundamental of these," the right to a job, and informing his radio audience of the plan he had submitted to Congress to ensure full employment with sixty million jobs in the postwar economy. "Others of the economic rights of American citizenship," such as housing or education, would also serve this overriding goal of "achieving adequate levels of employment."[127]

In his last two addresses, Roosevelt had crystallized the moral economy of the home front and reshaped it into an image of postwar society that would inspire and guide liberals for years afterward. A large section of American society shared a version of this vision as well—at least that part of it promising full employment. The wartime experience of a booming economy had cemented the government's legitimacy as a guarantor of the most basic form of economic security that most Americans expected: a job and the opportunity to improve one's standard of living through it.

As early as February 1943, when the uncertainties of the war had made citizens most attentive to world affairs, a poll showed that the question of employment and its guarantee in the postwar period was the top concern of three times as many people as was the goal of world peace. The concern with employment naturally increased as one went down the economic scale. But a conviction had emerged among people of all income levels by the end of the coal strike in June 1943 that "government, business and labor should get together *now* and make plans to try to do away with unemployment after the war." Republicans and Democrats, union workers and nonunion, rich and poor—84 percent or more of respondents falling into these categories agreed with this prescription. In a book examining these trends in public opinion, Jerome Bruner, a budding young pollster at the *Public Opinion Quarterly*, concluded, "The Government has a mandate from the people. The public wants jobs. It is counting on business and Government to work out plans—bold ones if need be—to that end."[128]

Despite the popular support, neither full nor fair employment would be institutionalized after V-J Day, even after concerted efforts by the Truman administration to build on the New Deal legacy in precisely these areas.[129] National service also never caught on, despite the wistful efforts of liberals who dreamed of a revived CCC or a domestic Peace Corps; neither did universal military training. Instead over the course of two decades the draft became increasingly skewed toward the working class in its selectivity. By the 1960s it had become a viable career path for poor Americans who lacked the educational opportunities or investment capital to rise into the middle class. By the Vietnam War, the armed forces would be so heavily skewed toward the lower end of the economic spectrum—thanks to the economic desperation that drove recruitment and the lack of social capital that made poor men more vulnerable to the draft lottery— that it would be widely understood to be a "working-class war."[130]

If full and fair employment failed to materialize as national policy, the memory of this promise continued to inform visions of full citizenship throughout the postwar period. High employment rates, sustained by Keynesian growth policies, would have to serve as an approximate substitute for full employment, a political compromise that mostly worked until the postwar political economy fell apart in the early 1970s. Civil rights activists and their liberal allies pushed for a permanent FEPC, the necessary complement to the full-employment bill. Although they met with failure at the hands of congressional conservatives, they would prevail in a dozen state legislatures that would establish their own versions of fair employment law, laying the grounds for the challenge to employment discrimination that would come with affirmative action in the 1960s.[131] Long after the equipment produced by the arsenal of democracy had rusted away on distant shores, the memory of a more vital social citizenship continued to haunt the memories of erstwhile soldiers of production.

6

Citizen-Soldiers

During the first week of July 1943, an item appeared in the op-ed pages of the *Los Angeles Times* that captured a growing mood of resentment among servicemen. In his regular and widely read column, Lee Shippey recounted a scene intended to shame his readers into action:

> When Lieut. Pat Milson, Canadian navy hero who helped get our boys to Africa arrived here Sunday he was shocked to see more motorcars full of pleasure drivers streaming through Hollywood than he had ever seen before. When he asked where people got all that gasoline he was told: "Oh, we can easily get gas on the black market." For two years he had been facing death, enduring hardship, suffering privation on the theory that this was everybody's war.

Recent headlines, Shippey noted, had reported the brazen activities of black marketeers whose activities around the country and "right here" in Los Angeles often went unchecked. "Are our honor and our devotion to our fighting men so cheap," asked Shippey, "that we will sell both of them for a few gallons of gas or a thick juicy steak?" He admonished his readers with words that subsequent events would make prescient: "Let us stop sneering at enemies abroad till we have quit condoning enemies at home."[1]

Two days later, American fighting men stationed in Los Angeles struck out at a figure whom many considered an enemy at home. Acting on the mounting sense of outrage Shippey had identified, the servicemen set things straight through force during the Zoot Suit riots that engulfed Los Angeles in the first ten days of June 1943. During the violent outbreak, which set off a summer of rioting and racial tension nationwide, servicemen banded together in impromptu gangs and "taxicab brigades," hunting down dwellers of what was perceived to be a criminal underworld.

To the rioting white servicemen, the zooters were sinister figures who wore the emblems of their subversive intent on their backs: flamboyant "zoot suits" whose excessive use of cloth qualified them as black market items, according to War Production Board regulations. In the eyes of most soldiers and white civilians, the zooters' suits, and the lifestyle they advertised, were a defiant rejection of the moral economy of the home front, a perversely inverted uniform that mocked the soldier's sacrifice. Their very presence in public places seemed to flaunt an unpatriotic self-indulgence. Through orchestrated attacks the soldiers reasserted the moral authority of the soldier as a culture hero before cheering crowds of white civilians who egged them on.[2]

The Zoot Suit riots were not the only outlet for the soldiers' impatience. The mass experience of military service during World War II fostered a distinctive mixture of resentment and prerogative that ran beneath the surface of the curt, frank, even stoic ethos for which the "silent generation" has become famous. Although no more than one out of every ten would ever see a shot fired in anger, all sixteen million who served in the armed forces had placed their lives at the disposal of their country, and each was held to the masculine standard of the idealized combat soldier. The more than three years, on average, that servicemen spent in the armed forces during the war only reinforced the contradictory expectations fostered by the role of the GI, cultivating an identity within the ranks that was often disconnected from, if not at odds with, the civilian identity left behind at induction. Such tensions posed a threat that concerned the War Department, which hired the University of Chicago sociologist Samuel Stouffer to lead an elaborate research team of social scientists to monitor fluctuations of morale and attitudes toward various facets of military service among servicemen.[3]

Because American GIs seemed so different from their fascist opponents, postwar social scientists concluded that their defining quality was a nonideological commitment to their buddies, families, and country.[4] This framing was itself a liberal ideological construct. In fact, American GIs *were* indoctrinated, quite heavily and successfully—by civilian propaganda before their service, and by a regimen of education and training during boot camp and afterward. In both civilian and military propaganda, American soldiers appeared as tolerant individualists, down-home democrats, rights-loving paragons of a free society in which self-interest and patriotism mixed in just the right proportions to place home, Mom, and apple pie on the lips of every fighting man given a celluloid soliloquy.[5]

As the racial animosities unleashed during the Zoot Suit riots would demonstrate, the nobler sentiments conveyed in training films and USO revues did not always sink in. But the GIs did selectively appropriate some central themes of wartime political culture to make sense of their experiences. Although divided into the separate branches of the army and the navy, segregated by race into Jim Crow units, stratified by class into enlisted and officer ranks, and dispersed to theaters of combat around the world, American servicemen shared a set of experiential coordinates that oriented them toward each other, the military, and the nation. To a man, nearly all resented the "rear echelon" of other soldiers and civilians who were more removed from the fighting than they were. This was true at the same time that servicemen clung to memories of home and relished any contact with family or friends while on leave or through the mail. The ambivalent mixture of longing and affection for a lost civilian identity and resentment of bearing most of the burden of wartime sacrifice had powerful effects on servicemen's identity. Almost universally, they regarded their military service—fraught as it was with ambivalence, boredom, and frustration—as a crucible of both their manhood and their national citizenship, which together established their Americanism.

Selecting Men for the Nation

The nation's first peacetime draft took effect in October 1940, marked by little of the controversy that had attended the divisive debate over intervention in preceding years. The position adopted by draft advocates was that "total war requires total registration."[6] As Roosevelt observed in his proclamation of the first registration in the fall of 1940, "Time and distance have been shortened. A few weeks have seen great nations fall. . . . The terrible fate of nations whose weakness invited attack is too well known to us all." The president expressed his confidence that "our young men will come from the factories and the fields, the cities and the towns, to enroll their names on registration day" in order to "hold high the torch of freedom in this darkening world so that our children and their children may not be robbed of their inheritance."[7] Apparently millions shared this sentiment. Unlike the draft for World War I, resistance was almost nonexistent and conscientious objectors were mostly compliant with demands for some sort of national service. Permanent peacetime mass conscription took root in the United States with almost no controversy or question.

In this respect the popularity of the film *Sergeant York* betrayed itself as a revealing prop for the ideology of voluntarism. Alvin York, the erstwhile conscientious objector from Tennessee whose sharpshooting and derring-do had made him the most decorated hero of the Great War, enjoyed a second act when Gary Cooper portrayed him in the eponymous 1941 film. The dramatic climax to the film's plot came when York wrestled with his conscience over whether to obey his induction notice, exercising an improbable degree of personal discretion in answering the "selective" call to service. Few American men during World War II had the opportunity to search their consciences when confronted by the demands of the U.S. government to place their bodies in the service of not one but two foreign wars. Nonetheless, the government had to tailor its appeals to a populace that fancied itself a nation of Gary Coopers—individualists all, and plucky ones at that.[8]

Notwithstanding the voluntaristic imagery, the unyielding reality remained that there were three bureaucratic gates through which all American men passed on their way to military service: the draft board, the induction center, and boot camp. Each marked a man's life, calibrating his fitness for the sternest demands of manhood and citizenship, and channeling him into a fate over which he had little control. The 15 percent or so who volunteered for the army or the navy might evade the indignities of the draft board, but they had little say in what happened thereafter.

Local draft boards thus decided the fate of most adult men between October 1940, when the Selective Service Act of that year took effect, and March 1947, when the act expired and inductions were halted for a period of months. For most of the war, every man between the ages of eighteen and sixty-five was required to register and was classified into four categories: I, available for service, graded into subcategories, with I-A indicating immediate availability for service; II, deferred due to occupational status, also graded into categories, with war work and farm labor receiving greater deferment than civilian work necessary to the war effort; III, deferred due to dependents, with those who also worked in essential war jobs deferred before those not working in war jobs; and IV, with several grades of unfitness or unsuitability for military service, ranging from officials (IV-B), nondeclarant aliens (IV-C), and ministers of religion (IV-D), to conscientious objectors (IV-E) and men deemed "physically, mentally, or morally unfit" (IV-F).[9] Out of the more than forty-five million registrants, nineteen million were selected for service, of which the army and the navy accepted just over ten million for induction.[10]

These classifications had momentous consequences for the manhood and the patriotic status of the men subjected to them. The draft placed a bureaucratic badge upon them—particularly for the dreaded IV-F classification—that would follow them through the rest of their lives. For those who went on to induction into the army or navy, a further set of finely graded inspections for physical, mental, and occupational ability awaited them, further winnowing them into classifications that would affect the structure of their opportunity, and their liability for dangerous assignments, throughout the rest of their time in the military. The draft and the armed services thus institutionalized finely graded definitions of manhood that would define a broader normative Americanism enframing national citizenship in the war years and beyond.[11]

The Selective Service System's more than six thousand boards were staffed by 184,000 volunteers, most of whom had been selected before the war according to their prestige within their local communities. They were given the authority to determine the draft status of each eligible man within their jurisdiction, which the appeals system of the Selective Service, headed by General Lewis B. Hershey, rarely overrode. Fewer than 10 percent of all I-A classifications were ever appealed—most initiated at the request of the employer—and in two-thirds of these cases the local decision was upheld.[12] Local pressures also explained the somewhat low proportion of African American men inducted to serve, as white board chairmen denied them the "right to fight" and thereby demonstrate their fitness for full citizenship.[13]

As John J. Corson, former director of the U.S. Employment Service, explained with more than a hint of frustration, the decentralized system of Selective Service boards worked against an effective national manpower allocation system. Local board members were not chosen for their expertise in occupational placement, nor was assigning vital war workers their main responsibility. Rather, he observed, "their chief concern is avoiding undue hardship. . . . They defer men on a *sentimental* rather than an occupational basis." Corson, writing in 1943, applauded the War Manpower Commission's growing authority over manpower policy, but his enthusiasm for greater central control over local draft boards and the labor market in general would ultimately be frustrated, as would the best exertions of Paul McNutt, who directed the WMC. Local boards ignored the WMC's efforts in early 1943 to force them to adhere to its detailed schedule of occupational deferments for essential war workers. For the remainder of the war, local boards continued to defer men on the basis of their family status rather than their occupation, national manpower priorities notwithstanding.[14]

Local boards could also undermine the best efforts of the WMC by agreeing to cancel the deferments of "undesirable" workers when local employers requested it, as sometimes happened to unfortunates working in the California shipyards. If workers went on strike, local boards could cancel strikers' II-B deferment for essential war work and reclassify them as I-A. This tactic occurred infrequently because of its limited effectiveness; nearly half of all industrial workers were classified IV-F, unfit for service, while many others had deferments due to dependents. However, reclassification could be a potent symbolic weapon, a trump card that overruled the growing sense of entitlement among workers.[15]

Mass compliance with the draft revealed a strikingly high degree of legitimacy for a policy with such a shaky past in the United States. There was no equivalent to the draft riots that had convulsed New York City in 1863, nor the widespread criticism and evasion of the draft that had elicited repression in World War I.[16] As with so many other aspects of the war mobilization in the 1940s, the draft and even its opposition were bureaucratized.

Conscientious objectors (COs) defined the outer limits of normative Americanism and manhood, as they had in World War I. Overwhelming majorities in national polls indicated their disapproval of COs, although the proportion declined slightly from 74 percent near the climax of the war in March 1944 to 65 percent in April 1945, when victory over Germany was at hand and the conclusion of the Pacific war in sight. Yet running beneath the surface of received attitudes were surprising indications of tolerance, as the Princeton psychologist Leo Crespi discovered. In the same polls that indicated predominant disapproval of COs, Crespi discovered large majorities, ranging between 60 and 70 percent, in favor of treating the COs fairly—allowing pay for their work, assignment to jobs making use of their skills and training, federal support for their dependents, even assignment overseas to help in war relief work—if they would submit to national service. Even more surprisingly, the proportion of respondents saying they *supported* the COs increased from 20 to 25 percent over the same time frame. These responses indicated not acceptance but a crucial tolerance that had been absent in the previous world war.[17]

Perhaps this less categorical outlook reflected a shift in the requirements of national belonging made possible by the meliorative effects of the interwar debate over neutrality and the popularization of critical views of war put forth by the peace movement and in films such as the popular *Big Parade* (1925). Certainly the laws governing the obligations for military service had loosened slightly since the previous war. The criteria to determine eligibility for CO status were broadened somewhat to emphasize individual conscience, not simply membership in a particular peace church, although the latter remained an essential foundation for a successful appeal. COs willing to serve in noncombat roles received a I-A-O classification and were inducted into the armed services, enjoying the full status of a soldier (if not necessarily the acceptance of his comrades). Those not willing to serve were classified IV-E and required to perform some work of use to the nation. At least 25,000 men with I-A-O classification were inducted (some estimates ranged as high as 50,000), while 11,950 with IV-E status were assigned to alternative service in civilian camps. Of this last group, 1,624 were convicted and sent to prison for refusing to serve even in the camps.[18]

Some aspects of the CO program's implementation also suggested that the interwar period and the New Deal had made a critical, if modest, difference in the treatment of dissenting citizens. Section 5(g) of the Selective Service and Training Act of 1940 made generic provisions for alternative service for COs. Under an agreement worked out between Roosevelt (who urged far stricter treatment), Selective Service director Hershey (who wanted to avoid the cost and trouble of running CO camps), and the churches, COs who refused noncombat service in the armed forces were to perform conservation work for the Department of Agriculture and the Department of the Interior, housed in defunct camp sites from the Civilian Conservation Corps (CCC) that were turned over to the newly created Civilian Public Service (CPS). The peace churches administered and funded the camps, taking orders from Hershey's old army buddy Col. Lewis F. Koch, a former CCC official.[19]

The rehabilitative vision of the CPS was grounded in the New Deal's programs to conserve the nation's manhood as well as its soil through militarized national service.[20] With its militaristic overtones, inherited from the CCC, and troubling similarity to other nations' youth programs during the interwar period, the CPS revealed the unintended consequences of a "thick" institutional definition of national belonging.[21] Unlike in World War I, apparently, there was room for a qualified toleration of dissent from war so long as COs devoted their bodies and minds to the nation in some constructive fashion.

CO policy was not, in the end, fully determined by New Deal precedents or tolerant strains of public opinion. General Hershey, whose sensibilities dated to the previous world war in which he had made his military career, ensured that COs felt the full stigma of their classification. Listening to the concerns of veterans lobbyists and their allies in Congress, he ensured that their lot would be a difficult one. He acted decisively to deny them any pay for their work, support for their dependents, compensation for injury during service, or opportunity to assist with overseas relief that would be commensurate with their desire to work against war. His spite for the COs persisted to the bitter end, making their postwar return to civilian life more trying than it needed to be. A few weeks after V-J Day, a poll showed 43 percent support for releasing COs immediately, with another 40 percent accepting release for "those who have done useful work."[22] Yet Hershey dragged his heels until October before releasing any COs from CPS camps, and did not free the last men until the day before the Selective Service Act of 1940 expired, at the end of March 1947.[23]

As the treatment of COs indicated, military service remained a central obligation of men's citizenship.[24] Virile Americanism was a primary requirement of the ideal "red-blooded" GI, and its prescriptions applied as universally as the draft itself. Indeed, masculine prescriptions for a militarized notion of full citizenship extended far beyond the laws, administrative offices, and local boards that constituted the draft system, reaching deep into the political culture.

The foremost articulators of the masculine and martial norm of citizenship were the draftees and soldiers themselves. Men feared they might not measure up, and consequently the rumors they shared concerning draft dodgers and 4-Fs attributed an exaggerated sickliness and even effeminacy to the "defectives," who were imagined to remain behind with the women. Soldiers sang "Four-F Charlie" as they marched on exercises, or they learned the verses while reading *Yank* or *Life*. "A sad case of humanity," the "sick and always ailing" Charlie would "never amount to anything," could "never be a father," had "blood as thin as water," and was even "taking a body-toner / so he can be a blood bank-donor."[25] Jokes ran along similar lines, featuring stock characters who got caught while cravenly trying to avoid their duty: the fool sent to the Near East, despite his attempt to evade the draft by cross-dressing, because "anybody who can wear a truss upside down can ride a camel for the duration"; the fellow who took his friend's advice (offered while strolling down Broadway) to feign mental illness, yet wound up classified 1-A because his friend forgot to mention the corollary requirement, that he actually have "heart trouble"; and the "yellow-livered" draft dodger who was cornered by his suspicious eye doctor in the back row of Radio City Music Hall and who attempted to maintain the pretense of myopia by asking tremulously, "Could you tell me if I am on the right bus for Jamaica?" Mostly jokes emphasized the pathetic lack of virility presumed to define the man who remained a civilian, such as the one about a new "5-B" classification: "bifocals, bald head, bridgework, bay window, and bunions."[26]

Suspicious neighbors, coworkers, and acquaintances filled the mailbags of the FBI, the Selective Service, and other agencies with letters naming local men who seemed to have evaded the draft. One anonymous writer sent a letter to the FBI wondering, "Why? A young man whose physical condition & ability seems O.K. and who passes remarks such as; why should I fight for Johnny Bull. [He] is allowed to work and not fight for this country." The author went on to name the man's employer and badge number, concluding, "He is not long in the U.S.A." A woman from Decatur, Illinois, wrote to the FBI to complain about her son-in-law, Donald, who had been loafing for "quite some time," refusing to work for less than 73 cents per hour and insisting on sitting "around the house read[ing] books [and] quarrel[ing] with" her daughter.[27] The avidity with which Americans reported their friends, family, and neighbors for draft evasion may explain the one big success enjoyed by the FBI's American Legion Contact Program. Over the course of the war the FBI pursued 445,649 cases of apparent draft evasion, convicting 11,320 men while resolving most of the other cases by working directly with the Selective Service to secure induction or legitimate deferral. These cases were brought to the attention of the FBI by letters and through the initiative of Legionnaires and contacts drawn from other civic groups.[28] Without the mass surveillance of everyday life instilled by the government to safeguard morale, the job of policing draft compliance would have been far more difficult.

Becoming GIs

If habituation to the state was a hallmark of World War II America, then military service was the stamp that impressed it onto the social fabric. A generation of young men encountered a cross section of the nation produced through the social engineering of Selective Service classification, screening procedures, testing, training, and assignment to a unit whose relationship to the local communities from which its men were drawn was far more tenuous than had been the case in earlier conflicts. GIs made their transition from civilian to military life during induction and basic training. No longer civilians pursuing their individual fates within a fluid and mobile American society, they landed at the bottom of a "new world" defined by its "authoritarian organization," "highly stratified social system," and "traditional" customs, as Stouffer and his team characterized the army.[29] A very similar, if more elite, characterization might have been made of the navy's training program. Beyond training and indoctrination, boot camp in both the army and navy also served to further heighten the masculine values that suffused martial citizenship, with official trials of physical endurance and skill, and unofficial hazing rituals that could border on the sadistic.

The central purpose of boot camp was, of course, to make soldiers of young men through drilling, training, indoctrination, hazing, physical and mental exhaustion, and constant subjection to discipline and authority. They learned that they belonged to the army or navy, not to the democratic society they were to defend. Above all, soldiers had to learn to take orders. Unconditional acceptance of authority and the chain of command was foundational, if artificial. Draftees largely had no military experience, but often did have educational preparation superior to that of their commanding officers, who came predominantly from the ranks of the regular army.[30]

As might be expected in such a situation, trainees disliked many aspects of boot camp and particularly resented the petty authority of their commanding officers. On the whole, GIs viewed noncoms as ignorant, incompetent, and poor teachers. What rankled the most was lack of the freedom to which civilian life had accustomed them—and, beyond the basic facts of regimentation, not being treated like an individual. At the end of a survey completed for Stouffer's research staff, one GI wrote that "the 'why' should always be explained. This is rarely done." Another wrote that "a soldier should be allowed to give his viewpoint on different occasions." In his first month at camp he had been allowed to offer up his views, but soon he was told to "shut up," and now he found himself trying "to keep suggestions to myself" and "just take orders." A third trainee felt that "the Army officers don't get out enough with the men to find out who is and who is not capable."[31]

These gripes would wash away with time, as the greater challenges of life in the field supplanted their memory. Combat veterans interviewed by Stouffer's staff in early 1944 admitted that the rigors of their training had either been "about right" (51 percent) or "not tough enough" (30 percent), particularly regarding practical matters such as physical training and war games. But when asked what they regarded the least helpful aspect of their training for actual combat, they listed exercises in obedience for its own sake: close order drill, marches and hikes, and military courtesy and inspections (in that order).[32]

This chafing at military authority did not necessarily represent its outright rejection. Stouffer and his staff concluded that it "existed side by side with a desire to achieve status within the system." This was why petty authority and the privileges officers enjoyed rankled so—they highlighted the many layers of experience, rank, and bureaucratic procedure that lay between privates or seamen and their ambitions to advance according to their ability. Unlike army regulars in the same position, enlistees found the army's overt system of rank and privilege highly objectionable. As one wrote in a "free comment" at the end of his survey response, "I thought the caste system was restricted to India. These officers think they are tin gods or the next thing to it."[33] What selectees most resented was the "bootlicking," favoritism, and "pull" that often seemed to determine promotion.

A more personalized sense of the flavor of life in boot camp can be gleaned from the missives of Robert "Jerry" Calhoun, a farm boy from just outside of Pittsburgh who was unusually dutiful in writing home to his parents. Calhoun had received some technical preparation in the Army Services Training Program at Carnegie Tech, where he and his fellow trainees cheerfully sang "Goldbrick, goldbrick, goldbrick in the ASTP" to the tune of "My Bonnie Lies over the Sea." He then shipped out for basic training at Camp Fannin, located on the outskirts of Tyler, Texas, in late May 1944.[34] His first reaction was disorientation—caused as much by the bleak "mud, sand, [and] heat" that characterized the landscape as by pulling KP duty at 4:20 in the morning, followed by gas mask training in chambers filled with laughing gas, and practice with live grenades.[35]

Although he eventually attained the certification for sharpshooter, Jerry Calhoun did not receive the kind of deferential treatment and solicitation of conscience that greeted Gary Cooper's Alvin York on the silver screen. Within a fortnight Calhoun was complaining of "chicken-shit . . . flying thick and fast" and other abuses of authority, although he quickly became inured to it. By the first of July he was sufficiently alienated to refuse his lieutenant's suggestion that he spend $18.75 out of his monthly pay of $51.22 to buy a war bond, although he backed down despite his miserly disposition by promising to start a $5.00 stamp book when he saw the "disconcerted" look on the officer's face. A week later he and his fellow trainees rebelled by refusing to buy any bonds when they were required to attend a bond rally until nine in the evening after a hard day's marching in the wet heat of the east Texas sun, which left them no time even to clean their rifles. "Only one" of the group bought any bonds—and, he added, "that one fellow's a 'brown-noser' anyway." By the time of his graduation from infantry basic training at midmonth he was likening his experience—sitting in muddy foxholes while tanks rolled above—to that of damned souls in hell up to their necks in "cowflop," hoping "Old Nick" wouldn't crack his whip.[36]

Green enlistees had to adjust to the outlooks and expectations of men from other parts of the country, or to the southern communities in which they were mostly based. Even before Calhoun left Pennsylvania, he wrote home to his parents that "almost every night, the Yankees and the Southerners fight the Civil War over again. That's no fooling, either. The arguing gets quite spirited at times."[37]

If basic training provided servicemen with their initiation into military tradition, orientation sought to inject some basic ideological content into the broader process of re-education. The films, officers' speeches, and small-group discussions that constituted orientation took up only a small proportion of a soldier's time every week, but they exposed servicemen to carefully framed messages about the purposes of the war and of major policies.

Government propagandists in World War II strove mightily to convince GIs that they were not issuing propaganda—and that even if they were, the GIs were preternaturally immune, as Americans, to the kinds of persuasion that had hypnotized their fascist enemies. The War Department's Division of Education and Information, which was responsible for much of the material GIs encountered during their orientation, posited fundamental differences between the nonideological G.I., who pined for Mom and apple pie, and the fanatical soldiers of Nazi Germany and Imperial Japan, whose indoctrination or racial inferiority were presumed to have reduced them to automatons easily incorporated into the fascist war machine.[38]

A prime specimen of this propaganda was provided by the film series Why We Fight, directed by the popular Hollywood auteur Frank Capra. Since the series drew on all the conventions of Hollywood in which Capra was versed, it is not surprising that these films shared some of the features of the far more prevalent and commercially more sophisticated films that greeted soldiers overseas under the sponsorship of the USO and other hospitality outfits.[39]

For all their notoriety, Capra's orientation films did not strike a chord among the GIs who were forced to watch them, as Stouffer's research staff discovered. Stouffer's men discovered that the GIs, like their civilian counterparts, rarely internalized the precise messages the government sought to convey, but rather selectively accepted or even misconstrued the images and messages to which they were exposed. Watching the Battle of Britain installment of the Why We Fight series improved soldiers' belief that aiding the British was necessary because "we would have been next," but only by raising this kind of response from 30 percent of those who had not seen the film to 44 percent among those who had.[40]

Unsurprisingly, GIs preferred entertainment to didacticism. From the first studies in December 1941 onward, the "great majority" of them "preferred shows put on by *outsiders*."[41] The most compelling orientation films, in the eyes of the GIs, came from the Private Snafu series, produced by Warner Brothers in the style of their beloved Bugs Bunny and other Looney Tunes cartoons. The goofy Snafu was a hapless army private who always managed to screw things up and get himself killed (or in deep trouble).

One 1943 Private Snafu episode, titled *Gripes*, was tested in an experiment that compared it to four other orientation films: one about amphibious training, another about civilian war work in a machine shop, a third that included first-person testimony and documentary footage about the desperate fighting on Corregidor, and the last about the Women's Army Auxiliary Corps (WAAC). As they watched, GIs recorded their moment-by-moment reactions by pushing a "like" or "dislike" button, allowing the research team to aggregate their responses into charts indicating overall preference for each scene and for each film overall.

Not only did *Gripes* outscore the other shorts by a dramatic margin, but all of its scenes outscored all of the scenes in the other shorts, with only four exceptions—each of them featuring authentic battle footage, a perennial favorite of military and civilian audiences. The film short *Back Home* was by far the least appealing of the five tested. It featured a small Connecticut tool-and-die shop recently awarded the Navy E Award for excellence in production. It never attained scores even one-third as high as the lowest score for the scenes in *Gripes*, and its appeal ranked somewhere around half as interesting as the first-person account from Corregidor.

Apparently the fond identification that home-front soldiers of production cultivated for the combat soldier went unrequited. The consensus among the GI viewers, according to the research team, was an instinctive revulsion at what they perceived to be "pseudo-patriotism" among civilians, who enjoyed high-paying war jobs and did not face the hardships of military life. As one GI stated, "That rubs a soldier the wrong way. They don't like to see civilians getting credit." Another explained, "We are at war, and everybody should do his duty, whether in the Army or not. They are getting $90 and $100 (per week) for the work they are doing."[42]

The plot of the Private Snafu short that beat out the other orientation films provides a window onto the GI sensibilities that made them susceptible to laughter, and thus to persuasion. *Gripes* opened like most other Private Snafu cartoons, with the trademark Loony Tunes boing and marquee featuring Snafu's goofy grin, followed by a narrator who spelled out the acronym that was his surname, pausing for comedic effect: "Situation Normal, All . . . Fouled Up."[43] His name, a mockery of military acronyms, reflected his irreverent attitude toward the army, which he displayed in the opening scene by griping about having to do kitchen patrol (KP) duty. In a rhymed refrain that got at many soldiers' frustrations, he moaned, "I joined this here army to join in the fun of jabbing the Jap and hunting the Hun, and look at the job they handed to me—KP! KP! KP! KP! KP!"

Soon Snafu's complaints were answered. As he recovered from a fever in the sick ward, an unkempt, cigar-chomping "technical fairy, first class" waved his wand and promoted him instantly to "master sarge, super-sarge, boss of the woiks." Once in charge, Snafu announced that the camp was under "new management," whose policy was "relaxation, more money," unlimited leisure, and a "new GI issue—each guy gets two dames." Soon soldiers were driving around camps with buxom "Victory Girls," the local PX was converted to a juke joint called Jake's that served liquor in the middle of the day, partying couples were carousing in the camp field, and Snafu was lounging in bed with a three-woman harem tending to his every need. The new policies earned high marks from the men, who cheered, "Hooray for Snafu gives us all limousines no more drill no salutes no more cleaning latrines." A jiving, bebopping soldier in a modified military uniform confided to the viewer, "Look me over Jackson, this is really all root, Snafu lets you dress up in a suit that is zoot."

Soon enough, the moral of the story arrived in the form of a swastika-labeled bomb. "Where are my troops?" Snafu asked, roused from his bed by the drone of approaching German aircraft. "No use," the technical fairy replied, "they ain't trained, and they got no morale." Snafu woke up from the reverie just as the bomb hit him in the dream. Duly chastened, he rushed straight from his sickbed—apparently he had been goldbricking—to eagerly return to his KP duty, where he agreed with the technical fairy: "The harder you woik, the sooner we're going to beat Hitler, that joik." Despite the hijinks, *Gripes* contained clear messages about morale and military discipline—and the kind of man who evaded work—even as it invoked the ideological aims of the war through references to Hitler and Nazism.

Just how deeply orientation films and speeches managed to lodge their ideological payload in the minds of GIs is difficult to discern. Some servicemen, particularly those with sharply formed political views, were willing to bluntly reject a New Deal for the world, as one GI did in the comment he added to the end of the survey he completed for Stouffer's field researchers in March 1945:

> I am not fighting to give freedom to the world. Freedom is something that must be earned. It can't be of any value when taken as a gift. I am fighting to keep America on top and to help Great Britain. If Roosevelt thinks he is going to flood this country with the scum of the world after the war he has a lesson coming. This is a white fighting Christian Country and we intend to keep it that way! We earned our freedom. All help to those who want to do the same. But no lies about handing it to them—And the least Government is the best Government.[44]

Relatively few soldiers responded in this fashion, repudiating outright the ideological agenda of a New Deal for the world. Only 16 percent of white enlisted soldiers in August 1942 agreed with the statement "We are not responsible for saving the world. We are in this war solely to defend the United States of America," whereas 38 percent said they disagreed.[45] Some larger, ill-defined proportion also sought to limit their personal exposure to danger overseas, and so also expressed discomfort with or aversion to a broad mandate for the war's objectives or for postwar peacekeeping. For still others, skepticism of an expansive military mission to defend freedom in the world was of a piece with their larger distaste for the army and its regimentation.

It was quite possible for soldiers to hold conflicting or even contradictory positions toward the war. When surveyed, a clear majority (between 66 and 75 percent, depending on combat experience) indicated that they never or only rarely questioned whether the war was worth fighting. Just under two-thirds (65 percent) accepted the idealistic proposition that America was "fighting to guarantee democratic liberties." Even among those who had doubts about whether the war was worth fighting, nearly half (47 percent) felt that the job they were doing for the army was "worthwhile." But prick the surface of these received attitudes with questions about the specifics of the war effort and one would discover, Stouffer reported, that "the more closely men approached the real business of the war, the more likely they were to question its worthwhileness, particularly as it applied to their personal experience."[46]

Despite the ingrained cynicism of the fighting troops and the outright criticism of liberal internationalist goals by conservatives and others who distrusted military authority, there were many indications that a large proportion of soldiers embraced, or at least accepted, the role of liberal international policeman for the U.S. military. Although roughly three out of ten enlisted men surveyed in the summer of 1943 claimed never to have heard of Roosevelt's Four Freedoms, nearly six out of ten did indicate some kind of recognition, and nearly a third could name two of the four. That so many were able to identify two of the freedoms because they overlapped with the Bill of Rights does not take away from the significance of the findings for the popular embrace of the liberal imaginary.[47]

Beyond the superficial indications provided by survey research, there is evidence of support for liberal internationalism in the songs sung by marines in the Pacific theater that the Archive of American Folksong collected from the field during the war. One song, composed in March 1944 by Kyle Kinzer, seaman first class on the SS *William Floyd*, snuck war aims into a work song sung to the tune of "The Wabash Cannonball." Although it emphasized their central mission in nationalistic terms—"our country we will save" by bringing food and ammunition "for the boys in foreign lands"—it also gave those nationalistic aims a Rooseveltian twist:

We will fight our country's battle
To set all people free
And when this war is over
How happy we will be!
Tojo and Hitler's disappointed
This is one thing that we know
So let's keep on a-rolling
And keep them on the go.[48]

Unlike other marching songs that labeled Axis enemies with pat monikers such as "old Mikado" or "the little corporal" (Hitler), or even explicitly mentioned them by name, such as Tojo or Mussolini, but did not mention freedom or other liberal ideological keywords, this song referred to the enemy as a stand-in for fascism.[49] Doubtless Kinzer's liberal proclivities, revealed by the very fact of his donating these songs to Lomax's outfit in the Library of Congress, explain his vocal and coherent articulation of liberal war aims. As was the case with his ideological opposite—the soldier fighting to "keep America on top"—this soldier's ideological orientation allowed him to articulate views that others left implicit, if they understood them at all.

Ideological commitment does not, however, explain how similar themes worked their way into other songs popular among marines in the Pacific theater. For example, the "Doctrine of the Raider Battalion," reported from Camp Elliott, San Diego, opened with this unlikely amalgam of Marine derring-do and liberal idealism:

We are Raiders of the Land and Sea.
We work together for Democracy
Gung Ho! Gung Ho! Gung Ho! Ho!
We are tough; we are just;
We fight when e'er we must
For the right to be free.[50]

Another song, "Modern Cannon Ball," centered on the "score to settle" with Japan after Pearl Harbor and Luzon. But it also included refrains that claimed the war was being fought to "make this country safe for those who love democracy": "Our Chinese friends and allies will see freedom in their land / When we lick those Fascist bullies from the island of Japan."[51]

Some of this military folklore sought to use Christian imagery to sanctify war aims. "You Better Get Ready"—a work song adapted by black soldiers—referred to a judgment day that loomed for the fascists, with one refrain placing the fascists in a deeper circle of hell than Old Scratch himself:

> The devil opened up his big black book,
> SING ON, BROTHER, SING!
> He opened it up and he took a look!
> SING ON, BROTHER, SING!
> He read off Adol[f] Hitler's name,
> And said, Old Hell just ain't the same,
> Compared to the Fascists, brother, I'm tame!
> SING ON, BROTHER, SING![52]

Another song enjoined the listener to read the Bible to "see how Joshua won" by praying to the Lord. In the last stanza, which devoted four of five lines to reiterating Christ's admonition "to watch and pray," the middle line altered the pattern, lending otherworldly sanction to worldly authority: "Government told the people all go [out into] the street / To hear the President speak."[53]

When singers referred explicitly to the enemy as fascist, they often indicated an ideological slant that appropriated liberal rhetoric for the singer's purposes. This was clearly the case for the song "You Fascists Bound to Lose," which had a strong Popular Front inflection. After gloating about Russian victories on the Eastern Front, its middle stanza prophesied a kind of international Popular Front revived by the fight against fascism:

> You cannot divide us nor keep us split apart,
> Us common folks is on the march, got freedom in our heart,
> You're bound to lose,
> You fascists bound to lose!
> People of every color fighting side by side
> Marching cross the fields where a million fascists died!
> You're bound to lose, you fascists bound to lose![54]

This song seemed to be aimed at southerners as much as it was at the Axis. A similar message pervaded "The Little Brown Jug Goes Modern," although its overtones had less to do with racial comity and more to do with a defense against the fascist critique of liberal democracy. Its last stanza bragged:

> They said our freedom had made us weak,
> They said our system had made us meek,
> But we'll answer them now with planes and tanks,
> If Hitler says "Peace," we'll say, "no, thanks."
> We've got about a billion friends and relations,
> We've got our buddies in the United Nations,
> When we get through with our Axis foe,
> They just won't be there no mo'![55]

Some songs used echoes of slave spirituals to give the contemporary struggle against fascist "slavery"—a common trope of liberal propaganda—a historical and racial twist. "Certainly Am," a call and response adapted from the eponymous Woody Guthrie song, sounded like something that might have been sung during Reconstruction, with its central refrain, "I'm gonna fight for my freedom, certainly am!"[56] Even more explicit was "What Are We Waiting On?" with its opening refrain:

> There's a great and bloody fight round the whole wide world tonight
> In the battle the bombs and shrapnel rain
> Hitler told the world around, he would break our freedoms down,
> United Nations gonna break those slavery chains, Great God!
> United Nations gonna break those slavery chains.

Later stanzas spoke of the Nazi defeat at Stalingrad, thanked the "Soviets and the mighty Chinese vets / And the Allies this whole wide world around," and even lauded the "battling British," portraying a rising of "all the people in the whole wide world" as if the war were a union organizing campaign, underscored by the refrain, "That's the union that'll tear old Hitler down."[57]

In "A Message to Hitler," the singer depicted the soldier's call to arms in personal, familial terms that linked personal obligations to public ones. After bragging about the might of the navy, he related that his father and sister both had called him to remind him of "what you are fighting for"—"the good old American way." He concluded that "Mr. Hitler must be crazy" to think he could "take this land of mine." "Now Mr. Roosevelt don't you get worried," the last stanza begins, "We will be home before long ... But don't you look for us / Until you hear that Hitler's gone."[58]

Mass military service had seemed to present an ideal opportunity for indoctrination into the central tenets of the American way, as articulated in *Why We Fight* and other orientation materials. The marine songs and Stouffer surveys revealed that liberal ideals did sometimes resonate, although more often they were reappropriated in idiosyncratic ways that served GIs' purposes. Veterans' survey responses also suggested an unexpected, even dark side to the meanings they took away from their training and military service. In September 1945, veterans of overseas service in the infantry told researchers that the army experience had changed them, but not necessarily for the better. Roughly 10 percent said that it had induced poor health, another 10 percent said it had resulted in poor mental health, and an equal proportion said that it had instilled cynicism in them, while slightly fewer said it had aged them "beyond their years" (7 percent) or made them "given to greater moral laxity" (6 percent).[59] The school of the army taught several lessons, some of them ideological, others personal, but all, in one way or another, formative of the GIs' broader political outlook on military life and their relationship to the nation and to the world.

Dividing Lines

As U.S. troops issued forth from stateside bases they brought with them an icon whose unlikely ubiquity soon became legendary. Men told stories of storming impossible beachheads, only to find on pushing back the enemy that another American soldier had beaten them there, leaving a scrawled cartoon of a man peering over a fence or ledge with the caption "Kilroy was here." Others found Kilroy's mark drawn on latrines, scrawled on walls, and even, as one joke had it, written on the underwear of freshly disrobed romantic conquests. Kilroy captured the peculiar sensibility of the midcentury American GI. Irreverent in a slightly goofy sort of way, tickling the same funny bone that made Private Snafu appealing, his mere presence suggested superhuman feats of daring or guile. Yet the partially obscured appearance of the man behind the fence suggested he was a cipher for the everyday Joe, who, driven to the brink of loopy madness by the arcane and meaningless drudgery of military life, had been inspired to evade the strictures of standard procedure that GIs were forced to obey.[60]

Back home, the iconography of the soldier in popular culture was too hallowed and too infused with personal worry to afford much in the way of humor or irreverence. But in the service, particularly among the rank and file, irreverence was a democratizing balm that soothed the injuries of rank and the arbitrariness of bureaucracy. Routine and petty authority defined everyday life for GIs, who learned in basic training and troop assignment to look to their buddies to help them survive the assaults of regimentation that bonded them together long before they reached an overseas bivouac or dock.[61] The privileges of rank, and the power enjoyed by those who could pull it, marked the most immediate and personally consequential dividing line in the daily life of the soldier. Petty use of rank also provided soldiers with their most immediate and regular encounter with military authority. Unsurprisingly, this made such abuses, derided as "chickenshit," eternal targets of the GIs' contempt.

Like their civilian friends and family, soldiers articulated their disillusionment by drawing on the social experiences that formed their local view on the war. Thousands of soldiers filled up the "free comment" sections on the War Department surveys of morale with complaints about incompetent "ninety-day wonders" and tyrannical officers who had obtained their positions through "connections" and "pull," leaving few opportunities for enlisted men to advance. Stouffer's analysis of the comments found, not surprisingly, that "well over half the comments concerned officers"—specifically their privileges and their relations with enlistees—"and almost all were unfavorable." Other, more systematically measured responses indicated clearly that "those with unfavorable attitudes toward officers outnumbered those with favorable attitudes," and that these unfavorable attitudes derived most of their force from serving in an army that "sanctioned and encouraged a *system* of special privilege."[62] One frustrated soldier's scrawled complaint articulated why ordinary perquisites seemed an undemocratic abuse of authority:

> I have never seen an organization so polluted with petty politics as the U.S. Army. Truthfully speaking, and you want the truth, I have seen only a few rare cases where a man was chosen for his ability and not because of his years of service or his political connections.[63]

Frustrations with the army's rigid hierarchy emerged in responses to a War Department survey of enlisted infantry in the Mediterranean theater who in the late spring of 1944 were invited to complete the prompt "If I were the CO . . ." The commanding officer (CO) was the most immediate and intimate representation of the chain of command for enlisted men. But these were seasoned troops who had been in battle since the landing in North Africa in late 1942 and had seen intense fighting as Allied forces made their way up the Italian peninsula.

"The Brass," by soldier Victor Lundy, showing soldiers stationed at Fort Jackson, South Carolina, on June 6, 1944, "D-Day." Lundy, an architectural student, was surprised to find himself transferred from the Army Special Training Program (ASTP) into the U.S. Army's 26th Infantry Division for the D-Day buildup. After the war Lundy went on to become an acclaimed architect. The image is taken from his World War II sketchbooks, now in the Victor A. Lundy Archive. (Courtesy of the Library of Congress, LC-DIG-ppmsca-24169)

Although nearly all enlisted men chafed at chickenshit, seasoned combat veterans were particularly resistant to it. They cultivated a rough democratic camaraderie that thrived on criticism of officers' prerogatives.

The troops' responses overwhelmingly emphasized the need to foster a more democratic atmosphere, reduce barriers between officers and enlisted men, and improve consideration for the morale of ordinary soldiers. The most common response, as paraphrased by the survey researchers, was "I would be democratic; I would be a buddy to my men" and treat them as a "comrade in arms." Many used the word "regular" to describe how officers should comport themselves, implicating the high-and-mighty attitude too many had learned in Officer Candidate School. "I would act like a human being and that would remedy everything," one respondent quipped. This insistence on respect manifested itself in particular suggestions for providing the men with more off-duty time ("more freedom" was the revealing term used), securing "the best possible" clothing and equipment, and demonstrating an overall concern with the "welfare" of the men under their command. GIs wished officers would take their suggestions more seriously and share their hardships more equally. Above all, they wanted officers to "treat them as men, not serial numbers, treat them as individuals not as a herd of cattle."[64]

The bitterness instilled by the insults of rank came out in a marching song that altered the folk ballad "Frankie and Johnnie." The soldiers' version told the story of two lovers separated by the orders of a "Colonel who wanted Frankie / Wanted her for his own girl / And when he popped her the question / He gave her a necklace of pearl." When Johnnie found out, he shot the colonel and went to jail, unmourned by the callous Frankie, who promptly "got another pilot." The refrain at the end of each stanza, "She was his gal, but she done him wrong," must have struck a chord among the men who sang it together. This concluding refrain reversed the central point of the traditional folk ballad, which, as Lomax's file in the Library of Congress documented, had Frankie shooting her two-timing Johnnie because "he was her man, but he done her wrong." The original version claimed "this story has no moral" except to show that "there ain't no good in men." By reversing the gender of the treacherous lover and having a corrupt colonel, rather than an unfaithful lover, wind up with a bullet in his heart, the soldiers added a moral and made the tragedy their own.[65]

Like class and rank, race marked a sharp dividing line fostering irreconcilable expectations among servicemen.[66] Both the army and the navy were committed to a long tradition of systematic racial segregation that began at induction and, with few exceptions, never relented. African Americans would make no more progress within the military during World War II than they had during the previous world war, but the emergence of an interwar civil rights movement bolstered by the Popular Front, the New Deal, and the prominence of racially inclusive messages in the Roosevelt administration's propaganda raised the expectations black soldiers had of military routes to citizenship.

Elevated black expectations came into violent confrontation with white soldiers' and civilians' expectations of black deference and invisibility in and around southern military bases. "Hitlerism at home" would spark concerted opposition among black troops, boosting enrollment in the NAACP and turning southern camp towns into battlegrounds.[67] Many of the bitterest fights involved black soldiers in uniform (especially officers) whose presence on the streets failed to elicit salutes or whose consumer dollars in restaurants were refused with icy stares and worse.[68] Over the course of 1943, the peak year of wartime racial violence, there were more than 240 violent racial incidents in forty-seven cities around the country.

In some camps, racial tensions boiled over into race war. At Camp Stewart, Georgia, conditions had deteriorated so badly by June 1943 that black soldiers took it upon themselves to fire on white MPs from hidden lookouts in organized raids—a state of affairs that army historians deemed "typical" of such racial outbreaks. Although the mounting violence grew surprisingly organized, it was simply the culmination of a process by which black soldiers contested segregation, escalating tactics and strategy as the army sought to crack down on them.[69] By 1944 the army had devised policies to dampen conflict, including the more proactive use of black military police, that defused some of the tension.[70] But for much of the war, on both the home front and the battlefront, racial tension and conflict was the norm.

This state of affairs, and black soldiers' views of it, are revealed in thousands of letters written to Judge William Hastie, the civilian aide for race relations in the War Department, and his successor, Truman Gibson. One black soldier wrote of "this hell hole," Camp Livingston, Louisiana: "Brother, if you are colored, you don't stand a chance down here." These reports catalogued a wide range of abuses visited upon black troops by white officers, from being excluded from USO shows and special training to watching in outrage as "even the German prisoners of war have more freedom and opportunities than us." The author was driven to distraction reflecting on how black soldiers, many of them highly skilled and educated, were "led like lambs to the slaughter to die for a democracy that doesn't exist down here."[71]

Hastie and Gibson were deluged with letters complaining of segregation, mistreatment by officers and other army staff, exclusion from special training, cruel insults, and being treated "like dogs." Citing the wanton disregard for basic decency exhibited by southern noncoms, most black letter writers took pains to emphasize the contradiction between their unequal treatment and the idealistic war aims publicized throughout civilian society and military orientation. In May 1944, Pvt. Charles Wilson of the Army Air Force wrote an eloquent letter directly to President Roosevelt, noting the "extreme pride" with which he had read FDR's "affirmation of our war aims" at a press conference:

> The United Nations are fighting to make a world in which tyranny, and aggression cannot exist; a world based upon freedom, equality, and justice; a world in which all persons, regardless of race, color and creed, may live in peace, honor and dignity.[72]

Wilson, echoing Roosevelt's rhetoric, reveled in the role the United States played in "driving back" fascism around the world and freeing peoples in North Africa, Sicily and Italy from "tyranny and aggression." But, he confided, these heroic efforts were in danger of being undermined by a refusal of democracy in the armed forces and back home. He knew through personal experience and from reports in the black press that the army and the navy consistently forced black servicemen into service units kept from combat, even though it meant a great underutilization of manpower. This left America "wide open for sowers of disunity":

> Nothing would suit Hitler, Tojo, and our own native fascists better, than disunity. . . . The lead editorial of the *Afro American* . . . [related] two cases of *tyranny* against two Negro soldiers. . . . [The editorial] went on to say: "This is terrorism, and the army has no answer for it. Have the soldiers themselves an answer? There are thousands of them and only a few police or bus drivers. . . . Disunity and civil strife would only weaken our fight against the German and Japanese fascists. A victory [for them] would only mean a victory for our own native fascists, who are at the bottom of this whole program of "white supremacy," race hatred, jim-crowism, and segregation. It would mean victory . . . for the Rankins, Bilbos, Smiths, Hearsts, McCormicks, Peglers, and Dies.

Wilson cited Ruth Benedict's pamphlet *The Races of Mankind* to debunk "the anti-democratic doctrine of 'race-superiority,'" and pointed to black war hero Dorie Miller to refute military officials' claims that black men made inferior soldiers. He closed by asking Roosevelt to issue an executive order that would do for the armed services what the order creating the FEPC had intended for war production, where black men and women could work "side by side" with whites.[73]

Even some rather dire cases could reveal improbably high expectations of fair treatment by the military. An African American private named Stanley West wrote to the adjutant general from New York City, where he had gone AWOL after being falsely accused of bringing liquor to his company's bivouac in Louisiana. "I enjoy serving in the Army and am willing to serve whatever sentence might be imposed," he wrote, but only on the condition that he not be sent back to the South. He wasn't deserting, he promised, but only trying to ensure that he was "going to be treated as a human being," in hopes that he would "feel within that it is a joy to serve my country rather than feel that I am in slavery." He signed off, "I am still a Law abiding citizen of the United States, and one of Uncle Sam's chosen men." West's next letter, from the brig in Camp Blanding, Florida, recorded the dashing of his hopes. It appears he received a "blue discharge" that excluded him from qualifying for the veterans' benefits that accrued to an honorable discharge.[74] Although such harsh outcomes for minor infractions were common enough for black soldiers, whom white officers often thought needed extra discipline, so too were West's initial expectations of fair treatment and full citizenship.

The disillusionment induced by encountering such systematic and violent repudiations of the idealistic war aims prompted many black soldiers to question whether they could go on. Even Wilson dropped his optimistic guard, asking the president, "How can we convince one tenth of the Armed Forces, the Negro members, that your pronouncement of the war aims of the United Nations means what it says, when their experience with one of the United Nations, the United States of America, is just the opposite?"[75] Private Bert B. Babero wrote to Gibson from Camp Barkeley, Texas, in January 1944, complaining of the extreme privations caused by Jim Crow. "All of us are loyal Americans who believe in the democracy for which we are supposed to be fighting," Babero wrote. "What better place should the execution of democracy be practiced than an Army camp," he reasoned, "where soldiers are actually offering their lives, if necessary, for the cause." He concluded that "the south is trying to win the war on one flank and helping the axis on their other."[76]

Over time, many black soldiers grew bitter. Pvt. Willie M. Purdue wrote to Truman Gibson from Camp Lee, Virginia, in extreme disillusionment. "Discrimination! Segregation! Prejudice! And God knows what" had all led him to give up hope. "I've swallowed all of this stuff that I can hold, of equality and freedom," he wrote, but he concluded, "if so much can be demanded for so little, truly justice must be asleep."[77] George S. Johnson of Baltimore wrote on behalf of his brother stationed at Camp Claiborne, Louisiana, where things were so bad that black soldiers were deserting "by the dozens." "The way things are here we should be fighting the white people instead of the Japs and the Germans."[78]

The letters to Gibson and Hastie were not simply desperate pleas. They revealed a strong sense among black troops that during this war in particular they should be able to realize their right to serve their country and claim full citizenship. The cultivation among black soldiers of a pride in uniform would have longer-term consequences; it was not a coincidence that black veterans played such a central role in leading the early civil rights movement.[79]

The most universal boundary, shared by nearly all servicemen regardless of their rank or race, was the imaginary line that divided fighting men from the "rear echelon," which included everybody standing behind them and out of harm's way. Although three-fourths of all servicemen in World War II served overseas, probably no more than one out of ten entered forward positions where they were exposed to battle. For the minority who bore the brunt of the war this was a source of great bitterness, particularly since the supply troops behind the lines, and the men stationed safely at home in the United States, all enjoyed the status of being identified with the symbol of the combat soldier without suffering the great peril of facing actual combat.

Where war propaganda dwelled on the figurative supply of matériel, the overseas need was concrete and decisive. For troops who had been through campaigns that suffered from problems with supply lines, as happened frequently in the vast Pacific, a missed shipment or a damaged pallet could be the source of enduring recrimination.[80] In Europe, too, an overwhelming majority (85 percent) of ground combat troops stationed in the Mediterranean theater in May and June 1945 believed that their comrades in arms felt "resentful" about troops with rear-area jobs. This resentment was tinged with envy, as many of the men assigned to combat felt that they should be able to switch places with rear-echelon men. But, knowing they could not, they indulged in what Stouffer believed was a compensatory conviction in the moral superiority of the most dangerous assignments and positions, which they esteemed most highly (even if they did not wish to fill them).[81] Here in the crucible of battle was the symbolic center of wartime political culture.

At the other extreme, standing at the outermost reaches of the rear echelon, was the civilian home front, whose defense was the ostensible reason servicemen were fighting in the first place. Servicemen regularly worried aloud that they might be sacrificing their lives only to protect troubling corruption or injustice back home. Depending on their political sensibilities, GIs were obsessed by the prospect of "fat cats," "strikers," and farmers living high on the war boom while they slogged away at the real work of winning the war. Although two-thirds of soldiers agreed with a survey item stating that "most or all of the people back home are doing all they should to help win the war,"[82] many wondered if an unpatriotic minority was nonetheless playing them for fools:

> I feel that everyone should be called upon to make as nearly equal [a] sacrifice as possible. Too many defense workers & industrialists are piling up huge sums of money while men in the armed forces are hardly able to get along on their earnings yet are called upon to risk their lives daily.[83]

It is possible to track with finer subtlety the complicated mixture of sentimental reminiscence and smoldering resentment that soldiers felt toward civilians by following the correspondence of the Servicemen's Committee at the National Broach and Machine Company of Detroit, set up to maintain ties between war workers and their former coworkers who had enlisted. Some of the early letters reflected the continued identification of former war workers with their civilian buddies, affirming the "soldier of production" and equipment imagery so prevalent in wartime propaganda. Sgt. Edmund C. Borysiewicz's letter home in early 1945 read as if it had been written by a tripartite factory committee for a plant bond drive:

> It's really swell to know that you are not forgetting the boys. Here's hoping that by serving our country we all repay you [for] turning out the thoughts and products that will bring us a faster victory. . . . It's good to know that the plant I worked for once is turning out equipment of the best quality—so fellows overseas will have the best to carry on with.[84]

Another letter, signed only "Andy," enjoined, "You do your part and we'll do ours. 'Let's Beat 'Em,'" almost as if he were calling down from the end of the production line in an Army-Navy Production Award poster. "The sooner we get the material," Michael Bahrie enjoined, "the quicker we get home."[85] Yet another letter conveyed its author's pride at "wearing the uniform of the greatest army fighting for [the] greatest country fighting for the greatest principles that mankind has ever or will ever know."[86] When they complained, it was usually to compare their current lot unfavorably to their lives in the plant. Carl Barnes wrote from naval training school at Cornell that he had gained a new appreciation for his "good bosses" at National Broach because he had to swallow the indignity of taking orders from a "former hotshot shoe salesman."[87]

The early letters sent back by the newly minted GIs adopted a chummy tone, but homesickness could quickly verge into bitterness tinged with jealousy. Some indulged a sentimental affection for National Broach, relating that they were "lonesome for the place" and claiming that "the place is just like home to me," as Carl Barnes wrote in 1944.[88] The reason for homesickness was not only nostalgia, but also the difficulty of facing the new realities of the army. As Ed Borysiewicz wrote of his position as an engineer armorer and aerial gunner, "If the fellows and gals think they have a tough time working those long hours at the company, just listen what a combat crew member goes through."[89]

If lifted out of context, Borysiewicz's words would have warmed Eddie Rickenbacker's heart. But the letter arrived at National Broach with warm thanks for recently received copies of the plant newsletter, the *Red Ring*, and inquiries into

Mail was a vital lifeline to the normalcy of home for soldiers, whether they were mired in the horrors of battle or simply tortured by the boredom and regimentation of military life. In this photo the men of Navy bombing squadrons VB104 and VB106 gather around their chief yeoman to receive their mail on Munda, New Georgia Island, February 2, 1944. (Courtesy of the National Archives Still Picture Records Section, ARC #520909)

life back home. Chuck Clinton admitted he would be "very happy to go back to the shop and work for the same pay I'm getting right now: $50 per month." (This was a suggestion often floated by antilabor spokesmen, especially when wildcat strikes crested.) But his reason for writing this was that he disliked being bossed around and prohibited from thinking for himself, as he had in his job at National Broach. "Sure would like to hear about the shop," he concluded without a trace of bitterness. "I miss it like hell."[90]

As the former employees of National Broach made their way into forward theaters of combat, their letters assumed a more critical tone. News of civilian complaints about deprivations and "sacrifices" such as rationing garnered little sympathy. Six months after his earlier, friendlier letter, Chuck Clinton wrote from "sunny Italy":

> You people back home have heard people complain about this and that. Things you can't buy—things you can't do because of the war. But, believe me, you are so very very lucky. You all have nice warm homes to live in. The people over here have had their homes bombed clear out. They don't have food, clothing or anything like that.[91]

Another former coworker, nicknamed "Royal," was blunter. From the Philippines, where MacArthur's forces were in the process of taking back the islands with some of the most brutal fighting in the Pacific theater, he wrote with bitter understatement, "I understand that you folks are having a tough time, getting fine steak chops, and smokes." He confessing being able to get all the smokes he needed, but the closest he could come to eating steak, or even remembering what it tasted like, was by gulping down the Spam in his ration. "If you know of anyone who might like to swap, they are welcome to this hell."[92] Even with these words of recrimination, Royal included warm thanks for Christmas presents recently received, and obviously cherished this precious tie back to the normalcy of civilian life.

Above all, writing home mingled idealizations of past and present. The former coworkers to whom these servicemen wrote represented everything they had lost to their new military identity, even as they also represented everything they hoped to regain—but never could, fully—once it was all over. Several letters conveyed worry about postwar employment at the plant. Carl Barnes wondered if the foreman, Jim Rankin, would "put a Chemical Engineer to work in the shop." "I bet he can find a spot for one around," he reassured himself.[93] "What'n'ell will all us former night shift lads do," he wrote in another letter, if they returned home to no more night shift, thanks to the female war workers whose productivity had been used to rationalize dropping the second shift. "Nice going, girls," he griped.[94] Chuck Clinton revealed his anxiety over his prospects after mustering out when he promised that he'd be back at work no more than two days after his discharge. "That will be vacation enough for me."[95]

Although soldiers tended to be generous in their views of the civilians they knew, it was much easier for them to vent frustrations when expressing opinions about civilians in the abstract, particularly those who could be stereotyped. Censors' reports on morale-threatening developments picked up in the V-mail the GIs sent home provide a window onto the resentments that servicemen, particularly those serving overseas, harbored toward civilians. The "most persistent and emphatic grievance" noted by the censor "was directed against alleged civilian selfishness, luxury, and indifference to the war effort. This feeling has been most bitter where strikes are involved." There was a notable increase in "hostility toward civilians" when soldiers returned to the theater from home leave.[96] When troops in the European theater were asked in April 1945 whether there were any groups that had "taken advantage of the war to further their own selfish interests," nearly half said yes. (The proportion declined to 40 percent by August, when the war's triumphant end may have made GIs more generous.) Asked to specify who took advantage, 19 percent pointed to business, 11 percent fingered Jews, 9 percent blamed labor unions, 7 percent suspected communists or other radicals, and 6 percent looked askance at African Americans.[97] These categories delineated the main scapegoats that had haunted the politics of prejudice in the GIs' civilian lives.

When white servicemen encountered civilians who fit these categories and so seemed to embody the most egregious features of the unworthy civilians safely profiting from their sacrifice in the hindmost rows of the rear echelon, they struck out at them. This, at least, was what happened in the violent summer of 1943.

The Serviceman and the Zoot

The resentments that churned both military and civilian life came to a boiling point in the last half of the war, starting with the race riots that erupted in the summer of 1943. Simmering indignation toward the rear echelon boiled to the surface when GIs met civilians on leave, particularly when such encounters crossed racial lines. In those violent confrontations, rioters got a chance to act out the fantasies of annihilation they had rehearsed in telling wartime racial rumors. The most violent conflicts of the war years, in Detroit and Harlem, were set off or escalated by rumors envisioning moral outrages crystallized by racially coded images of servicemen.

In the Detroit riot, which occurred in the middle of June 1943, twin rumors spread through the white and black communities, stoking an already tense and violent summer day into an all-out race war.[98] Whites, passing the rumor along by telephone (with army intelligence listening in), heard that black ruffians had "slit a white soldier's throat and raped his girlfriend." Blacks heard that it was white sailors who had "thrown a Negro woman and her baby into the lake." Here the contested visions of soldiers and what they represented split the community apart. White rioters tried to exorcise the racial demons rumored to threaten "their" soldiers and women by attacking blacks who refused to remain "in their place" (that is, out of sight). Those set upon by black rioters experienced their worst racial nightmare come true. To black Detroit, the white sailors and soldiers who joined lustily in the rioting seemed to give physical form to the merciless hypocrisy of a segregated war against fascism.[99] The conflagration proved to be one of the nation's worst race riots, taking the lives of 34 people—25 of whom were African American—and injuring 675.[100]

Rushing to post-riot Detroit to investigate, Martin Dies drew on a language that would be familiar to those who had followed his investigation of Japanese "subversion" in the camps. The Detroit riots were caused, he claimed, by "un-American propaganda activities and the coddling of races by politically minded people in this country." Fat paychecks from war work and too much unrestricted leisure on Belle Isle Park, where the riot had begun, had left the motor city's black migrants susceptible to agitation, according to Dies.[101]

The Harlem riot broke out at the start of August, unleashing the frustrations that had been building with each indignity visited upon black soldiers through-out the war. The trigger was an altercation that led to the shooting of a black MP by a white policeman, a clash soon transformed by rumor into the cold-blooded killing of a black soldier defending his mother. As the story spread, a broad cross section of Harlem vented its rage in a commodity riot that decimated more than a thousand local stores.[102] By smashing storefronts and looting, the black citizens of Harlem struck out at the symbols of their exclusion from war prosperity, link-ing it to the flagrant subordination of black soldiers.[103]

The Zoot Suit riot that launched the orgy of racial violence that summer also involved a contest over the meaning of the GI, but it was so propulsive precisely because it was not only a race riot. It was fueled by conflict whose symbolic vio-lence was just as important as its physical destruction.

For five days in the first week of June 1943, during the same week in which the Dies Committee held its hearings on "Jap pampering," white servicemen stationed throughout southern California spontaneously reasserted the sense of honor they felt was threatened by a conspicuous lack of sacrifice among a certain group of civilians. The zoot suits worn by Mexican Ameri-can youths known as pachucos provided white servicemen with precisely the sort of racialized icon for which they had cultivated a burning hatred while enduring the rigors of basic training or the tedium of noncombat service. The youths' baggy, pleated trousers, porkpie hats, dangling watch fobs, and other extravagances seemed to be emblems of a menacing counterculture. Banding together in impromptu gangs and "taxicab brigades"—a makeshift rioting army—servicemen hunted down and attacked figures who wore the emblems of their subversive intent on their backs. When the sailors, soldiers, and marines caught their quarry, they enacted a ritual whose stylized violence pointed to the moral violation they felt they were authorized to purge from civilian society.[104]

A typical episode unfolded in front of the Orpheum Theater in downtown Los Angeles on the night of Monday, June 7, at the peak of the rioting. A gang of sailors dragged Enrico Herrera out onto the street along with the other young

Gangs of American sailors and marines armed with sticks during the Zoot Suit Riots, Los Angeles, California, June 1943. The riots broke out as tensions rose between servicemen stationed in the city and Latino youths, amongst whom zoot suits were the latest fashion. (Courtesy of the Hulton Archive/Getty Images, #85374826)

Mexican Americans whom they had plucked from seats in the theater. A crowd of white civilians made room for the servicemen to enact the spectacle. While the sailors stripped and then beat the youths, the crowd hooted in approval. The laughter and cheering swelled to a deafening howl when the sailors methodically destroyed the zoot suits they had torn from the pachucos' backs, and then cast the shredded "drapes" into the dirt of the street. Some of them had come to the theater that night to see Glenn Miller and his orchestra, but this performance gave them more than their money's worth.[105]

The evening after Herrera and the others were beaten, a widely read Hearst newspaper, the *Los Angeles Evening Herald and Express*, spelled out the formula for "de-zooting":

Procedure was standard.

Grab a zooter.

Take off his pants and frock coat and tear them up or burn them.

Trim the "Argentine ducktail" haircut that goes with the screwy costume.[106]

The ritual seemed less clinical when experienced from within the suit, as a young pachuco eyewitness made clear in his retelling of the riots to a sympathetic observer:

> Some sailors near us called, "Come on you Pachucos, you yellow bastards, we'll get you . . . all of you." The crowd laughed and moved, pushing every way and everybody. They were all trying to get someplace down the street. Then we heard a roar and somebody yelled, "They got 'em, they got 'em. They got those goddamned zootsuiters." And from the corner in front of the theater a mob of sailors poured out with a couple of kids wearing finger-tip coats, pulled along in the middle of them. Those kids were getting it all right, with busted heads and bleeding faces, those kids were getting it. Pretty soon, a black coat was thrown up and got passed around with people catching it and tossing it. Then the pants came and another coat, a tan one. Each time the crowd yelled and packed tighter to the center. The police were standing along the sides holding their night sticks, looking pleased about the whole thing. Or maybe they were gazing at the stars in the sky. They didn't do nothing to stop that mob, nothing. A blonde girl near us jumped and caught the tan coat that went sailing by. She grabbed it, then she squirmed until she got it on. She danced around in a circle yelling, "I'm a Pachuca, I'm a Pachuca." She was laughing and kissing the sailor next to her like she was nuts.[107]

Significantly, these "de-zootings" unfolded primarily in public places of amusement, entertainment, and consumption where servicemen and zooters had clashed before, when the deference servicemen expected from civilians was flouted by assertive pachucos willing to take a stand.[108] Also worth noting was the predominance of symbolic over physical violence, at least in the first few days of rioting. There were no fatalities, rapes, or other extreme rampages, as would be the case in Detroit. Apparently some zooters were given the choice of disrobing rather than having their zoot suits torn off them; the servicemen appear to have been as outraged by the suits as they were by their wearers.[109]

Commentators of all political stripes adopted conspiracy as the cause of the riots, with predictable variations on which villain had hatched the conspiracy. When the riots subsided, conservatives blamed agitators for fanning resentment over white discrimination and encouraging delinquency among disaffected

Mexican American youths.[110] This perspective was shared by investigators in the Joint Fact-Finding Committee on Un-American Activity, headed by California state senator Jack Tenny, whose hearings suggested that the racial disturbances surrounding zoot suiters were encouraged by fascist and communist agitators.[111] Carey McWilliams, one of the "agitators" identified by the Tenny Committee for his public defense of the maligned pachucos in the sensational Sleepy Lagoon trial the previous fall, also detected the machinations of conspiracy in the riots, although in his account the police were the guilty party.[112] Liberal leaders within the Mexican community attributed the riots to the fifth column plots of Mexican fascists known as *sinarquistas*.[113]

No conspiracy was required to provoke the servicemen to spontaneous attacks on zooters. As the Office of Naval Intelligence (ONI) realized almost immediately, "The recent Los Angeles disturbances seem to have been the result of local economic, social, and police conditions," not the product of fifth column activity. While ONI was far from liberal in its take on the riots, it acknowledged that the riots emerged from the wide range of social problems besetting the Mexican community in wartime Los Angeles.[114] A subsequent report on the riots released by the navy in 1951 admitted that racial animus played a role among the white rioters.[115] Over time, historians have confirmed the original interpretation put forth by those such as McWilliams and others sympathetic to the Mexican community. The Zoot Suit Riots were indeed race riots in which white servicemen and civilians acted out their aggressions toward a stigmatized minority.[116]

Yet racism alone does not explain the why servicemen should have focused so intensely and pointedly on the zoot suit to channel their rage against Mexicans. Whites in Detroit did not require zoot suits to justify or direct their attacks on African Americans a few weeks later. Curiously, in Los Angeles there were no fatalities, despite rioting among thousands of civilians and pachucos that spread widely throughout the city and persisted over the course of almost two weeks. None of the 112 victims requiring hospitalization—18 of whom were servicemen—sustained life-threatening injuries, although one black defense worker did lose an eye.[117] Rioters inflicted so little property damage that the loudest economic complaint came from civic leaders who protested the "out of bounds" order that ended the rioting, since it temporarily cut off a significant source of business for the local establishments who catered to servicemen on leave.[118] All of these considerations suggest that something more than ordinary racial tensions must have been involved in the rioting.

From the first crowd actions in Oakland and Venice Beach earlier that spring, and continuing throughout the subsequent riots, servicemen acted as if the zoot suit made its wearer an effigy whose proud vestments had to be stripped away and destroyed to restore the moral order of urban public spaces. Frustrated white servicemen and civilians performed the "de-zootings" to emasculate and otherwise humiliate zooters so that their challenge to the norms of wartime society could be put to rest.[119] As *Newsweek* observed two weeks after the riots, "The sight of a young man in a zoot suit in wartime was probably enough to infuriate many servicemen."[120] Why was a suit of clothes so provocative that it moved thousands of ordinary soldiers and civilians to riot?

At times it seemed that the suit itself was the villain, a threatening talisman whose simple existence could not go unchecked. Nearly all accounts describe servicemen physically destroying the clothing of those they deemed zooters, in most cases by tearing them to shreds or burning them. Clearly a moral point was being made, and it was sharpened as much by those whom the servicemen left alone as by those whom they attacked. On the first Saturday evening of the riots, a group of sailors hunting for zooters walked ominously through one of many East Side bars and places of amusement searched that night, pointedly scrutinizing the appearance of the patrons. When they found two men in zoot suits drinking beer at a table, they ordered the men to disrobe. One complied and had his "drapes" torn to pieces before his face. The other would not agree to this humiliation and so had his suit torn from his body as the sailors beat him.[121] *Newsweek* likewise reported that, early in the rioting, sailors roved the East Side "harrying all zoot suiters they met, thrashing those who refused to discard their fancy clothes."[122]

The defiant decision to wear a zoot suit rather than a military uniform came off as a pathological provocation. An alienist provided his professional opinion of the situation, probing into the criminal mind with a smug conjecture: "The zoot-suiter says to himself, 'I haven't had attention. . . . Uniforms are cropping up everywhere. I am too young for service, or, even though I am old enough, I already have a delinquency record and will not be accepted. Or I am in 4-F. I will design my uniform.'" Faced with such unwholesome effrontery, the soldiers simply showed their moral fiber. "Uncle Sam," the alienist pronounced, "you are of sound mind and body. You are a picture of the real American youth. . . . The service man feels a righteous pride in his military garb. He comes to resent any class which gives a distorted impression of the Americanism which he represents."[123]

Newspaper accounts reinforced the public approval of the soldiers' repudiation of the zooters as their opposites by drawing a sharp contrast between the zooters and their tormentors, applauding the changed public demeanor produced by the rough judgment meted out by servicemen. On Monday, June 7, the *Los Angeles Times* crowed, "those gamin' dandies, the zoot suiters, having learned a great moral lesson from servicemen, mostly sailors, who took over their instruction three days ago, are staying home nights."[124] The copy in the *Herald and*

Express rang with glee. One story painted a mental picture of infantilization for its readers: "Throughout the east side district erstwhile wearers of the fantastic frock coat and exaggerated peg-top pants took advantage of the lull in the fighting to slink home in diapers or coverings hastily improvised from newspapers."[125] Zoot suits, and dandyism more generally, had always given off more than a whiff of gender subversion; now they only stoked the rioters' antagonism to greater extremes.[126]

Drawing on masculinist imagery linked to Americanism, headlines and cover stories consistently described the actions of the rioting servicemen in martial overtones. The *Herald and Express* reported an early night of rioting as if it were a military maneuver: "Two hundred Navy men sailed up the Los Angeles River early today, and in a task force of taxicabs launched a reprisal attack on 'zoot suit' gangsters in the East Los Angeles area."[127] An enlarged photo dominated the front page of the *Los Angeles Times* on June 8, displaying the naked body of a boy wearing only a hat, crouched over the body of a fallen companion. The caption read, "Unconditional Surrender: two zoot suiters, beaten and stripped in front of a theater at 8th and Main Sts. in the war declared on them by servicemen."[128] Some liberal newsmen, such as the writer for *Time*'s coverage of the riots, suggested that the martial spirit was more appropriate to "Panzer divisions" than patriotic "brigades" or "task forces."[129] But most invoked military imagery to underline the righteousness of the rioting servicemen.

The reassertion of moral order within public spaces that had been corrupted by "unwholesome" and "subversive" figures focused so heavily on the consumer behavior and flamboyant style affected by the zooters for a reason. The zoot suit was a black market item that drew attention to itself, an antiuniform that expressed a young man's individuality, flair, and freedom at a time when young men were expected to be serving their country through conformity to military service.[130] The zoot suit lifestyle directly challenged a central aspect of wartime political culture: the ritual affirmation of the serviceman's sacrifice, and the consumer patriotism citizens were expected conspicuously to embrace as evidence that they were "doing their part" to back that sacrifice.

Very few of the youths who wore the zoot suit were confirmed members of the semicriminal counterculture the Hearst press derided almost nightly.[131] But enough were to make the stereotype stick. Unfortunately for the great number of youths who embraced the fashion sense but not necessarily the militancy or the criminality, the cocky stance of the zooter came at a terrible price.[132]

Many black and Mexican youths did not see an inherent incompatibility between military service and zoot style. Black GIs brought the zoot suit over to Britain and introduced a generation of working-class youth to a consumerist vision of American popular culture that helped spawn a postwar youth culture.[133] Some black soldiers even took the liberty of having their uniforms tailored to suggest the signature features of the zoot suit, including elongated coattails and looser-fitting "drapes." Despite this sartorial rebellion, which went against army regulations, the soldiers were not involved in any disruptive behavior. Indeed, the zooted uniforms were their only infraction of military conduct—one that the army soon forbade.[134] At least some of the pachuco youths Beatrice Griffith interviewed after the riots saw military uniforms as a type of status-conferring outfit that might resemble a zoot suit. One eyewitness fancied wearing "those army zootsuits" as a paratrooper.[135] Despite the wide range of meanings that might be attributed to the zoot suit style by its enthusiasts and emulators, it represented only an intolerable menace, if not subversion, to most whites.[136]

Defenders of the zooters responded to their wholesale condemnation by affirming the GI, emphasizing the deep patriotism among Mexican Americans that had been obscured by the riots. They stressed the loyal military service so many Mexican American youths gave to their country. This was the point implicitly made by Beatrice Griffith in naming her paean to Chicano youth *American Me* and opening it with the eyewitness account of a pachuco whose trip to Los Angeles to report for induction was interrupted by the Zoot Suit Riots.[137] Ruth Tuck provided an equally sympathetic assessment of the situation in "Behind the Zoot Suit Riots" for *Survey Graphic*. She bemoaned the lost opportunity among pachucos, for whom "patriotism and military action had a strong appeal," as reflected by enlistments that "swelled" in Mexican districts and by younger boys who "played at war among the gangs." Observing the lowered morale of the barrios overrun by rioting, Tuck added, "What their many sons in the armed services think has not been revealed."[138] This counteraffirmation of the sacrifice of Chicano soldiers had resonance among commentators who stood outside the small circle of sympathizers. State attorney general Robert Kenny admitted of the zooters, "There are lots of good kids among them." Then, to bring his point home, he added, "Most of them have brothers in the Army."[139]

One especially articulate pachuco defended the zoot suit by linking it to the sacrifices of Chicano servicemen. He had been one of the defendants rounded up and put on display in the show trial that followed the Venice riots in May. Though the judge had dismissed the case on grounds of insufficient evidence, the young man was still upset by the unfair treatment he had received:

> I was born in this country. Like you said, I have the same rights and privileges of other Americans. . . . Pretty soon I guess I'll be in the army and I'll be glad to go. But I want to be treated like everyone else. We're tired of being pushed around. We're tired of being told we can't go to

this show or that dance hall because we're Mexican or that we better not be seen on the beach front, or that we can't wear draped pants or have our hair cut the way we want to. . . . My people work hard, fight hard in the army and navy of the United States. They're good Americans and they should have justice.[140]

This recourse to the rhetoric of American rights and liberties—so pervasively tied to the "American standard of living" during the war through ads, propaganda, and diverse encounters with federal authority—was a powerful statement to those who sympathized with the young man's plight.[141] One of the youths Beatrice Griffith interviewed after the riots echoed his line of reasoning by recounting the rage of an embittered friend: "Is this what we are fighting for? What Emelio takes his pennies and nickels to school for to buy a jeep? Democracy doesn't work at home. . . . Tonight they beat us up . . . beat us up while our guys are overseas fighting."[142]

From this perspective, wearing a zoot suit, or articles of clothing styled to approximate that look, was one of the few ways in which pachucos could assert their rights in public and thereby gain some respect, instill some fear, or at the very least garner some recognition. If pachucos couldn't go to all of the same theaters or dance halls that white Angelenos took for granted, they could at least assert their presence in public, in their own style, for their own amusement—the most tangible way they could realize the democratization of daily life produced by the war effort.

Freedom to adopt the lifestyle of one's choice would eventually be embraced by the generation of baby boomers just coming into the world by the end of the war. But it did not pass muster with the generation that fought the war. The American standard of living had proven too provocative when sported by assertive Chicano and black youths. This was because that standard was still in the process of becoming an entitlement to which American citizens might lay claim. During the war, this claim was restricted to those who best identified themselves with the sacrifice of the combat soldier—whether through essential war work, patriotic consumption, or, best of all, military service. The military uniform had been too thoroughly glorified to brook any challenge, which the zoot suit provided by its mere existence.

Who, then, had more authority to put the zooters in their place than the servicemen whose sacrifice was the polar star for an entire home-front culture? In the copy of the Ad Council, the war may have been fought to protect the individual choice of the citizen-consumer in his right to an American standard of living.[143] But such individualism could never challenge the sacrifice of the serviceman. When it did, wartime expectations of patriotic consumerism transformed the zoot suit into a sinister mask of subversive intent that had to be torn from its wearer and destroyed in order to put down the threat to the legitimacy of the emerging national political culture.

Turning the Tables in Demobilization

The GIs' sense of entitlement revealed itself again in the winter of 1945–46, when the "army mutiny of 1946" broke out over the slow pace of demobilization. Popular pressure on Congress in the months after V-J Day had pushed the armed services to release men far more rapidly than anticipated. At the same time, Truman had felt obliged to cut inductions drastically, leaving greatly diminished and demoralized forces overseas. From a peak strength of 12.3 million in May 1945, when 7.6 million servicemen were stationed overseas, the total number of men under arms by the end of 1945 fell to 5.5 million. The pace of demobilization was so rapid it overwhelmed shipping lines, forcing the army to announce in early January 1946 that overseas soldiers would have to stay at their posts to sustain force levels in critical hotspots throughout the still-volatile postwar world. After months of waiting and idling about, writing letters to congressmen emblazoned with the slogan "No boats, no votes," while their wives back home organized Bring Back Daddy Clubs that mailed hundreds of baby shoes to Congress, more than a million men who qualified for release discovered they would have to remain at their stations until shipping conditions and military recruitment improved.[144]

The response among the troops was immediate and spontaneous, although it became more organized and politically potent over the weeks that followed. On Christmas Day 1945 a rowdy group of four thousand soldiers stationed in Manila marched on the replacement depot headquarters. They were sent back to their barracks by Col. J. C. Campbell, who barked, "You men forget you're not working for General Motors" (where the UAW had shut down operations with a massive strike). On January 6, a mob of perhaps twenty thousand soldiers converged on the command headquarters at City Hall to confront the local commander, Lt. Gen. William Steyer.

Protests soon spread from the Pacific, where they were most intense, to other theaters. When a crowd in London's Grosvenor Square was confronted by a sergeant who asked if they knew "who we got on this side" of the Atlantic—i.e., the ally Britain—five hundred unruly GIs responded, "Eleanor." They promptly marched to the Claridge Hotel, where Eleanor Roosevelt was staying to attend the first meeting of the General Assembly of the United Nations, but all they got was her promise to "do all I can." In Paris the

Champs-Elysées were mobbed by a crowd of several hundred soldiers wielding flares and denouncing those who did not protest as "slackers" and "scabs." Other protests and mass meetings erupted in Austria, India, Korea, and even on bases in the United States.[145]

The unrest spread even to the occupation troops, "who should have known better," according to *Time*. When Secretary of War Robert Patterson visited Yokohama on an inspection tour of the Pacific, he was greeted with boos. In Frankfurt, Germany, two thousand men entered the army headquarters and harangued their commanding officer, Lt. Gen. Joseph T. McNarney, goading him to come out and meet his troops. When they were informed that he was attending a meeting of the Four Powers in Berlin, they booed and hissed, mocking him.

Predictably, army officials charged treachery and subversion. Maj. Gen. Clovis Byers, chief of staff for the Eighth Army in Japan, claimed, "It appears that subversive forces are deliberately at work, for obscure reasons, attempting to undermine the morale of our Army."[146] Byers was not alone in his conviction. The newly resurrected House Committee on Un-American Activities began an investigation of communist subversion among protesting GIs and left-leaning veterans' organizations. Committee counsel Ernie Adamson claimed that "Communist agitators actually went into the Army for the sole purpose of causing trouble." The Catholic journal *Commonweal* noted that Communist Party organs and "fellow-traveling sheets" provided "an abundance of slogans for orientating the protest."[147] Yet in the end, none of the mutineers was court-martialed, even as accusations of treason and sabotage were hurled at striking workers who participated in the great strike wave of 1945–46 that shut down much of American industry. The GIs were too politically organized, and their image too sacred, to warrant consistent treatment.

The problem was geopolitical. The armed forces could not occupy Germany and Japan while policing other reclaimed battle zones if the force level fell below 1.55 million. Discounting official warnings that troop strength was deteriorating dangerously, the servicemen didn't see why the burden had to fall on their shoulders. As the liberal magazine the *Nation* summarized the soldiers' complaint, they did not see "why they should be forced to rot in idleness in countries which are not conquered territory, and in no need of our policing—in France, in the Philippines, in the Caribbean, in China, even here at home."[148]

More was at work than simple criticism of army policy or even grand strategy. The army mutineers of 1946 condensed all the wartime frustrations over chickenshit, military hierarchy, and the rear echelon into a single indictment leveled en masse. As the *Nation* paraphrased their complaint, postwar strategy did not "warrant the use of veteran airmen to fly empty Coke bottles over the dangerous 'hump' of the Himalayas or to bring tile from Bombay to Karachi to build an officers' club." The rioting servicemen were striking back in the only way they could at the officers who kept them "polishing the brass" on their hats, convinced that "those who have the power to move them about the world like so many pawns lack the slightest idea of what they are doing."[149] The mid-Pacific edition of *Stars and Stripes* provided a more direct indictment:

> Enlisted men have had all they want of being treated as "second-class citizens." . . . A caste system inherited from Frederick the Great of Prussia and the 18th-Century British Navy is hardly appropriate to the U.S. . . . The aristocracy-peasantry relationship characteristic of our armed forces has a counterpart nowhere in American life. Such privileges and preferences actually destroy respect for rank, undermine morale and efficiency.[150]

GIs were inclined to make critical observations about postwar grand strategy as a way to reframe their personal obligations. Letters sent by angry soldiers to their congressmen—accounting for half of all their mail by January—made this point bluntly. One group cabled from Manila wondering "why 230,000 troops are necessary to occupy friendly and allied Philippines" when only 200,000 were needed in Japan, according to General MacArthur. A sergeant stationed in Puerto Rico asked, "What are we doing with 100,000 men in the Caribbean area? If we really need occupation forces send us to Germany and Japan." From London twenty-three enlisted men complained of the use of army personnel for the operation of commercial concerns such as Pan American Airways, when many of them owned small businesses back home that did not benefit from the low wages paid to privates and petty officers.[151]

Pfc. John Janes of the marines demanded a justification of his assignment when interviewed by *Time*. "What I want," he said of his post guarding Bridge 21 on the railroad route between Tientsin and Chingwangtao in China, was "an explanation of what I'm doing here. Then I'll sleep better. . . . We're buttering somebody's bread, riding these coal trains. Why don't these Chinese National Troops run the railroads?" Fear of communist takeover in China did not worry American GIs stationed there, according to *Time*. Their reasoning was that "when we leave, the Communists will take it anyway—so why not let them have it now?" Soldiers had become disillusioned by the incompetence and mismanagement prevalent in Nationalist territory, for which the marines had coined a new acronym, "JACFU," short for "joint American-Chinese foul-up."[152] (Private Snafu would have been honored by the resemblance.)

Beneath their unwillingness to conduct U.S. foreign relations personally, lay a deeper frustration with army brass and an abiding resentment of civilians who remained in the comforts of home rather than volunteer or press for heightened draft quotas. GIs resented the constant recalibration of the point system by which their release was determined. Based on extensive research by Stouffer's team into the criteria the GIs felt would make for the fairest demobilization policies, the point system awarded priority for combat, length of service (particularly overseas), and family dependents. Here was a precise, arithmetical calculation of a man's moral worth within the wartime political culture. By caving into political pressure for rapid demobilization and progressively changing the number of points that guaranteed release, then reneging on the system altogether in January 1946, the army had abrogated the fictive social contract under which mass conscription was deemed legitimate.[153] In response, soldiers turned the tables on their superiors to demonstrate their displeasure and lack of consent.

There was an exquisite irony in this state of affairs. The soldiers considered themselves to be second-class citizens, as *Stars and Stripes* put it, and risked being court-martialed for mutiny in order to challenge that status and return themselves to a civilian life devoid of the "aristocracy-peasantry relationship." Yet the society to which they returned guaranteed them—or at least the fourteen million who were white and male—a first-class citizenship in the GI Bill of Rights whose scope and comprehensiveness were unparalleled in the history of the U.S. welfare state. The imagined moral bonds connecting civilians' hero worship of the combat soldier to the GIs' assertion that they were entitled to full citizenship because of their sacrifice for the nation formed a perfect closed circuit. It was that circuit of legitimation within the national political culture, as much as the maneuvering of interest groups and politicians who fed off it to serve their constituencies, that sustained the bifurcated postwar welfare state.[154]

A militarized national citizenship was not the only legacy of the citizen-soldiers who fought the Second World War. As a vast demographic presence within postwar society, formers GIs quickly assumed leading roles in business, politics, and nearly every other realm of American public life. Their influence helped cement acceptance of the government whose orders they had learned to take during the war. Of course, shared experience did not breed a commensurately homogeneous or uncomplicated orientation toward the military. Because the army or the navy had sent them into harm's way, sometimes under the leadership of sadistic noncommissioned officers or inexperienced commissioned officers with pull, enlisted men articulated an elaborate culture of distaste for military hierarchy and regimentation.

Yet GIs also learned to obey government authority in its most extreme forms and accept its ultimate purposes, which in turn legitimized their claims to full citizenship when they returned to society as veterans. Despite all the high sentiment about "the individual" and "freedom of choice" in wartime celebrations of the American way of life, the silent generation produced few iconoclasts or nonconformists, as reviled conscientious objectors knew well. Mass conscription inculcated obedience as well as entitlement, making the veterans of World War II among the most ardent defenders of government authority and the most vocal critics of those baby boomers who chose to repudiate the draft and the military establishment during the Vietnam War a generation later. Their normative sense of Americanism—institutionalized by screening, loyalty oaths, and training, even as it was fostered by the male camaraderie of the platoon and the broader GI culture—became a litmus test of national citizenship, first outlined in the GI Bill of Rights and other servicemen's legislation, and subsequently affirmed by the veterans and their myriad civilian supporters as they dominated postwar life.

Conclusion: Legacies of
the Warfare State

In the last three months of 1945, demobilization suddenly descended upon the United States. Although the industrial mobilization had reached its peak in the early spring, when victory over Germany was within sight, it was not until a few weeks prior to the surrender of Japan that war contracts were terminated en masse. In August the War Department cancelled nearly 71,000 contracts. By the end of the year nearly all of the more than 300,000 war contracts had been settled, accounting for $64 billion even after massive discounts. Consequently, employers laid off more than 2.5 million workers in September alone. In some industries, such as aircraft, ammunition, and shipbuilding, employment fell to half of what it had been in May. Virtually all of the civilian war agencies wound down their operations in the last months of 1945, with only vestigial staffs continuing into 1946.[1] Popular clamor for demobilization extended even more passionately toward the soldiers, returning them home at a pace that was only just shy of ruinous. Within a year of V-J Day nine million servicemen had returned to civilian life, leaving another three million on active duty. By mid-1947, half as many again remained in uniform, leaving military personnel at only 13 percent of their peak levels two years earlier.[2]

Despite the great pressure to return to normalcy, and the pell-mell manner in which the Truman administration responded to popular demand, demobilization did not represent absolute retreat. At a million and a half strong, the postwar military at its smallest was still more than four times larger than the interwar armed forces at their most muscular.[3] (See Chart A.3.) Despite a vigorous debate over the extent and role of the military establishment during these immediate postwar years, Congress moved forward with the unification of the armed forces under the Department of Defense, while total military spending never fell below $11 billion, or roughly a third of all federal expenditures and over 4 percent of the GDP. While this was a big step back from peak mobilization in 1944–45, it still represented twice the proportion of federal spending and nearly three times the proportion of GDP spent in 1940—the peak for the interwar years, thanks to bolstered defense spending after the fall of France. (See Chart A.4.) These unprecedented expenditures underwrote the creation of a national security establishment backed by peacetime conscription and a large standing army that, along with the other branches, occupied a network of bases throughout the world.[4]

By the war's end, then, Americans had authorized a government far larger and more intrusive than the New Deal had ever been. Although this warfare state would not be finalized until the looming confrontations with the Soviet Union hardened into the Cold War, Americans had already learned to live with the leviathan and accept its demands as legitimate during the "good war," whose Manichean imagery and overtones of Armageddon lived on to define postwar political culture.

The unwinding of the war machinery only highlighted the question of what would become of the leviathan that had grown up during the conflict. The collapse of government presence in everyday life proved to be just as politicizing as had its expansion over the previous four years. In the 1930s, Americans had confronted the intractable puzzle of how government might somehow end the Depression. In the first half of the 1940s, they had faced the question of whether and, from 1941 onward, on what terms the United States should enter the world war to defeat the fascist threat. But in the second half of the decade, starting with the detonation of atomic weapons over Hiroshima and Nagasaki in early August 1945, Americans found themselves confronted with the dual specters of mass unemployment and the outbreak of another global conflict, both of which seemed likely in 1945 and 1946.[5] These worries would not find a programmatic solution until the Korean War, when a new global strategy, and a political economy of "limited war" to sustain it, were institutionalized within the Truman and Eisenhower administrations.

In the meantime, Americans of varying persuasions were left to their own devices to articulate their visions of what the postwar order should bring. Their assumptions, both divergent and convergent, provide insight into the terms on which federal authority could operate. Even when these visions were at odds with the dominant currents of postwar politics, they highlighted popular assumptions about government power and citizenship that had been fostered by the war.

The Unrealized Vision of a Fiscal Rollback

The Republican Party platform for 1944 pledged to reduce taxes on incomes and consumption—"as soon as the war ends"—to levels "consistent with the normal expenditures of government in the postwar period." Perhaps out of cockiness that stemmed from the conservative coalition's victory over Roosevelt's revenue bill earlier in the year, the platform echoed the slogan of a return to normalcy that had inaugurated the Harding administration's triumph over Wilson and all that he stood for in the previous world war. It looked beyond victory to a reestablishment of the Republican ascendancy that had defined the affluent 1920s. It also struck at the heart of what party stalwarts such as Robert Taft had long believed to be "the very heart of the New Deal"—deficit spending—by pledging to "reduce that debt as soon as economic conditions make such reduction possible." Elsewhere it called for tighter fiscal controls, linking them to an efficiency that was wanting in the Democratic administration, and suggesting that without such an effort to restore austerity and restrain unchecked "bureaucracy," the United States might lose the "trial throughout the world today" over whether "men can organize together in a highly industrialized society, succeed, and still be free."[6]

In the midterm elections of 1946, when Republicans took back control of Congress for the first time since Herbert Hoover's searing defeat in 1932, cutting taxes and balancing the budget remained a critical component of the party's winning slogan, "Had enough?" The Eightieth Congress, which took power after that election, placed tax cutting and budgetary conservatism at the center of its legislative agenda, with Robert Taft leading the way.[7]

Honing their rallying cry, Republicans continued to work the theme of fiscal conservatism, making it a central plank of their 1948 platform. In touting the Eightieth Congress's record of achievement, it listed "the budget balanced" and "taxes reduced" immediately after the first item, "the long trend of extravagant and ill-advised Executive action reversed." The party was committed to working to "reduce the enormous burden of taxation in order to provide incentives for the creation of new industries and new jobs." The very framework of constitutional government depended on fiscal policies that promoted "production and thrift" and a "reduction of the public debt," among other measures, as part of a larger effort to abolish "excessive centralization," promote "more efficient" government, and accomplish "the rooting out of Communism wherever found." "These things," the platform concluded, "are fundamental."[8] Cutting taxes and balancing budgets had become code words for rolling back the New Deal state, which Taft and his allies constantly conflated with "socialism."

By all rights, the fiscal citizenship established by Morgenthau's Treasury ought to have been the most vulnerable of the war's legacies, had the previous war's conclusion been any indicator. The Republican administrations of the 1920s, led by Secretary of the Treasury Andrew Mellon, had pushed back hard on the regime of class taxation inaugurated during the Wilson administration, introducing numerous loopholes that undermined its effective rates.

The mass fiscal citizenship created in the Second World War seemed to share the same vulnerabilities. If inflation threatened the rising standard of living, consumers would quickly spend more of their disposable income to make up for the change, and bond sales would suffer accordingly. Citizens would be further disinclined to buy bonds if their symbolic identification with soldiers was eroded, and if consumer durables appeared on the market to compete with bond purchases. Taxes would become politically toxic. For a time it seemed as if these developments, combined with the Republican Congress's programmatic efforts, might accomplish the same fiscal rollback that had cemented their party's hegemony in the 1920s. Only the looming threat of a return to total war that persisted through the end of the decade, followed by the war in Korea, prevented this recurrence.

Yet mass fiscal citizenship survived to underwrite the Cold War. By that time, even those who cashed in their war bonds continued to be influenced by the civic meanings they had ascribed to them. A series of postwar studies of Americans' liquid assets and consumer requirements (plans for spending) indicated that bondholders continued to set their war bonds apart from their ordinary finances. Very few said they planned to use them to pay for consumer purchases—and subsequent studies showed that few of them in fact did. They relied instead on growing postwar income and consumer credit to purchase the consumer goods that suffused the postwar landscape. Respondents almost universally said that war bonds were reserved to secure their families' expanded economic opportunity—one of the "freedoms" for which the war had been fought. When asked about their particular plans for these earmarked funds, "only two types of answers were made by large numbers": the money would go to purchasing a home or starting a business. This suggestive finding, corroborated in multiple studies relying on rigorous survey design, indicates an important factor influencing the conservative turn taken by postwar economic citizenship. Less valuable (on average) but far more prevalent than the GI Bill benefits that were also used to buy houses and launch small businesses and farms, war savings bonds not only pushed savings rates to historic highs during the war but also helped nudge a wide range of citizens toward middle-class pursuits in subsequent years.[9] Popular postwar notions linking property and economic entitlement were underwritten by the social and cultural practices of wartime fiscal citizenship.

The paying of income tax did not decline in the way that savings bonds did, a divergence that cannot be explained by state capacity or legal coercion alone. Taxes had acquired a legitimacy from the moral economy of the war that persisted into the postwar period, although the war's end removed the overwhelming sense of obligation to the soldier that had motivated wartime taxpayers. A Gallup poll taken on May 15, 1945, immediately after the formal surrender of Germany, asked whether "Congress should reduce income taxes this year, or should wait until after Japan is defeated." A whopping 77 percent said to wait. True to their word, most Americans changed their position on tax cuts soon after V-J Day. Roughly two-thirds of respondents in a national poll taken on August 16, 1945, said they thought it was a "good idea" to reduce personal income taxes (which Congress promptly did, with President Truman's blessing). This sentiment cut across income groups: indeed, a somewhat lower proportion of "prosperous" respondents than respondents with "lower middle" income wanted their taxes cut. The end of the war did not mean that citizens expected to escape taxation, however; they simply wanted a break. By 1946, roughly 60 percent of the population still felt that the taxes they paid were "fair," according to polls taken in February and again in November—when elections returned Republicans to the control of Congress on the platform of rolling back the New Deal. This popular acceptance of taxation was not as strong as the 85 to 90 percent who had said their taxes were fair when polled in 1944 and 1945, but it represented a solid majority nonetheless.[10]

Amazingly, the decade following World War II saw no tax revolts, although the Republican Party pushed successfully in 1947–48 and 1954 for significant tax cuts that largely benefited those in the upper income brackets. Despite these cuts, marginal tax rates remained dramatically higher than in the New Deal days of soaking the rich, and the mass foundations of the income tax remained firmly entrenched—a political fact that bipartisan majorities eventually institutionalized with the Internal Revenue Code of 1954. Yet in these years of unprecedented "resource extraction," nearly every major poll showed no more than 11 percent of respondents ever indicating that "high taxes" were their biggest concern, or among the most important problems facing the country.[11]

In the early years of the postwar period, the Republicans apparently failed to exploit the "confiscatory" taxation they claimed had been imposed upon the nation by "socialistic" New Dealers. Indeed, they exposed themselves to charges by Truman in the 1948 campaign that they were serving the interests of the rich while endangering the nation's fiscal soundness in a time of grave national security concerns.[12] The only period in the decade following World War II in which respondents noted a major concern about the fairness of their taxes was in the wake of the 1954 tax cuts, when a plurality of 44 percent indicated that *reduced* tax rates were unfair because they favored "certain groups."[13] Republicans would not successfully hammer away at the postwar fiscal regime until the tax revolt that began in the 1970s. The national impact of this strategy would not be felt electorally until the Reagan Revolution. After hovering around a negligible 2.5 to 3.5 percent for two decades (from 1952 to 1972), the proportion of respondents in the National Election Survey who cited taxes as the basis for their voting decisions jumped to 7.0 percent in 1976, and then doubled again to 14.8 percent in 1980, when Reagan successfully campaigned against "big government," whose excesses he blamed on "tax-and-spend Democrats."[14]

That it should have taken so long for the Republican Party to profit from its devotion to tax cuts and related attacks on New Deal spenders, attempted as early as the 1946 elections, is a testament to how profoundly the fiscal state had been legitimized by the social politics of World War II, and how enduringly ordinary Americans had learned its lessons of fiscal citizenship. With the onset of mass participation in public finance, the stage had been set for what sociologist Daniel Bell called the "revolution of rising entitlements," which increasingly dominated politics over the course of the postwar period.[15]

There was a contradiction built into the logic of entitlement embedded within the new fiscal citizenship. Canvassing voters for the 1950 elections, the political journalist Samuel Lubell discovered a striking pattern of complaint among those Democrats who expected to vote Republican that year. They said they intended to bolt because inflation and increased withholding taxes threatened their ability to meet their FHA-guaranteed mortgage payments, thus striking at the foundation of their standard of living. Inflation, Lubell noted, was the one issue that cut across class lines and jeopardized the New Deal coalition, prompting former Democrats to criticize government spending and complain, "We're being taxed to death!" Lubell concluded that "once the bite of taxes was felt, the Welfare State took on a new aspect."[16] With time and bracket creep, this trickle of defections would become a flood—but not until the bonds linking obligation and entitlement came undone a generation later, when inflation and economic stagnation threatened to torpedo standards of living, and severe civil strife over the Vietnam War abrogated the postwar social contract.

The Unrealized Vision of a Full-Employment Economy

The postwar prospects for social citizenship in the workplace—for "industrial democracy," as labor leaders framed it—seemed much more robust than they did for the continuation of mass fiscal citizenship. Yet the opposite proved to be the case. Unions and most of their members cemented the gains they had made during the war, but only at the cost of securing benefits whose privatization, dependence on bread-and-butter unionism, and exclusivity proved to be the downfall of labor's social power in the postwar period. Such a fate could not have been predicted on V-J Day.[17]

The most pressing problem in September 1945 was the prospect of unemployment. If the previous war was any indication, the recession widely expected to follow the war would be devastating, and it would be compounded by runaway inflation. Pent-up demand among frustrated home-front consumers and the mass layoffs caused by contract cancellations seemed to promise a repeat. In a bid to sustain the corporatism that had swollen labor's membership rolls and established its official role in the war effort, the CIO and the AFL pursued a

Labor-Management Charter with the Chamber of Commerce that pledged to sustain high wages, high employment, and acceptance of the Wagner Act in consonance with "private competitive capitalism" and managerial control over the factory floor.[18] This plan for reconversion would necessarily rely on the practice of arbitration that the War Labor Board had made so central to labor relations during the war.

Walter Reuther, vice president of the United Auto Workers, outlined an even bolder vision for government's role in guaranteeing postwar employment in a long essay titled "Our Fear of Abundance," published in the *New York Times Sunday Magazine* on September 16.[19] Heartened by the formation of the Atlee government in Britain and its central pledge to realize the comprehensive plan for social welfare that had been outlined by the economist William Beveridge during the war, Reuther proposed a plan by which the government would nationalize the vast capital plant that taxpayers had paid for since 1940. This would guarantee the full employment that the war mobilization had demonstrated was possible, and thereby avoid the crisis of underconsumption that the abrupt termination of the war economy seemed to portend. Rather than close factories, as the Ford Motor Company had done at its famous Willow Run bomber plant, the government should create a new agency modeled on the Tennessee Valley Authority (TVA). This agency could survey the more than $20 billion in "ultra-modern" war facilities that had been built during the war, supervise their conversion to the production of railway equipment and low-cost housing stock, and provide for their operation directly or through leasing to private corporations or even worker-owned collectives, whichever would guarantee "an equitable wage pattern, a good low-cost product and protection of the Government's investment." A future of affordable public housing and accessible public transit beckoned.

If these plans for the disposition of the war plant were combined with a guaranteed annual wage and geographical equalization of pay standards—the first attained through collective bargaining, the second presumably through wage controls, both impossible without government involvement—the shift to a high-demand, high-volume modern economy would be guaranteed. In a dig at Henry Ford and the political economy he represented, Reuther claimed that all that stood between taxpayers and the realization of this vision was the "disparity between our B-29 technology and our huffing and puffing Model T distributive system," the latter of which had "led to the crash of 1929 and ushered in a period of unprecedented waste of human and material resources." Acting to resolve this disparity would finally enable "economic democracy within the framework of political democracy." But if positive plans for the war plant were "too long delayed," out of concerns for the "contract termination pains of business" or the political discomfort of the Truman administration, they would quickly become "monuments to our fear of abundance," leaving "our free way of life" to "lie in ruins around them."

At the center of Reuther's proposal was a vision of government authority legitimized by its victory in war. His reference to the TVA reflected his dyed-in-the-wool faith in government planning, a legacy of his lifelong socialism, but it also reflected the extraordinary faith in government expertise and planning established by the Manhattan Project and other pioneering projects on sonar, radar, computing, electronics, and airframes:

> We have but to mobilize for peace the resourcefulness and technical know-how which put the B-29 in the skies over Tokyo and sent the atomic bomb crashing into Hiroshima—and we can wipe out the slums and sub-standard housing, both rural and urban, which sap the health and dignity of millions of American families.

If the United States failed to act on its opportunity to secure victory for economic as well as political democracy, it would deserve a grim epitaph: "We had the ingenuity to unlock the secrets of the universe for the purposes of destruction but we lacked the courage and imagination to work together in the creative pursuits of peace."[20]

Reuther's plans were a political impossibility. The lion's share of the war plant would be sold to industry—mostly former war contractors—for a song, providing perhaps the largest one-time capitalization of private industry in American history. Regional equalization of wages would proceed gradually over the course of decades, as the Southwest and then the South continued to attract defense dollars and private capital to states that guaranteed the "right to work," while rust-belt industrial workers suffered precisely the fate Reuther had hoped to forestall.[21] A guaranteed annual wage secured through collective bargaining was never in the offing, although Reuther would eventually secure a privatized, sectorally delimited version of it when he signed the "Treaty of Detroit" contract for the UAW in 1950.[22] Labor rights, though surging and muscular throughout the 1940s, would not gain further purchase within government, as Reuther and his fellow labor statesmen hoped, and so would not expand much beyond the beachheads established during the war.

The dream of full employment sustained liberals well into the postwar years, making "sixty million jobs" a catchword for economic planning that captured the imaginations of Henry Wallace, Alvin Hansen, and others who remained on the left wing of politics after the war.[23] The great majority of Americans also expected government guarantees of full employment, although they did not necessarily embrace planning as the way to accomplish that goal. When a poll in February 1944 asked respondents what government should do to avoid postwar unemployment, 74 percent said, in one form or another, that the government should provide jobs when the economy failed to do so. Two years later, with postwar unemployment a mounting fear, the response to this question was almost identical. In October 1944, 67.7 percent of people polled said they thought the federal government should "provide jobs for every one able and willing to work but who cannot get a job in private employment." In March 1945, 85 percent of respondents in yet another poll said Congress should begin immediately making plans for full employment, rather than waiting until after the war. Three months later, 76 percent said yes when asked by the Gallup Organization, "Should the government do anything about workers who lose their jobs and are unable to find work because there are not enough jobs?" In August, two-thirds of respondents in another poll indicated that full employment was a goal that the government ought to pursue. By September, with war contracts suddenly cancelled and millions of soldiers returning home, 79 percent felt "it should be up to the government" to ensure jobs "for everyone who wants to work." Although none of these polls indicated precisely how full employment should be accomplished, the great majority who affirmed government's responsibility to promote full employment split evenly between those who felt it should take the initiative through public works or other government employment, and those who felt it should be the employer of last resort, after private businesses had failed to employ everyone.[24]

Despite these high expectations, the goal of sixty million jobs would not be attained again until the early 1950s, when another war stoked the national economy. Indeed, the highest expectations inspired by the affluence and proliferating opportunities of the home front would be deferred for at least a generation, if not indefinitely. The planners had seen their final days in government when Congress cut the last of the New Deal public works and planning agencies in 1943. After the war, no central planning agency would emerge to plan for full employment in the sense intended by New Dealers. Not even the reconversion could be managed properly, as the agencies that had managed the war economy, including the NWLB, the WMC, and the WPB, shut down unceremoniously by the end of 1945, while the OPA lived on in an increasingly politicized twilight that ended disastrously with the final failure of price controls during the "beefsteak elections" in the fall of 1946. If full employment was to come, it would not be through central agencies like those that had managed the war economy.[25]

Unionized workers would also see their most extreme demands cast aside in the increasingly conservative climate of the mid-1940s. A postwar strike wave that dwarfed even the wartime wildcats sealed a public image of unions as dangerously militant in their demands for their members. Rising antilabor sentiment formed a solid bedrock of support for anticommunism, which had politically galvanized conservatives by the end of the war and grew increasingly compelling to liberals once the Cold War began. A direct line of rising militancy ran from the wildcat strikes to the authorized strikes of 1945 and 1946 in which union leaders finally were free to act on the mounting demands of their vastly enlarged membership. Running in parallel to that line was the path of labor-baiting and anticommunism, from the Smith-Connally Act in 1943 to the Taft-Hartley Act of 1947, which unified Southern Democrats and Republicans in their determination to thwart the political aspirations of the unions.

Union members would receive unprecedented compensation and job security in the postwar years, but not through guarantees from the federal government. Rather, these benefits resulted from the privatization of public provision for union workers, through contracts signed with large corporate employers that guaranteed job seniority, union work rules, pensions, health benefits, and wage increases pegged to inflation. Unionized workers attained the American standard of living during the postwar years, but the main supports for that standard were in the private sector.[26]

Mexican American and African American civil rights organizers would have to wait a generation before succeeding in getting the federal government to affirm the full citizenship of the workers they had represented during the war. After the militancy of 1943 died down, modest efforts to resist segregation and combat continuing employment discrimination provoked increased intransigence by whites that lasted well into the 1970s and beyond. A bid to make the FEPC permanent fell quickly before the determined opposition of businessmen and southern leaders, although twelve states (all in the North) did erect their own versions of the ill-fated agency, establishing a body of legal precedent that would form the basis for equal opportunity law after the Civil Rights Act of 1964. Perhaps more significant, activist networks—such as the NAACP organizers in the shipyard communities of the West Coast and the committees established by Mexican American community leaders to protest the Zoot Suit Riots—would form the organizational foundations for a later, more successful generation. The authority and state capacity of the federal government were central to their effectiveness in realizing those claims—by sending troops to enforce court rulings, assigning lawyers in the Department of Justice to litigate on minorities' behalf, and at the very least, by acting to ensure that America's image abroad was not tarnished by charges of apartheid.[27]

Despite the many ways in which the rising expectations unleashed by the war years were blocked or deferred, one basic expectation was met for most Americans in the immediate postwar period. Full employment—for whites, if not for everyone—was effectively accomplished in all but a few years of the two decades following the war. Thanks to the wide range of preferences created for them, white veterans enjoyed the strongest guarantees of employment. For most of the more than 100 million Americans who never saw military service during the war, the postwar years would also be a period of astonishing peacetime economic opportunity. In part, this was because the years following World War II were not truly years of peace; military spending kept the economy running at high capacity well into the 1970s.

The Social Citizenship That Was and Was Not

Virtually every organized group in public life sought to claim the returning GIs as their own. But claiming the veteran, or using him for political ends, could prove an unpredictable business, as postwar liberals discovered. First it was necessary to reclaim the mantle of everyman by attaching a political agenda to the returning veterans, the ultimate claimants of wartime citizenship. New Dealers had attempted this during the debates over the GI Bill in 1944, seeking unsuccessfully to broaden the legislation in ways that would provide security for veterans by guaranteeing the soundness of the entire social fabric.[28] The effort would continue into the postwar period, as liberals advanced proposals for housing, full employment, inflation control, and the extension of social insurance—all with comparably limited success, thanks to the clout of the conservative bloc in Congress.[29]

Though ultimately thwarted, expansive prescriptions for veterans provided a window onto a broadly popular vision of postwar government activism. The contours of that liberal vision were on display in an article by the notorious New Dealer and former head of the OPA, Leon Henderson. In July 1946, an *Atlantic Monthly* article by Henderson painted a bleak picture of a spreading black market that threatened to engulf the country in short order if discipline was not restored through public support of price control and rationing. The essay opened with an appeal to national pride, warning that America might be in danger of losing its superior way of life. "There was a time when Americans used to look down on foreigners for supporting a society in which the impossible could usually be obtained with a large enough bribe. Now we are rapidly evolving just such a system for ourselves." More than just a threat to national pride, the black market cut into the very fiber of society. The "prevalence of bribery and corruption" resembled an epidemic, spreading swiftly out of the back offices of a few unprincipled profiteers to infect each part of the social fabric, thereby "debasing the fundamental aspects of our personal relations."[30]

Henderson pointed to the hardships encountered by veterans and soldiers as a way to grab readers' sympathies, selecting examples to underline the moral dimensions of economic behavior and its ramifications for the national welfare. Citing incidents from around the country of price gouging, bribery, and other abuses that verged on racketeering, he described an especially harmful practice, the "tie-in sale," which "hurt the most" because it took advantage of "people with virtually no bargaining power," those in search of housing:

> A homeless veteran in Los Angeles, upon being told that a sunny furnished room was only $6 a week, said quickly, "Fine, I'll take it." His enthusiasm cooled when the landlady added, "And there'll be $9 extra each week, for rent of the garden out back." The OPA found the garden to be an alley full of refuse. . . .
>
> A landlady in Norfolk, showing two Navy officers a moderately priced apartment, announced that to get the apartment, the officers would first have to buy her paintings, a bargain at $300 each.

These anecdotes were chosen to outrage. No figure in wartime and postwar America had a more universally recognized entitlement to fair treatment than the soldier, whether serving on active duty or recently retired from service. Because their sacrifice was being exploited by opportunists, many veterans were becoming jaded by the new "gyp or be gypped philosophy" of the black market. Henderson somberly reported "mounting evidence" that veterans, gripped by bitter resentment and the "fever" to "get rich faster" that had advanced the black market throughout the country, were taking advantage of their ability to purchase government surplus and building materials, reselling those items on the black market. In such an atmosphere, where even paragons of citizenship were tempted to profit illicitly, "the weak decide that dishonesty is the best policy" and an expanding circle of people cast aside their sense of economic fair play in a "chain of profiteering tricks."

Henderson's appropriation of the hapless veteran seeking housing might have gained traction as a call for expanded OPA authority in 1944, when FDR included the right to housing as part of the larger security for which the GIs were then fighting. In the summer of 1946, it was a last salvo in a political war that Truman would lose and the OPA's enemies in Congress would win.[31]

Liberals weren't the only ones to use the veteran as a political football. One reason Henderson's gambit was a losing one was that veterans already enjoyed both private and public housing subsidies. Fixing the housing shortage did not require reviving the OPA's authority. By playing to the veteran, a group of congressmen and senators—including Bennett "Champ" Clark of Missouri and John Rankin of Mississippi—could preside over a congressionally dominated domain within the national state that ensured the convergence of federal largesse with their own needs for constituent service.[32]

Yet the appropriation of the veteran involved more than simply using him as a political football. Much like the GI, the veteran became a cultural figure who represented the coming postwar order, with all its uncertainties as well as promise.

The hopes and fears that attached to the returning veterans revealed much about the kind of society that Americans wanted the war to have won, and about the nature of the government they would tolerate to bring that society about.

In general, civilians conveyed unqualified support for the best treatment of "the boys" on their return. At least part of this affirmation of a positive veterans' program drew on the memory of World War I veterans marching on the Capitol for their deferred bonuses and selling apples on street corners during the Great Depression. A majority in a June 1943 Gallup poll thought veterans would have difficulty finding jobs after the war, even though unemployment was then heading toward an effective rate of zero. This fear, combined with the moral approbation showered on the soldiers, accounts for the broad-based support for generous veterans' benefits. Roughly three-fourths of National Opinion Research Center respondents questioned in April 1943 thought the government should guarantee jobs for veterans after the war. Polls in the summer of 1944 showed two-thirds of respondents accepting the idea of hiring preferences ("first choice of the jobs that are open") and 83 percent embracing unemployment benefits guaranteed by the government. More than 85 percent of respondents to a *Fortune* poll in April 1945 said they thought the government should provide even more educational aid than was already provided by the original GI Bill.[33]

When pushed by OWI researchers to identify particular areas of concern or hope, civilians provided a more complicated, ambivalent response. A report summing up trends prevalent within correspondence panels observed that "civilians feel a debt and a corresponding responsibility to the veteran," but the indebtedness was "tinctured" with fears that veterans would form a political bloc, override legitimate civilian needs, and perhaps sow an element of instability and lawlessness into society. The fifth of correspondents who thought the GIs would return as improved citizens were counterbalanced by the third who expected them to be restless, nervous, or irritable, and by the fifth who worried their "education in killing" would make them dangerous. More realistically, some correspondents noted that veterans had become politically organized since the interwar nadir. "They won't sell apples," the report paraphrased, and "they know how to march."[34]

Civilian criticisms of veterans' programs centered on economic concerns. A handful of correspondents on every OWI panel made some noise regarding the cost of veterans' benefits—except, significantly, the labor editors' panel, which had only one member make the point. A social worker captured the ambivalence embedded within this complaint:

> When these fears [of the cost of veterans' pensions] are challenged they are willing enough to admit that we as a nation must help men with their adjustments, but practically in the same breath they say, we must also stop these laws which allocate money for the services to soldiers.[35]

Support for particular programs varied according to their nature: rehabilitation of bodies and minds directly harmed by combat enjoyed acceptance "as uncritical and undifferentiated as it is enthusiastic." A common refrain was "we can't do too much for the boys"—although a variation on that statement appended a meaningful "but" to the end. Everything, the report concluded, was "contingent upon full employment." As one businessman corresponded, civilians' recognition of the "legitimacy of the veteran's claim," and their knowledge that it was "too popular to be directly contested," only amplified their anxiety over veterans' reemployment preferences.[36]

GIs shared these civilian anxieties about the postwar economy, and were determined not to wind up on street corners selling apples. Before they became veterans, servicemen revealed a mutually constitutive mixture of entitlement and fear in the expectations they held for their return to civilian life, as Samuel Stouffer's researchers discovered when conducting planning surveys for demobilization. Most men interviewed in the European theater in September 1945 did not think their postwar prospects worse than before the war—only two out of ten said so, although the youngest and oldest respondents were more pessimistic. The greatest concern, even for those who were not pessimistic, was employment and security, mentioned by 38 percent of the sample. The proportion worried more generally about finding a "good job" and settling down to a stable life was even higher.[37] Even so, a sizable portion of soldiers felt they had clear plans: 85 percent of soldiers posted in the Central Pacific told interviewers in the summer of 1944 that they had made at least tentative plans for their postwar lives.[38]

Whether they were asked about the GI Bill, rehabilitation, reemployment rights, tax status, or dependents' benefits, soldiers apparently agreed with the elevation of the combat soldier to a special place of prominence in national life. The demand for substantial readjustment assistance and special treatment for returning veterans was unabashed: just over 50 percent of respondents in an October 1944 army study indicated that they considered their mustering-out pay insufficient, while nearly half thought it was merely adequate and only 2 percent said it was too generous. Another study in June 1944 found that 86 percent of enlisted whites thought veterans should enjoy hiring preferences in government, with nearly half supporting preferences even for less-qualified veterans.[39] A majority of white GIs (six out of ten) in the European theater could identify the GI Bill of Rights when asked in May 1945, just weeks after the German surrender. Those who had a clear idea of what the government planned for the veteran were most likely to think it was doing a good job. More than one out of five thought it could be improved upon, with the provisions for loans (for education, housing, businesses, and farms) and bonuses receiving the most concern.[40]

Once they had settled back in at home, veterans as a group seemed to feel that they had received their due. More than 70 percent indicated to Gallup's interviewers in September 1946 that they thought the government had provided them personally with all the help they thought it should.[41] This largely positive assessment is understandable, even in light of the real sacrifices so many veterans had made. White male veterans came the closest of any group to realizing the fuller national citizenship Roosevelt had promised in his economic bill of rights in 1944. The politics of the GI had institutionalized the convergence of civilians' hero worship and the soldier's sense of entitlement. It made veterans into first-class citizens entitled to a comprehensive welfare state that included guarantees of health care, reemployment, retraining, education, tax breaks, retirement pensions, survivors' benefits, home loans, loans for businesses and farms, and a host of preferences that placed them at the front of the line in public life.[42] These unprecedented benefits reflected the tremendous moral claim the GIs could make on the nation.[43]

The claims veterans could make were not, of course, unlimited. First and foremost, they were constrained by the decentralized structure of federalism, on which the GI Bill's framers had relied heavily to ensure its independence from executive control. The accessibility of benefits was determined by the integration of the Veterans Administration (VA) with state and local politics, and the public-private cooperation on which so much of the "hidden state" relied. Postsecondary education had to be pursued at institutions accredited and incorporated according to criteria shaped by the states, a problem for black and female veterans. Loans for homes, businesses, and farms had to be secured through private banks, which could reject applicants according to criteria of creditworthiness that reinforced the hierarchies of race, class, and gender that had long kept private capital segmented. Unemployment benefits, retraining, and job placement reflected the conventions of the family wage, which disqualified female veterans once they married and discouraged even those who didn't. When contemplating how or whether to pursue the GI Bill's educational offerings, working-class veterans of all races and ethnicities were limited by their prior educational attainment and their access to educational resources.[44]

Despite these significant limitations, veterans' benefits opened extraordinary horizons for an entire generation of men. The Eightieth Congress's defeat of Truman's health care proposal left most Americans without a safety net against the hazards of illness and poor health, but the VA hospital system guaranteed veterans a modicum of coverage. Unemployment benefits and preferences for job hiring, placement, advancement, and retention, often augmented by state law, doubtless contributed to the greater opportunities that both black and white veterans of World War II experienced over the course of decades.[45] Demographic research has revealed a major improvement in life chances for veterans, especially those who served in World War II—even for minorities with diminished access to veterans' benefits.[46] Education allowed veterans to pursue real opportunities for economic mobility within their social stratum, if not necessarily at a higher class level.

Minority veterans' encounter with military service armed them with formidable practical and moral resources. A wave of civil rights organizing swept throughout the South immediately after the war, led by black veterans who prompted voter registration drives that momentarily rocked the region before their efforts were put down in a wave of lynchings and other forms of racial policing. Even in the face of this violent intimidation, returning veterans of African, Mexican, Japanese, and Native American backgrounds would assume leading roles in their respective communities' postwar civil rights organizations. Some of them joined the progressive American GI Forum before it was investigated by HUAC for communist infiltration.[47] As postwar embodiments of the combat soldier, their moral claim to national citizenship exerted a legitimacy strong enough to challenge the entrenched customs of racial prejudice that had shaped the nation for hundreds of years.

If veterans of World War II had the moral authority to expand and challenge the boundaries of national citizenship in the postwar years, they drew on the same authority to police those boundaries by personally applying the logic of Americanism. Much like the World War I veterans who founded the American Legion, conservative postwar veterans served as foot soldiers in the culture war that was anticommunism. This time the stakes were higher, for the target in the 1940s was nothing less than the entire federal government: bureaucrats in the State Department and the Treasury who had advised Nationalist China (John Service), participated in Bretton Woods (Harry Dexter White), and presided over the San Francisco conference that chartered the United Nations (Alger Hiss); radar workers in the Army Signal Corps and low-level employees on the Manhattan Project (Julius and Ethel Rosenberg); even David Lilienthal, former head of the TVA, and Robert Oppenheimer, illustrious atomic scientist.

Postwar anticommunism evolved beyond the old nativist countersubversion that had produced the first attorney general's list at the turn of the century and brought about the deportation to Russia of Emma Goldman and other radicals during the Red Scare after World War I. Expelling aliens was not enough, although the Smith Act of 1940 built on that legacy. Now the challenge was rooting out "internal subversion" by American "dupes" who were indistinguishable—save by their convictions and their character—from loyal citizens. The task involved no less than policing the interior boundaries of national identity—the sovereign self—through an elaborate bureaucratic apparatus that extended well beyond the Truman administration's loyalty program to infiltrate the remotest corners of local communities, cultural discourse, and personal practice in everyday life during the Cold War.[48]

In this endeavor to police loyalty, veterans were able to draw on some of the popular machinery of surveillance set up during the war years. FBI director J. Edgar Hoover revived the American Legion Contact Program at the onset of the Korean War in 1950, after having left it largely dormant throughout the second half of the 1940s. Although still denied the FBI badges they coveted, and forced into the virtuous anonymity of their covert status, by March 1953 a total of 100,880 Legionnaires in 16,577 posts had become official "contacts." Writing to FBI field staff to impress upon them the magnitude of the political opportunity, Hoover noted that the Legion, with its three million members, could be found "in practically every community of the United States . . . its members with varied nationality backgrounds are employed in practically every type of industrial, communications, transportation, and utilities facility."[49] The grassroots network formed by this and other contact programs provided the FBI with many eyes and ears throughout the country.[50]

In the end, the volunteer spies of the American Legion were more of a resource for public relations with veterans' groups than they were intelligence assets. As Hoover noted in a confidential memo to the special agent in charge in Seattle, "I know of very few instances in which such contacts were of vital interest in connection with Bureau investigations although the program was of inestimable value along other lines."[51] Yet the significance of the program should not be judged solely according to its effectiveness or publicity, for each and every one of the thousands of Legionnaires enlisted in the program thought of himself as working for the FBI. As one veteran contact proudly indicated in applying for clearance to attend a "Counter-Subversive School" held by the American Legion in November 1947, his qualifications included "special investigative work" he had done during World War II "on several cases re: Naziism and subversive work in sub-contract factories."[52] The ubiquity of the FBI's presence and its insinuation into the American Legion and other veterans' organizations lent it an aura of omniscience that would prove critical to its credibility in the anticommunist social politics of the Cold War.

The Paradox of Rights in the Warfare State

In the Reagan eighties, when rhetorical and programmatic assaults on "big government" began to dominate national political life, Democratic senator Fritz Hollings liked to tell a parable about the paradox that had taken over national politics by then:

A veteran returning from Korea went to college on the GI Bill; bought his house with an FHA loan; saw his kids born in a VA hospital; started a business with an SBA loan; got electricity from TVA and, later, water from an EPA project. His parents, on Social Security, retired to a farm, got electricity from REA and had their soil tested by USDA. When his father became ill, the family was saved from financial ruin by Medicare and a life was saved with a drug developed through NIH. His kids participated in the school lunch program, learned physics from teachers trained in an NSF program and went to college with guaranteed student loans. He drove to work on the Interstate and moored his boat in a channel dredged by Army engineers. When floods hit, he took Amtrak to Washington to apply for disaster relief, and spent some time in the Smithsonian museums. Then one day he got mad; he wrote his congressman an angry letter. "Get the government off my back," he wrote. "I'm tired of paying for all those programs created for ungrateful people!"[53]

Although exaggerated, something in that story rang true in the 1980s. In light of recent reports of widespread dependence on pensions and other government benefits among politically organized opponents of "big government," it seems we are no less immersed in the paradox of rights talk and state power today than we were then, or indeed have been since World War II. Of course, many things have changed since then. The end of the Cold War and of the militarized national citizenship that it fostered has wrought profound changes. Perhaps that explains why, for the first time since the age of Robert Taft, "socialism" has become a political keyword shaping national politics—even as entitlements continue to expand unchecked, defying both fiscal and political gravity.

Although entitlements have gained considerable traction through support from interest groups and bureaucratic inertia, the idealistic rights talk fostered by the imaginary of the warfare state has proven insufficient in itself to preserve, much less advance, rights in practice. Nationalism—spurred by a nearly constant state of emergency generated by the Depression, World War II, the Cold War, and terrorism—has overridden the rights of the individual in countless ways. Yet rights talk has persisted and come to dominate national political culture.

Starting in World War II, rights claims directed at the federal government became an increasingly pervasive, even paradigmatic feature of politics because national power rested more firmly than ever on a state that obscured the sources of its power—unleashing the growth of the mixed economy while branding it the "free market"; concentrating national and global power in a military establishment disarmingly named the Department of Defense and authorized to safeguard the "free world"; constantly surveilling the loyalty of citizens to preempt internal subversion of a "free society." The pervasive imagery of freedom, which abetted this early rights revolution, obscured the nature of public power by individualizing it. Rights—even precious rights to enlist, vote, work, or consume without discrimination—were the coin of that realm, more payment than prize in the 1940s. But they provided ways to conceptualize public benefits and claim political leverage that gained a critical foothold in both society and government, opening an approach to national citizenship that a later generation would claim as its prize.

APPENDIX

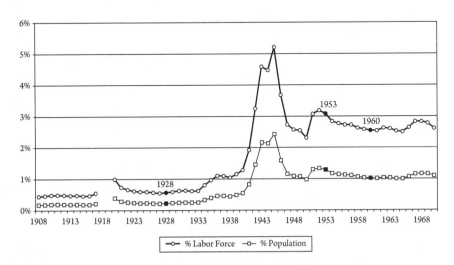

Chart A.1. United States Federal Employment (Civilian non-Postal) as a Percentage of the Labor Force and Population, 1908–1970. Source: U.S. Bureau of the Census, *Historical Statistics of the United States, Colonial Times to 1970* (Washington, DC: USGPO, 1975), series A6, A7, D1, D12, Y308, Y314.

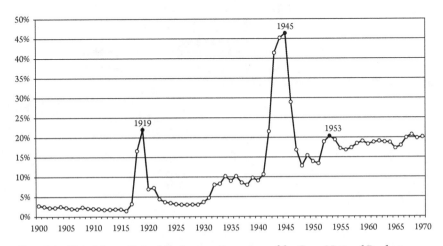

Chart A.2. United States Federal Outlays as a Percentage of the Gross National Product, 1900–1970. Source: U.S. Bureau of the Census, *Historical Statistics of the United States, Colonial Times to 1970* (Washington, DC: USGPO, 1975), series F1, Y457.

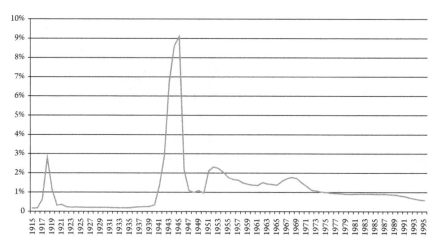

Chart A.3. Military Personnel as a Proportion of the U.S. Population, 1915–1995. Source: Susan B. Carter et al., eds., Historical Statistics of the United States—Millennial Edition (New York: Cambridge University Press, 2006), series Ed26, Aa7.

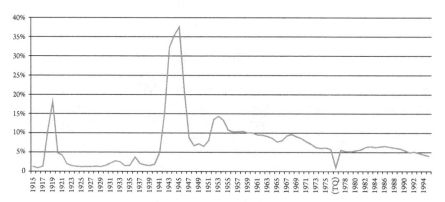

Chart A.4. US Military Spending as a Proportion of the GDP, 1915–1995. Source: Susan B. Carter et al., eds., Historical Statistics of the United States—Millennial Edition (New York: Cambridge University Press, 2006), series Ed146, Ca10.

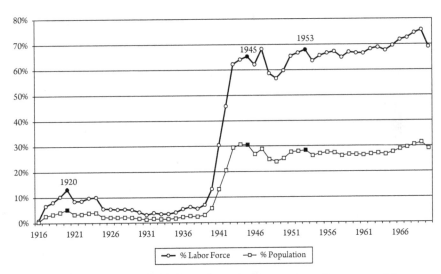

Chart A.5. United States Federal Personal Income Taxpayers as a Percentage of the Labor Force and Population, 1916–1970. Source: U.S. Bureau of the Census, *Historical Statistics of the United States, Colonial Times to 1970* (Washington, DC: USGPO, 1975), series A6, A7, D1, D12, Y394, Y403.

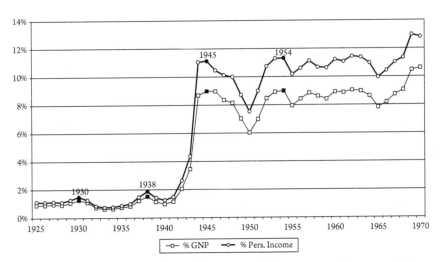

Chart A.6. United States Federal Personal Income Tax Payments as a Percentage of the Gross National Product and of Personal Income, 1925–1970. Source: U.S. Bureau of the Census, *Historical Statistics of the United States, Colonial Times to 1970* (Washington, DC: USGPO, 1975), series F1, F8, Y359.

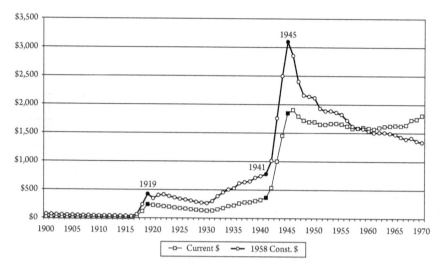

Chart A.7. United States Federal Debt per capita, 1900–1970 (1958 Constant Dollars, Adjusted for Inflation). Source: U.S. Bureau of the Census, *Historical Statistics of the United States, Colonial Times to 1970* (Washington, DC: USGPO, 1975), series A6, A7, Y493; deflator derived from series F1 and F3.

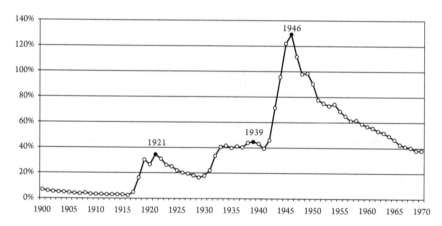

Chart A.8. United States Federal Debt as a Percentage of the Gross National Product, 1900–1970. Source: U.S. Bureau of the Census, *Historical Statistics of the United States, Colonial Times to 1970* (Washington, DC: USGPO, 1975), series F1, Y493.

ABBREVIATIONS FOR SOURCES CONSULTED

Archives

{**11th Naval Dist. Recs.**} Records of the Commandant's Office, Eleventh Naval District, Records of Shore Establishments and Naval Districts, RG 181, National Archives—Pacific Region, Laguna Niguel, California.

{**Allport MS**} Gordon W. Allport Papers, HUG 4118.15, Harvard University Archives, Cambridge, Massachusetts.

{**Army Censor Reports**} Theater Censor Reports, G-2, U.S. Army Force, Far East, Records of General HQ, Southwest Pacific Area and United States Army Forces, Pacific (World War II), RG 496, National Archives, College Park, Maryland.

{**Amer. Soldier Studies**} Research Reports, Information and Education Division, Research Branch of the U.S. Army, in Records of the Assistant Secretary of Defense (Manpower, Personnel and Reserve), Research Division, Attitude Reports of Overseas Personnel, 1942–1953, RG 330, National Archives, College Park, Maryland.

{**BAE Reports**} Likert Studies, Bureau of Agricultural Economics. Collected in three binders, box 22, Historical Files, 1941–69, Savings Bond Division, Office of the National Director, General Record of the Department of the Treasury, RG 56, National Archives, College Park, Maryland.

{**BAE Studies**} Project Files, 1940–45, Records of the Division of Program Surveys, Bureau of Agricultural Economics, Department of Agriculture, RG 83, National Archives, College Park, Maryland.

{**BASR-Kate Smith**} Kate Smith Bond Drive Records (B–0200), Bureau of Applied Social Research (BASR), Columbia University, New York.

{**Calhoun MS**} Robert J. Calhoun Papers, 42nd Infantry Division Collection, U.S. Army Military History Institute, Carlisle Barracks, Pennsylvania.

{**FBI FOIA Recs. Marquette**} Records of the American Legion Contact Program, Federal Bureau of Investigation, Special Collections, Marquette University, Milwaukee, Wisconsin.

{**FERA Appeals**} Appeals and Appointments for Employment, Old General Subject Series, March 1933–Jan. 1935, Central Files, Federal Emergency Relief Administration, RG 69, National Archives, College Park, Maryland.

{**Hastie/Gibson Recs.**} Records of the Civilian Aide to the Secretary of War, General Subject File, 1940–1947, National Archives, College Park, Maryland.

{**LC Lomax War Coll.**} Lomax MS, American Folklife Center, Library of Congress, Washington, D.C.

{**LC Marine Recordings**} Marine Corps Combat Recordings, Division of Recorded Sound, Library of Congress, Washington, D.C.

{**LC Rumors**} World War II Rumor Collection, AFC 1945/001, American Folklife Center, Library of Congress, Washington, D.C.

{**Natl. Broach-USAMHI**} National Broach and Machine Co. Collection, United States Army Military History Institute, Carlyle Barracks, Pennsylvania.

{**NEC State Dir. Reports**} State Directors' Reports on Surveys of Public Opinion, 1937–42, Division of Field Operations, National Emergency Council (NEC), stored in the Records of the Office of Government Reports (OGR), RG 44, National Archives, College Park, Maryland.

{**NORC-Reports**} Printed reports on public opinion, National Opinion Research Center (NORC) Archives, University of Chicago.

{**Odegard MS**} Peter Odegard Papers, FDR Library, Hyde Park, New York.

{**Odum Rumors**} Rumor transcripts for Race and Rumors of Race, Howard Washington Odum Papers #3167, Southern Historical Collection, Wilson Library, University of North Carolina at Chapel Hill.

{**OWI-Intell.**} Intelligence Reports, OWI Surveys Division, boxes 1805–6, 1855–58, in OGR Recs., RG 44, National Archives, College Park, Maryland.

{**OWI-Polls**} Reports, OWI Extensive Surveys Division, boxes 1796–1804 in OGR Recs., RG 44, National Archives, College Park, Maryland.

{**OWI-Research**} Reports and Memoranda, OWI Research Division, boxes 1708–1719, 1842, in OGR Recs., RG 44, National Archives, College Park, Maryland.

{**OWI-Surveys**} Reports, OWI Surveys Division, boxes 1784–6 in OGR Recs., RG 44, National Archives, College Park, Maryland.

{**Pickens MS**} William Pickens Papers, Microfilm R993–997, Schomburg Center, New York Public Library.

{**Selective Svc.**} Records of the Selective Service System, RG 147, National Archives, College Park, Maryland.

{**Treas. Films**} Department of the Treasury, film records in Motion Picture, Sound, and Video Division, RG 56, National Archives, College Park, Maryland.

{**"What the Soldier Thinks"**} Special Service Division, Research Branch and Services of Supply, War Department, "What the Soldier Thinks: A Monthly Digest of War Department Studies on the Attitudes of American Troops," 1942–1945. Internal memoranda, typed ms., circulated as "classified" until September 1945. Bound and stored in the general holdings of the Regenstein Library, University of Chicago.

{**WPA Mail**} Central Files: General 1935–1944, Work Projects Administration, RG 69, National Archives, College Park, Maryland.

Microfilm

{**Amer. Soldier Free Comments**} [Formerly] Security-Classified Microfilm Copy of Records Relating to the Morale of Military Personnel, 1941–45 (44 rolls, negative, 16 mm), Records of the Information and Education Division, War Department, RG 165, National Archives, College Park, Maryland.

{**FDR-OF**} President's Office Files, FDR Library, Hyde Park, New York.

{**FEPC Recs**} Selected Documents from the Records of the Committee on Fair Employment Practice (FEPC), RG 228, National Archives and Records Management, College Park, Maryland.

{**Morgenthau Diaries**} Morgenthau Diaries, FDR Library, Hyde Park, New York.

Online Archives

{**Ad*Access**} Ad*Access Collection (online exhibit), Duke University Library, http://scriptorium.lib.duke.edu.

{**American Presidency Project**}, {**PID # | platindex #**} John T. Woolley and Gerhard Peters, The American Presidency Project (online). University of California, Santa Barbara (hosted), Gerhard Peters (database). Available from World Wide Web: http://www.presidency.ucsb.edu/ws/?pid=# (presidential speech) or http://www.presidency.ucsb.edu/showplatforms.php?platindex=[R/DYEAR] (party platform).

{**LC Amer. Mem.**} American Memory (online exhibit). Library of Congress, Washington, D.C., http://memory.loc.gov.

{**LC Dear Mr. President Collection**} "Dear Mr. President" interview transcripts conducted January-February 1942, AFS 6397–6452, 6455–6463, American Folklife Center, Library of Congress, Washington, D.C., http://memory.loc.gov/ammem/afcphhtml/afcphhome.html.

{**LC MacLeish-Evans**} MacLeish/Evans Collection, Manuscript Division, Library of Congress, Washington, D.C., http://hdl.loc.gov/loc.mss/mff.003004.

{**LC Man on the Street Collection**} "Man-on-the Street" interview transcripts conducted December 8–10, 1941, AFS 6357–6375, 6453–6454, American Folklife Center, Library of Congress, Washington, D.C., http://memory.loc.gov/ammem/afcphhtml/afcphhome.html.

{**LC Radio Research Project**} Radio Research Project Manuscript Collection, Archive of Folk Culture, American Folklife Center, Library of Congress, Washington, D.C., http://hdl.loc.gov/loc.afc/afc1941005.ms006.

{**MacLeish MS**} Papers of Archibald MacLeish, 1907–1981, Manuscript Division, Library of Congress, Washington, D.C., http://hdl.loc.gov/loc.mss/mff.001002, http://hdl.loc.gov/loc.mss/mff.001043.

{**NARA-Digital**} Digital Collections available via ARC online finder. National Archives and Records Administration, Washington, D.C., http://nail.nara.gov.

{**NMAH Victory Posters**} "Produce for Victory" (online Exhibit). National Museum of American History, Washington, D.C., http://americanhistory.si.edu/victory.

{**NWU WWII Posters**} World War II Poster Collection. Northwestern University Library, Chicago, IL, http://www.library.northwestern.edu/govpub/collections/wwii-posters.

Government Documents and Published Sources

{**CR**} *Congressional Record.*

{**FDR Papers**} *The Public Papers and Addresses of Franklin D. Roosevelt.* Ed. Samuel I. Rosenman. 13 vols. New York: Random House, 1938–50.

{**Fireside Chats**} *FDR's Fireside Chats.* Ed. Russell D. Buhite and David W. Levy. Norman: University of Oklahoma Press, 1992.

{**Hist. Stat. US**} *Historical Statistics of the United States, Colonial Times to the Present.* Washington, D.C.: USGPO, 1975.

{**Hist. Stat. US—ME**} *Historical Statistics of the United States, Earliest Times to the Present: Millennial Edition.* Ed. Susan B. Carter, Scott Sigmund Gartner, Michael R. Haines, Alan L. Olmstead, Richard Sutch, and Gavin Wright. New York: Cambridge University Press, 2006, http://hsus.cambridge.org.

{**Ickes, Secret Diary**} Harold L Ickes, *The Secret Diary of Harold L. Ickes,* 2 vols. (New York: Simon and Schuster, 1953).

{**Letters of A. MacLeish**} *Letters of Archibald MacLeish, 1907 to 1982.* Ed. R. H. Winnick. Boston: Houghton Mifflin, 1983.

{**RACON**} *The FBI's RACON: Racial Conditions in the United States during World War II,* ed. Robert A. Hill. Boston: Northeastern University Press, 1995.

{**WRA Hearings**} "Investigation of Un-American Propaganda Activities in the United States," House Special Committee on Un-American Activities, 78th Congress, 1st Session, Volume 15, 9044–9070.

{**Treas. Rpt. 1950**} U.S. Treasury. *Annual Report of the Secretary of the Treasury on the State of the Finances for the Fiscal Year Ended June 30.* Washington, DC: U.S. Government Printing Office, 1951.

Newspapers

Boston Herald-Examiner
California Eagle
The NAACP Crisis
Los Angeles Daily News
Los Angeles Eastside Journal
Los Angeles Herald and Express
Los Angeles Times
Minute Man
Monthly Labor Review
New Republic
New York Times
Newsweek Magazine
Philadelphia Inquirer
PM Magazine
San Francisco People's World
Stars and Stripes
Survey Graphic
Survey Midmonthly
Time Magazine
Washington Post
Yank

NOTES

Introduction

1. Fireside chat, November 1, 1944, in Russell D. Buhite and David W. Levy, eds., *FDR's Fireside Chats* (Norman: University of Oklahoma Press, 1992), 293.
2. *FDR Papers*, 9:670.
3. See Hope Tisdale Eldridge, "Problems and Methods of Estimating Postcensal Population," *Social Forces* 24, 1 (October 1945): 41–46, esp. 44.
4. *Hist. Stat US—ME*, Table Bf663–678, sum of cases/employed for Bf663–Bf670, includes all figures for FERA, FSA, CCC, NYA, WPA, CWA, and other federal emergency projects.
5. Special Committee on the Termination of the National Emergency, *Senate Report 93-549*, 93rd Congress, 1st Sess. (1973). Repeal of most economic controls occurred in the First Decontrol Act of 1947.
6. Alan Brinkley, *The End of Reform: New Deal Liberalism in Recession and War* (New York: Knopf, 1995); Paul Koistinen, *Arsenal of World War II: The Political Economy of American Warfare, 1940–1945* (Lawrence: University Press of Kansas, 2004).
7. Fred J. Cook, "Juggernaut: The Warfare State," *The Nation*, October 28, 1961; Cook, *The Warfare State* (New York: Macmillan, 1962); Cook, "The Warfare State," *The Annals of the American Academy of Political and Social Science* 351 (1964): 102–9. The thesis of "capture" by "corporate liberals" is most closely associated with James Weinstein, *The Corporate Ideal in the Liberal State, 1900–1918* (New York: Farrar, Straus & Giroux, 1971), and Gabriel Kolko, *The Triumph of Conservatism* (New York: Free Press, 1977).
8. Harold Lasswell, "The Garrison State," *American Journal of Sociology* 46, 4 (January 1941): 455–68.
9. Michael Sherry, *In the Shadow of War: The United States Since the 1930s* (New Haven: Yale University Press, 1995), quote on xi.
10. Bruce Cumings, *Dominion from Sea to Sea: Pacific Ascendancy and American Power* (New Haven: Yale University Press, 2009), 501–13, esp. 504–6.
11. Christopher Capozzola, *Uncle Sam Wants You: World War I and the Making of the Modern American Citizen* (New York: Oxford University Press, 2008), provides a vivid exploration of how entrenched these institutions of self-governance were, and how momentous it was for the federal government to encroach upon them in World War I.
12. *West Virginia State Board of Education v. Barnette* 319 U.S. 624 (1943); Richard Ellis, *To the Flag: The Unlikely History of the Pledge of Allegiance* (Lawrence: University Press of Kansas, 2005), 81–120.
13. Ellis Hawley, *The Great War and the Search for Modern Order* (New York: St. Martin's Press, 1979).

14. William J. Novak, "The Myth of the 'Weak' American State," *American Historical Review* 113, 3 (June 2008): 752–72; Brian Balogh, *A Government Out of Sight: The Mystery of National Authority in Nineteenth-Century America* (Cambridge: Cambridge University Press, 1998); Richard R. John, "Governmental Institutions as Agents of Change: Rethinking American Political Development in the Early Republic, 1787–1835," *Studies in American Political Development* 11 (Fall 1997): 347–80.

15. Robert Pippin, *Hollywood Westerns and American Myth: The Importance of Howard Hawks and John Ford for Political Philosophy* (New Haven: Yale University Press, 2010); Daniel Carpenter, *Reputation and Power: Organizational Image and Pharmaceutical Regulation at the FDA* (Princeton: Princeton University Press, 2010). This topic has a more established pedigree in social psychology; see Tom Tyler, *Why People Obey the Law* (Princeton: Princeton University Press, 2006 [1990]). This is not to say that historians have neglected political culture per se. For an exceptionally sophisticated approach to using political culture and language, see Michael Kazin, *The Populist Persuasion: An American History* (New York: Basic Books). Nor have they neglected popular encounters with the state; exemplars include Lizabeth Cohen, *Making a New Deal: Industrial Workers in Chicago, 1919–1939* (Cambridge: Cambridge University Press, 1990); Brinkley, *The End of Reform*; Bryant Simon, *A Fabric of Defeat: The Politics of South Carolina Millhands* (Chapel Hill: University of North Carolina Press, 1998); Meg Jacobs, "'How About Some Meat?': The Office of Price Administration, Consumption Politics, and State Building from the Bottom Up, 1941–1946," *Journal of American History* 84, 3 (December 1997): 910–41.

16. Caroline Ware, "Introduction," in *The Cultural Approach to History*, ed. Caroline Ware (New York: Columbia University Press, 1940), 12. The cultural approach outlined by Ware is compatible with the scholarly literature on *mentalités*, everyday life, and governmentality. This book is informed by all four veins of thought, although its focus remains on the cultural and institutional politics, rather than the psychology, of the national state's formation.

17. Robert Westbrook, *Why We Fought: Forging American Obligations in World War II* (Washington, DC: Smithsonian Books, 2004); Mark H. Leff, "The Politics of Sacrifice on the American Home Front in World War II," *Journal of American History* 77, 4 (March 1991): 1296–318. See also Brinkley, *End of Reform*; Nelson Lichtenstein, *Labor's War at Home: The CIO in World War II* (Cambridge: Cambridge University Press, 1982), ch. 6; Roland Young, *Congressional Politics in the Second World War* (New York: Columbia University Press, 1956), 6; James Kloppenberg, *The Virtues of Liberalism* (New York: Oxford University Press, 1998); and especially Kloppenberg, "From Hartz to Tocqueville: Shifting Focus from Liberalism to Democracy in America," in *The Democratic Experiment: New Directions in American Political History*, ed. Meg Jacobs, William Novak, and Julian Zelizer (Princeton: Princeton University Press, 2003), 350–80.

18. This point is most dramatically made by Harvard Sitkoff in his recent reassessment of black "militancy" and what he now considers its relative absence during World War II; see Sitkoff, "African American Militancy in the World War II South: Another Perspective," in *Remaking Dixie: The Impact of World War II on the American South*, ed. Neil R. McMillen (Jackson: University Press of Mississippi, 1997), 70–92; Sitkoff, "Racial Militancy and Interracial Violence in the Second World War," *Journal of American History* 58, no. 3 (December 1971): 661–81.

19. Max Weber, *Economy and Society: An Outline of Interpretive Sociology*, ed. Guenther Ross and Claus Wittich (Berkeley: University of California Press, 1978), 2:941–55.

20. For a select group of distinguished studies in a crowded field, see Arthur Meier Schlesinger, *The Age of Roosevelt*, 3 vols. (Boston: Houghton Mifflin Company, 1957–1960); James MacGregor Burns, *Roosevelt: The Lion and The Fox* and *Roosevelt: Soldier of Freedom* (New York: Harcourt, Brace, 1956, 1970); Frank Freidel, *Franklin Delano Roosevelt* (Boston: Little, Brown, 1952); William Leuchtenburg, *Franklin D. Roosevelt and the New Deal* (New York: Harper and Row, 1963); David Kennedy, *Freedom from Fear: The American People in Depression and War* (New York: Oxford University Press, 1999).

21. Making everyday life the analytic focus of historical studies of power has earned a prominent place in histories of Europe and Asia, particularly for the period examined by this study (the 1930s and 1940s). For a brief sampling, consult Sheldon Garon, *Molding Japanese Minds: The State in Everyday Life* (Princeton: Princeton University Press, 1997); Sheila Fitzpatrick, *Everyday Stalinism: Ordinary Life in Extraordinary Times, Soviet Russia in the 1930s* (New York: Oxford University Press, 1999); John Dower, *Embracing Defeat: Japan in the Wake of World War II* (New York: W. W. Norton, 1999); Peter Fritzsche, *Life and Death in the Third Reich* (Cambridge, MA: Harvard University Press, 2008); Shannon Fogg, *The Politics of Everyday Life in Vichy France: Foreigners, Undesirables, and Strangers* (Cambridge: Cambridge University Press, 2008); David Kynaston, *Austerity Britain 1945–1951* (New York: Walker, 2008); Michael Geyer and Sheila Fitzpatrick, *Beyond Totalitarianism: Stalinism and Nazism Compared* (Cambridge: Cambridge University Press, 2009); Nick Hubble, *Mass Observation and Everyday Life: Culture, History, Theory* (New York: Palgrave Macmillan, 2010). On everyday life as a category of historical analysis, see Henri Lefebvre, *Critique of Everyday Life*, trans. John Moore (London: Verso, 1991 [1947]); Michel de Certeau, *The Practice of Everyday Life*, vol. I: *Introduction*, trans. Steven Rendall (Berkeley: University of California Press, 1984); Alf Ludtke, ed., *The History of Everyday Life*, trans. William Templer (Princeton: Princeton University Press, 1995); Leora Auslander, *Cultural Revolutions: Britain, North America, and France* (Berkeley: University of California Press, 2009).

22. I am informed here by the notion of an "eventful temporality" in William Sewell, "Three Temporalities: Toward an Eventful Sociology," in *the Logics of History: Social Theory and Social Transformation* (Chicago: University of Chicago Press, 2005), 81–123; and by the conceptualization of "turning points" in Andrew Abbott, "On the Concept of Turning Point," in *Time Matters: On Theory and Method* (Chicago: University of Chicago Press, 2001), 240–60.

23. Westbrook, *Why We Fought*; Eric Foner, *The Story of American Freedom* (New York: W. W. Norton, 1998).

24. On the larger project of liberal "governmentality" and its "ideology of freedom," see Michel Foucault, *Security, Territory, Population: Lectures at the Collège de France, 1977–1978*, ed. Michel Senallart (New York: Palgrave Macmillan, 2009), 48, 108–10; and Foucault, *The Birth of Biopolitics: Lectures at the Collège de France*, ed. Michel Senallart (New York: Palgrave Macmillan, 2008).

25. *FDR Papers*, 9:670.

26. On gendered citizenship, see Margot Canaday, *The Straight State: Sexuality and Citizenship in Twentieth-Century America* (Princeton: Princeton University Press, 2009); Alice Kessler-Harris, *In Pursuit of Equity: Women, Men, and the Quest for Economic Citizenship* (New York: Oxford University Press, 2001); Theda Skocpol, *Protecting Soldiers and Mothers: The Political Origins of Social Policy in the United States* (Cambridge, MA: Harvard University Press, 1992); Elaine Tyler May, *Homeward Bound: American Families in the Cold War Era* (New York: Basic Books, 1988); Ruth Milkman, *Gender at Work: The Dynamics of Job Segregation by Sex during World War II* (Urbana: University of Illinois Press, 1987); Alice Kessler-Harris, *Out to Work: A History of Wage-Earning Women in the United States* (New York: Oxford University Press, 1982).

27. Benedict Anderson, *Imagined Communities: Reflections on the Origin and Spread of Nationalism* (London: Verso, 1991 [1983]).

Chapter 1

1. Archibald MacLeish, "Deposit of the Magna Carta," speech draft, November 28, 1939, 1, 3, 5, in box 787, Magna Carta, 1939–53, History 10, LC-MacLeish/Evans.

2. FDR to MacLeish, November 4, 1939, LC-MacLeish/Evans.

3. On the tendency to obscure power by cloaking it in the mists of time, see J. G. A. Pocock, *The Ancient Constitution and the Feudal Law: A Study of English Historical Thought in the Seventeenth Century* (Cambridge: Cambridge University Press, 1957).

4. Foner, *The Story of American Freedom*, 219–61; Cass Sunstein, *The Second Bill of Rights: FDR's Unfinished Revolution* (New York: Basic Books, 2004). See also Michael Kammen, *A Machine That Would Go of Itself: The Constitution in American Culture* (New York: Knopf, 1986); Daniel Rodgers, *Contested Truths: Keywords in American Politics Since Independence* (New York: Basic Books, 1987). The language of rights had of course defined earlier periods as well, most notably the Revolution and Civil War.

5. Roosevelt famously opened his first inaugural address with the observation that in confronting the Great Depression, "the only thing we have to fear is fear itself." Franklin Delano Roosevelt, "Inaugural Address," March 4, 1933, in FDR Papers (1933), 11.

6. Hadley Cantril, *Invasion from Mars*, ed. Albert H. Cantril (New Brunswick: Transaction Publishers, 2005 [1940]), 19–31, 57–63; quotes on 21, 23–24, 30.

7. For Cantril's subsequent articulation of these concerns into a research agenda, see *The Psychology of Social Movements* (New York: Wiley, 1941), and *The Politics of Despair* (New York: Basic Books, 1958). For scholarly discussion of this development in political thought and culture, consult Edward A. Purcell Jr., *The Crisis of Democratic Theory: Scientific Naturalism and the Problem of Value* (Lexington: University Press of Kentucky, 1973), esp. ch. 7; Benjamin L. Alpers, *Dictators, Democracy, and American Public Culture: Envisioning the Totalitarian Enemy, 1920s–1950s* (Chapel Hill: University of North Carolina Press, 2003), esp. 121–27; and David Ciepley, *Liberalism in the Shadow of Totalitarianism* (Cambridge, MA: Harvard University Press, 2006), passim, e.g., 141–45.

8. The first sketches of this dangerous "character structure" may be found in Erich Fromm, *Escape from Freedom* (New York: Farrar and Rinehart, 1941). The theory was subsequently elaborated in Theodore Adorno et al., *The Authoritarian Personality* (New York: Harper and Row, 1950); and Hannah Arendt, *The Origins of Totalitarianism*, 2nd ed. (New York: Meridian Books, 1958).

9. Cantril, *Invasion from Mars*, 51–52, 53–54.

10. "Mass Murder in Guernica," *NYT*, April 29, 1937, 20; Jonathan Mitchell, "Death Rides the Wind, *New Republic*, May 26, 1937, 63–64; photograph, captioned "Bombing that Stirred the World," *Chicago Tribune*, May 10, 1937, back page. On the public reception of these events, see Ian Patterson, *Guernica and Total War* (Cambridge, MA: Harvard University Press, 2007), 16–48; Judy Yung, *Unbound Feet: A Social History of Chinese Women in San Francisco* (Berkeley: University of California Press, 1995), ch. 5; Brenda Gayle Plummer, *Rising Wind: Black Americans and U.S. Foreign Affairs, 1935–1960* (Chapel Hill: University of North Carolina Press, 1996), ch. 2; James H. Merriwether, *Proudly We Can Be Africans: Black Americans and Africa, 1935–1961* (Chapel Hill: University of North Carolina Press, 2002), ch. 1.

11. "Army Is Perturbed over Fear of War," *NYT*, November 6, 1938, 24. The subhead for the story read, "Alarmist Attitude May Force Hasty Changes in Defense Set-Up, Officers Say— 'Radio Panic' an Instance—Requests Pour In from All Parts of Country for Anti-Aircraft Protection." On the class of 1938 in Congress, see James T. Patterson, *Congressional Conservatism and the New Deal: The Growth of the Conservative Coalition in Congress, 1933–1939* (Lexington: University of Kentucky Press, 1967), esp. ch. 8.

12. James MacGregor Burns, *Roosevelt: The Lion and the Fox* (San Diego: Harcourt, Brace, 1956), 385 and ch. 19 passim.

13. Brinkley, *End of Reform*; Patterson, *Congressional Conservatism in the New Deal*; Jeff Shesol, *Supreme Power: Franklin Roosevelt vs. The Supreme Court* (New York: W. W. Norton, 2010).

14. Sidney Milkis, *The President and the Parties: The Transformation of the American Party System Since the New Deal* (New York: Oxford University Press, 1993), chs. 3–6; Peter Fearon, *War, Prosperity and Depression: The U.S. Economy 1917–45* (Lawrence: University Press of Kansas, 1987), 207, Table 12.2.

15. Mark F. Hawkins to FDR, April 14, 1938, reprinted in *The People and the President: America's Conversation with FDR*, ed. Lawrence and Cornelia Levine (Boston: Beacon Press, 2002), 228; emphasis in the original.

16. Burns, *Soldier of Freedom*.

17. William Leuchtenburg, "The New Deal and the Analogue of War," rev. ver. in *The FDR Years: On Roosevelt and His Legacy*, ed. Leuchtenburg (New York: Columbia University Press, 1995), ch. 2; Alan Brinkley, *The End of Reform: New Deal Liberalism in Recession and War* (New York: Alfred A. Knopf, 1995).

18. Wayne Cole, *Roosevelt and the Isolationists, 1932–45* (Lincoln: University of Nebraska Press, 1983); Justus Doenecke, *Storm on the Horizon: The Challenge to American Intervention, 1939–1941* (Lanham, MD: Rowman and Littlefield, 2000).

19. "Quarantine the Aggressors," October 5, 1937, American Presidency Project, PID #15476.

20. Wayne S. Cole, *Roosevelt and the Isolationists 1932–45* (Lincoln: University of Nebraska Press, 1983), 237–52; quote on 247.

21. Brownie Dressler to "My dear President Roosevelt," October 16, 1937, in Levine, ed., *The People and the President*, 211–12.

22. Leila Susman, *Dear FDR: A Study in Political Letter-Writing* (Totowa, NJ: Bedminster Press, 1963), 66.

23. Nayan Shah, *Contagious Divides: Epidemics and Race in San Francisco's Chinatowns* (Berkeley: University of California Press, 2001).

24. "Quarantine the Aggressors," October 5, 1937.

25. Commonwealth Club address, September 23, 1932, American Presidency Project, PID #88391.

26. Claire Bond Potter, *War on Crime: Bandits, G-men, and the Politics of Mass Culture* (New Brunswick, NJ: Rutgers University Press, 1998).

27. On the yacht episode, see John Morton Blum, *From the Morgenthau Diaries*, vol. 1: *Years of Crisis, 1934–38* (Boston: Houghton Mifflin, 1959), 335.

28. Minutes of meeting, late October 1944, *Morgenthau Diaries*, 786:1ff.

29. Patterson, *Congressional Conservatism in the New Deal*.

30. Walter Goodman, *The Committee: The Extraordinary Career of the House Committee on Un-American Activities* (New York: Farrar, Straus & Giroux, 1968); Jason Scott Smith, *Building New Deal Liberalism: The Political Economy of Public Works, 1933–1956* (New York: Cambridge University Press, 2006), 160–89; Ellen Schrecker, *Many Are the Crimes: McCarthyism in America* (Boston: Little, Brown, 1998).

31. Susman, *Dear FDR*, 23–50.

32. Ibid., 87; Levine, ed., *The People and the President*, ix.

33. This practice was in contrast to the Hoover White House, which had employed only one person in the mailroom to handle eight hundred letters a day on average, and adopted an approach modeled more on public relations and market research than on plebiscitary or constituent service methods. Susman, *Dear FDR*; Levine, ed., *The People and the President*; Brian Balogh, "'Mirrors of Desires': Interest Groups, Elections, and the Targeted Style in Twentieth-Century America," in *The Democratic Experiment: New Directions in American Political History* (Princeton: Princeton University Press, 2003), 222–49. On Hoover's grounding in market modes of knowledge production and distribution, see William Leach, *Land of Desire: Merchants, Power, and the Rise of a New American Culture* (New York: Pantheon, 1993), 349–70.

34. Ira Smith, *"Dear Mr. President": The Story of Fifty Years in the White House Mail Room* (New York: Messner, 1949), 159.

35. Richard R. John, *Spreading the News: The American Postal System from Franklin to Morse* (Cambridge, MA: Harvard University Press, 1995).

36. Susman, *Dear FDR*, 64–65. On Hoover's broad approach to political communication, which was less intensive and followed the approach of advertising and trade or interest groups, see Balogh, "'Mirrors of Desires.'"

37. Susman, *Dear FDR*, 63–64.

38. *NYT*, January 21, 1934; quoted in Susman, *Dear FDR*, 78.

39. Levine, ed., *The People and the President*.

40. Ibid., intro; on white father, see Gary Gerstle, *American Crucible: Race and Nation in the Twentieth Century* (Princeton: Princeton University Press, 2001).

41. Another such informant, who reported with her eyes rather than her reporter's ear, was Dorothea Lange. Linda Gordon, *Dorothea Lange: A Life Beyond Limits* (New York: W. W. Norton, 2009); Anne Whiston Spirn, *Daring to Look: Dorothea Lange's Photographs and Reports from the Field* (Chicago: University of Chicago Press, 2008).

42. Lorena Hickok, *One Third of a Nation: Lorena Hickok Reports on the Great Depression* (Urbana University of Illinois Press, 1981).

43. Ibid., 78.

44. Ibid., 51–52.

45. Hopkins MS FDRL, boxes 15–84 (Hickok's reports are in boxes 67–68).

46. Hickok, *One Third of a Nation*, e.g., 103, 107.

47. NEC Director to "The Executive Officer" [FDR], October 25, 1940, NEC State Dir. Reports.

48. Jean M. Converse, *Survey Research in the United States: Roots and Emergence, 1890–1960* (Berkeley: University of California Press, 1987).

49. See, e.g., Hugh O'Donnell, [FERA] administrative assistant, to Mr. Thomas Adams, January 31, 1935; memorandum "Possible Personnel," March 18, 1935; both in box 2, FERA Appeals.

50. Benjamin Jonah to the President, December 7, 1938; Jonah to the Works Progress Administration, Attention: Harry L. Hopkins, December 22, 1938; both in folder "020 Gp—L July 38," box 46, WPA Mail.

51. On "legibility," consult James C Scott, *Seeing Like a State: How Certain Schemes to Improve the Human Condition Have Failed* (New Haven: Yale University Press, 1998).

52. Converse, *Survey Research*.

53. George H. Gallup, *The Pulse of Democracy: The Public Opinion Poll and How It Works* (New York: Simon and Schuster, 1940); on the journalistic tradition informing the founding of survey research, see Converse, *Survey Research*.

54. William Stott, *Documentary Expression and Thirties America* (Chicago: University of Chicago Press, 1973).

55. Benjamin Alpers, *Dictators, Democracy, and American Public Culture: Envisioning the Totalitarian Enemy, 1920s–1950s* (Chapel Hill: University of North Carolina Press, 2003), 77–156; Michael Denning, *The Cultural Front: The Laboring of American Culture in the Twentieth Century* (London: Verso, 1997), 1–50.

56. Frankfurter to Roosevelt, May 11, 1939, container 8, "Frankfurter, Felix," in MacLeish MS.

57. MacLeish to Frankfurter, May 15, 1939; MacLeish to Roosevelt, May 28 and June 1, 1939; both in *Letters of A. MacLeish*, 299–303.

58. *NYT*, June 7 and 8, 1939, as quoted in Signi Lenea Falk, *Archibald MacLeish* (New York: Twayne, 1965), 102, 176 n. 7.

59. Quoted in D. A. Saunders, "The Dies Committee: First Phase," *Public Opinion Quarterly*, April 1939, 237.

60. MacLeish to Sandburg, June 13, 1940, in container 20, "Sandburg, Carl," MacLeish MS.

61. Goodman, *The Committee*; Jane De Hart, *The Federal Theater, 1935–39: Plays, Relief, and Politics* (Princeton: Princeton University Press, 1967); Jerre Mangione, *The Dream and the Deal: The Federal Writers' Project, 1935–1943* (Boston: Little, Brown, 1972).

62. Ed Kahn, "The Early Collecting Years—Introduction," in *Alan Lomax: Selected Writings, 1934–1997*, ed. Ronald D. Cohen (New York: Routledge, 2003), 1–2; Lomax, "Music in Your Own Back Yard," in ibid., 47–55.

63. Fletcher Collins Jr., to Alan Lomax, December 11, 1941, AFC 1941 005 ms007, LC Radio Research Project.

64. For more on these connections as they pertained to the institutionalization of folklore in the Library, see Jerrold Hirsch's incisive *Portrait of America: A Cultural History of the Federal Writer's Project* (Chapel Hill: University of North Carolina Press, 2003), 231–35.

65. Lomax to Spivacke, "In re contribution of the Archive of American Folk Song in event of conscription," n.d. [1940], folder "Hemphill Songs," box 13, LC Lomax War Collection.

66. Antonio Gramsci, *Selections from the Prison Notebooks of Antonio Gramsci*, ed. and trans. Quintin Hoare and Geoffrey Nowell Smith (London: Lawrence and Wishart, 1971), 5–23.

67. B. A. Botkin and Charles Seeger, "Tradition as a Factor in Cultural Strategy," marked "Confidential," "Copy for Dr. Spivacke," n.d. [probably winter 1941–42], folder "Hemphill Songs," box 13, LC Lomax War Collection.

68. Ibid., 1–2.

69. Ibid., 2.

70. Hirsch, *Portrait of America*, 235.

71. Alan Lomax and Charles Seeger, "American Songster" [proposal, n.d.]; handwritten and typewritten notes on "Star-Spangled Banner" pamphlet, n.d.; "Tunes Good for Marching or Community Singing," n.d.; Lomax to Music Division [Spivacke], September 18, 1942; all in folder "Hemphill Songs," box 13, LC Lomax War Collection.

72. Alan Lomax, memorandum to Spivacke, "In re contribution of the Archive of American Folk Song in event of conscription," n.d. [1940], in folder "Hemphill Songs," box 13, LC Lomax War Collection,.

73. Lieut. William H. Price, USNR, to Harold Spivacke, October 4, 1943; Spivacke to Price, October 22, 1943; both in folder "Hemphill Songs," box 13, LC Lomax War Collection.

74. Robert W. Bloch, Staff Sergeant, USMC, "A Report on the Marine Corps Record Collection at the Library of Congress," typed ms., August 20, 1953, in LC Marine Recordings.

75. Fireside chat, May 26, 1940, in Russell D. Buhite and David W. Levy, eds., *FDR's Fireside Chats* (Norman: University of Oklahoma Press, 1992).

76. Fireside chat, December 29, 1940, in Buhite and Levy, eds., *FDR's Fireside Chats*.

77. Hadley Cantril, *The Human Dimension: Experiences in Policy Research* (New Brunswick: Rutgers University Press, 1967), 35–36.

78. Robert Divine, *Second Chance: The Triumph of Internationalism in America During World War II* (New York: Atheneum, 1967), 6–28.

79. Hadley Cantril, *Gauging Public Opinion* (Princeton: Princeton University Press, 1947); Steven Casey, *Cautious Crusade: Franklin D. Roosevelt, American Public Opinion, and the War Against Nazi Germany* (New York: Oxford University Press, 2001), 18–19.

80. Reprinted in *FDR Papers*, 9:663–72.

81. Elizabeth Borgwardt, *A New Deal for the World: America's Vision for Human Rights* (Cambridge, Mass: Belknap Press of Harvard University Press, 2005).

82. Virtually all of the enormous literature on Roosevelt in the war years discusses (or at least mentions) the Four Freedoms and the Atlantic Charter. For two vivid accounts, see Frank Freidel, *Franklin D. Roosevelt: A Rendezvous with Destiny* (Boston: Little, Brown, 1990), 360–61, 387–90; and James MacGregor Burns, *Roosevelt: The Soldier of Freedom* (New York: Harcourt, Brace, Jovanovich, 1970), 33–35, 128–31. On the U.N. Universal Declaration of Human Rights, see Mary Ann Glendon, *A World Made New: Eleanor Roosevelt and the Universal Declaration of Human Rights* (New York: Random House, 2001), xviii, 10, 42, 165, 176, 238. On the pervasiveness of the Four Freedoms in government propaganda and domestic political culture, see Richard Westbrook, "Fighting for the American Family: Private Interests and Political Obligations in World War II," in *The Power of Culture: Critical Essays in American History*, ed. Richard W. Fox and T. J. Jackson Lears (Chicago: University of Chicago Press, 1993), 195–221; and Foner, *The Story of American Freedom*, ch. 10, esp. 221–29.

83. *FDR Papers*, 9:670–71.

84. Hadley Cantril, ed., *Public Opinion 1935–1946* (Princeton: Princeton University Press, 1951), 1083, items 5 and 8. See also John M. Blum, *V Was for Victory: Politics and American Culture During World War II* (New York: Harcourt, Brace, 1976), 46. Apparently citizens of the United States were not alone in their professed ignorance of war aims: 86 percent of Canadians polled late in January of 1943 could name no war aims stated in the Atlantic Charter, while 5 percent or fewer mentioned self-determination of nations, freedom from fear, freedom from want, or other specifics; Cantril, ed., *Public Opinion*, item 10.

85. MacLeish to Roosevelt, May 16, 1942, quoted at length in Blum, *V Was for Victory*, 29.

86. All Youth Club of Waterbury, CT, to Hershey, Western Union telegram, June 12, [1941], in folder "Protests Against 'Work or Fight' Order," box 33, "General Protests—Age Limits; 'Work or Fight,'" Operations and Executive Office, Selective Service System, RG 147, National Archives, Suitland Records Center, Maryland.

87. Geo. Miller of Noble, Ohio, to Chester Bowles, n.d. [processed August 9, 1945], in the "Complaints" folder, box 2, Records of the Racial Relations Advisor, Staff Operations, Office of Price Administration, RG 188, National Archives, College Park.

88. Brett Gary, *The Nervous Liberals: Propaganda Anxieties from World War I to the Cold War* (New York: Columbia University Press, 1999), esp. 15–53; Ellen Herman, *The Romance of American Psychology: Political Culture in an Age of Experts* (Berkeley: University of California Press, 1995), 48–81.

89. On the tension between romantic nationalism and cultural pluralism within the New Deal cultural programs, see Hirsch, *Portrait of America*, 1–13.

90. Westbrook, *Why We Fought*.

Chapter 2

1. Ickes, *Secret Diary* II:445; Thomas P. Wolf, "McCloy, John Jay, Jr.," *American National Biography* (2000); Walter Isaacson and Evan Thomas, *The Wise Men: Six Friends and the World They Made* (New York: Simon and Schuster, 1988); Melvyn Leffler, *A Preponderance of Power: National Security, the Truman Administration, and the Cold War* (Stanford: Stanford University Press, 1992), 58; Michael Sherry, *The Rise of American Air Power: The Creation of Armageddon* (New Haven: Yale University Press, 1987), 317–20, 414 n. 50.

2. Ickes, *Secret Diary* II:445.

3. Clayton R. Koppes and Gregory D. Black, *Hollywood Goes to War: How Politics, Profits, and Propaganda Shaped World War II Movies* (New York: Free Press, 1987), 51–53.

4. On the larger project of liberal "governmentality" and its "ideology of freedom," see Michel Foucault, *Security, Territory, Population: Lectures at the Collège de France, 1977–1978*, ed. Michel Senallart (New York: Palgrave Macmillan, 2009), 48, 108–10; and Foucault, *The Birth of Biopolitics: Lectures at the Collège de France*, ed. Michel Senallart (New York: Palgrave Macmillan, 2008).

5. On the concept of a public sphere, see Jürgen Habermas, *The Structural Transformation of the Public Sphere: An Inquiry into a Category of Bourgeois Society*, trans. Thomas Burger (Cambridge: MIT Press, 1989). On the "laboring" of the public sphere in the 1930s and 1940s, told—without reference to Habermas—from a laborite perspective, see Michael Denning, *The Cultural Front: The Laboring of American Culture in the Twentieth Century* (London: Verso, 1997), 3–159, esp. 39–50, 77–83.

6. Wendy Wall, *Inventing the American Way: The Politics of Consensus from the New Deal to the Civil Rights Movement* (New York: Oxford University Press, 2009); Eric Foner, *The Story of American Freedom* (New York: W. W. Norton, 1998), 249–73; Robert Griffith, "The Selling of America: The Advertising Council and American Politics, 1942–1960," *Business History Review* 57 (Autumn 1983): 388–412; Kenneth Osgood, *Total Cold War: Eisenhower's Secret Propaganda Battle at Home and Abroad* (Lawrence: University Press of Kansas, 2006), 28–150.

7. MacLeish to Sherwood, December 9, 1941, in *Letters of A. MacLeish*, 307–8.

8. William James, "The Moral Equivalent of War," *International Conciliation*, no. 27 (New York: American Association for International Conciliation, 1910).

9. Roosevelt revised the speech throughout the day. See his comments to Stephen Early in "The Seven Hundred and Ninetieth Press Conference—First Wartime Press Conference (Excerpts)," December 9, 1941, in *FDR Papers* (1941), 10: 516. On Sherwood's central

role in drafting the address, see *The People and the President: America's Conversation with FDR,* ed. Lawrence and Cornelia Levine (Boston: Beacon Press, 2002), 397.

10. Pvt. Juan N. Cavazos to Roosevelt, December 10, 1941; "A Michigander" to [Stephen] Early, December 10, 1941; both reprinted in Levine, ed., *The People and the President,* 402–3, 405.

11. Text of fireside chat in Russell D. Buhite and David W. Levy, eds., *FDR's Fireside Chats* (Norman: University of Oklahoma Press, 1992), 197–205. See also Levine, ed., *The People and the President,* 397, on audience; and Potter, *War on Crime.*

12. On early uses of patriotic sacrifice for political ends, see Sarah J. Purcell, *Sealed with Blood: War, Sacrifice, and Memory in Revolutionary America* (Philadelphia: University of Pennsylvania Press, 2002).

13. Lenore Parker to Roosevelt, December 10, 1941; Mamie O. Tew to Roosevelt, December 10, 1941; both reprinted in Levine, ed., *The People and the President,* 403–4, 406.

14. Gary Gerstle, *American Crucible: Race and Nation in the Twentieth Century* (Princeton: Princeton University Press, 2001), 185.

15. Cavazos to Roosevelt, Parker to Roosevelt, and Ryan to Roosevelt, December 11, 1941, all in Levine, ed., *The People and the President,* 401, 402–3, 406.

16. Mark H. Leff, "The Politics of Sacrifice on the American Home Front in World War II," *Journal of American History* 77, 4 (March 1991): 1296–318. See also Nelson Lichtenstein, *Labor's War at Home: The CIO in World War II* (Cambridge: Cambridge University Press, 1982), ch. 6; and Roland Young, *Congressional Politics in the Second World War* (New York: Columbia University Press, 1956), 6.

17. "Civilians Speculate about the Veterans of World War II," report no. C48 (March 7, 1945), 1, box 1719, OWI-Research.

18. Cf. Robert Westbrook, *Why We Fought: Forging American Obligations in World War II* (Washington, DC: Smithsonian Books, 2004).

19. William H. Gramfort to Roosevelt, n.d. [December 10, 1941]; Arthur Gahiner to Roosevelt, n.d. [December 10, 1941]; both in Levine, ed., *The People and the President,* 404–5, 407–8.

20. Hadley Cantril, "Comparison of Opinions of Those Who Do and Do Not Listen to the President's Radio Talks," confidential report, September 17, 1941, FDR-OF 32:0571–76.

21. J. T. Dahlstrom and N. N. Quinn to Roosevelt, December 9, 1941, in Levine, ed., *The People and the President,* 405.

22. Adam Berinsky, *In Time of War: Understanding American Public Opinion from World War II to Iraq* (Chicago: University of Chicago Press, 2009), 33–60; Hadley Cantril, *The Human Dimension: Experiences in Policy Research* (New Brunswick: Rutgers University Press, 1967); see also, e.g., Cantril to Anna M. Rosenberg, May 20, 1941, FDR-OF 32:00581–83, esp. analysis of chronological trends and regional breakdowns in responses to the question of which was more important, "keep out of war ourselves, or To help England win, even at the risk of getting into the war?"

23. Berinsky, *In Time of War,* 45–51.

24. On the persistent strength of anti-British attitudes, see Steven Casey, *Cautious Crusade: Franklin D. Roosevelt, American Public Opinion, and the War against Nazi Germany* (New York: Oxford University Press, 2001).

25. AFS 6375B, December 9, 1941, LC Man on the Street Collection.

26. AFS 6454B, December 1941, LC Man on the Street Collection.

27. AFS 6370B, December 9, 1941, LC Man on the Street Collection.

28. AFS 6368B, December 9, 1941, LC Man on the Street Collection.

29. AFS 6370B, December 9, 1941, LC Man on the Street Collection.

30. AFS 6366B, December 8, 1941, LC Man on the Street Collection.

31. AFS 6357A, December 8, 1941, LC Man on the Street Collection.

32. AFS 6367A, December 9, 1941, LC Man on the Street Collection; Susan Zeiger, *In Uncle Sam's Service: Women Workers with the American Expeditionary Force, 1917–1919* (Ithaca: Cornell

University Press, 1999); Christopher Capozzola, *Uncle Sam Wants You: World War I and the Making of the Modern American Citizen* (New York: Oxford University Press, 2008), ch. 3.

33. AFS 6375A, December 9, 1941, LC Man on the Street Collection.

34. AFS 6368B, December 9, 1941, LC Man on the Street Collection.

35. AFS 6371B, December 9, 1941, LC Man on the Street Collection.

36. AFS 6361A, December 1941, LC Man on the Street Collection.

37. Brenda Gayle Plummer, *Rising Wind: Black Americans and U.S. Foreign Affairs, 1935–1960* (Chapel Hill: University of North Carolina Press, 1996); Penny von Eschen, *Race Against Empire: Black Americans and Anticolonialism, 1937–1957* (Ithaca, NY: Cornell University Press, 1997); Gerald Rosenberg, *How Far the Promised Land? World Affairs and the American Civil Rights Movement from the First World War to Vietnam* (Princeton: Princeton University Press, 2006).

38. AFS 6360B, December 10, 1941, LC Man on the Street Collection; apparently this interview was conducted before word of Germany and Italy's declarations of war had reached the newsstand.

39. AFS 6454B, December 1941, LC Man on the Street Collection.

40. AFS 6371B, December 9, 1941, LC Man on the Street Collection.

41. AFS 6370B, December 9, 1941, LC Man on the Street Collection.

42. Warren Kimball, *Swords or Ploughshares? The Morgenthau Plan for Defeated Nazi Germany, 1943–1946* (Philadelphia: Lippincott, 1976).

43. AFS 6369A, December 9, 1941, LC Man on the Street Collection.

44. AFS 6371A, December 9, 1941, LC Man on the Street Collection.

45. AFS 6452A, January or February 1942, LC Dear Mr. President Collection.

46. AFS 6439A, January or February 1942, LC Dear Mr. President Collection; see also Nikhil Pal Singh, *Black Is a Country: Race and the Unfinished Struggle for Democracy* (Cambridge, MA: Harvard University Press, 2004).

47. AFS 6439B, January or February 1942, LC Dear Mr. President Collection.

48. AFS 6427A, Cut A6, January or February 1942, LC Dear Mr. President Collection.

49. AFS 6415A, Cut A2, January or February 1942, LC Dear Mr. President Collection; see also Gary Gerstle, *Working-Class Americanism: The Politics of Labor in a Textile City, 1914–1960* (Cambridge: Cambridge University Press, 1989).

50. AFS 6449A, Cut A2, January or February 1942, LC Dear Mr. President Collection.

51. AFS 6406A, January or February 1942, LC Dear Mr. President Collection.

52. AFS 6405A, January or February 1942, LC Dear Mr. President Collection.

53. AFS 6425A; see also AFS 6423A; both January or February 1942, LC Dear Mr. President Collection.

54. AFS 6401B, January 8, 1942, LC Dear Mr. President Collection.

55. AFS 6399A, January 8, 1942, LC Dear Mr. President Collection.

56. AFS 6403A, January or February 1942, LC Dear Mr. President Collection.

57. AFS 6463A, January or February 1942, LC Dear Mr. President Collection.

58. AFS 6429B, January or February 1942, LC Dear Mr. President Collection.

59. This was the title track to the Almanac Singers' *Dear Mr. President* (Keynote Records, 1942).

60. Pete Seeger, "Dear Mr. President," a talking blues song sung by Peter Bowers (Pete Seeger), January or February, 1942, AFS 6408A, LC Dear Mr. President Collection.

61. Alan Lomax to Pete Bowers [Seeger], February 10, 1942, AFC 1941 005 ms023, LC Radio Research Project.

62. Alan Lomax to Mrs. Wilhelmina Waters, April 3, 1942, AFC 1941 005 ms028, LC Radio Research Project.

63. Almanac Singers, "C for Conscription," "The Ballad of October 16," and "The Ballad of Billy Boy," on *Seven Songs for John Doe*, Almanac 1102-A, May 1941. See scathing review in *Time*, June 16, 1941. On the FBI's involvement see David King Dunaway, *How Can I Keep from Singing: Pete Seeger* (New York: Da Capo Press, 1990), 105.

64. Ellen Herman, *The Romance of American Psychology: Political Culture in the Age of Experts* (Berkeley: University of California Press, 1995), 17–81.

65. Noel Silver, "Pope, Arthur Upham," *Encyclopaedia Iranica Online* (February 20, 2005), available at http://www.iranica.com/articles/pope-arthur-upham.

66. Ladislas Farago, *German Psychological Warfare; Survey and Bibliography* (New York: Committee for National Morale, 1941); Ickes, *Secret Diary*, II:419.

67. Susan A. Brewer, *Why America Fights: Patriotism and War Propaganda from the Philippines to Iraq* (New York: Oxford University Press, 2009), 98–104; Allan M. Winkler, *The Politics of Propaganda: The Office of War Information, 1942–1945* (New Haven: Yale University Press, 1978), 23; Herman, *The Romance of American Psychology*, 48–50; Benjamin Alpers, *Dictators, Democracy, and American Public Culture: Envisioning the Totalitarian Enemy, 1920s–1950s* (Chapel Hill: University of North Carolina Press, 2003), 159.

68. Arthur Upham Pope, "The Importance of Morale," *Journal of Educational Sociology* 15, 4 (December 1941): 195–205, quotation on 195.

69. Alexander Leighton, *Human Relations in a Changing World* (New York: E. P. Dutton, 1949), 78–79, emphasis in the original; modified from Leighton, "A Working Concept of Morale for Flight Surgeons," in *The Military Surgeon* 92, 6 (June 1943).

70. Alexander Leighton, *The Governing of Men: General Principles and Recommendations Based on Experience at a Japanese Relocation Camp* (Princeton: Princeton University Press, 1945), 362–63; Leighton, "Training Social Scientists for Post-War Conditions," *Applied Anthropology* 1, 4 (July–September 1942): 25–30.

71. The results of that study were written up in Alexander H. and Dorothea Cross Leighton, *The Navaho Door: An Introduction to Navaho Life* (Cambridge, MA: Harvard University Press, 1944). See also Wade Davies, "Cornell's Field Seminar in Applied Anthropology: Social Scientists and American Indians in the Postwar Southwest," *Journal of the Southwest* 43 (Autumn 2001): 317–41.

72. Ruth Benedict, *The Chrysanthemum and the Sword: Patterns of Japanese Culture* (Boston: Houghton Mifflin, 1946); Margaret Mead, *And Keep Your Powder Dry: An Anthropologist Looks at America* (New York: William Morrow, 1942).

73. David Lloyd Jones, "The U.S. Office of War Information and American Public Opinion During World War II, 1939–1945," Ph.D. thesis, State University of New York at Binghamton, 1976, 130–43. See also Clayton Koppes and Gregory D. Black, *Hollywood Goes to War: How Politics, Profits and Propaganda Shaped World War II Movies* (New York: Free Press, 1987), esp. chs. 3 and 4; Thomas Doherty, *Projections of War: Hollywood, American Culture, and World War II* (Columbia: Columbia University Press, 1993), 11; Michele Hilmes, *Radio Voices: American Broadcasting, 1922–1952* (Minneapolis: University of Minnesota Press, 1997), ch. 8; and Barbara Dianne Savage, *Broadcasting Freedom: Radio, War and the Politics of Race, 1938–1948* (Chapel Hill: University of North Carolina Press, 1999), 118–19.

74. Roland Marchand, *Creating the Corporate Soul: The Rise of Public Relations and Corporate Imagery in American Big Business* (California: University of California Press, 1998), esp. chs. 6–8; Frank W. Fox, *Madison Avenue Goes to War: The Strange Military Career of American Advertising, 1941–45* (Provo: Brigham Young University Press, 1975), chs. 2 and 3; Theodore S. Repplier, "Advertising Dons Long Pants," *Public Opinion Quarterly* 9, 3 (Autumn 1945): 269–78; Jean M. Converse, *Survey Research in the United States: Roots and Emergence, 1890–1960* (Berkeley: University of California Press, 1987), chs. 4–6; Susan Herbst, *Numbered Voices: How Opinion Polling Has Shaped American Politics* (Chicago: University of Chicago Press, 1993), ch. 5. Hadley Cantril's memoir of the unofficial polling he did for FDR during the war provides a vivid account of the tentative and covert way in which the federal government began to make use of the black art of public opinion research; see his *The Human Dimension*, esp. 35–96.

75. Michael Kammen, *Mystic Chords of Memory: The Transformation of Tradition in American Culture* (New York: Knopf, 1991).

76. Quoted in Doherty, *Projections of War*, 168.

77. Foner, *Story of American Freedom*, 224; Kammen, *Mystic Chords of Memory*; Doherty, *Projections of War*.

78. Stuart Svonkin, *Jews Against Prejudice: American Jews and the Fight for Civil Liberties* (New York: Columbia University Press, 1997); Deborah Dash Moore, "Jewish GIs and the Creation of the Judeo-Christian Tradition," *Religion and American Culture* 8, 1 (Winter 1998): 31–53; Marc Dollinger, *Quest for Inclusion: Jews and Liberalism in Modern American* (Princeton: Princeton University Press, 2000).

79. On public opinion research, see Jean M. Converse, *Survey Research in the United States: Roots and Emergence, 1890–1960* (Berkeley: University of California Press, 1987), chs. 4–6; Susan Herbst, *Numbered Voices: How Opinion Polling Has Shaped American Politics* (Chicago: University of Chicago Press, 1993), ch. 5; Cantril, *The Human Dimension*, 35–96.

80. Daniel Katz, "The Surveys Division of OWI: Governmental Use of Research for Informational Problems," In *How to Conduct Consumer and Opinion Research: The Sampling Survey in Operation*, ed. Albert Blankenship (New York: Harper and Brothers, 1946), 247.

81. George Roeder, *The Censored War: American Visual Experience During World War Two* (New Haven: Yale University Press, 1993), 59–61, 72, 111.

82. Leff, "The Politics of Sacrifice."

83. "What Did You Do Today . . . for Freedom?" Magazine Publishers of America, 1943, object III.E.3; "The Five Sullivan Brothers 'Missing in Action' Off the Solomons: They Did Their Part," Division of Public Inquiries, OWI, 1943; object III.E.1; both in NWU WWII Posters.

84. Warren I. Susman, "Culture Heroes: Ford, Barton, Ruth," in *Culture as History: The Transformation of American Society in the Twentieth Century* (New York: Pantheon, 1984), 122–210.

85. Westbrook, *Why We Fought*, 13–37; Ben Alpers, "This Is the Army: Imagining a Democratic Military in World War II," *Journal of American History* 85 (June 1998): 129–63.

86. Leff, "The Politics of Sacrifice"; also discussed in Young, *Congressional Politics in the Second World War*, and Lichtenstein, *Labor's War at Home*.

87. Allan M. Winkler, *The Politics of Propaganda: The Office of War Information, 1942–1945* (New Haven: Yale University Press, 1978).

88. Ibid., chs. 1 and 2; John M. Blum, *V Was for Victory* (New York: Harcourt, Brace, 1976), 21–45.

89. Winkler, *Politics of Propaganda*, 66–67.

90. Marchand, *Creating the Corporate Soul*, ch. 8; Jackson Lears, *Fables of Abundance: A Cultural History of Advertising in America* (New York: Basic Books, 1994), 247–58; Fox, *Madison Avenue Goes to War*, chs. 4 and 5; Robert Griffith, "The Selling of America: The Advertising Council and American Politics, 1942–1960," *Business History Review* 57, 3 (Autumn 1983): 388–412; Sydney Weinberg, "What to Tell America: The Writers' Quarrel in the Office of War Information," *Journal of American History* 55, 1 (June 1968): 73–89; Chester J. La Roche et. al., "Should the Government Advertise?" *Public Opinion Quarterly* 6, 4 (Winter 1942): 511–36; J. A. R. Pimlott, "Public Service Advertising: The Advertising Council," *Public Opinion Quarterly* 12, 2 (Summer 1948): 209–19.

91. Elizabeth Borgwardt, *A New Deal for the World: America's Vision for Human Rights* (Cambridge, MA: Belknap Press, 2005).

92. John Dower, *War Without Mercy: Race and Power in the Pacific War* (New York: Pantheon Books, 1986); Mae M. Ngai, *Impossible Subjects: Illegal Aliens and the Making of Modern America* (Princeton: Princeton University Press, 2004), 93–201; Geoffrey R. Stone, *Perilous Times: Free Speech in Wartime from the Sedition Act of 1798 to the War on Terrorism* (New York: W. W. Norton, 2004), 235–411. The more selective internment policies directed at German and Italian enemy aliens attested further to the racial nature of the violation.

93. MacLeish to Allen, October 12, 1943, in *Letters of A. MacLeish*, 318–20.

Chapter 3

1. FDR, "On the Declaration of War with Japan," December 9, 1941, American Presidency Project, PID #16056.

2. "Andrews Spikes Rumor: Brands as 'Fantastic' Stories of Ships with Pearl Harbor Dead," *NYT*, February 2, 1942, 3. For other such rumors see Gordon W. Allport and Leo Postman, *The Psychology of Rumor* (New York: Henry Holt, 1947), 3–7, which classifies them as "bogeys."

3. Wayne S. Cole, *Roosevelt and the Isolationists, 1932–45* (Lincoln: University of Nebraska Press, 1983), 502.

4. Doris Kearns Goodwin, *No Ordinary Time: Franklin and Eleanor Roosevelt: The Home Front in World War II* (New York: Simon and Schuster, 1994), 319–20.

5. FDR, "On the Progress of the War," February 23, 1942, American Presidency Project, PID #16224.

6. Allport and Postman, *Psychology of Rumor*, 1.

7. "Attack upon Pearl Harbor by Japanese Armed Forces," Senate doc. no. 159, submitted January 28, 1942, 77th Cong., 2nd Sess.

8. Greg Robinson, *By Order of the President: FDR and the Internment of Japanese Americans* (Cambridge, MA: Harvard University Press, 2001), 73–124.

9. Massachusetts Report [August 1942], transcription of conversation overheard in a Boston restaurant, folder 83, box 5; Utah Report [August 1942], transcription of rumor heard in Salt Lake City, folder 66, box 4; both in LC Rumors.

10. The literature on conspiracy theory and conservatism is too vast to cite here. Although it has died many critical deaths, the classic statement remains Richard Hofstadter, *The Paranoid Style in American Politics: And Other Essays* (New York: Knopf, 1965), 3–40. For a similar argument that provides broader chronological coverage, see Seymour Martin Lipset, *The Politics of Unreason: Right Wing Extremism in America, 1790–1970* (New York: Harper and Row, 1970). My analysis in this chapter does not share their insistence on an irrational or psychologically deficient core to right-wing rumor and conspiracy theory, but it does benefit from their attention to the thematic preoccupations, shared assumptions, and verbal legerdemain such groups have employed. A more recent take on conspiracy theory that emphasizes its antistatist uses in the twentieth-century United States is Kathryn S. Olmsted, *Real Enemies: Conspiracy Theories and American Democracy, World War I to 9/11* (New York: Oxford University Press, 2009), 45–81. A more extended analysis of the political maneuvering behind the original Pearl Harbor conspiracy theories and their long-lived perpetuation can be found in Emily S. Rosenberg, *A Date Which Will Live: Pearl Harbor in American Memory* (Durham, NC: Duke University Press, 2003).

11. John Dower, *War Without Mercy: Race and Power in the Pacific War* (New York: Pantheon, 1986); Gerald Horne, *Race War: White Supremacy and the Japanese Attack on the British Empire* (New York: New York University Press, 2004).

12. Jan H. Brunvand, *American Folklore: An Encyclopedia* (New York: Garland Publishing, 1996); Erving Goffman, *Forms of Talk* (Philadelphia: University of Pennsylvania Press, 1981); James C. Scott, *Domination and the Arts of Resistance: Hidden Transcripts* (New Haven: Yale University Press, 1990).

13. On governmentality, see Michel Foucault, *Security, Territory, Population: Lectures at the Collège de France, 1977–78*, trans. Graham Burchell (Basingstoke: Palgrave Macmillan, 2007), 347–58 and passim. On legibility, see James C. Scott, *Seeing Like a State: How Certain Schemes to Improve the Human Condition Have Failed* (New Haven: Yale University Press, 1998), 2–3 and passim. On the shift from responsible speech to free speech in World War I, see Christopher Capozzola, *Uncle Sam Wants You: World War I and the Making of the Modern American Citizen* (New York: Oxford University Press, 2008), 144–72. On liberal concern about repeating the excesses of World War I, see Brett Gary, *The Nervous Liberals: Propaganda Anxieties from World War I to the Cold War* (New York: Columbia University

Press, 1999). On Hoover's trial by fire in the early 1920s and the lessons he learned by the late 1930s and 1940s, see Richard Gid Powers, *Secrecy and Power: The Life of J. Edgar Hoover* (New York: Free Press, 1987), 93–129, 253–57.

14. Michael Dobbs, *The Saboteurs: The Nazi Raid on America* (New York: Knopf, 2004).

15. Utah and Iowa reports [August 1942], in "Civilian Front: Security and Treatment of Enemy Aliens," folder 66, box 4, LC Rumors.

16. Memo, A. H. Belmont to D. M. Ladd, File #66-9330-204, July 31, 1950; Memo, D. M. Ladd to the Director [JEH], File #66-9330-130, September 11, 1943; Memo, JEH to SACs, File #66-9330-70, October 7, 1941; all in FBI FOIA Recs. Marquette (hereafter, FBI files from this collection will be cited using only the standard FBI file number). On the broader history of the contact program, see Athan Theoharis, "The FBI and the American Legion Contact Program, 1940–1966," *Political Science Quarterly* 100, 2 (Summer 1985): 271–86.

17. "Memorandum: The American Legion Backs Up the FBI," File #66-9330-150, July 17, 1945, 3–4; Memo, J. Edgar Hoover to Special Agents in Charge, File #66-9330-12, December 4, 1940, 2; Memo, JEH to SACs, File #66-9330-134, October 27, 1943, 2.

18. "Loose Lips Might Sink Ships," Office for Emergency Management, 1941, ARC no. 513543, Office of Government Reports (RG 44), NARA-Digital.

19. "Bits of careless talk are pieced together by the enemy: convoy sails for England tonight," U.S. War Dept., Army Service Forces, Adjutant General's Dept, Monthly Catalog, 1944, Object no. II.4, NWU WWII Posters.

20. "Careless Talk Got There First," U.S. War Dept., Army Service Forces, Adjutant General's Dept.—Monthly Catalog 1944, 597, Object no. II.8; "Careless Talk—Got There First," U.S. War Dept., Army Service Forces, Adjutant General's Dept.—Monthly Catalog 1944, 1092, Object no. II.9; "Someone Talked!" U.S. President, Emergency Management Office, War Information Office—Monthly Catalog 1943, 208, Object no. II.23; "Because Somebody Talked!" U.S. War Dept. Army Service Forces, Adjutant General's Dept.—Monthly Catalog 1944, 881, Object no. II.7; all in NWU WWII Posters.

21. "Wanted! For Murder: Her Careless Talk Costs Lives," Adjutant General's Office—Monthly Catalog 1944, 1092, Object no. II.12; "If You Talk Too Much, This Man May Die," War Information Office—Monthly Catalog 1943, 95, Object no. II.21, both in NWU WWII Posters.

22. "Warning, Sabotage: Treason Is Punishable by Death," U.S. Office of the Provost Marshall, 1943, Object no. II.10, NWU WWII Posters. The connection between talk and sabotage could be made through a broad reading of the law, which forbade "deliberately doing any act which may injure, interfere with, or obstruct the United States or any allied nation in carrying on the war, by injuring or destroying war material, war premises, or war utilities."

23. "Memorandum on Rumors and Rumor-Control Groups," January 16, 1943, "OWI—Rosten January 16, 1943" folder, Box 1855, OWI-BOI Reports. See esp. 1 ("circulate the very rumors … denied") and 10 ("never repeat a rumor").

24. Victor E. Devereux to Leo Rosten, November 21, 1943 and Rosten reply to Devereux, November 25, 1943, in "RUMOR: Devereux, Victor E." folder, Box 1855, OWI-BOI Reports.

25. Hadley Cantril, H. Goudet, and H. Herzog, *The Invasion from Mars* (Princeton: Princeton University Press, 1940). See Edmund P. Russell III, "'Speaking of Annihilation': Mobilizing for War Against Human and Insect Enemies, 1914–1945," *Journal of American History*, March 1996, 1505–29, for the cultural impulse to conceive of external threats as invading pests requiring annihilation, though surely the viral model of invasion runs deeper than the connections drawn in Russell's perceptive article.

26. "Contribution of Enemy Sources Section to Study of 'Rumors' in the United States," "SOURCES/Contribution of Enemy Sources" folder, box 1851, OWI-BOI Reports.

27. Ibid., esp. 4, 6. Howard Odum, *Race and Rumors of Race: Challenge to American Crisis* (Chapel Hill: University of North Carolina Press, 1943) remains the most perceptive treatment of "anti-Negro" rumors. Classification poses a problem since terms such as

"wedge-driver" subsume a wide variety of stories under a common heading simply because they reveal resentment against something.

28. "Wartime Rumors in Two Eastern Cities," September 12, 1942, "Surveys Special Report #21, September 12, 42" folder, box 1784, OWI-Surveys.

29. For a perceptive account of how deeply this question troubled wartime liberals, see Benjamin Alpers, *Dictators, Democracy, and American Public Culture: Envisioning the Totalitarian Enemy, 1920s–1950s* (Chapel Hill: University of North Carolina Press, 2003); Brett Gary, *The Nervous Liberals: Propaganda Anxieties from World War I to the Cold War* (New York: Columbia University Press, 1999).

30. On MacLeish, Davis, and OWI's predisposition toward "government information," see Allan Winkler, *The Politics of Propaganda: The Office of War Information, 1942–1945* (New Haven: Yale University Press, 1978), 8–37.

31. See, e.g., Eugene L. Horowitz, "The Development of Attitude Toward the Negro," *Archives of Psychology* 194 (January 1936); Horowitz, "'Race' Attitudes," in *Characteristics of the American Negro*, ed. Otto Klineberg (New York: Harper and Brothers, 1944), 139–247.

32. Leo P. Rosten [Leonard Q. Ross, pseud.], *The Education of H*Y*M*A*N K*A*P*L*A*N* (New York: Harcourt, Brace and World, 1937).

33. Estimate of thirty to forty rumor clinics around the country in "Why We Have Rumors," transcript of broadcast on WMEX, Boston, December 22, 1942, in "Notes, lectures, speeches" folder 143, box 4, Allport MS. The number of prominent and established clinics was smaller, just under a dozen, as estimated by Eugene Horowitz in memo to Leo Rosten, October 13, 1942, "Administrative Information and Correspondence, September–December 1942," folder 5, box 1, LC Rumors. The OWI quickly realized the potential for misunderstanding posed by the proliferating clinics, and issued a guide that discouraged all but the most circumspect techniques; see "Memorandum on Rumors and Rumor-Control Groups," January 16, 1943, box 1855, OWI-Intell.

34. Transcripts of more than three thousand rumors collected in this study are kept in the LC Rumors collection, filed by state and by topic. In addition to using their own field agents and civilian defense volunteers, the OWI relied on employees of local U.S. Employment Service and Social Security Board offices. Although they have their limitations, they have the benefit of having been passively recorded at "listening stations" rather than prompted by the questions of pollsters and government-employed social scientists conducting surveys. For problems among rumor collectors regarding rumor definition, see Eugene Horowitz memo to Eugene Katz, August 26, 1942, folder 13, box 2; and reports from Kansas City, Florida, and Alabama, boxes 2–3, LC Rumors.

35. For an exhaustive account of OWI and its internal workings, see David Lloyd Jones, "The U.S. Office of War Information and American Public Opinion during World War II, 1939–1945," Ph.D. dissertation, State University of New York at Binghamton, 1976.

36. The classic study of rumor is Allport and Postman, *Psychology of Rumor*, which was based on the rumors reported to the Boston rumor clinic, directed by Allport. As Tamotsu Shibutani has pointed out in his also classic *Improvised News: A Sociological Study of Rumor* (Indianapolis: Bobbs-Merrill, 1966), Allport's conceptualization of rumors as distorted messages overlooks the communal and improvised nature of rumors, in which the "content" of the rumor—its meaning, as opposed to its factual validity—is produced through the social processes of hearsay and conversation.

37. Floyd Allport and Milton Lepkin, "Wartime Rumors of Waste and Special Privilege: Why Some People Believe Them," *Journal of Abnormal and Social Psychology*, January 1945, 3–36. This study, which presented the most rigorous measure of credence, estimates that 23.3 percent of respondents believed the rumors they heard. A much higher proportion (69–76 percent) was reported in "Wartime Rumors in Two Eastern Cities," Special Report No. 21, September 12, 1942, 30, Table 14, in box 1784, OWI-Surveys. This result may have been biased by its reliance on government interviewers, who generally commanded more respect than private interviewers. It should be noted that all such measures are inherently

flawed: "belief" or "credence" was measured by listing a discrete set of rumors and asking if respondents believed them. The number believed divided by the total number of rumors presented yields the percentage of belief. Left out of the calculation are all of the other possible rumors floating around that investigators could not identify in their study, a source of selective bias.

38. Allport and Lepkin, "Wartime Rumors of Waste and Special Privilege." This measure is also tainted by the problem of recall—perhaps those who remembered rumors did so because they were predisposed to accepting them on first hearing. Unappealing rumors might be forgotten, especially if the phrasing was altered.

39. "Wartime Rumors in Two Eastern Cities"; on women and the gendered construction of gossip in early modern England, where this stereotype originated, consult B. S. Capp, *When Gossips Meet: Women, Family, and Neighbourhood in Early Modern England* (Oxford: Oxford University Press, 2003).

40. Gordon Allport, "Comments on Special Report No. 21"; Allport and Lepkin, "Wartime Rumors of Waste and Special Privilege," 12–14, 28 (Table 1), found that readers of the Syracuse *Post-Standard* were significantly more resistant to rumors they had seen debunked in the weekly column.

41. On free speech during World War II, see Geoffrey R. Stone, *Perilous Times: Free Speech in Wartime from the Sedition Act of 1798 to the War on Terrorism* (New York: W. W. Norton, 2004), ch. 4; Gary, *The Nervous Liberals*, ch. 6; Richard Polenberg, *War and Society: The United States, 1941–1945* (Philadelphia: J. B. Lippincott, 1972). On the difficulty the federal government encountered trying to stifle its critics on the right, consult Stone, *Perilous Times*, 252–83, and Polenberg, *War and Society*, ch. 2, esp. 48–49.

42. For regional distribution of anti-Semitic and antiblack rumors, see Robert H. Knapp, "A Psychology of Rumor," *Public Opinion Quarterly*, Spring 1944, 22–37, Table 1, "Rumors Reported During September, 1942," columns for New England, Atlantic Seaboard, Midwest, and South. Anti-Japanese rumors in the West are not captured in this table, but from the federal government's study of them it is clear that such rumors were most frequent in communities within a few hundred miles of internment and re location camps.

43. The proportion agreeing that Jews had "too much power and influence" rose from 44 percent in July 1942 to 58 percent in November 1945; Hadley Cantril, ed., *Public Opinion 1935–1946* (Princeton: Princeton University Press, 1951), 382–83, esp. items 17 and 18. In a subsequent discussion of wartime efforts to measure public opinion, Cantril noted that the proportion answering yes to this question was roughly 10 percent higher (66 percent) when questions were conducted through secret ballot, although these findings were based on smaller, less representative samples; Cantril, *Gauging Public Opinion* (Princeton: Princeton University Press, 1947), 79. For the broader climate of anti-Semitism, see Theodore Hamerow, *Why We Watched: Europe, America, and the Holocaust* (New York: W. W. Norton and Co, 2008), 261–85.

44. Over half of all anti-Semitic rumors collected by the Boston rumor clinic pertained to "Jewish draft boards"; one-third involved "Jewish doctors." See "Anti-Semitic Rumors," folder 128, Allport MS.

45. For an early indication that the military was concerned about this rumor, see Samuel A. Stouffer to R. Keith Kane, June 1, 1942, box 1, LC Rumors. John M. Blum, *V Was for Victory* (New York: Harcourt, Brace, 1976), 174–75, mentions government suspicions of an Axis campaign against the Jews, as well as Hershey's denial.

46. According to one national estimate done by Robert H. Knapp, who worked with Allport at the Boston rumor clinic at the start of the war, anti-Semitic rumors accounted for nearly 14 percent of all rumors reported in the states of New England and the Atlantic seaboard as of September 1942. This was almost twice the rate for states in the other regions (South, 5.2 percent; Midwest, 7.7 percent; West, 8.0 percent). It is not clear whether these rates reflect the frequency of anti-Semitic rumor in these regions or a heightened sensitivity to the

same, which would suggest an opposite interpretation, i.e., that states with higher rates were more tolerant, not less. What these numbers do suggest, however, is that anti-Semitic rumors were more *noticeable* in New England and the Atlantic seaboard; for this reason they provide an indication of how anti-Semitic rumors crystallized public sentiments in this region, regardless of acceptance. Robert H. Knapp, "A Psychology of Rumor," *Public Opinion Quarterly*, Spring 1944, 22–37. OWI research showed that anti-Semitic rumors also cropped up with comparable frequency in the Midwest, and to a lesser extent in the Pacific Northwest. See relevant state folders, LC Rumors.

47. Reported by Robert H. Knapp, Massachusetts Committee on Public Safety, November 5, 1942, in Massachusetts folder, LC Rumors.

48. Massachusetts folder, LC Rumors. Unlike "The First American," these two poems were not known to circulate widely outside of Boston.

49. Stone, *Perilous Times*, 236–310; Glen Jeansonne, *Gerald L. K. Smith, Minister of Hate* (New Haven: Yale University Press, 1988); Neil Baldwin, *Henry Ford and the Jews: The Mass Production of Hate* (New York: Public Affairs, 2001), 304–8; Gary, *Nervous Liberals*, 207–42; Leo Ribuffo, *The Old Christian Right: The Protestant Far Right from the Great Depression to the Cold War* (Philadelphia: Temple University Press, 1983), 77–79.

50. For a detailed discussion of the monitoring and prosecution of native fascists by liberals in OWI and the Department of Justice, see Gary, *Nervous Liberals*, ch. 6. For background on the extreme right in World War II, see Ribuffo, *The Old Christian Right*; and Glen Jeansonne, *Women of the Far Right: The Mothers' Movement and World War II* (Chicago: University of Chicago, 1996) as well as his *Gerald L. K. Smith, Minister of Hate*. Allport had a professional interest in anti-Semitism. He would rely on his wartime research to compile examples for his postwar classic *The Nature of Prejudice* (Reading, MA: Perseus Books, 1979 [1954]).

51. Direct, verbatim reports of "The First American" were received by OWI from Missoula, Montana; Duluth and Minneapolis, Minnesota; Chicago and Springfield, Illinois; Rutland, Vermont; Boston, Massachusetts; New York City and Long Island, New York; Chester, Pennsylvania; and Richmond, Virginia. For OWI tracking, see folder for "Rumor: Roosevelt, Nicholas," box 1856, OWI-Intell. Early reports are in the Pennsylvania field office folder, OWI Reports on Rumors, first half of August 1942, "Local Rumor Control Projects: [Alabama to Wyoming]," State Rumors by Subject, boxes 2–3, LC Rumors. See also "Anti-Semitic Rumors," March 1943, in folder 128, "Psychology of Rumor—Misc. Material," box 5, Allport MS.

52. Bennett Cerf, ed., *The Pocket Book of War Humor* (New York: Pocket Books, 1943), 145.

53. Letter from A.C., "Philadelphia Inquirer" folder, box 1857, OWI-Intell.

54. "Anti-Semitic Rumors," March 1943, Allport MS.

55. Ibid. The same rumor crops up repeatedly in LC Rumors.

56. Arizona folder, LC Rumors.

57. Minnesota folder, LC Rumors.

58. "Anti-Semitic Rumors," March 1943, Allport MS.

59. Ibid.

60. Indiana folder, LC Rumors.

61. "Rumors in Massachusetts, July 6–13, 1942," and "Rumors in the Boston Region: March 20–May 25, 1942," both in folder 126, box 5; "Anti-Semitic Rumors," March 1943. All three reports in Allport MS.

62. "Smuggling Christians" in New York and Massachusetts folders, LC Rumors.

63. Quote attributed to an anonymous person in Utica, New York. "Anti-Semitic Rumors," March 1943, Allport MS; see also numerous other statements to the same effect in this report, e.g., those reported from Cleveland, Ohio; Louisiana; Utica, New York; Arlington, Virginia; and Seattle, Washington. For other statements claiming that Washington was run by Jews, or claiming that certain prominent administrators were Jewish, see LC Rumors, folder 108, Chicago, Illinois; St. Paul and Minneapolis, Minnesota; and state folders (e.g., comments made in Memphis, Tennessee; Cleveland, Ohio; Harrisburg, Pennsylvania; Detroit, Michigan; Yonkers, Jamaica, and Buffalo, New York; and Indianapolis, Indiana).

64. Folder 65, box 4, LC Rumors.

65. Theodor Adorno, Else Frenkel-Brunswick, Daniel J. Levinson, and R. Nevitt Sanford, *The Authoritarian Personality* (New York: American Jewish Committee, 1950), ch. III, Table 13 (III), item 72 of A-S Scale. This item was used in the most concentrated version of the scale; it was chosen for its ability to reflect anti-Semitism more powerfully than other items without raising suspicions in interviewees. Interview dates given on 21–22.

66. On preempting racial tensions by countering rumors, see William H. Weber (OWI Chicago office), "Special Report on Counter-Propaganda," memo to Eugene Katz (OWI Bureau of Intelligence), September 4, 1942. The OWI's investigation of "Eleanor Clubs" and other racial rumors is described in Weber to Eugene Katz, September 1, 1942; Don M. Lochner (OWI Florida field representative) to Weber, August 25, 1942; Paul Duncan (Alabama field representative) to Weber, August 29, 1942; Don M. Lochner (Florida field representative) to Weber, August 27, 1942; E. Leight Stevens (Richmond, Virginia, field representative) to Katherine Blackburn (chief, OWI Bureau of Public Inquiries), August 28, 1942; all in folder 5, box 1, LC Rumors.

67. Odum, *Race and Rumors of Race*.

68. Bryant Simon, "Introduction," in Odum, *Race and Rumors of Race*, vii–xxxii.

69. RACON, 1–72; Powers, *Secrecy and Power*, 239–74.

70. Reported by Nancy Hirsch, Agnes Scott College, February 24, 1943, folder 3, "Observational Reports on Black/White Relations," boxes 58–59 (hereafter "Obs. Reports"), Odum Rumors.

71. Anonymous report from Tulane, January 12, 1943, folder 5, Obs. Reports, Odum Rumors.

72. Anonymous report from Georgia State Women's College at Valdosta, February 8, 1943, folder 1, Obs. Reports, Odum Rumors.

73. Emphasis added, anonymous report from the University of Alabama, February 2, 1943, folder 1, Obs. Reports, Odum Rumors; Jacqueline Jones, *Labor of Love, Labor of Sorrow: Black Women, Work and the Family, from Slavery to the Present* (New York: Basic Books, 1985), 55–68, 236–38, 256–60.

74. Alabama folder, LC Rumors.

75. Bridge party and federal official in Folder 107, box 7, LC Rumors. Although social security, relief, and Aid to Dependent Children did not originate in the war, their mention here is of a piece with other complaints largely centered on wages and working conditions in war plants.

76. In the August 23, 1943, Minutes of the Committee on Subversive Propaganda and Rumor, Dade County Rumor Clinic folder, General Reports R-W, Rumor Clinics, OWI-Intell. Reports and Special Memoranda, 1942–1943. On Hoover's southern upbringing and antipathy to the civil rights movement, see Powers, *Secrecy and Power*, 5–35, 323–32.

77. Illinois folder, LC Rumors.

78. See, e.g., Alabama folder, LC Rumors. Memo on race tensions in Richmond from James H. Woodall, Regional Representative, USES, Washington, D.C., to OWI Special Services, August 18, 1942, Virginia Folder, LC Rumors.

79. Alabama folder, [first half of August 1942], LC Rumors.

80. Florida folder, [first half of August 1942], LC Rumors.

81. See, e.g., "Congress Upheld by Rickenbacker: Call for Leader Who Will Not 'Coddle' Minorities, Pressure Groups," *NYT*, March 9, 1944, 34; "Call Youth Court a Plan to 'Coddle," *NYT*, March 25, 1942, 24. This usage appears to have been a survival from the interwar period, as reflected in "Miss Perkins to 'Coddle' Reds," *NYT*, October 26, 1938, 12.

82. OWI investigations summarized in Webber to Katz, September 1, 1942, and enclosed field reports, LC Rumors. FBI investigations reported in RACON, 81, 244, 255, 259, 274, 281, 289, 298, 306, 338, 344.

83. For Eleanor Club rumors tracked by OWI that were nearly identical to those reported to Odum, see state folders, LC Rumors (VA, FL, AL, TX, SC). For investigation which established that no conspiracy existed, see William H. Webber summary memo to Eugene Katz,

September 1, 1942 and memos from OWI field reps. to Webber dated August 25 and August 27, 1942 (FL), August 28, 1942 (VA), August 29, 1942 (AL); all memos in "Administrative Information and Correspondence," folder 5, box 1, LC Rumors.

84. Bryant Simon, "Introduction," in Odum, *Race and Rumors of Race*, xxvii–xxix. See also Robin D. G. Kelley, "We Are Not What We Seem: Rethinking Black Working-Class Opposition in the Jim Crow South," *Journal of American History* 80, 1 (June 1993): 75–112.

85. See, e.g., rumor that "Eleanor Club will not allow her to do general work," reported by S. Spurlock, Agnes Scott College, February 26, 1943, folder 3; list of club "rules" in report by K. Virginia Bell, University of Florida, April 3, 1943, folder 1; both in Obs. Reports, Odum Rumors.

86. Reported by D. Dozier, University of Alabama, January 29, 1943, folder 1, Obs. Reports, Odum Rumors. See almost identical report from Jacksonville, Florida, folder 107, box 7, LC Rumors. See also Odum, *Race and Rumors of Race*, 69–70.

87. Bryant Simon, "Fearing Eleanor: Wartime Rumors and Racial Anxieties, 1940–1945," in *Labor in the Modern South*, ed. Glen Eskew (Athens: University of Georgia Press, 2001), 83–101; Goodwin, *No Ordinary Time*; Gil Troy, *Mr. and Mrs. President: From the Trumans to the Clintons* (Lawrence: University of Kansas Press, 2000), 8–11, 23, 24. See also Odum, *Race and Rumors of Race*, Ch. X, on Eleanor Roosevelt's folkloric image and the rumors.

88. Anonymous report, Wesleyan College, Georgia, February 22, 1943, folder 2, Obs. Reports, Odum Rumors.

89. Reported by Louise Terash, Georgia State College for Women, Milledgville, February 10, 1943, folder 4, Obs. Reports, Odum Rumors.

90. Anonymous report, Georgia State Women's College, Valdosta, February 9, 1943, folder 2, Obs. Reports, Odum Rumors.

91. Odum, *Race and Rumors of Race*, 148; 142–55.

92. James H. Woodall, USES, memo to OWI Special Services, August 18, 1942, Virginia folder, boxes 2–3, LC Rumors.

93. Stephen Hahn, *A Nation Under Our Feet: Black Political Struggles in the Rural South from Slavery to the Great Migration* (Cambridge, MA: Harvard University Press, 2003), 116–59.

94. Robert A. Hill, "Introduction," in RACON.

95. *Los Angeles Times*, June 1, 1943.

96. William Gellermann, *Martin Dies* (New York: John Day, 1944), 16–30.

97. Martin Dies, *The Trojan Horse in America* (New York: Dodd, Mead, 1940).

98. Walter Goodman, *The Committee: The Extraordinary Career of the House Committee on Un-American Activities* (New York: Farrar, Straus and Giroux, 1968), 128–29.

99. Committee on Wartime Relocation and Internment of Civilians, *Personal Justice Denied* (Seattle: University of Washington Press, 1997 [1982]), 93–96; Robinson, *By Order of the President*, 193.

100. Committee on Wartime Relocation and Internment of Civilians, *Personal Justice Denied*, 224–26; Goodman, *The Committee*, 152–54; Robinson, *By Order of the President*, 192–94.

101. For conditions in the camps, see Committee on Wartime Relocation and Internment of Civilians, *Personal Justice Denied*, 158–67, esp. 157, Table 2, and162–63, on diet and the mess halls.

102. Townsend's testimony was entered into the public record during hearings on June 10, 1943. Townsend testimony, WRA Hearings.

103. Ibid., 9054, 9057, 9068.

104. Ibid., 9052, 9055, 9058.

105. Ibid., 9048–49, 9054–55.

106. Ibid., 9060.

107. Ibid., 9069.

108. Committee on Wartime Relocation and Internment of Civilians, *Personal Justice Denied*, 226; Robinson, *By Order of the President*, 193. The hearings did unearth some minor administrative inefficiencies that the WRA moved quickly to address.

109. Committee on Wartime Relocation and Internment of Civilians, *Personal Justice Denied*, 178–79; see matter of Townsend's false testimony on 226.

110. Testimony by Dillon Myer, July 6 and July 7, 1943, WRA Hearings; "lies or half-truths" correction in Committee on Wartime Relocation and Internment of Civilians, *Personal Justice Denied*, 226.

111. John W. Jeffries, *Wartime America: The World War II Home Front* (Chicago: Ivan R. Dee, 1996), 27–31, 85–87.

112. Amy Bentley, *Eating for Victory: Food Rationing and the Politics of Domesticity* (Urbana: University of Illinois Press, 1998), 86–87, 94, 96, 111–13; Meg Jacobs, "How About Some Meat? The Office of Price Administration, Consumption Politics, and State Building from the Bottom Up, 1941–1946," *Journal of American History* 84, 3 (December 1997): 934–41.

113. OPA pamphlet, January 1943, as cited in Bentley, *Eating for Victory*, 85.

114. "First call" and broader discussion of menu in testimony of Thomas Cavett, former investigator, California State Legislature, 9266–76; see also Townsend testimony, testimony by Townsend's supervisor, Augustus Empie, June 9, 1943, WRA Hearings, 8937–42; "there wasn't a meat shortage" from Gelvin testimony, WRA Hearings, 8872.

115. Goodman, *The Committee*, 153.

116. Testimony of Jim Washum, June 18, 1943, WRA Hearings, 9377; also mentioned briefly in Goodman, *The Committee*, 155.

117. Myer testimony, WRA Hearings, 9652.

118. Empie testimony, WRA Hearings, 8937–42.

119. Transcript from August 1942 in Arizona folder, LC Rumors. The same rumors of Japanese privilege and pampering were also reported in "Rumors on Rationing, Conservation, and Salvage," December 1942, Memorandum No. 24, and in "Rumors on Minority Groups," February 11, 1943, Memorandum No. 39; both in Box 1842, OWI-Intell.

120. Idaho folder, LC Rumors.

121. Arizona folder (Phoenix), LC Rumors. Brian Masaru Hayashi, *Democratizing the Enemy: The Japanese American Internment* (Princeton, NJ: Princeton University Press, 2004), 17–18.

122. Arizona folder, LC Rumors.

123. OWI Field Reports, Phoenix, Arizona. On the role of white migratory workers vis-à-vis nonwhite workers in determining racial hierarchies in the southwestern states, see Neil Foley, *White Scourge: Mexicans, Blacks, and Poor Whites in Texas Cotton Culture* (Berkeley: University of California Press, 1999).

124. Testimony of J. W. Buzzell, WRA Hearings, 9281–83.

125. *Los Angeles Times*, June 4, 1943; Committee on Wartime Relocation and Internment of Civilians, *Personal Justice Denied*, 163–67. Army pay started at $25 per month. Unskilled laborers in the camps were paid $12 per month, skilled laborers got $16 for the same, and professionals earned $19.

126. Transcript from August 1942, Wisconsin folder, LC Rumors.

127. Transcript from August 1942, Texas folder, LC Rumors.

128. Wendy Wall, *Inventing the American Way: The Politics of Consensus from the New Deal to the Civil Rights Movement* (New York: Oxford University Press, 2008).

129. Arizona folder and Miscellaneous folder no. 92, box 6, LC Rumors.

130. Allport and Poston, *Psychology of Rumor*, 174.

131. John M. Blum, *V Was for Victory: Politics and American Culture During World War II* (New York: Harcourt, Brace, Jovanovich, 1976), 296–98; Richard N. Smith, *Thomas E. Dewey and His Times* (New York: Touchstone, 1982), ch. 12.

132. Smith, *Thomas E. Dewey and His Times*, 409–10, 433–34.

133. Warren Moscow, "Dewey Predicts 'Red Menace' Rise if Roosevelt Wins," *NYT*, November 2, 1944.

134. *CR*, September 11, 1944, 7649, and September 18, 1944, 7866–67, as quoted in Roland Young, *Congressional Politics in World War II* (New York: Columbia University Press, 1956), 173.

135. Rosenberg, *A Date Which Will Live*, 38–52.

136. Transcripts recorded mid-1942, in Minneapolis and New York folders, "Local Rumor Control Projects," boxes 2–3, LC Rumors.

Part II

1. Michael Walzer, "The Communitarian Critique of Liberalism," in *Thinking Politically: Essays in Political Theory*, ed. Michael Walzer (New Haven: Yale University Press, 2007), 101–5.

2. Hist. Stat. US—ME, series Ac424-6, Ed1, Ed27.

3. *Edwards v. California*, 314 U.S. 160 (1941). The right to move was first affirmed in *Crandall v. Nevada*, 73 U.S. 35 (1868), but subsequently fell into neglect along with much of Reconstruction-era jurisprudence.

4. Charles Chamberlain, *Victory at Home: Manpower and Race in the American South During World War II* (Athens: University of Georgia Press, 2003), 69–96.

5. Hist. Stat. US—ME, Ca9-10, Ea705; U.S. Department of Labor, *Industrial Disputes and Wage Stabilization in Wartime*, vol. I of *The Termination Report of the NWLB* (Washington, DC: USGPO, [1948]), 547–59, esp. Tables 2 and 5, Chart 3, and 551.

6. W. S. Woytinsky et al., *Employment and Wages in the United States* (New York: Twentieth Century Fund, 1953), 398–99, Fig. 31 and Tables 169–70.

7. "Wartime Expansion of the Labor Force," *Monthly Labor Review* 61, 2 (August 1945): 234–36.

8. John W. Jeffries, *Wartime America: The World War II Home Front* (Chicago: Ivan R. Dee, 1996), 61–64.

9. Carole Shammas, "A New Look at Long-Term Trends in Wealth Inequality in the United States," *American Historical Review* 98, 2 (April 1993): 412–31, esp. 425, Table 5.

10. James T. Patterson, *Grand Expectations: Postwar America, 1945–1974* (New York: Oxford University Press, 1996), 14, 76.

11. *Smith v. Allwright*, 321 U.S. 649 (1944); Kraig Beyerlein and Kenneth Andrews, "Black Voting During the Civil Rights Movement: A Micro-level Analysis," *Social Forces* 87, 1 (September 2008): 68.

12. Henry Lee Moon, *The Balance of Power: The Negro Vote* (New York: Doubleday, 1948), 197; Steven Lawson, *Running for Freedom: Civil Rights and Black Politics in America Since 1941* (New York: McGraw-Hill, 1990), 33–39; Thomas Sugrue, *Sweet Land of Liberty: The Forgotten Struggle for Civil Rights in the North* (New York: Random House, 2008), 87–129.

Chapter 4

1. "Kate Smith, First Spot on the Network," Tuesday, September 21, 1943, typed transcript, 4–5, in BASR-Kate Smith; Robert K. Merton, *Mass Persuasion: The Social Psychology of a War Bond Drive* (New York: Harper and Brothers, 1946), 3, 60–64.

2. Spot 7, BASR-Kate Smith. Confirmed as most influential in Merton, *Mass Persuasion*, 53, n.7.

3. Spot 6, BASR-Kate Smith; Merton, *Mass Persuasion*, 52–53.

4. Hist. Stat. US, Series F1, Y457. The starting point for any history of this regime is W. Elliot Brownlee, *Federal Taxation in America: A Short History*, 2nd ed. (Cambridge: Woodrow Wilson Center Press, 2004); and Brownlee, ed., *Funding the Modern American State: The Rise and Fall of the Era of Easy Finance* (Cambridge: Woodrow Wilson Center Press, 1996), esp. chs. 1 and 2. See also Herbert Stein, *The Fiscal Revolution in America*, 2nd ed. (Washington, DC: American Enterprise Institute, 1996); John F. Witte, *The Politics and Development of the Federal Income Tax* (Madison: University of Wisconsin Press, 1985); Bartholomew Sparrow, *From the Outside In: World War II and the American State* (Princeton: Princeton

University Press, 1996); Jarvis M. Morse, "Paying for a World War: The United States Financing of World War II," 1975, U.S. Treasury Library, Washington, D.C.; Harold Vatter, *The U.S. Economy in World War II* (New York: Columbia University Press, 1985); Julian Zelizer, *Taxing America: Wilbur D. Mills, Congress, and the State, 1945–1975* (Cambridge: Cambridge University Press, 1998).

5. J. R. Vernon, "World War II Fiscal Policies and the End of the Great Depression," *Journal of Economic History* 54, 4 (December 1994): 850–68.

6. Stein, *The Fiscal Revolution in America*, ch. 8; Robert M. Collins, *More: The Politics of Economic Growth in Postwar America* (New York: Oxford University Press, 2000), 10–16.

7. My approach to resource extraction emphasizes the centrality of what Margaret Levi calls ruler credibility and taxpayer expectations of equal cooperation (i.e., equity), rather than treating them as mere constraints on rulers' designs; cf. her *Of Rule and Revenue* (Berkeley: University of California Press, 1988), 52–67.

8. On the mutually constitutive nature of obligation and entitlement in forging citizenship, see Linda Kerber, *No Constitutional Right to Be Ladies: Women and the Obligations of Citizenship* (New York: Hill and Wang, 1998).

9. *Hist. Stat. US*, 224 and 1114, Series Y457 and F1; Vatter, *The U.S. Economy in World War II*, 103; Richard Polenberg, *War and Society: The United States, 1941–1945* (Philadelphia: J. B. Lippincott, 1972), 27; John M. Blum, *V Was for Victory* (New York: Harcourt, Brace, 1976), 91. Sparrow, *From the Outside In*, 287 and 301, Table 7.6, provides numbers indicating that World War II was nine times more expensive than World War I, but qualifies that by observing that a stronger dollar in the 1940s meant that the difference in the cost of the two wars was even greater than his estimate suggests. For a slightly different figure for total defense expenditures 1941–1945, ca. $350 billion, see U.S. Bureau of the Budget, *The United States at War: Development and Administration of the War Program by the Federal Government*, repr. ed. (Washington, DC: U.S. Government Printing Office, 1946), 112, Chart 12.

10. The First Revenue Act of 1940 lowered personal income tax exemptions, raised surtax rates on individual incomes, especially on middle incomes, and increased most tax rates by 10 percent for five years. The Revenue Act of 1941 lowered the personal exemption even further and raised rates sharply for nearly all brackets. The Revenue Act of 1942 again lowered exemptions and raised normal rates sharply, while adding a 5 percent Victory Tax to all net annual incomes over $624: with a range of minimum and maximum surtax rates between 13 percent (for annual incomes of $2,000) and 82 percent (for incomes above $200,000) and exemptions as low as $1,200 for a childless family head and $500 for a single person, this act set the basic contours of the wartime income tax structure. The Current Tax Payment Act of 1943 established withholding of income tax at the source for nearly all incomes. Brownlee, *Federal Taxation in America*, 89–97; Henry C. Murphy, *The National Debt in War and Transition* (New York: McGraw-Hill, 1950), 19, 51; Vatter, *The U.S. Economy in World War II*, 109; Treas. Rpt. 1950, Exhibit 26, 251.

11. Canada paid for 57 percent of its war costs through taxation, while the figure for Britain was 52 percent. Murphy, *The National Debt in War and Transition*, 250–56; Vatter, *The U.S. Economy in World War II*, 104, 111 (Table 6.3). The term "tax regime" comes from Brownlee, *Federal Taxation in America*, now the standard account of the federal income tax in this period; see 89–100 on World War II, which he says marked a new regime, "the era of easy finance."

12. John Morton Blum, *From the Morgenthau Diaries*, 3 vols. (Boston: Houghton Mifflin, 1959–67), and Blum, *V Was for Victory*, 16–21, 228–30.

13. Randolph E. Paul, *Taxation in the United States* (Boston: Little, Brown, 1954), 294–379; John F. Witte, *The Politics and Development of the Federal Income Tax* (Madison: University of Wisconsin Press, 1985), 114–23; Brownlee, *Federal Taxation in America*, 96; Blum, *From the Morgenthau Diaries*, III:76; Roland Young, *Congressional Politics in the Second World*

War (New York: Columbia University Press, 1956), ch. 5. See Treas. Rpt. 1950, tables IV–VI, 248–50, for effective rates.

14. Brownlee, *Federal Taxation in America*, 26–30, 46–59, 73–88. Two recent studies in political science detail the centrality of the tariff to the economic fates and political interests of farmers and workers: Richard Franklin Bensel, *The Political Economy of American Industrialization, 1877–1900* (Cambridge: Cambridge University Press), ch. 7, and Elizabeth Sanders, *Roots of Reform: Farmers, Workers, and the American State 1877–1917* (Chicago: University of Chicago Press, 1999), 217–30.

15. The OASI tax began at 1 percent in 1937 and rose to 3 percent by 1939, with employers paying half in the form of a payroll tax and employees paying the other half in deductions from their paychecks. Edward D. Berkowitz, "Social Security and the Financing of the American State," in *Funding the Modern American State, 1941–1995: The Rise and Fall of the Era of Easy Finance*, ed. W. Elliot Brownlee (New York: Cambridge University Press, 1995), ch. 4. Constitutionality of Social Security taxes upheld in *Steward Machine Co. v. Davis* and *Helvering et al. v. Davis* (1937). Number of workers covered by Social Security in *Hist. Stat. U.S.*, 342, Series H51, H54, H55.

16. *Hist. Stat. US*, 8, 126, 1110; Series A6 for total resident population; Series D1 for total number of people in the workforce (civilian and military); Series Y394 and Y403 for number of taxable individual income tax returns. When generalizing about the wartime and postwar workforce, I make the assumption that those paying income tax are part of the workforce, when in fact a few were not. This small overestimate of taxpayers in the workforce is negligible, and unavoidable given the numbers provided by the Treasury and the Bureau of the Census.

17. Total wartime taxes in Vatter, *The U.S. Economy in World War II*. Other numbers from *Hist. Stat. US*, 224 and 1107; Series F1 for GNP, Series F8 for personal income, Series Y359 for internal revenue collections for personal income tax.

18. In 1942, when the tax base grew from 17.5 million to 27.6 million, covering millions of people previously excluded due to their low incomes, per capita income taxes more than doubled, to $24.19, which in constant, inflation-adjusted dollars was 100 percent higher than the prewar peak in 1937. In 1943 the tax base expanded again, from 27.6 to 40.2 million, and once again per capita income taxes doubled, to $48.49, an 87 percent increase after inflation. The next year, 1944, saw income tax payments shoot up to $131.95 per capita, a real increase of 166 percent after inflation, just a few dollars shy of the wartime high that would be set in 1945.

19. Per capita income tax payment is a measure that captures the intensity of taxation for the population as a whole, including both taxpayers and nontaxpayers. The rationale for such a measure is that all citizens are affected by the fact of income tax payment, even if they do not pay taxes, and that the average amount of tax spent by the state on behalf of the entire population reflects what might be called "state presence," for stakeholders and spectators alike.

20. Witte, *The Politics and Development of the Federal Income Tax*, 128–29, Figure 6.4.

21. Treas. Rpt. 1950, 245–50, tables II, III, V, VI. I use the masculine pronoun because it describes the great majority of wage earners and taxpayers during World War II.

22. Ratio of taxpayers to BIR staff calculated by diving total number of taxpayers by total BIR staff on payroll (including clerks): *Hist. Stat. US*, series Y394, Y403, 1110; Sparrow, *From the Outside In*, Table 4.3. For BIR state capacity in 1950, see Sparrow, Table 4.3, and the testimony on February 5, 1951, by George J. Schoeneman, commissioner of Internal Revenue, in Paul, *Taxation in the United States*, 598.

23. "Pretest Results on Form 1040A Income and Victory Tax," Special Memorandum #91, October 13, 1943, 4; "Pretest Results on Four Proposed 1040A Income Tax Blanks," Special Memorandum #101, January 23, 1944, 22–24; in boxes 1798 and 1803, OWI Polls.

24. Carolyn C. Jones, "Split Income and Separate Spheres: Tax Law and Gender Roles in the 1940s," *Law and History Review* 6, 2 (Fall 1988): 259–310; Alice Kessler-Harris, *In Pursuit*

of Equity: Women, Men, and the Quest for Economic Citizenship in 20th-Century America (New York, 2001), 170–202.

25. Carolyn C. Jones, "Mass-Based Income Taxation: Creating a Taxpaying Culture, 1940–1952," in *Funding the Modern American State, 1941–1995* (Cambridge: Cambridge University Press, 1996), 107–10.

26. Staff meeting and quote in Morgenthau Diaries, 615:147, FDR Library, Hyde Park; Morgenthau quoted and discussed in Jones, "Mass-Based Income Taxation," 107–9, 139. Her discussion omits the staffer's retort, thus significantly recasting the significance of the exchange.

27. Sparrow, *From the Outside In*, 124; Young, *Congressional Politics in the Second World War*, 124–25.

28. Stein, *The Fiscal Revolution in America*, chs. 8–9, esp. 169–70, 180–82, 220–32; see also Sparrow, *From the Outside In*, 98.

29. Vatter, *The U.S. Economy in World War II*, 102–7. The $49 billion figure includes all bonds purchased by individuals, not just E bonds (cf. figure on E bond sales in the next paragraph).

30. Note that most, but not all, war bonds sold to individuals were E bonds; the higher-denomination F and G bonds were purchased by wealthy individuals, trusts, banks, and other institutions. This analysis focuses on E bonds because they formed the popular basis of the war finance program. The First War Loan Drive occurred between November 30 and December 23, 1942; the Second, April 12–May 1, 1943; the Third, September 9–October 2, 1943; the Fourth, January 18–February 15, 1944; the Fifth, June 12–July 8, 1944; the Sixth, November 20–December 16, 1944; the Seventh, May 14–June 30, 1945; Victory, October 29–December 8, 1945. Figures in Murphy, *The National Debt in War and Transition*, 38–41, 106–9, 195; and *Minute Man*, February 1946, 2–6, 18. E bond features were in contrast to the negotiable Liberty Bonds of World War I, which came in only one large denomination ($100), and whose value fell into the low $80s during the immediate postwar period. The *Minute Man* was the official organ of the volunteer sales staff in the War Savings Program; often this was the only published source of official figures for bond sales, provided by the Federal Reserve banks which processed bond transactions.

31. For 1944 income tax expenditures, see Chart 1.5. For bond sales in 1944, see Murphy, *National Debt in War and Transition*, 196. Here I refer to total sales of series E, F, and G bonds. This is a departure from the meaning of the word "bond" used throughout the rest of this chapter. It is appropriate because numbers for income taxes include all incomes and thus are biased upward due to high marginal rates on top brackets (the maximum was 91 percent, 1944–45). E sales reflect the investments of mainly small investors, whereas wealthier investors were more likely to buy F and G bonds. Of course, F and G bonds were also purchased by institutions, so the comparison is imperfect.

32. *Minute Man*, February 1946, 5.

33. Murphy, *The National Debt in War and Transition*, 197–98.

34. Blum, *From the Morgenthau Diaries*, III:16–22. On the coerciveness of World War I bond drives, see Russell A. Kazal, *Becoming Old Stock: The Paradox of German-American Identity* (Princeton: Princeton University Press, 2004), 151–95.

35. Blum, *From the Morgenthau Diaries*, III:33, 38–39, 43–48, 52–58, 65–73.

36. The top five states bought over $1 billion each: New York, Pennsylvania, Illinois, Ohio, and Michigan; *Minute Man*, February 1946, 6, 12–13. On volunteers and personal solicitation, see Morse, "Paying for a World War," 179, 185–86. Civilian employment for the federal government was 3.01 million in 1943, 3.06 million in 1944, and 3.55 million in 1945; Hist. Stat. U.S. 1102, Series Y308. A summary of wartime studies of bond sales and buyer motivation can be found in "An Appraisal of the Victory Loan Drive," Report #41, March 9, 1946, in box 22, Historical Files, 1941–69, Savings Bond Division, Office of the National Director, General Records of the Department of the Treasury, RG 56, National Archives—

College Park. Dorwin Cartwright, "Some Principles of Mass Persuasion: Selected Findings of Research on the Sale of United States War Bonds," *Human Relations* 2 (1949): 253-67, Table 2.

37. Murphy, *The National Debt in War and Transition*, 87, acknowledged that that despite Treasury policy, the system of quotas adopted for each bond drive ensured that in practice, "much coercion actually occurred in the field."

38. Because they were aimed primarily at the less affluent, payroll plans accounted for a large proportion of bond and tax transactions but collected a smaller proportion of total funds collected by the Treasury: more than $15 billion of the $40 billion invested in E bonds throughout the war, and $10.3 billion of the $19 billion in income taxes collected in 1944; Treas. Rpt. 1950, 483; Morse, "Paying for a World War," 163-70; Sparrow, *From the Outside In*, 111-12, 141-42; Lawrence R. Samuel, *Pledging Allegiance: American Identity and the Bond Drive of World War II* (Washington, DC: Smithsonian Institution Press, 1997), 30, 88-92. Between 1943 and 1945 the number of workers on the war bond payroll plan was very close to the number whose income taxes were withheld by July 1943: between 25 and 27 million. Murphy, *National Debt in War and Transition*, 199-200; Blum, *From the Morgenthau Diaries*, III:21; Brownlee, *Federal Taxation in America*, 97; Paul, *Taxation in the United States*, 348-49.

39. Morse, "Paying for a World War," ch. IX; Samuel, *Pledging Allegiance*, 20-25, 32-33, 37-42.

40. Samuel, *Pledging Allegiance*, 3-73.

41. William Pickens, "How Would You Feel?" typescript for editorial, n.d. [late 1939 or early 1940]; in reel 2, microfilm R993-997, William Pickens MS, Schomburg Center, NYPL.

42. "Report of the Interracial Section for 1943"; "Report" for 1944, p. 70; both in Treasury Papers, Pickens Microfilm R-4463.

43. Pickens to Kathryn Close, *Survey Graphic*, September 14, 1941, box 19, Treasury Papers, Pickens Microfilm R-4463.

44. Morse, "Paying for a World War," 315-16.

45. Ibid., 17-18; Blum, *From the Morgenthau Diaries*, III:16-22, quote on 19. See also Blum, *V Was for Victory*, 15-21.

46. Jones, "Mass-Based Income Taxation"; Donald T. Critchlow, "The Political Control of the Economy: Deficit Spending as a Political Belief, 1932-1952," *Public Historian* 3, 2 (Spring 1981): 5-22; Samuel, *Pledging Allegiance*; Kessler-Harris, *In Pursuit of Equity*, ch. 4. See also Blum, *V Was for Victory*; Alan Brinkley, *The End of Reform: New Deal Liberalism in Recession and War* (New York: Knopf, 1995).

47. Morse, "Paying for a World War," 302-10. Officials within the Treasury chafed at the OWI's insistence that it clear all significant releases to the press, other media, and entertainment outlets. The OWI felt the Treasury enjoyed too large a share of the free advertising donated by private industry, and entertained proposals to reallocate it to other agencies that enjoyed less favor among businessmen.

48. Blum, *From the Morgenthau Diaries*, III:76; Young, *Congressional Politics in the Second World War*, 17-18; Morse, "Paying for a World War," 234-36; "Greatest Promotional Campaign 'Backs the Attack,'" *Minute Man*, September 15, 1943, 9.

49. Frank W. Fox, *Madison Avenue Goes to War: The Strange Military Career of American Advertising 1941-45* (Provo: Brigham Young University Press, 1975), 46, 55-66, 71-74; Wendy Wall, *Inventing the American Way: The Politics of Consensus from the New Deal to the Civil Rights Movement* (New York: Oxford University Press, 2008), 103-62; Roland Marchand, *Creating the Corporate Soul: The Rise of Public Relations and Corporate Imagery in American Big Business* (Berkeley: University of California Press, 1998), 321-29; Stuart Ewen, *PR! A Social History of Spin* (New York: Basic Books, 1996), 339-46.

50. Fox, *Madison Avenue Goes to War*, 34-35.

51. Morse, "Paying for a World War," 210-36; Samuel, *Pledging Allegiance*, ch. 3. On automobile salesmen, see Harold Graves to Morgenthau, February 11, 1942, Morgenthau Diaries

495:420, On Hollywood cooperation and local theater support for bond drives, see Carlton Duffus memo to Harold Graves, February 2, 1942, Morgenthau Diaries 491:391; and Thomas Doherty, *Projections of War: Hollywood, American Culture, and World War II* (New York: Columbia University Press, 1993), 81–82.

52. Emphasis in the original. Amos Parrish and Company, New York, "Wartime Dividend," printed portfolio, 1943, Library of Congress.
53. Poster reproduced in *Minute Man*, December 1, 1944, 7.
54. "A Grim Exhibit," *Minute Man*, February 15, 1943, 7–8.
55. On the tendency to dehumanize the Japanese enemy with racial stereotyping, see John Dower, *War Without Mercy: Race and Power in the Pacific War* (New York: Pantheon, 1986).
56. *What Makes a Battle*, n.d. [1944], Treas. Films 13.1/2.
57. For a discussion of the increasing willingness of government authorities toward the end of the war to release shocking material to the public in order to counteract civilian complacency, see George H. Roeder Jr., *The Censored War: American Visual Experience During World War Two* (New Haven: Yale University Press, 1993), esp. 19–25, 34, 37.
58. *My Japan*, n.d. [1945], Treas. Films 56.30.1/2.
59. Jones, "Mass-Based Income Taxation," 107–28.
60. Education Section, Savings Bonds Division, U.S. Department of the Treasury, *School Savings in Action* (Washington, DC: USGPO, 1943), frontispiece.
61. Morse, "Paying for a World War," 170–77; Samuel, *Pledging Allegiance*, 34–37.
62. Both NEA and *Parents' Magazine* excerpts quoted in Robert Kirk, "Getting in the Scrap," 224; *Parents' Magazine*, November 1944, 24; Isaac L. Kandel, *The Impact of the War upon American Education* (Chapel Hill: University of North Carolina Press, 1948), 20–21. See also Morse, "Paying for a World War," 171.
63. Education Section, Savings Bonds Division, U.S. Department of the Treasury, *Schools at War: Handbook of Suggestions for School Administrators* (Washington, DC: USGPO, 1944), 6.
64. Ibid., 8–11; *School Savings in Action*, 4.
65. Education Section, Savings Bonds Division, U.S. Department of the Treasury, *War Savings Programs for Schools at War: Tested Plays, Program Ideas* (Washington, DC: USGPO, 1944), 31–37.
66. Ibid., 38–52.
67. William Tuttle, *"Daddy's Gone to War": The Second World War in the Lives of America's Children* (New York: Oxford University Press, 1993), 113–15, 124–26, 130–33; Robert W. Kirk, "Getting in the Scrap: The Mobilization of American Children in World War II," *Journal of Popular Culture* 29, 1 (Summer 1995): 223–33.
68. On movie attendance, Victory Film distribution, and the widespread technique of using battle footage, see Doherty, *Projections of War*, 9–11, 80–82.
69. Roeder has referred to this ubiquitous association as the "homefront analogy"; see *Censored War*, 59–61.
70. *Bonds at War*, n.d. [1943?], Treas. Films 56.4.
71. *Mission Completed*, 1945, Treas. Films 56.33.2.
72. *Midnight*, 1945, Treas. Films 56.28.
73. *It Can't Last*, 1944, Treas. Films 56.15. MacLeish's authorship of the screenplay is noted in *Minute Man*, October 15, 1944, 8–9.
74. Morgenthau to Knox, December 17, 1943, and Morgenthau to Henry Stimson, Secretary of War, December 17, 1943, and April 26, 1944, in Morgenthau Diaries 685:48 and 724:184. Morse, "Paying for a World War," 214, 310.
75. *Minute Man*, March 15, 1944, 12.
76. *Minute Man*, October 15, 1943, 9; March 15, 1944, 17.
77. *Minute Man*, December 1, 1944, 8–9.
78. Psychological Corporation, "A Study of People's Motives for Buying Defense Bonds and Stamps," submitted January 12, 1942, Morgenthau Diaries 485:137–63. Because this study

was based on an unscientific survey, it precludes precise generalizations about patterns of motivation among bond buyers.

79. "'Our War' in Bridgeport," Study 99, in box 10, BAE Studies.

80. On negative reactions to commercialism, see "Participation in the War Savings Program, Preliminary Report," BAE Report #4, October 15, 1942, 2; "Reactions to Current Appeals in the Sale of War Bonds," BAE Report #7, January 8, 1943, 3; "An Appraisal of the Second War Loan Drive, Identification and Motivation," BAE Report #15, August 9, 1943, 3. For other references to this mounting disgust with war advertising, see Merton, *Mass Persuasion*, 82–83, 186–87; Fox, *Madison Avenue Goes to War*, 33–38. "Trapeze" quote in Merton, 83 n. 6.

81. Gamble to Morgenthau, February 2, 1945, Eccles to Morgenthau, June 12, 1942, both in Morgenthau Diaries, 815:157 and 538:169; Merton, *Mass Persuasion*, 46–47, 76, on "sacred" versus "profane" transactions.

82. U.S. Treasury Department, Defense Savings Staff, *Our America* (Washington, DC: USGPO, 1942).

83. "Reader Reactions to Treasury Pamphlet *Our America*," Special Report No. 14, June 25, 1942, in box 1784, OWI—Surveys.

84. Dorwin Cartwright, "Some Principles of Mass Persuasion: Selected Findings of Research on the Sale of United States War Bonds," *Human Relations* 2 (1949): 253–67.

85. Jean M. Converse, *Survey Research in the United States: Roots and Emergence, 1890–1960* (Berkeley: University of California Press, 1987), 72–73, 154–74.

86. Patterns in all six drives analyzed in "Appraisal of the Victory Loan Drive," Program Surveys Report #41, March 1946, 11–12, Tables 3 and 3a, in BAE Reports.

87. Ibid., 13–15, Tables 4, 4a, 5, 5a.

88. Hadley Cantril, ed., *Public Opinion 1935–46* (Princeton: Princeton University Press, 1951), items 64, 76, 92, 320–21, 323.

89. "Bond Redemptions in March, 1944," Program Surveys Study 93–I, April 7, 1944, 1, 2, 11; "Factors Involved in Plans to Pay Income Taxes in 1943," Program Surveys Memo by Gould, January 12, 1943, 6–7, both in box 1, Dorwin Philip Cartwright MS, Bentley Historical Library, University of Michigan—Ann Arbor.

90. See the discussion of earmarking in Viviana Zelizer, *The Social Meaning of Money: Pin Money, Paychecks, Poor Relief, and Other Currencies* (Princeton: Princeton University Press, 1997), 6–30; Nelson Lichtenstein, *The Most Dangerous Man In Detroit: Walter Reuther and the Fate of American Labor* (New York: Basic Books, 1995), ch. 10.

91. Lendol Calder, *Financing the American Dream: A Cultural History of Consumer Credit* (Princeton: Princeton University Press, 1999), 18–22, 274–91.

92. *Minute Man*, February 15, 1943, 8. Equipment price list was probably compiled in 1944; in "War Finance Program—Background" folder, box 30, Odegard MS. Napa and El Paso bombers mentioned, along with sixteen others named after cities, in Ted Gamble memo to Morgenthau, May 7, 1942, Morgenthau Diaries 525:47.

93. Education Section, Savings Bonds Division, U.S. Department of the Treasury, *Schools at War: Teachers' Bulletin*, December 1943, 8.

94. Army policy mentioned in equipment price list, cited above; navy policy in Gamble memo to Morgenthau, May 7, 1942, Morgenthau Diaries, 525:47.

95. "An Appraisal of the Fourth War Loan Drive, the Conduct and Results of the Drive in Selected Plants," Program Surveys Report #24, April 11, 1944, 13–15, in BAE Reports.

96. Education Section, Savings Bonds Division, U.S. Department of the Treasury, *School at War: Teachers' Bulletin*, October 1943.

97. See correspondence between Morgenthau and R. W. Coyne, January 17 and January 18, 1945, in Morgenthau Diaries 810:165, 263.

98. Roosevelt letter to Morgenthau discussed in Morgenthau letter to Roosevelt, May 1, 1943, Morgenthau Diaries 630:66. For the original suggestion from the Canadian John Franklin Carter, forwarded by Roosevelt, see entry 630:69.

99. During the war employment levels approached 100 percent, real wages rose by a third, and personal consumption rose by 15 percent, despite shortages.
100. "A Case Book on the Ten Percent Plan," [August 31, 1942]," "Payroll Savings Promotion" folder, box 19, Odegard MS.
101. "Personal Solicitation in the Third War Loan," n.d., 11–12, in folder "Advertising: Third War Loan—Personal Solicitation—1943," box 9; "A Case Book on the Ten Percent Plan," both in Odegard MS.
102. Minutes, March 10, 1943, Morgenthau Diaries, 615:150.
103. "An Appraisal of the Third War Loan Drive, Part IV: Solicitation in the Third War Loan," BAE Report #19, December 7, 1943, 2–3; "Appraisal of the Victory Loan Drive," 8–9, Tables 1 and 1a.
104. Merton, *Mass Persuasion*, chs. 2–6.
105. Robert B. Westbrook, *Why We Fought: Forging American Obligations in World War II* (Washington, DC: Smithsonian Books, 2004), ch. 3.
106. Merton, *Mass Persuasion*, Appendix C, Tables I–A, I–B.
107. Quoted in "Size," November 21, 1944, 2, BASR-Kate Smith.
108. Merton, *Mass Persuasion*, 79–89, 94–96, 101–2 (Chart III), 146–52.
109. Interview transcript #022, 3, answer to question 14, BASR-Kate Smith. Merton, *Mass Persuasion*, 111, determined that sixty-three out of seventy-five interviews displayed such deep involvement.
110. Merton, *Mass Persuasion*, 45–54.
111. "Appraisal of the Victory Loan Drive," 16–17, Tables 6 and 6a.
112. Transcript of radio address in Randolph Paul to Morgenthau, March 17, 1943, Morgenthau Diaries 617:83.
113. Fireside Chats, 270.
114. Reprinted in Lawrence and Cornelia Levine, *The People and the President: America's Conversation with FDR* (Boston: Beacon Press, 2002), 460.
115. Cantril, ed., *Public Opinion 1935–1946*, 311, item 2; see also 314, items 5, 7, 9; Nelson Lichtenstein, *Labor's War at Home: The CIO in World War II* (Cambridge: Cambridge University Press, 1982), ch. 6.
116. Reprinted in Levine and Levine, *The People and the President*, 466–67.
117. Frank Martel, editor, *AFL Daily News*, Labor Temple, Detroit, MI, to Clyde Hart, OWI, November 17, 1943, 1–2, in OWI, box 1747.
118. Harry B. Winkeler, St. Louis *Labor Tribune*, to Clyde Hart, OWI, November 16, 1943, 1–2, in OWI, box 1748.
119. On earmarking, see Zelizer, *The Social Meaning of Money*, 6–30.
120. David M. Kennedy, *Freedom from Fear: The American People in Depression and War, 1929–1945* (New York: Oxford University Press, 1999).
121. See, e.g., "Income and Savings in Buffalo," BAE Report #1, August 22, 1942, 13.
122. "Appraisal of the Sixth War Loan, Part II: Identification and Motivation," BAE Report #32, February 1, 1945, 2; "Appraisal of the Victory Loan Drive," 13, Tables 4 and 4a.
123. "Attitudes Toward Income Taxes," Special Memo #67, July 10, 1943, es 8, 10, OWI-Polls box 1802.
124. Blum, *V Was for Victory*, 92–100; *HistStatUS*, F543, G416; Vatter, *The U.S. Economy in World War II*, 108, Chart 6.2, 138–42.
125. Fireside Chats, 288–89; Cass Sunstein, *The Second Bill of Rights: FDR's Unfinished Revolution and Why We Need It More than Ever* (New York: Basic Books, 2004); J. Sparrow, "Fighting over the American Soldier," 320–22.
126. "The Sale of War Bonds in Urban Areas," BAE Report # 12, June 4, 1943, 6–7, Tables 3–4.
127. "Reasons People Give For and Against Buying Bonds," BAE Report #11, June 3, 1943, 16.
128. Morse, "Paying for a World War," 170.
129. "The Buying of War Bonds and Stamps," Study 55, October 9, 1942, 1, OWI-Surveys box 1784A.

130. Interview transcript, "non-buyer 101," 1, question 3, BASR-Kate Smith. Emphasis in the original. On others who felt they couldn't give more for bonds, see Merton, *Mass Persuasion*, 112–13, 137–38.

131. Ibid., 6, "free answer."

132. "The Buying of War Bonds and Stamps," 2; 10 percent goal among the wealthy corroborated in Merton, *Mass Persuasion*, 112–13. "Participation in the War Savings Program: Public Attitudes with Respect to Spending or Saving," BAE Report #4, December 29, 1942.

133. "Table II—Sales to Individuals," *Minute Man*, February 1946, 7.

134. Ibid.

135. For overall bonds sales, see U.S. Treasury, *Annual Report of the Secretary of the Treasury on the State of the Finances for the Fiscal Year Ended June 30* (Washington, DC: USGPO, 1951), Table 30, 561; inflation and percentage of the GNP calculated based on *Hist. Stat. U.S.*, Series F1, F3, F5, 224.

136. "Appraisal of the Victory Loan Drive," BAE Report #41, March 1946, Table 5, 14. The figures given are for nonfarm respondents; farm respondents gave similar, although not identical, responses (see Table 5a, 15).

137. Treas. Rpt. 1950, Tables 28, 33. Redemption rates generally ran in the opposite direction of size of bond issue, reflecting the different reasons for investing (immediately moral vs. long-term financial). The highest redemption rates in 1947 were for $10 issues, at 72 percent. None of the yearly issues of $1,000 E bonds ever attained redemption rates over 30 percent during the first 7 years of issue, while F and G bond redemptions stayed even lower, at 20 percent or less by 1947. Murphy, *The National Debt in War and Transition*, 201–5, 225–26.

138. George Katona, *Psychological Analysis of Economic Behavior* (New York: McGraw-Hill, 1951), Table 3, 84, reprints findings from Survey Research Center study of Security Loan Drive (July 1948) and Opportunity Loan Drive (July 1949).

139. Murphy, *The National Debt in War and Transition*, 225–26.

140. Jones, "Mass-Based Income Taxation," 128, 139–46.

141. Treas. Rpt. 1950, Table 28, 558.

142. Andrea Louise Campbell and Kimberly J. Morgan, "Financing the Welfare State: Elite Politics and the Decline of the Social Insurance Model in America," *Studies in American Political Development* 19 (Fall 2005): 173–95; Sven Steinmo, *Taxation and Democracy: Swedish, British and American Approaches to Financing the Modern State* (New Haven: Yale University Press, 1993).

143. Survey Research Center, *Foreign Affairs Study*, June 1951, Study #ICPSR-7219, variable no. 10 [computer file], Ann Arbor, Michigan: Inter-University Consortium for Political and Social Research [distributor].

Chapter 5

1. United News Reel 90/95, Office of War Information, RG 208, National Archives—College Park.

2. "Worker Morale in Five Shipyards," Report 44, January 18, 1943, 22, in box 1798, OWI-Polls.

3. T. H. Marshall, "Citizenship and Social Class," in *Class, Citizenship and Social Development* (Garden City, NY: Doubleday, 1964), 65–122, esp. 71–83, 113–15, 117–19; Charles Tilly, "Where Do Rights Come From?" in *Democracy, Revolution and History*, ed. Theda Skocpol (Ithaca: Cornell University Press, 1998); Anthony Giddens, *The Nation-State and Violence* (Berkeley: University of California Press, 1987), 198–209.

4. For a handy overview of the agencies that managed the war economy, see U.S. Bureau of the Budget, *The United States at War: Development and Administration of the War Program by the Federal Government* (Washington, DC: U.S. Government Printing Office, 1946), 39, Chart 4.

5. U.S. Department of Labor, *Industrial Disputes and Wage Stabilization in Wartime*, vol. I of *The Termination Report of the NWLB* (Washington, DC: USGPO, [1948]), 183–297, 480, 490, 504, 538. The WLB adjusted wages to compensate for "substandards of living," inter- and intraplant inequities, equal pay for equivalent work, and other criteria. Differences within plants were the most difficult for workers to accept, and thus provided some of the strongest equalizing pressure for wage adjustment; see Nelson Lichtenstein, *Labor's War at Home: The CIO in World War II* (Cambridge: Cambridge University Press, 1982), 112–16. As Lichtenstein points out, these adjustments did not fundamentally alter the wage structure, but rather made inequities less glaring. A good synopsis of the Little Steel agreement can be found in James B. Atleson, *Labor and the Wartime State: Labor Relations and Law During World War II* (Urbana: University of Illinois Press, 1998), 51, 130–31; and Richard Polenberg, *War and Society: The United States, 1941–1945* (Philadelphia: J. B. Lippincott, 1972), 25–27.

6. George Q. Flynn, *The Mess in Washington: Manpower Mobilization in World War II* (Westport: Greenwood, 1979), 66, 190; Marilynn S. Johnson, *The Second Gold Rush: Oakland and the East Bay in World War II* (Berkeley: University of California Press, 1993), 36–45; Alan Clive, *State of War: Michigan in World War II* (Ann Arbor: University of Michigan Press, 1979), 172–73.

7. Flynn, *The Mess in Washington*, 60–62, 68–70, 256.

8. U.S. Department of Labor, *Industrial Disputes and Wage Stabilization in Wartime*, 290–97; Flynn, *The Mess in Washington*, 174; William Chafe, *The Paradox of Change: American Women in the Twentieth Century* (New York: Oxford University Press, 1991), 132; Flynn, *The Mess in Washington*, 174–76, 178–79; Maureen Honey, *Creating Rosie the Riveter: Class, Gender, and Propaganda During World War II* (Amherst: University of Massachusetts Press, 1984), 28–58.

9. U.S. Department of Labor, *Industrial Disputes and Wage Stabilization in Wartime*, 150–55; Flynn, *The Mess in Washington*, 149–68, McNutt quoted on 153; Wynn, *The Afro-American and the Second World War*, 48–51.

10. Flynn, *The Mess in Washington*, 18; U.S. Department of Labor, *Industrial Disputes and Wage Stabilization in Wartime*, xxii, 297; Milkman, *Gender at Work*, 74–75; Kessler-Harris, *Out to Work*, 289–90; Chafe, *Paradox of Change*, 138–41; Wynn, *The Afro-American and the Second World War*, 50–55; Merl Reed, *Seedtime for the Modern Civil Rights Movement: The President's Committee on Fair Employment Practice, 1941–1946* (Baton Rouge: University of Louisiana Press, 1991), 74–76, 85–87, 267–317.

11. Bruce Nelson, "Organized Labor and the Struggle for Black Equality in Mobile during World War II," *Journal of American History* 80, 3 (December 1993): 952–88; Daniel Kryder, *Divided Arsenal: Race and the American State During World War II* (Cambridge: Cambridge University Press, 2000), 88–132; Reed, *Seedtime for the Modern Civil Rights Movement*, 117–22, 205–30.

12. U.S. Department of Labor, *Industrial Disputes and Wage Stabilization in Wartime*, 547–59, esp. Tables 2 and 5, Chart 3, and 551.

13. Weekly pay given in current dollars; Harold Vatter, *The U.S. Economy in World War II* (New York: Columbia University Press, 1985), 123, Table 7.2; Peter Fearon, *War, Prosperity and Depression: The U.S. Economy, 1917–1945* (Lawrence: University Press of Kansas, 1987), 279.

14. Lichtenstein, "The Making of the Postwar Working Class: Cultural Pluralism and Social Structure in World War II," *Historian* 51, 1 (November 1988), 42–43, 50–59; Gary Gerstle, "The Working Class Goes to War," in *The War in American Culture: Society and Consciousness During World War II*, ed. Lewis A. Erenberg and Susan E. Hirsch (Chicago: University of Chicago Press, 1996), 105–27; Gerstle, *American Crucible: Race and Nation in the Twentieth Century* (Princeton: Princeton University Press, 2001), 187, 199–201; Gerstle, *Working-Class Americanism: The Politics of Labor in a Textile City, 1914–1960* (Cambridge: Cambridge University Press, 1989), 289–302.

15. Howell John Harris, *The Right to Manage: Industrial Relations Policies of American Business in the 1940s* (Madison: University of Wisconsin Press, 1982); Lichtenstein, *Labor's War at Home*, 89–96. Giddens, *The Nation-State and Violence*, 206–7 and 322–23, identifies "the 'management' of production" as a form of surveillance by which social citizenship (he uses the term "economic citizenship") and its attendant rights are regulated and circumscribed in order to control workers; workers, in turn, tend to resist such surveillance through withdrawal or resistance of production. As will be discussed below, it was just such a contest over the moral significance of war production which shaped the content of production propaganda and guided workers' appropriation of the "soldier of production" iconography.

16. Daniel T. Rodgers, *The Work Ethic in Industrial America, 1850–1920* (Chicago: University of Chicago Press, 1978).

17. Gerstle, *Working-Class Americanism*, 293–302; Gerstle, "The Working Class Goes to War," esp. 110–11. See also Clive, *State of War*, 55, 60–61.

18. Fireside Chats, 198–205.

19. Fireside Chats, 220–29; "Survey of Intelligence Materials," No. 24, May 20, 1942, in box 1805, OWI-Intell.

20. Fireside Chats, 207–18 and 214 n. 11. Poll by National Opinion Research Center (NORC), March 2, 1942, in Hadley Cantril, ed., *Public Opinion 1935–1946* (Princeton: Princeton University Press, 1951), 588, item #7.

21. William L. Bird Jr. and Harry R. Rubenstein, *Design for Victory: World War II Posters on the American Home Front* (New York: Princeton Architectural Press, 1998), 12–13, 31–32, 38–41, 48, 66, 78.

22. "Worker Reactions to Incentives Used in War Industries," Report #17, July 7, 1942, 1–2, in box 1786, OWI-Surveys; and "War Worker Motivations," Intelligence Report, August 12, 1942, 17–18, in box 1805, OWI-Intell.

23. Steven Fraser, *Labor Will Rule: Sidney Hillman and the Rise of American Labor* (Ithaca, NY: Cornell University Press, 1991), 465–67; Maurice Isserman, *Which Side Were You On? The American Communist Party During the Second World War* (Middletown: Wesleyan University Press, 1984), 96–100; Lichtenstein, *Labor's War at Home*, 60–63.

24. "Your Ore Packs a Punch!" War Department Public Relations, 1943; object III.C, NWU WWII Posters.

25. "Do It Right: Make It Bite," Cecil Calvert Beall for Army Ordnance, 1942; object IIIC.44, NWU WWII Posters.

26. See, e.g., the shirtless worker whose image appeared in the *ITU News* in October 1940, featured on the cover of Gerstle, *Working-Class Americanism*; see 175 for another example and discussion of this "supermanlike" figure, which was intended to capture the "massive productive power" of industrial workers.

27. "Get Hot/Keep Moving," n.d. and unattributed, poster 163991.09, part of the National Museum of American History exhibit, "Produce for Victory, Posters on the American Home Front, 1941–1945." See also Bird and Rubenstein, *Design for Victory*, 72.

28. "Keep 'Em Coming!" U.S. Army Ordnance Department (Washington, DC: USGPO, 1942), object IIIC.37, NWU WWII Posters.

29. "Man the Guns," McClelland Barclay for the U.S. Navy, Recruiting Bureau, 1942; control number NWDNS-44-PA-24; "Keep 'Em Fighting." National Safety Council, n.d.; control number NWDNS-44-PA-1171B; both in Still Picture Branch, National Archives—College Park.

30. Honey, *Creating Rosie the Riveter*, 13 and passim.

31. "Strong in the Strength of the Lord," OWI, 1942, object IIIE.12, NWU WWII Posters; "It's a Two-Fisted Fight," poster 164393.07, NMAH Victory Posters, reproduced in Bird and Rubenstein, *Design for Victory*, 67.

32. "It's today's production that counts!" Navy Ordnance [1942], object IIIC.4., NWU WWII Posters.

33. On placement of production posters, see Bird and Rubenstein, *Design for Victory*, 64.
34. "Pass the Ammunition—The Army Needs More Lumber," U.S. Army, 1943, object IIIC.42, NWU WWII Posters.
35. "Kinda Give It Your Personal Attention, Will You?" U.S. War Production Board, 1942, object IIIC.30, NWU WWII Posters.
36. "What You're Making May Save My Daddy's Life," WPB, 1942, object IIIC.35, NWU WWII Posters.
37. "Killing Time Is Killing Men," Reynold Brown for North American Aviation, 1943; poster 164814.01, NMAH Victory Posters, reproduced in Bird and Rubenstein, *Design for Victory*.
38. See photograph of workers taking their break next to this sign in Bird and Rubenstein, *Design for Victory*, 68.
39. Bird and Rubenstein, *Design for Victory*, 52–58, 64–66, 78.
40. "The War Worker's Point of View," report no. 21, July 28, 1942, Summary, Table 1, in box 1786, OWI-Surveys. For corroboration, see "Worker Morale in Five Shipyards," Memorandum no. 44, January 18, 1943, esp. 2, 31, box 1798, OWI-Polls. This study was based on a large, representative sample of shipyard workers.
41. "Survey of Intelligence Materials," no. 22, May 6, 1942, 5; "War Worker Motivations," Intelligence Report, August 12, 1942, Summary; both in box 1805, OWI-Intell. Workers in "low-morale" plants also yearned for a connection to the battlefront but felt bitterness rather than satisfaction. See "Worker Motivation in Time of War: Case Studies of Six Critical War Plants," Report #20, July 28, 1942, 18–19, 21, 31, in box 1786, OWI-Surveys.
42. "Worker Reactions to Incentives Used in War Industries," Report #17, July 7, 1942, Summary, in box 1786, OWI-Surveys.
43. "Worker Motivation in Time of War: Case Studies of Six Critical War Plants."
44. "The War Worker's Point of View," 22.
45. "Worker Reactions to Incentives Used in War Industries," 1.
46. "War Worker Motivations," Intelligence Report, August 12, 1942, Summary; "The War Worker's Point of View," Summary, 5, and Table 31.
47. "Control of Wages, Hours and Profits in the Furthering of War Production," Report no. 18, July 7, 1942, 1, in box 1786, OWI-Surveys.
48. "Survey of Intelligence Materials," no. 32, July 16, 1942, 10, in box 1805, OWI-Intell.; for corroboration, see also "War Worker Motivations," 7.
49. Cantril, ed., *Public Opinion, 1935–1946*, 1023, item 20.
50. Flynn, *The Mess in Washington*, 222–26.
51. Lichtenstein, *Labor's War at Home*, 82–109; Mark Leff, "The Politics of Sacrifice on the American Home Front in World War II," *Journal of American History* 77, 4 (March 1991): 1298–306.
52. "Survey of Intelligence Materials"; Cantril, *Public Opinion 1935–46*, 313–14, items 2, 3, 5, 8, 9, and 1006, item 1. The 64 percent figure was most likely derived from a National Opinion Research Center poll done in May 1942; see Cantril, ed., *Public Opinion, 1935–1946*, 313, item 2. On the symbolic resonance of the $25,000 salary cap for workers, see Leff, "The Politics of Sacrifice," 1298–306; Lichtenstein, *Labor's War at Home*, 99; on its decisive political defeat in the spring of 1943, see Roland Young, *Congressional Politics in the Second World War* (New York: Columbia University Press, 1956), 99–102.
53. Hadley Cantril, "Opinion Trends in World War II: Some Guides to Interpretation," *Public Opinion Quarterly* 12, 1 (Spring 1948): 30–44, esp. trend chart on 39; "What the Civilian Thinks," Memo 82, July 18, 1944, 27, in box 1800, OWI-Polls.
54. "The War Worker's Point of View," 11–13, 16. See also "War Worker Motivations" for confirmation of the connection between morale and perceptions of management's ability of promote full production. "Worker Motivation in Time of War: Case Studies of Six Critical War Plants," Report no. 20, July 28, 1942, 6, also concludes that the worker would accept personal sacrifice only "when he sees management doing the same."
55. "The War Worker's Point of View," 11 and Table 1C.

56. "Worker Morale in Five Shipyards," Memo 44, January 18, 1943, 23–31. This report was based on a large, scientific sample of workers in each shipyard, and thus provides some of the most generalizable opinion data produced by OWI, on part with Likert's work on bonds and taxes.

57. "Worker Motivation in Time of War," Summary.

58. Risa Goluboff, *The Lost Promise of Civil Rights* (Cambridge, MA: Harvard University Press, 2007); Kryder, *Divided Arsenal*, 88–132; 121, Table 4.5.

59. Case in Folder N, Reel 26, FEPC Recs.

60. Earl Lewis, *In Their Own Interests: Race, Class and Power in Twentieth-Century Norfolk, Virginia* (Berkeley: University of California Press, 1991), 182–83.

61. Freddie Barrett letter, March 6, 1943, in Houston Shipbuilding Case Folder, Reel 25, FEPC Records.

62. Herbert Cameron, report to NAACP, n.d. (late June 1944), folder "local-662," reel 84, closed cases, FEPC records.

63. Herbert Cameron, report to NAACP, n.d. (late June 1944), 6, folder "local-662," reel 84, closed cases, FEPC records.

64. Herbert Cameron, "Special News," press release, n.d. (June 1944), folder "local-662," reel 84, closed cases, FEPC records.

65. Thomas Madison Doram, sworn testimony dated November 18, 1943, in box 322, Los Angeles Complaints, Hearings 1941–1946, Legal Division, Records of the Committee on Fair Employment Practice, RG 228, National Archives—College Park.

66. Doram FEPC testimony, 11/181/19 43, 1–2.

67. Ibid., 2–3.

68. Ibid., 4–5.

69. Ibid., 6–7.

70. Ibid., 7.

71. Johnson, *The Second Gold Rush*, 67–76, quote on 74; Reed, *Seedtime for the Modern Civil Rights Movement*, ch. 9, esp. 315–17.

72. George Lipsitz, *Rainbow at Midnight: Labor and Culture in the 1940s* (Urbana: University of Illinois Press, 1994), ch. 3; Robin D. G. Kelley, "'We Are Not What We Seem': Rethinking Black Working-Class Opposition in the Jim Crow South," *Journal of American History* 80, 1 (June 1993): 89–102.

73. Lewis, *In Their Own Interests*, 176; Eric Arnesen, *Brotherhoods of Color: Black Railroad Workers and the Struggle for Equality* (Cambridge, MA: Harvard University Press, 2001), 181–202.

74. Martha Biondi, *To Stand and Fight: The Struggle for Civil Rights in Postwar New York City* (Cambridge, MA: Harvard University Press, 2003); Reed, *Seedtime for the Modern Civil Rights Movement*.

75. Lewis, *In Their Own Interests*, 167–98. Also see Biondi, *To Stand and Fight*; Arnesen, *Brotherhoods of Color*, 181–229.

76. *Tunstall v. Brotherhood of Locomotive Firemen and Enginemen*, 323 U.S. 210 (1944).

77. *Steele v. Louisville and N.R. Co.*, 323 U.S. 192 (1944).

78. Arnesen, *Brotherhoods of Color*, 234; Jennifer Klein, *For All These Rights: Business, Labor, and the Shaping of America's Public-Private Welfare State* (Princeton: Princeton University Press, 2003).

79. Nelson, "Organized Labor and the Struggle for Black Equality"; Lichtenstein, *Labor's War at Home*, 125–26; Allan M. Winkler, "The Philadelphia Transit Strike of 1944," *Journal of American History* 59, 1 (June 1972): 73–89; Mauricio Mazón, *The Zoot-Suit Riots: The Psychology of Symbolic Annihilation* (Austin: University of Texas Press, 1984), 55–56, notes the connection between the Zoot Suit Riots and the UMW wildcat strikes at that time, but makes no specific mention of hate strikes.

80. Nelson, "Organized Labor and the Struggle for Black Equality," 955, 971–78, 982–88; Lichtenstein, *Labor's War at Home*, 125.

81. "The Negroes' Role in the War: A Study of White and Colored Opinions," Memo #59, July 8, 1943, 4, 21, 29, 51, in box 1799, OWI-Polls.

82. Ibid., 23, 35–36, 38–39; "Workers and the War," Report #12, April 28, 1942, table xxiii, in box 1786, OWI-Surveys.

83. "The Negroes' Role in the War"; Cantril, ed., *Public Opinion 1935–1946*, 510, item #18.

84. The seminal article in this vein is Harvard Sitkoff, "Racial Militancy and Interracial Violence in the Second World War," *Journal of American History* 58, 3 (December 1971): 661–81, esp. 669–71.

85. Important exceptions to this tendency to separate hate strikes and wildcats that were not racially motivated is Joshua Freeman, "Delivering the Goods: Industrial Unionism During World War II," *Labor History* 19, 4 (Fall 1978): 570–93, esp. 586–87; Lipsitz, *Rainbow at Midnight*.

86. Lichtenstein, *Labor's War at Home*, chs. 4 and 5, figures on 133–34, Tables 2 and 3; Atleson, *Labor and the Wartime State*, chs. 7 and 8, figures on 142, Tables 1 and 2. See also Lipsitz, *Rainbow at Midnight*; Martin Glaberman, *Wartime Strikes: The Struggle Against the No-Strike Pledge in the UAW During World War II* (Detroit: Bewick, 1980); Jerome E. Scott and George C. Homans, "Reflections on the Wildcat Strikes," *American Sociological Review* 12, 3 (June 1947): 278–87.

87. Atleson, *Labor and the Wartime State*, 146–47, Tables 5 and 6. I have combined figures for wages and hours since together these determined workers' pay.

88. Kevin Boyle, "Auto Workers at War: Patriotism and Protest in the American Automobile Industry, 1939–1945," in *Autowork*, ed. Robert Asher and Ronald Edsforth (Albany: State University of New York Press, 1995), 99–126, quotes on 100, 107, and grievance data on 106, Table 4; and Freeman, "Delivering the Goods," 592–93. Cf. Nelson Lichtenstein, "Auto Worker Militancy and the Structure of Factory Life, 1937–1955," *Journal of American History* 67, 2 (September 1980): 335–53.

89. Boyle, "Auto Workers at War," 99, 110–11, 118–19, 123–25; quote on 123.

90. Job satisfaction was second most important, after education. E. William Noland, "Worker Attitudes and Industrial Absenteeism: A Statistical Appraisal," *American Sociological Review* 10, 4 (August 1945): 503–10, esp. Table 3. This finding rested on three different rating methods: multiple regression, correlation coefficient, and average (mean) scale rank. See also Joel Seidman, *American Labor from Defense to Reconversion* (Chicago: University of Chicago Press, 1956), 161; "The Treatment of Absenteeism," Memo 53, April 27, 1943, and "Workers' Reactions to Absenteeism," Memo 53A, May 24, 1943, both in box 1799, OWI-Polls; "Tested Ways to Reduce Absenteeism," *Factory Management and Maintenance* 101, 2 (March 1943): 831; Eleanor V. Kennedy, "Absenteeism in Commercial Shipyards, 1942," *Monthly Labor Review* 56, 2 (February 1943), 212; Duane Evans, "Absenteeism in Relation to War Production," *American Labor Review* 56, 1 (January 1943): 1.

91. Richard Tansey and Michael Hyman, "Public Relations, Advocacy Ads, and the Campaign Against Absenteeism During World War II," *Business and Professional Ethics Journal* 11 (Fall 1993).

92. OWI Poster V-305, reproduced in John J. Corson, *Manpower for Victory: Total Mobilization for Total War* (New York: Farrar and Rinehart, 1943), 161.

93. Jones and Lamson Machine Co., "He's Not Celebrating!" 1945, advertisement no. W0276, Ad*Access Collection, Duke University Library.

94. Reported in the first half of August 1942, in Missouri folder, State Rumors by Subject, boxes 2–3, LC Rumors.

95. "Reactions to the War Economy," Report no. 16, June 16, 1942, 2, in box 1786, OWI-Surveys.

96. "Inflation and American Opinion," Special Intelligence Report, February 20, 1943, 3, in box 1806, OWI-Intell.

97. "The War Worker's Point of View," Report no. 21, July 28, 1942, Summary.

98. Minnesota folder, State Rumors by Subject, boxes 2–3, LC rumors. For other quotes to similar effect, see Oklahoma, Arizona folders.

99. Colorado and Utah folders, State Rumors by Subject, boxes 2–3, LC rumors.

100. "On the 'Special Privilege' of the Defense Worker," 5, folder 4, box 1, LC rumors.

101. Minnesota folder, State Rumors by Subject, boxes 2–3, LC rumors.

102. "He's Watching You," U.S. Office for Emergency Management, 1942, object II.22, NWU WWII Posters.

103. "Report on Reactions of War Workers to the Poster 'He's Watching You,'" Poster Study No. 2, box 1784A, OWI-Surveys.

104. "Loose Lips Might Sink Ships," Office for Emergency Management, 1941, stored in the records of the Office of Government Reports (RG 44), National Archives—College Park. Digital reproduction available at http://arcweb.archives.gov, ARC identifier 513543.

105. Rickenbacker quoted in Flynn, *The Mess in Washington*, 45–46.

106. "Coal Strike Aftermath," memo, February 8, 1943, box 1718, OWI-Research.

107. Cantril, ed., *Public Opinion, 1935–1946*, 1, item 2; Keith E. Eiler, *Mobilizing America: Robert Patterson and the War Effort, 1940–1945* (Ithaca, NY: Cornell University Press, 1997), 370–72, quote on 371; Flynn, *The Mess in Washington*, 44–46.

108. "Survey of Intelligence Materials," no. 21, April 29, 1942, 5, in box 1805, OWI-Intell.

109. "Personal Identification with the War," Intelligence Report, October 28, 1942, 12, and "Governmental Compulsion During the War: Do People Want to Be Told What to Do?" Report no. 28, October 13, 1942; both in box 1806, OWI-Intell.

110. Cantril, ed., *Public Opinion 1935–1946*, 1125, item 37; "Mobilizing American Manpower," August 18, 1942, Summary, in box 1786, OWI-Surveys.

111. Cantril, ed., *Public Opinion 1935–1946*, 823, items 56 and 58.

112. Ibid., 824, items 65–67.

113. Fireside Chats, 225.

114. Fireside Chats, 233–34; he repeated the phrase "essential justice and practical necessity" twice within two paragraphs, apparently to acknowledge that workers had legitimate concerns about wage controls.

115. Cantril, ed., *Public Opinion 1935–1946*, 822, item 53. On the coal strike and public reaction, see Polenberg, *War and Society*, 161–70; Joel Seidman, *American Labor from Defense to Reconversion* (Chicago: University of Chicago Press, 1956), 133, 142. On Roosevelt and the strike, see Frank Freidel, *Roosevelt: A Rendezvous with Destiny* (Boston: Little, Brown, 1990), 370–71; James MacGregor Burns, *Roosevelt: The Soldier of Freedom, 1940–1945* (New York: Harcourt, Brace, Jovanovich, 1970), 335–37.

116. Fireside Chats, 250–53.

117. Ibid., 253–54.

118. Ibid., 255–56.

119. Doris Kearns Goodwin, *No Ordinary Time: Franklin and Eleanor Roosevelt: The Home Front in World War II* (New York: Simon and Schuster, 1994), 440–43, quotes on 440 and 442.

120. Ibid.; Cantril, ed., *Public Opinion 1935–1946*, 822, item 51; Polenberg, *War and Society*, 166–70.

121. Fireside Chats, 283–93.

122. Hadley Cantril, *The Human Dimension: Experiences in Policy Research* (New Brunswick: Rutgers University Press, 1967), 95–96; FDR Papers, 14:43.

123. Fireside Chats, 293.

124. Ibid., 286–87.

125. Ibid., 287 n. 11; Rosenman, ed., *The Public Papers and Addresses of Franklin Delano Roosevelt*, 14:36.

126. Fireside Chats, 289–90.

127. Ibid., 307–15.

128. Jerome Bruner, *Mandate from the People* (New York: Duell, Sloan, and Pearce, 1944), 170–87, quote on 186.

129. Stephen Bailey, *Congress Makes a Law: The Story Behind the Employment Act of 1946* (New York: Columbia University Press, 1950).

130. Christian Appy, *Working-Class War: American Combat Soldiers in Vietnam* (Chapel Hill: University of North Carolina Press, 1993); Gerstle, *American Crucible*, 268–346.

131. Anthony Chen, *The Fifth Freedom: Jobs, Politics, and Civil Rights in the United States, 1941–1972* (Princeton: Princeton University Press, 2009).

Chapter 6

1. Lee Shippey, "Our Mess of Pottage," in column, "Lee Side o' L.A.," *Los Angeles Times*, June 1, 1943.

2. The ritualized attacks counted as an episode in the recurrent "regeneration through violence" that has been enacted imaginatively, through myths, folklore, and popular culture legends, throughout American history. Richard Slotkin, *Regeneration Through Violence: The Mythology of the American Frontier, 1600–1860* (Middletown, CT: Wesleyan University Press, 1973), 5 and passim.

3. After the war Stouffer and some of the social scientists whom he had supervised synthesized the findings of the scores of reports and data analyses they had performed for the War Department. These were combined into the four-volume series Studies in Social Psychology in World War II, whose first two volumes, gathered together under the heading *The American Soldier*, became a classic of postwar social science. See vol. 1, Samuel Stouffer et al., *The American Soldier: Adjustment During Army Life*; vol. 2, Stouffer et al., *The American Soldier: Combat and Its Aftermath*; vol. 3, Carl Hovland et al., *Experiments on Mass Communication*; vol. 4, Stouffer et al., *Measurement and Prediction* (Princeton: Princeton University Press, 1949, 1950).

4. This tradition was begun by American propaganda during the war, then operationalized and quantified by Samuel Stouffer in *The American Soldier*.

5. Benjamin Alpers, *Dictators, Democracy, and American Public Culture: Envisioning the Totalitarian Enemy, 1920s–1950s* (Chapel Hill: University of North Carolina Press, 2003); Robert B. Westbrook, *Why We Fought: Forging American Obligations in World War II* (Washington, DC: Smithsonian Books, 2004); Andrew Huebner, *The Warrior Image: Soldiers in American Culture from the Second World War to the Vietnam Era* (Chapel Hill: University of North Carolina Press, 2008).

6. U.S. Selective Service System, *Registration and Selective Service*, Special Monograph No. 3 (Washington, DC: USGPO, 1946), 123.

7. Ibid., 136–37.

8. *Sergeant York* (Warner Brothers, 1941); Alpers, "This Is the Army: Imagining a Democratic Military in World War II," *Journal of American History* 85 (June 1998): 129–63.

9. Selective Service Administration, *Selective Service Regulations*, vol. 3: *Classification and Selection* (Washington, DC: USGPO, 1940). Note that the legislation used Roman numerals in the classifications (e.g., IV-F), whereas popular usage tended to employ Arabic numerals (e.g., 4-F).

10. U.S. Selective Service System, *Registration and Selective Service*, 57, Table 1; George Q. Flynn, *The Draft, 1940–1973* (Lawrence: University Press of Kansas, 1993), 60. The Fourth Registration, conducted April 27, 1942, raised the upper limit to sixty-four, and the Fifth, on June 30, 1942, lowered it to eighteen.

11. Margot Canaday, *The Straight State: Sexuality and Citizenship in Twentieth-Century America* (Princeton: Princeton University Press, 2009), 137–73.

12. George Q. Flynn, *Lewis B. Hershey, Mr. Selective Service* (Chapel Hill: University of North Carolina Press, 1985), 86; Flynn, *The Draft, 1940–1973* (Lawrence: University Press of Kansas, 1993), 35, 54, 58–60.

13. Flynn, *The Draft*; Neil Wynn, *The Afro-American and the Second World War* (New York: Holmes and Meier, 1976).

14. John J. Corson, *Manpower for Victory: Total Mobilization for Total War* (New York: Farrar and Rinehart, 1943), foreword by Paul McNutt, xi–xii; 214–15, 234–75; Flynn, *Lewis B. Hershey*, 88–90; George Q. Flynn, *The Mess in Washington: Manpower Mobilization in World War II* (Westport: Greenwood, 1979), 200–5; Flynn, *The Draft, 1940–1972*, 82.

15. Flynn, *The Draft*, 80–85.

16. Christopher Capozzola, *Uncle Sam Wants You: World War I and the Making of the Modern American Citizen* (New York: Oxford University Press, 2008), 21–54; Russell Kazal, *Becoming Old Stock: The Paradox of German-American Identity* (Princeton: Princeton University Press, 2004); Iver Bernstein, *The New York City Draft Riots: Their Significance for American Society and Politics in the Age of the Civil War* (New York: Oxford University Press, 1990).

17. Leo P. Crespi, "Attitudes Toward Conscientious Objectors and Some of Their Psychological Correlates," *Journal of Psychology* 18 (July 1944): 81–117; Crespi, "Public Opinion Toward Conscientious Objectors: II. Measurement of National Approval-Disapproval," *Journal of Psychology* 19 (April 1945): 209–50; Crespi, "Public Opinion Toward Conscientious Objectors: III. Intensity of Social Rejection in Stereotype and Attitude," in *Journal of Psychology* 19 (April 1945): 251–76; Crespi, "Public Opinion Toward Conscientious Objectors: IV. Opinions on Significant Conscientious Objector Issues," *Journal of Psychology* 19 (April 1945): 277–310; Crespi, "Public Opinion Toward Conscientious Objectors: V. National Tolerance, Wartime Trends, and the Scapegoat Hypothesis," *Journal of Psychology* 20 (October 1945): 321–46. For corroborating polls indicating a tolerance for COs before the war and afterward, see Cantril, ed., *Public Opinion 1935–1946*, 135, items 2 (January 1940) and 5 (September 1945).

18. Mulford Q. Sibley and Philip E. Jacob, *Conscription of Conscience: The American State and the Conscientious Objector, 1940–1947* (Ithaca, NY: Cornell University Press, 1952), 83, Table V.

19. Ibid., 110–23.

20. Neil Maher, *Nature's New Deal: The Civilian Conservation Corps and the Roots of the American Environmental Movement* (New York: Oxford University Press, 2008).

21. Kieran Patel, *Soldiers of Labor: Labor Service in Nazi Germany and New Deal America, 1933–1945* (New York: Cambridge University Press, 2005); Wolfgang Schivelbusch, *Three New Deals: Reflections on Roosevelt's America, Mussolini's Italy, and Hitler's Germany, 1933–1939* (New York: Picador, 2006), 138–84, ch. 5.

22. Cantril, *Public Opinion 1935–1946*, 135, item 5.

23. Sibley and Jacob, *Conscription of Conscience*, 200–41.

24. For a thoughtful examination of the gender dynamics undergirding World War II COs, consult Timothy Stewart-Winter, "Not a Soldier, Not a Slacker: Conscientious Objectors and Male Citizenship in the United States During the Second World War," *Gender and History* 19, 3 (November 2007): 519–42.

25. Eric Posselt, ed., *G.I. Songs* (Great Neck: Granger Books, 1978 [1944]), 81. According to the editor, who compiled songs popular among GIs in World War I, "This noble song, mentioned variously by 'Yank,' 'Life,' and other magazines as one of the great favorites of our men, has many other amusing but unfortunately unprintable verses. Period.)" Songs in this book were selected by the editor based on their popularity among soldiers: commercial recordings were excluded.

26. Radio City joke in Bennett Cerf, ed., *The Pocket Book of War Humor* (New York: Pocket Books, 1943); other jokes in the same vein, 38, 39, 41.

27. M.Z. to "Mr. Edgar Hoover," June 2, 1943; "A Citizen" to the FBI, postmarked June 3, 1943, from New York City; both in folder "Fan Mail June 1–3," box 14, Selective Svc.

28. "Memorandum: The American Legion Backs Up the FBI," File #66–9330–150, July 15, 1945, 3. For other civic organizations who provided contacts, including the Chamber of Commerce, the Boy Scouts of America, the Knights of Columbus, and several others, see "Bureau Bulletin," File #66–03–707 November 26, 1945.

29. Stouffer et al, *Adjustment During Army Life*, 55.

30. Ibid., 61–63.

31. Ibid., 69–70.

32. "What the Soldier Thinks," March 25, 1944, 1, 2, 5.

33. Stouffer et al., *Adjustment During Army Life*, 72–74.

34. Robert J. Calhoun to parents, February 18 and May 29, 1944, in folder T/5, box 1, Calhoun MS.

35. On disorientation of soldiers, and the training in regional difference this provided, see Morton Sosna, "The GI's South and the North-South Dialogue During World War II," in *Developing Dixie: Modernization in a Traditional Society*, eds. Winifred Moore, Joseph Tripp, and Lyon Tyler (Westport: Greenwood Press, 1988), 311–26.

36. Calhoun to parents, June 14, July 1, 9, and 16, 1944, in folder T/5, box 1, Calhoun MS.

37. Calhoun to parents, February 22, 1944, in folder T/5, box 1, Calhoun MS; Sosna, "The GI's South and the North-South Dialogue During World War II."

38. Westbrook, *Why We Fought*, ch. 1; Alpers, "This Is the Army."

39. Thomas Doherty, *Projections of War: Hollywood, American Culture, and World War II* (New York: Columbia University Press, 1993); Clayton Koppes and Gregory Black, *Hollywood Goes to War: How Politics, Profits, and Propaganda Shaped World War II Movies* (New York: Free Press, 1987).

40. "What the Soldier Thinks," December 1943, 12–13. Cf. similar proportions for the other films in the series as reported in an earlier report: "What the Soldier Thinks," August 1943, 89–97. For a thorough treatment of the impact of orientation films on soldiers' motivation, see Hovland et al., *Experiments on Mass Communication*.

41. "What the Soldier Thinks," December 1942 (rev. printing February 1943), 56–57.

42. Hovland et al., *Experiments on Mass Communication*, 108–13; "polygraph" results for film shorts on 111, Figure 2; quotes on 113.

43. "Gripes," Pvt. Snafu series (Warner Bros., 1943), dir. Friz Freleng.

44. Amer. Soldier Free Comments, Survey 32 (March 9, 1945, on reel 9, third page [labeled 6], Q64.

45. Stouffer et al., *Adjustment During Army Life*, 432, Table 1.

46. Stouffer, *American Soldier*, I:434, 440–41, 460.

47. "Omnibus Survey of Attitudes," July–September, 1943, Q98A, Q98B, basic frequencies tabulated from S-63D, American Soldier dataset, USAMS1945-S63D [computer file], Storrs, CT: The Roper Center, University of Connecticut [distributor].

48. Untitled song composed by Kyle J. Kinzer, S 1/c, U.S. Navy, March 14, 1944, in WACO, box 13, 01.Hemphill Songs LC Lomax War Collection.

49. See, e.g., "Company 'C' Victory Song," [January 1943], song transcript reported from the headquarters of the Marine Raider Battalion Amphibious Force at Camp Elliott, San Diego, in WACO, box 13, 03.Marine Songs, LC Lomax War Collection. See also "Care of Uncle Sam," by Denver Darling, n.d., DECCA 6063-B, which refers in an offhand way to making "old Tojo" a "souvenir," and reducing "Mussolini and Hitler" to being "meek as a lamb," without really indicating what they stood for; in WACO, box 13, 04.World War II Songs, LC Lomax War Collection.

50. "Doctrine of the Raider Battalion," [January 1943], song transcript reported from the headquarters of the Marine Raider Battalion Amphibious Force at Camp Elliott, San Diego, in WACO, box 13, 03.Marine Songs, LC Lomax War Collection.

51. "Modern Cannon Ball," n.d., song transcript reported in WACO, box 13, 04.World War II Songs, LC Lomax War Collection.

52. "You Better Get Ready," n.d., song transcript reported in WACO, box 13, 04.World War II Songs, LC Lomax War Collection.

53. "Strange Thing Happen All Over the Land," n.d., song transcript reported in WACO, box 13, 03.Marine Songs, LC Lomax War Collection. Apparently these were wartime variations on the larger body of folksong termed "Roosevelt's Blues" by one scholar. Guido van Rijn, *Roosevelt's Blues: African-American Blues and Gospel Songs on FDR* (Jackson: University Press of Mississippi, 1997).

54. "You Fascists Bound to Lose," n.d., song transcript reported in WACO, box 13, 04.World War II Songs, LC Lomax War Collection.

55. "The Little Brown Jug Goes Modern," n.d., song transcript reported in WACO, box 13, 04.World War II Songs, LC Lomax War Collection.

56. "Certainly Am," n.d., song transcript reported in WACO, box 13, 04.World War II Songs, LC Lomax War Collection.

57. "What Are We Waiting On?," n.d., song transcript reported in WACO, box 13, 04.World War II Songs, LC Lomax War Collection.

58. "A Message to Hitler," by Dock U. Reese, January 1943, to be sung to the tune of "Old Hannah," song transcript reported in WACO, box 13, 04.World War II Songs, LC Lomax War Collection.

59. "What the Soldier Thinks," September 1945, 13.

60. The best discussion of the absurdity and irreverence of GI culture is still Paul Fussell, *Wartime: Understanding and Behavior in the Second World War* (New York: Oxford University Press, 1989); see ch. 17, esp. 260–62 on Kilroy and other GI favorites.

61. Fussell, *Wartime*, 79–95.

62. Stouffer et al., *The American Soldier: Adjustment During Army Life* (Princeton: Princeton University Press, 1949): 369, 373, 379 and ch. 8 generally.

63. "Planning Survey II, Schedule A–1, Free Comments, I and E Questionnaires, May 12, 1942," entry unnumbered (7th), roll 1, box 1, "Formerly Security-Classified Microfilm Copy of Records Relating to the Morale of Personnel (1941–45), 1942–46," Amer. Soldier Free Comments.

64. "What the Soldier Thinks," July 25, 1944, 1–4. For similar views in other theaters, see "What the Soldier Thinks," February 1945, 1–5; and June 1945, 8–10.

65. For all of the stanzas, see the full version in Posselt, ed., *G.I. Songs*; "Frankie and Johnnie" folder, Lomax MS, LC AFS. Note that the source here uses the spelling "Johnnie" instead of the more commonly seen "Johnny."

66. For purposes of compression I focus here on black-white racial relations, but of course the dividing lines were much more complex, although often centered around white-nonwhite. See Beth Bailey and David Farber, *The First Strange Place: The Alchemy Of Race and Sex in World War II Hawaii* (New York: Free Press, 1992); Tamotsu Shibutani, *The Derelicts of Company K: A Sociological Study of Demoralization* (Berkeley: University of California Press, 1978); Deborah Dash Moore, *GI Jews: How World War II Changed a Generation* (Cambridge, MA: Belknap Press, 2004); Jeremi Suri, *Henry Kissinger and the American Century* (Cambridge, MA: Belknap Press, 2007), 52–92.

67. Bailey and Farber, *First Strange Place*; Richard Dalfiume, *Desegregation of the U.S. Armed Forces: Fighting on Two Fronts, 1939–1953* (Columbia: University of Missouri Press, 1969), 64–81.

68. Bailey and Farber, *First Strange Place*; Lizabeth Cohen, *A Consumer's Republic: The Politics of Mass Consumption in Postwar America* (New York: Alfred A. Knopf, 2003), 90–96; Robin D. G. Kelley, *Race Rebels: Culture, Politics, and the Black Working Class* (New York: Free Press, 1996), chs. 1–3.

69. Daniel Kryder, *Divided Arsenal: Race and the American State During World War II* (Cambridge: Cambridge University Press, 2000), 168–207.

70. Kryder, *Divided Arsenal*, 3, 133–207; see 155, Figure 5.2, for monthly totals and seasonal patterns of violence, 1942–44.

71. Pvt. James Pritchell to the Asst. Civilian Aide to the Secretary of War, January 12, 1944, Camp Livingston, Louisiana, folder, box 186, Hastie/Gibson Recs.

72. Pvt. Charles Wilson to President Franklin Delano Roosevelt, May 9, 1944, folder "Attitudes of Negro Soldiers," box 181, Hastie/Gibson Recs.

73. Ibid.

74. Pvt. Stanley West to Adjutant General, U.S. Army, September 23, 1941; West to "Jim," [mid-October 1941]; both in folder "Camp Bowie, TX," blue discharges series, box 185, Hastie/Gibson Recs.

75. Wilson to Roosevelt, 3.

76. Pvt. Bert B. Babero to Truman K. Gibson, January 13, 1944, folder "Attitudes of Negro Soldiers," box 181, Hastie/Gibson Recs.

77. Pvt. Willie M. Purdue to T. K. Gibson, [ca. August 1943] folder "Camp Lee, VA (3)," blue discharge series, box 185, Hastie/Gibson Recs.

78. Letter to "Afro," n.d., in folder "Camp Clairborne, LA. (4)," blue discharge series, box 185, Hastie/Gibson Recs.

79. John Dittmer, *Local People: The Struggle for Civil Rights in Mississippi* (Urbana: University of Illinois Press, 1994), 1–9, 13–18, 19–40; Charles M. Payne, *I've Got the Light of Freedom: The Organizing Tradition and the Mississippi Freedom Struggle* (Berkeley: University of California Press, 1995), 13, 24, 30–31, 47–48, 56–57, 66, 87, 136–37, 177, 181–82, 188, 404; Steve Lawson, *Black Ballots: Voting Rights in the South, 1944–1969* (New York: Columbia University Press, 1976), 102–15, 341.

80. Stouffer et al., *Combat and Its Aftermath*, 292–99.

81. Stouffer et al., *Combat and Its Aftermath*, 299–316; Research Branch, Information and Education Section, ETOUSA, "What ETO Soldiers Think of: The Attitudes of Civilians, The Fact That Some Soldiers Have Never Been Overseas, Combat Men's Resentment of Rear-Echelon Troops," report no. 124-M-10 (August 8, 1945).

82. Ibid., Table 15, 475.

83. Amer. Soldier Free Comments, entry unnumbered (37th).

84. Ed Borysiewicz letter, [January] 1945, Natl. Broach-USAMHI.

85. "Andy" letter, February 12, 1943; Michael Bahrie letter, June 18, 1943, Natl. Broach-USAMHI.

86. Pat B. Messina letter, n.d., Natl. Broach-USAMHI.

87. Carl Barnes letter, September 28, 1944, Natl. Broach-USAMHI.

88. Carl Barnes letter, September 29, 1944, Natl. Broach-USAMHI.

89. S/Sgt. Edmund Borysiewicz, January 15, 1943, Natl. Broach-USAMHI.

90. Chuck Clinton letter, unaddressed, [July 1944], Natl. Broach-USAMHI.

91. Chuck Clinton to "Dear Friends," December 28, 1944, Natl. Broach-USAMHI.

92. "Royal" to the "Gang," January 17, 1945, Natl. Broach-USAMHI.

93. Carl Barnes letter, September 28, 1944, Natl. Broach-USAMHI.

94. Carl Barnes to the "Gang," October 22, 1943, Natl. Broach-USAMHI.

95. Chuck Clinton to Scotty, January 21, 1945, Natl. Broach-USAMHI.

96. "The Censorship Survey of Morale (June 1943 to August 1945)," n.p. (section K), box 24 [formerly T-1429], Army Censor Reports.

97. Stouffer et al., *Combat and Its Aftermath*, 585, Table 3.

98. Janet L. Langlois, "The Belle Isle Bridge Incident: Legend Dialectic and Semiotic System in the 1943 Detroit Race Riots," *Journal of American Folklore* 96, 380 (1983): 183–99.

99. Marilynn S. Johnson, "Gender, Race, and Rumors: Re-examining the 1943 Race Riots," *Gender and History* 10, 2 (August 1998): 264, 268.

100. Dominic Capeci and Martha Wilkerson, *Layered Violence: The Detroit Riots of 1943* (Jackson: University Press of Mississippi, 1991) provides the most thorough analysis of the Detroit riots.

101. Goodman, *The Committee*, 156.

102. Johnson, "Gender, Race, and Rumors," 252–77; Dominic Capeci, *The Harlem Riot of 1943* (Philadelphia: Temple University Press, 1977); Capeci and Wilkerson, *Layered Violence*.

103. For a perceptive analysis of the link between race relations, consumer politics, and commodity riots in World War II and during the 1960s, see Cohen, *A Consumer's Republic*, 83–100, 371–79. On the link between rumor and riot in the Vietnam era, when rumor clinics modeled on the World War II era were also used, see Terry Ann Knopf, *Rumors, Race and Riots* (New Brunswick: Transaction, 1975).

104. Luis Alvarez, *The Power of the Zoot: Youth Culture and Resistance During World War II* (Berkeley: University of California Press, 2008); Eduardo Pagán, *Murder at the Sleepy*

Lagoon: Zoot Suits, Race, and Riot in Wartime L.A. (Chapel Hill: University of North Carolina Press, 2003), chs. 6–8; Mauricio Mazón, *The Zoot-Suit Riots: The Psychology of Symbolic Annihilation* (Austin: University of Texas Press, 1984); Edward Escobar, *Race, Police, and the Making of a Political Identity: Mexican Americans and the Los Angeles Police Department, 1900–1945* (Berkeley: University of California Press, 1999), chs. 8–12; Zaragosa Vargas, *Labor Rights Are Civil Rights: Mexican American Workers in Twentieth-Century America* (Princeton: Princeton University Press, 2005), ch. 5.

105. Orpheum event reported in *Time*, June 21, 1943, 18; the San Francisco *People's World*, June 10, 1943; and the California *Eagle*, June 10, 1943. Glen Miller listed in advertisement for Orpheum Theater in the *Los Angeles Times*, June 7, 1943.

106. *Los Angeles Evening Herald and Express* June 8, 1943, A13. Emphasis in the original.

107. Beatrice Griffith, *American Me* (Boston: Houghton Mifflin, 1948), 8. According to Griffith, x, this eyewitness account and others like it in her book "are the children's own stories, told to me by them and written with their encouragement."

108. "Report on Attack on Naval Personnel by Zoot-Suiters," Records of the Commandant's Office, Eleventh Naval District, Records of Shore Establishments and Naval Districts, RG 181, National Archives—Pacific Region (Laguna Niguel). Episodes occurring in consumer sites include the El Portel, June 6, 1943; pool hall, May 29; Venice Boulevard, "first part of April"; Casino Ballroom, "middle of April," Admiral Theater, May 29; Paramount Theater, May 22; Arcade Bowling Alley, April 17; theater district, June 5 and 6; Orpheum, June 5; Hollywood Roller Bowl, June 5; Majestic Ballroom, June 5; Lincoln Park, date unknown; Palladium, "first part of April"; Tip Toe Inn, "middle of April." Pagán, *Murder at the Sleepy Lagoon*, ch. 5, provides a thorough analysis of these confrontations that confirms both their escalation prior to the riots and their profound effect on perceptions of the zoot suiters as a criminal menace.

109. Pagán, *Murder at the Sleepy Lagoon*, 180, suggests the low casualty rate may also have been the result of the zooters' ability to evade capture on their home turf.

110. Griffith, *American Me*, 25.

111. Mauricio Mazón, *The Zoot-Suit Riots: The Psychology of Symbolic Annihilation* (Austin: University of Texas Press, 1984), 97–99.

112. Carey McWilliams, *North from Mexico: The Spanish-Speaking People of the United States* (Philadelphia: J.B. Lippincott, 1948), 235–39, 245–48.

113. Mazón, *The Zoot-Suit Riots*, 81–82; Escobar, *Race, Police, and the Making of a Political Identity*, 184, 221–22. McWilliams's early reporting on the riots also implicated the *sinarquistas*, a connection he later dropped. See his report "The Zoot Suit Riots" in the *New Republic*, June 21, 1943, 818–20.

114. "Counter-Intelligence Summary," District Intelligence Office, Section B-7, Eleventh Naval District, June 1943 (date-stamped July 5, 1943). Box 248, Chief of Naval Operations, ONI Security Classified Administrative Correspondence 1942–1946, RG 38, National Archives—College Park.

115. Discussed in Mazón, *The Zoot-Suit Riots*, esp. 81.

116. McWilliams, *North from Mexico*; McWilliams, "The Zoot Suit Riots"; McWilliams, "Hearst Press Incited Campaign Against Mexicans" and "Zoot Suit Riots Served Purpose," *PM*, June 11 and June 13, 1943; Chester Himes, "Zoot Riots Are Race Riots," *Crisis*, July 1943, 200–1, 222; Griffith, *American Me*. Historical scholarship in this vein includes Escobar, *Race, Police, and the Making of a Political Identity*; George Sanchez, *Becoming Mexican American: Ethnicity, Culture, and Identity in Chicano Los Angeles, 1900–1945* (New York: Oxford University Press, 1993); Rodolfo Acuña, *Occupied America: A History of Chicanos*, sixth ed. (New York: Pearson Longman, 2007).

117. Mazón, *The Zoot-Suit Riots*, 78–81; Pagán, *Murder at the Sleepy Lagoon*, 276–77; "Counter-Intelligence Summary," 19, for numbers on injuries.

118. McWilliams, "Hearst Press Incited Campaign Against Mexicans" and "Zoot Suit Riots Served Purpose"; Griffith, *American Me*, 26; Escobar, *Race, Police, and the Making of a Polit-*

ical Identity, 246. See Solomon Jones, *The Government Riots of Los Angeles, June 1943* (San Francisco: R and E Research Associates, 1973), 33, for a discussion of a Chamber of Commerce study estimating that the order cost the city as much as $1 million for each weekend servicemen were barred from visiting it on leave.

119. Mazón, *The Zoot-Suit Riots*, introduction, esp. 1–2, 12–14.

120. *Newsweek*, June 21, 1943, 38.

121. McWilliams, *North from Mexico*, 247.

122. *Newsweek*, June 21, 1943, 36.

123. *Los Angeles Evening Herald and Express*, June 9, 1943.

124. *Los Angeles Times*, June 7, 1943, II–1.

125. *Los Angeles Evening Herald and Express*, June 8, 1943.

126. Catherine S. Ramirez, *The Woman in the Zoot Suit: Gender, Nationalism, and the Cultural Politics of Memory* (Durham: Duke University Press, 2009).

127. *Los Angeles Evening Herald and Express*, June 5, 1943.

128. *Los Angeles Times*, June 8, 1943.

129. *Time*, June 21, 1943, 18. One of the eyewitnesses in Griffith, *American Me*, 10, echoes this often-repeated observation.

130. Mazón, *The Zoot-Suit Riots*.

131. Robin D. G. Kelley, "The Riddle of the Zoot: Malcolm Little and Black Cultural Politics During World War II," in *Race Rebels: Culture, Politics, and the Black Working Class* (New York: Free Press, 1994): 161–81, esp. 171–73 on draft dodging, and 173–78 on hustling, pimping, thieving, and how "the illicit economy 'schooled'" Malcolm Little (aka Malcolm X); Stuart Cosgrove, "The Zoot-Suit and Style Warfare," *History Workshop Journal* 18 (Autumn 1984): 77–91; Steve Chibnall, "Whistle and Zoot: The Changing Meaning of a Suit of Clothes," *History Workshop Journal* 20 (Autumn 1985): 56–81; Shane White and Graham White, *Stylin': African American Expressive Culture from Its Beginnings to the Zoot Suit* (Ithaca: Cornell University Press, 1998), 256.

132. It does not appear that most wearers of the zoot suit considered themselves to be as militantly opposed to the dominant culture as Kelley and White would suggest, although clearly there was a dedicated subculture of zooters for whom their depiction of resistance is quite accurate. See, for example, Fritz Redl's classification of zooters into four "types": members of an "expressional dance cult," youths wishing to make an individualistic "declaration of independence," youths identifying themselves as part of "a spontaneous youth movement," and a small number "for whom the zoot suit is a disguise for delinquent gang formation." Redl, "Zoot Suits: An Interpretation," 259–61.

133. Chibnall, "Whistle and Zoot," 64–74.

134. White and White, *Stylin',* 257–58. Here I take a different view from the authors: rather than seeing this episode as an example of "bucking authority," I take the "impeccable" behavior of these troops (the authors' description) to indicate a less confrontational motive among the trainees. This seems especially clear when compared with the many incidents of racial violence on southern bases and in nearby towns, which erupted when black soldiers protested discrimination, unfair treatment, and Jim Crow expectations of deference.

135. Griffith, *American Me*, 5, 14.

136. Pagán, *Murder at the Sleepy Lagoon*, xxv–xxxv, 67–73, explains that the zoot suit was worn by youths of many different ethnicities. This contributed to its transgressive quality in the eyes of most whites and minorities aspiring to the "respectable" middle class.

137. Griffith, *American Me*, 3–14.

138. Ruth Tuck, "Behind the Zoot Suit Riots," *Survey Graphic*, August 1943, 314, 313; for a similar point, see McWilliams, "The Zoot Suit Riots," *New Republic*, June 21, 1943, 618–20; McWilliams, *North from Mexico*, 259.

139. *New York Times*, June 11, 1943.

140. Quoted in Sanchez, *Becoming Mexican American*, 253.

141. Eric Foner, *The Story of American Freedom* (New York: W. W. Norton, 1998), ch. 10, esp. 230–31.

142. Griffith, *American Me*, 12–13.

143. Meg Jacobs, *Pocketbook Politics: Economic Citizenship in Twentieth-Century America* (Princeton: Princeton University Press, 2005); Cohen, *A Consumer's Republic.*

144. R. Alton Lee, "The Army 'Mutiny' of 1946," *Journal of American History* 53, 3 (December 1966): 555–71; John C. Sparrow, "History of Personnel Demobilization in the United States Army," typescript, Office of the Chief of Military History, Department of the Army, 1951, 143–354.

145. "Morale," *Time*, January 21, 1946, 20; *New York Times*, January 10, 1946; Lee, "The Army 'Mutiny' of 1946," 562–63.

146. "Morale," 20–21.

147. As quoted in Lee, "The Army 'Mutiny' of 1946," 568.

148. "Why G.I.'s Demonstrate," *Nation*, January 19, 1946, 60.

149. Ibid. The original uses "coke" and "officer's club"; I have changed these to "Coke" and "officers' club" for ease of reading.

150. As quoted in "Morale," 21.

151. Soldiers' letters to congressmen in "Unrest of Veteran Troops: What Homesick Soldiers Say," *United States News*, January 25, 1946, 19–21.

152. "Morale," 21–22.

153. For a technical account of the point system and an analysis of the soldiers' response to its collapse, consult Stouffer et al., *Combat and Its Aftermath*, 520–95. See also Sparrow, "History of Personnel Demobilization in the United States Army," 30–308.

154. Kathleen J. Frydl, *The GI Bill* (New York: Cambridge University Press, 2009).

Conclusion

1. War Records Section, Committee on Records of War Administration, *The United States at War: Development and Administration of the War Program by the Federal Government* (Washington, DC: USGPO, 1946), 472, 475–77, 500.

2. Robert A. Pollard, *Economic Security and the Origins of the Cold War, 1945–1950* (New York: Columbia University Press, 1985), 20–23.

3. Hist. Stat. US—ME, series Ed26, comparison for 1939 and 1948. The trend when viewed as a proportion of the population, rather than in absolute troop levels, is consistent; postwar military personnel never dipped below 10 per 1,000 population, whereas interwar deployments at their highest never exceeded 2.5 per 1,000. See series Aa7 and Ed26, as demonstrated in Figure Ed-A, in Scott Sigmund Gartner, "National Defense, Armed Forces, Wars, and Veterans," Hist. Stat. US—ME.

4. Hist. Stat. US-ME, series Ed146, Ed153, Ed154; Michael Hogan, *A Cross of Iron: Harry S. Truman and the Origins of the National Security State, 1945–1954* (New York: Cambridge University Press, 1998).

5. Hadley Cantril, ed., *Public Opinion 1935–1946* (Princeton: Princeton University Press, 1951), 903–4, items 102 (September 15, 1945), 103 (September 1945), 108 (September 6, 1945), show only a minority of respondents anticipating that business would provide "enough jobs for nearly everyone" (42 percent, item 102), or that there would be "enough jobs for everybody" within five years (29 percent, item 103) or that unemployment would be better within a year (44 percent, item 108).

6. Republican Party platform of 1944, American Presidency Project, PID #25835; James T. Patterson, *Mr. Republican: A Biography of Robert A. Taft* (Boston: Houghton Mifflin, 1972), 190.

7. Jonathan Bell, *The Liberal State on Trial: The Cold War and American Politics in the Truman Years* (New York: Columbia University Press, 2004), 47–55; Patterson, *Mr. Republican*, 372–75.

8. Republican Party platform of 1948, American Presidency Project, PID #25836.

9. Findings of the Survey of Consumer Finances summarized in George Katona, *Psychological Analysis of Economic Behavior* (New York: McGraw-Hill, 1951), 72–81; full reports in the June issues of *Federal Reserve Bulletin*, 1947–1949; first study done in January 1946.

10. Cantril, ed., *Public Opinion 1935–1946*, items 76, 89, 92, 321–23.

11. See question ID USGALLUP.50–460, QTP03A (5%, Gallup, August 1950); USGAL-LUP.50–461, QK04A (10%, Gallup, September 1950); USGALLUP.50–461, QK04A (10%, Gallup, September 1950); USGALLUP.52–488, Q03B (3%, Gallup, March 1952); USGALLUP.52–495, Q03 (6%, Gallup, July 1952); USGALLUP.54–528, QK03 (3%, Gallup, March 1954); USGALLUP.060454, RK23B (4%, Gallup, June 1954); USORC.54SEP, R04 (3%, Opinion Research Corporation, September 1954); USORC.55SEP, R57 (8%, Opinion Research Corporation, September 1955), in Public Opinion Online, Roper Center, University of Connecticut, via Lexis-Nexis, http://web.lexis–nexis.com [electronic file accessed January 15, 2006]. (The sole exception was a poll taken in the inflation-plagued winter of 1950, prior to mid-term Congressional elections, when the proportion doubled but still amounted to only 26 percent insisting on a tax cut: USGALLUP.50–451, QK13A (Gallup, January 1950), ibid; note that this question simply asked respondents "What do you think will be the main problem which will be discussed," to which 26 percent responded "taxes" or "tax reduction."

12. Herbert Stein, *The Fiscal Revolution in America*, 2nd ed. (Washington, DC: American Enterprise Institute, 1996), 206–22.

13. USORC.55SEP, R31 (Opinion Research Corporation, July 1955), ibid. See USORC.54SEP, R17 (Opinion Research Corporation, September 1954) for corroboration with almost identical responses (44% said unfair "because favored some groups too much," 35% said fair, 20% had no opinion). The combination of inflation and rising taxes appears to have helped induce strategically located Democrats to vote Republican in 1950, although the particular reasons for this—pinched budgets that forced retirees and new families to choose between making mortgage payments and paying taxes—would not shape the broad contours of national politics until the 1970s. See Samuel Lubell, *The Future of American Politics* (New York: Harper and Brothers, 1952), 216–18.

14. Susan B. Hansen, *The Politics of Taxation: Revenue Without Representation* (New York: Praeger, 1983), Figure 6.1, 177. Note also that by the 1970s and 1980s the tax revolt had become intertwined with the broader racial legacies of the New Right. See Joseph Crespino, "Civil Rights Versus the Religious Right: Desegregation, Christian Schools, and Religious Freedom in the 1970s," in *Rightward Bound: Making America Conservative in the 1970s* (Cambridge, MA: Harvard University Press, 2008).

15. Daniel Bell, *The Cultural Contradictions of Capitalism* (New York: Basic Books, 1996), 227–36.

16. Lubell, *The Future of American Politics*, 216–18.

17. Nelson Lichtenstein, *The Most Dangerous Man in Detroit: Walter Reuther and the Fate of American Labor* (New York: Basic Books, 1995), 248–98.

18. Ibid., 225.

19. Walter P. Reuther, "Reuther Challenges 'Our Fear of Abundance,'" *New York Times*, September 16, 1945, SM5.

20. The definitive work on the Manhattan Project in American culture in these formative early years is Paul Boyer, *By the Bomb's Early Light: American Thought and Culture at the Dawn of the Atomic Age* (New York: Pantheon, 1985).

21. Matthew Lassiter and Joseph Crespino, eds., *The Myth of Southern Exceptionalism* (New York: Oxford University Press, 2010), introduction; Matthew Lassiter and Kevin Kruse, "The Bulldozer Revolution: Suburbs and Southern History Since World War II," *Journal of Southern History*, August 2009, 691–706; Bruce Schulman, *From Cotton Belt to Sunbelt: Federal Policy, Economic Development, and the Transformation of the South, 1938–1980* (New York: Oxford University Press, 1991).

22. Lichtenstein, *The Most Dangerous Man in Detroit*, 271–98.

23. Alan Brinkley, *The End of Reform: New Deal Liberalism in Recession and War* (New York: Alfred A. Knopf, 1995), 227–64; Alonzo Hamby, "Sixty Million Jobs and the People's Revolution: The Liberals, the New Deal, and World War II," *The Historian* 30, 4 (August 1968): 578–98.

24. Cantril, ed., *Public Opinion 1935–1946*, 900–4, items 72, 88, 93, 96, 99, 104, 109.

25. Michael Flamm, "Price Controls, Politics, and the Perils of Policy by Analogy: Economic Demobilization After World War II," *Journal of Policy History* 8, 3 (1996): 335–55; Meg Jacobs, "How About Some Meat? The Office of Price Administration, Consumption Politics, and State Building from the Bottom Up, 1941–1946," *Journal of American History* 84, 3 (December 1997): 934–41; Barton Bernstein, "The Truman Administration and Its Reconversion Wage Policy," *Labor History* 6, 3 (Fall 1965): 214–31, and "The Removal of War Production Controls on Business, 1944–1946," *Business History Review* 39, 2 (Summer 1965): 242–60.

26. George Lipsitz, *Rainbow at Midnight: Labor and Culture in the 1940s* (Urbana: University of Illinois Press, 1994), 99–181; Lichtenstein, "From Corporatism to Collective Bargaining: Organized Labor and the Eclipse of Social Democracy in the Postwar Era," in *The Rise and Fall of the New Deal Order, 1930–1980*, ed. Steve Fraser and Gary Gerstle (Princeton: Princeton University Press, 1989), 140–45; Barton Bernstein, "Walter Reuther and the General Motors Strike of 1945–1946," *Michigan History* 49, 3 (September 1965): 260–77; Barton Bernstein, "The Truman Administration and the Steel Strike of 1946," *Journal of American History* 52, 4 (March 1966): 791–803.

27. Risa Goluboff, *The Lost Promise of Civil Rights* (Cambridge, MA: Harvard University Press, 2007); Mary L. Dudziak, *Cold War Civil Rights: Race and the Image of American Democracy* (Princeton: Princeton University Press, 2000); Chandler Davidson and Bernard Grofman, eds., *Quiet Revolution in the South: The Impact of the Voting Rights Act, 1965–1990* (Princeton: Princeton University Press), 32–33, 47–48, 52, 110, 340, 344, 381–82.

28. David R. B. Ross, *Preparing for Ulysses: Politics and Veterans During World War II* (New York: Columbia University Press, 1969); Kathleen J. Frydl, *The GI Bill* (New York: Cambridge University Press, 2009); Glenn Altschuler and Stuart Blumin, *The GI Bill: A New Deal for Veterans* (New York: Oxford University Press, 2009).

29. Ira Katznelson, Kim Geiger, and Daniel Kryder, "Limiting Liberalism: The Southern Veto in Congress, 1933–1950," *Political Science Quarterly* 108, 2 (Summer 1993): 283–306; Bell, *The Liberal State on Trial*, 1–45; Cohen, *A Consumer's Republic*; Meg Jacobs, *Pocketbook Politics: Economic Citizenship in Twentieth-Century America* (Princeton: Princeton University Press, 2005); David Freund, *Colored Property: State Policy and White Racial Politics in Suburban America* (Chicago: University of Chicago Press, 2007); Edward Berkowitz, *Mr. Social Security: The Life of Wilbur J. Cohen* (Lawrence: University Press of Kansas, 1995).

30. Leon Henderson, "How Black Is Our Market?" *Atlantic Monthly*, July 1946, 46–53.

31. Jacobs, *Pocketbook Politics*.

32. Frydl, *GI Bill*.

33. Cantril, ed., *Public Opinion 1935–1946*, 1001, item 1 (under Education), items 1, 6, 9, 10.

34. OWI Research Division, Bureau of Special Services, "Civilians Speculate About the Veteran of World War II," Report no. C48 (March 7, 1945), i, viii, 19, in boxes 1718–19, OWI-Research.

35. Ibid., 24.

36. Ibid., 15, 21.

37. "What Enlisted Men in the ETOUSA Think the Biggest Problems Are That They Will Be Facing after the War," Report 124-M-7, September 8, 1945, 13 (Table 12), and 14, in folder "MTO-68 What EM MTOUSA th big prob fac after War," box 1030, Amer. Soldier Studies.

38. "Post-War Job Plans of Enlisted Men in the Central Pacific," preliminary report, Report no. 10, [probably August or September 1944]; for similar levels elsewhere, see Samuel Stouffer et al., *The American Soldier: Combat and Its Aftermath* (Princeton: Princeton University Press, 1949), 603, Table 1.

39. AMSO-S106E, Q41, June 1944; AMS0159, Q50, October 1944, basic frequencies tabulated from American Soldier datasets, USAMS1944-S106E and USAMS1944-S159 [computer files], Storrs, CT: The Roper Center, University of Connecticut [distributor].

40. "Summary of Enlisted Men's Answers to Several Questions on 'The GI Bill of Rights,'" Report ETO-80, June 1945, in folder "ETO-80 Sum EM Ano Ques on 'G. I. Bill Rts,'" box 1015, Amer. Soldier Studies.

41. Cantril, ed., *Public Opinion 1935–1946*, 1000, item 11.

42. The depth and persistence of veterans' benefits, which were often reinforced by state law and local ordinances, provided an important edifice for white male privilege well into the last decades of the century, as discussed in Linda Kerber, *No Constitutional Right to Be Ladies: Women and the Obligations of Citizenship* (New York: Hill and Wang, 1998). On World War II veterans' benefits more generally, see Mark D. Van Ells, *To Hear Only Thunder Again: America's World War II Veterans Come Home* (Lanham, MD: Lexington Books, 2001); Michael Gambone, *The Greatest Generation Comes Home: The Veteran in American Society* (College Station: Texas A&M University Press, 2005); Ira Katznelson, *When Affirmative Action Was White: An Untold History of Racial Inequality in Twentieth-Century America* (New York: Oxford University Press, 2005); Altschuler and Blumin, *The GI Bill*; Frydl, *The GI Bill*.

43. Ross, *Preparing for Ulysses*, 36–38, 70–73, 78–88, 89–124, 148–57, 224–37, 238–74.

44. Frydl, *GI Bill*; Katznelson, *When Affirmative Action Was White*; Robert Lieberman, *Shifting the Color Line: Race and the American Welfare State* (Cambridge, MA: Harvard University Press, 1998); and Lieberman, *Shaping Race Policy: The United States in Comparative Perspective* (Princeton: Princeton University Press, 2005).

45. John Modell, Marc Goulden, and Sigurdur Magnusson, "World War II in the Lives of Black Americans: Some Findings and Interpretation," *Journal of American History* 76, 3 (December 1989): 838–48.

46. John Modell et al., "World War II in the Lives of Black Americans."

47. Merl Reed, *Seedtime for the Modern Civil Rights Movement: The President's Committee on Fair Employment Practice, 1941–1946* (Baton Rouge: University of Louisiana Press, 1991), 315–17; Marilynn S. Johnson, *The Second Gold Rush: Oakland and the East Bay in World War II* (Berkeley: University of California Press, 1993), 72–81; John Dittmer, *Local People: The Struggle for Civil Rights in Mississippi* (Urbana: University of Illinois Press, 1994), 1–9, 13–18, 19–40; Escobar, *Race, Police, and the Making of a Political Identity: Mexican Americans and the Los Angeles Police Department, 1900–1945* (Berkeley: University of California Press, 1999), ch. 12; Charles M. Payne, *I've Got the Light of Freedom: The Organizing Tradition and the Mississippi Freedom Struggle* (Berkeley: University of California Press, 1995), 13, 24, 30–31, 47–48, 56–57, 66, 87, 136–37, 177, 181–82, 188, 404; Steve Lawson, *Black Ballots: Voting Rights in the South, 1944–1969* (New York: Columbia University Press, 1976), 102–15, 341.

48. George Chauncey, *Gay New York: Gender, Urban Culture, and the Makings of the Gay Male World, 1890–1940* (New York: Basic Books, 1994), 360; Elaine Tyler May, *Homeward Bound: American Families in the Cold War Era* (New York: Basic Books, 1988); Ellen Schrecker, *Many Are the Crimes: McCarthyism in America* (Boston: Little, Brown, 1998); David Caute, *The Great Fear: The Anticommunist Purge Under Truman and Eisenhower* (New York: Simon and Schuster, 1978); Robert Goldstein, *American Blacklist: The Attorney General's List of Subversive Organizations* (Lawrence: University Press of Kansas, 2008).

49. Memo, R. D. Simpson to F. J. Baumgardner, File #66-9330-319, April 22, 1953; reactivation in Memo, JEH to All Investigative Employees, File #66-9330-204, August 1, 1950.

50. On the popular appeal of anticommunism, see Richard Fried, *The Russians Are Coming! Pageantry and Patriotism in Cold-War America* (New York: Oxford University Press, 1998); on networks of informers and the crucial role the FBI played in covertly providing leads and information to anticommunist investigators, see Ellen Schrecker, *Many Are the Crimes: McCarthyism in America* (Boston: Little, Brown, 1998).

51. Memo, JEH to SAC Seattle, File #66-9330-188, May 23, 1947.
52. Applications attached to Memo from Mr. Ladd to L. R. Pennington, File #66-9330-197, January 20, 1948; applicant's name obscured by FOIA edits, only identifier given was age, fifty-three, and occupation, "Executive Selling."
53. Special thanks to Alan Petigny for suggesting this anecdote. Text of anecdote provided by Hollings' office, email dated January 30, 2003. For a reminiscence of Hollings's favorite story, see Clifford Adelman, "I Was Closed Down," *Washington Post*, November 22, 1995, which places its moral in the context of the Republican shutdown of Congress in its confrontation with the Clinton administration at that time.

ACKNOWLEDGMENTS

As a child of the 1980s, for whom soaring federal deficits and scandalous credit card limits have seemed merely a part of the natural order of things, I have developed an intimate understanding of debt. Yet, during the years in which this dissertation was researched and written, I have accumulated a new type of debt, one that runs quite counter to the Reagan-era memories of my youth. At every step in my career, my teachers and colleagues, kith and kin, have shown a generosity of spirit and willingness to invest in character (my own) that runs directly against the inflationary ethos. I am hopelessly in their debt, and the interest continues to compound daily.

At Brown University I found an intimate and collegial community in which I was free to pursue my interests as best I saw fit. My advisor, James Patterson, exercised a combination of thoughtfulness and unswerving scrupulosity that few other advisors would have taken the pain to emulate. Astonishingly responsive and quick to return a draft covered with incisive comments, always balanced and fair in his assessments, and ready to hold even the minutest of assertions to the light of critical inspection, he has demonstrated the full meaning of the term "high standards." I thank him for his example and his patience. The late Jack Thomas did me the great favor of "calling them as he saw them." Fortunately, his sight was better than mine, and after reading more drafts than I had the right to inflict upon him, he showed me a view of my own work that otherwise would have remained obscure to me. Thanks are also due to Howard Chudacoff, whose perceptive comments improved this thesis.

Others at Brown also greatly enriched my studies there. Volker Berghahn, Mari Jo Buhle, Naomi Lamoreaux, and Gordon Wood provided four distinct but equally admirable models of scholarly engagement and intellectual rigor. Mary Gluck and Lajos Chasy exemplified the very best that the Brown community had to offer—both intellectually and morally, as scholars and as friends. Exchanges with Thomas Gleason, Joan Richards, and Philip Benedict enlightened me and encouraged me to consider adopting a more comparative and multidisciplinary approach. Thanks to the kindness of Anthony Molho, James McClain, Burr Litchfield, Joan Lusk, and Michael Diffily, my passage through the graduate program at Brown was far pleasanter and more productive than it might otherwise have been. My time in Providence was also made infinitely more worthwhile by conversations in seminar and over coffee with fellow students Jerry Davila, Robert Fleegler, L. E. Hartmann, Ari Kelman, Josh Marshall, Zach Morgan, Alan Petigny, Sarah Purcell, and Josh Zeitz.

After leaving Providence I had the privilege of working among an extraordinary group of people at George Mason University. At the Center for History and New Media (CHNM), Roy Rosenzweig exercised a ceaseless intellectual curiosity, generosity of spirit, and awe-inspiring work ethic that I can only hope to emulate one day. A large universe of people looked to Roy as a model and a guide; I'm grateful that he included me in his orbit. The world is a far poorer place without him. My time in Fairfax was also enriched and enlivened by conversations with John Cheng, Dan Cohen, Matt Karush, Alison Landsberg, the late Larry Levine, Mike O'Malley, and Elena Razlogova, all of whom were generous enough to listen to my ideas or read my work, making suggestions that have expanded my horizons. Before joining the center, I was lucky to work with Jack Censer, Dee Ann Holisky, and Daniele Struppa, whose vision of the liberal arts sustained the broader academic environment that made CHNM such a vital intellectual community.

At the University of Chicago I have been fortunate to find myself in the midst of that rare thing, a genuine community. It is a true community in the best sense of that word because of the many salutary ways in which intellectual engagement, moral support and civic responsibility are allowed to combine. Needless to say, Chicago has provided an ideal environment in which to expand and refine the ideas that lie at the heart of this book. It has also proved to be a wonderfully sustaining place to live, through the best and the worst of times. A number of my colleagues have been unstintingly generous with their time and good advice, especially Leora Auslander, Dain Borjes, Mark Bradley, George Chauncey, Lis Clemens, Jane Dailey, Sheila Fitzpatrick, Michael Geyer, Ramón Gutiérrez, Neil Harris, Tom Holt, Adrian Johns, Emilio Kouri, Mae Ngai, David Nirenberg, Julie Saville, Amy Dru Stanley, Chris Stansell, Alison Winter, and Salim Yaqub. Applying institutional leverage to amplify intellectual support, John Boyer, Jim Chandler, Kathy Conzen, Bruce Cumings, Prasenjit Duara, and Mark Hansen arranged abundant leave time, ample research funding, amenable teaching arrangements, and sparingly light service obligations. From my very first days in Hyde Park I have benefitted from the vitality and seriousness of my students, beginning with the rock-solid research assistance provided by Alison Lefkovitz, Sarah Miller-Davenport, Susannah Engstrom, Sameer Popats, and Peter Simons.

That I was able to draw on such capable assistance was thanks, in part, to Diane Brady and Cyndee Breshock, who so ably managed the department's research assistants, along with their many other charges.

As I have presented portions of this book at conferences, symposia, and in talks, I have received a wealth of feedback from a wide range of scholars who have read and commented on portions of my work, including Thomas Adams, Beth Bailey, Alan Brinkley, Joe Crespino, Don Critchlow, Emmanuel Didier, Doug Flamming, Linda Kerber, Robert Lieberman, William Leuchtenburg, William Link, Isaac Martin, Ajay Mehrotra, Sidney Milkis, Gautham Rao, Elizabeth Sanders, Bryant Simon, Ed Wehrle, and Julian Zelizer. An intrepid cadre of generous souls has ventured to read all or most of my manuscript at various stages of its drafting—in some cases, more than once. To these good friends and colleagues—Brian Balogh, Chris Capozzola, Josh Ditelberg, Gary Gerstle, Matthew Lassiter, Bill Novak, Bat Sparrow, and Jeremi Suri—I owe a special debt of gratitude.

As this book attests on many levels, institutions matter. At a critical stage, Jesse Ausubel of the Alfred P. Sloan Foundation provided grant support to a young scholar proposing to explore an untested new methodology. As one of many salutary consequences of Jesse's generosity and vision, David Kirsch became a treasured interlocutor and good friend whose many insights, analytical and practical, have informed the making of this book. In my first summer at Chicago, the National Endowment for the Humanities (NEH), upon the nomination and support of my chair, Kathy Conzen, provided funds that allowed me to complete my research for chapter 6. A few years later, Jim Chandler at the Franke Institute, in concert with Mark Hansen and John Boyer, sponsored my residential fellowship during a year that saw some of the most important pieces of this book come together. My writing and ideas gained a sharper edge thanks to talks and workshops at Cambridge University's American History seminar, at the invitation of Tony Badger and Josh Zeitz; at Sussex University's American Studies workshop, at the invitation of Richard Godden; at the Miller Center, University of Virginia, at the behest of Brian Balogh and Sid Milkis; and at the Remarque Institute's Kandersteg Seminar, at the invitation of Katy Fleming. At the final stage of editing my submitted manuscript, one institution in particular became especially important: my publisher, Oxford University Press. That was because within OUP there is a one-woman institution unto herself—my editor, Susan Ferber—whose judicious eye and impeccable instincts proved invaluable. Thanks also go to Joellyn Ausanka, who provided expert copyediting and ensured the highest standards in the production process.

Portions of this book have appeared in print elsewhere. Parts of chapter 4 appeared in "'Buying Our Boys Back': The Mass Foundations of Fiscal Citizenship in World War II," *Journal of Policy History* 20, 2 (2008): 263–86. They are reprinted here courtesy of Cambridge University Press. Other parts of chapter 4, and the introductory text to part II, appear in somewhat different form in "Freedom to Want: The Federal Government and Politicized Consumption in World War II," in *Mobilizing the Movement: Civil Rights and the Second World War*, ed. Kevin Kruse and Stephen Tuck (New York: Oxford University Press, 2011). Portions of chapter 6 initially appeared in "A Nation in Motion: Norfolk, the Pentagon, and the Nationalization of the Metropolitan South, 1941–1953," in *The Myth of Southern Exceptionalism*, ed. Matthew Lassiter and Joseph Crespino (New York: Oxford University Press, 2010). Material from both essays is reprinted here courtesy of Oxford University Press.

The community of archivists, curators, and librarians perform essential work that makes historical scholarship possible. I count myself lucky to be able to rely on the world-class offerings of the Regenstein Library at the University of Chicago—not least of which have included the expert advice of Frank Conaway and Julia Gardner. I am also grateful to the following institutions for granting me access to their collections: the National Archives in College Park, Maryland (where Wayne DeCeasar, Walter Hill, and David Pfiffer were exceptionally helpful), and Laguna Niguel, California; the Harvard University Archives and Widener Library; the FDR Library in Hyde Park; the Louis Round Wilson Special Collections of the University of North Carolina–Chapel Hill (where Matthew Turi provided timely and accurate assistance); the Bancroft Library in California; the American Folklife Center at the Library of Congress; Columbia University Library; the Schomburg Center at the New York Public Library; Georgetown University Library; Stanford University Library; the Library at the University of Maryland, College Park; Brown University Library; and the outstanding public libraries in Boston, Chicago, New York City, San Francisco, and Denver.

My longest-standing debts lie with my friends and family, who have patiently endured the seemingly endless quest to finish this dissertation. Claire Ward was the first person to plant the insidious idea that a Ph.D. might lie in my future. Barbara Rose and the late Frank Rose encouraged me along similar lines, demonstrating an abiding commitment to language, literature, and scholarship whose example continues to guide me. I only wish Frank could have seen this book reach publication, given how profoundly his critical sensibility shaped my intellectual development. Josh Ditelberg and Dan Edelstein humored late-night flights of philosophical speculation, endless offhand observations, and non sequiturs, all without ever betraying our pact of mutually suspended disbelief. If it were not for the support, guidance, and expert advice of Hilliard Farber—none of which was deserved by me—there are many crucial decisions I might not have made, including this career. Hill, you made all the difference.

Finally, my family has sustained me and endured more inconvenience than I had any right to inflict. Everly Conway de Macario and Alberto Macario have been model in-laws, always standing at the ready to help me advance my studies. Alex and Sue Macario have humored and accommodated me on countless family vacations when work had to take precedence over recreation. Patricia Conway provided vital support, intellect and moral, during her yearly visits. When confronted with the same kinds of unreasonable demands in the service of the book, Jennifer Botsford, Nancy Scruggs, and Terry and Ann Sparrow have never wavered in their support and understanding. Perhaps this is because they, too, fell under the influence of Madeline Rudolph, who first implanted in me an unreasonable love of books and the life of the mind they unlocked. Her great-granddaughter Elena Sparrow has grown to the cusp of adolescence while awaiting an answer to the fair but difficult question, "Daddy, when is your book going to be done?" Elena's brother Dylan has also learned to ask this question, although fortunately most of *his* childhood will be free of its weight. Their brother Simon Sparrow, to whom this book is dedicated, did not live to see it into print, but he lightened our spirits and filled our hearts with a vital, necessary buoyancy. In our memories, he still does. And through it all, on the face of the earth in the night and the day, there has been Everly Macario, the first source of my inspiration. A truer heart and soul mate I never will find.

INDEX

CPSIA information can be obtained
at www.ICGtesting.com
Printed in the USA
BVHW030719290821
615176BV00003B/161